The Rehabilitation of Partner-Violent Men

Erica Bowen

The Rehabilitation of Partner-Violent Men

WILEY-BLACKWELL
A John Wiley & Sons, Ltd., Publication

This edition first published 2011

Wiley-Blackwell is an imprint of John Wiley & Sons, formed by the merger of Wiley's global Scientific, Technical, and Medical business with Blackwell Publishing.

Registered Office
John Wiley & Sons Ltd, The Atrium, Southern Gate, Chichester, West Sussex, PO19 8SQ, UK

Editorial Offices
The Atrium, Southern Gate, Chichester, West Sussex, PO19 8SQ, UK
9600 Garsington Road, Oxford, OX4 2DQ, UK
350 Main Street, Malden, MA 02148-5020, USA

For details of our global editorial offices, for customer services, and for information about how to apply for permission to reuse the copyright material in this book please see our website at www.wiley.com/wiley-blackwell.

Library of Congress Cataloging-in-Publication Data

Bowen, Erica, 1976-
The rehabilitation of partner-violent men / Erica Bowen.
p. cm.
Includes bibliographical references and index.
ISBN 978-0-470-99771-0 (cloth) -- ISBN 978-0-470-99772-7 (pbk.)
1. Abusive men--Rehabilitation. 2. Women--Violence against--Prevention. 3. Family violence--Law and legislation. 4. Family violence--Prevention. I. Title.
HV6626.B679 2011
362.82'925--dc22

2010035874

A catalogue record for this book is available from the British Library.

Set in 10/12 pt Minion by Toppan Best-set Premedia Limited
Printed in Singapore by Ho Printing Singapore Pte Ltd

1 2011

To the most important people in my life:
My family – past and present.

Contents

About the Author

Dr Erica Bowen is Senior Lecturer in Psychology at Coventry University. Erica completed her PhD at the University of Birmingham in 2003 which consisted of an evaluation of a community based rehabilitation programme for male perpetrators of intimate partner violence. During the last seven years, Erica has produced a number of publications from this and associated research, which examine methodological aspects of evaluation, as well as expanding the knowledge base concerning the factors associated with the process and outcome of rehabilitation in this client group. Dr Bowen can be contacted via her personal website at www.ebpsychology.co.uk.

Acknowledgements

Writing a book such as this, one relies primarily on the research and practice of others. Consequently, I would like to thank all the academics and practitioners who have invested their time and resources in examining the issue of intimate partner violence and how we can intervene to prevent reoffending, and whose work is cited herein. In addition, along the way several people contributed uniquely through helping to find or provide resources. My thanks therefore go to the following: Sinead Bloomfield, Dr Ruth Hatcher, Vicky Nealon, Gareth Ross, Chris Fry, Dr Steve Goode, CBE, Dr Danny Clarke, Ian Garrett, and the Crown Prosecution Service for permission to include table 2.1.

Special mention is deserved by several of my colleagues who provided support and perspective throughout the process of writing this book. In particular, I would like to thank Dr Clare Wood, Dr Sarah Brown, Dr Gail Steptoe-Warren and Kate Walker for their friendship, support, guidance and humour during the many stressful moments, and Kate in particular for her feedback on the (very) rough drafts. Special mention goes to Dr Becki Jenks, who by a random twist of fate has been unfortunate enough to share an office with me both during the writing up of my PhD thesis, and seven years later this book, and has not once requested me to leave, or a transfer – you are a true friend without whom I am certain I would not have had the emotional strength to complete this book. I would also like to thank Professor Tony Beech for his influence on my thinking about evaluation. A final mention must go to Professor Liz Gilchrist, without whom I would never have happened upon a field of research that I feel more passionate about now than I did a decade ago – thank you.

Finally, for their seemingly unquestioning and unconditional love and support, I would like to thank my family. My husband Dan has provided unyielding support and perspective and has been a more than tolerant sounding board when required, and our son Morgan who simply makes the world a better place.

Acknowledgements

1

Introduction

Violence within intimate relationships is by no means a modern phenomenon. In fact the earliest documented British case of violence against a woman by her husband is that of Margaret Neffield from York in 1395 (described by Lunn, 1991, cited in Mullender 1996). Margaret appeared with witnesses in front of the Ecclesiastical court and presented a case that her husband had attacked her with a dagger, inflicting several wounds including broken bones. Despite the supporting statements from the witnesses, the court found that a legitimate case for a judicial separation had not been made. The final ruling was that Margaret should continue to live with her husband (Lunn, 1991).

Although this account is more than 600 years old, the nature of the violence used, injury inflicted, and attitudes of the judiciary towards such behaviours, are representative of domestic violence scenarios occurring well into the 1990s. Indeed, even today, in the early part of the 21st century, the national and local press is littered with stories of domestic violence in which decisions (or lack thereof) taken by statutory agencies lead to the release of a known victim back into the hands of her abuser with fatal consequences. It is perhaps not surprising that media coverage of domestic violence issues is dominated by such stories, given the media's general preoccupation with 'bad news'. Although these stories do well to highlight domestic violence as an ongoing social issue, identify persisting flaws within the current system and exert pressure on relevant parties, they fail to acknowledge the extent to which the statutory response to domestic violence has changed.

Indeed, when considering the title of this book *The Rehabilitation of Partner-Violent Men*, it is clear that a great deal has changed in Britain since the fourteenth-century case of Margaret Neffield, with regard to society's response to domestic violence in

The Rehabilitation of Partner-Violent Men, by Erica Bowen

general and, more specifically, the response of statutory and criminal justice agencies, which has been prioritized by recent Government initiatives and which form the focus of this book. At the time of writing, offenders who are arrested for a domestic violence motivated offence may be referred to a rehabilitation programme either as part of a prison sentence, or as a condition of a community rehabilitation order supervised by probation services. This is a far cry from the situation even in the 1970s where the police and other statutory agencies failed at every opportunity to acknowledge domestic violence incidents (Dobash & Dobash, 1992). This does not mean, however, that the Government has been particularly forward looking in its approach to domestic violence. On the contrary, much of the evident policy change is a direct reflection of the long-term and continuing pressure placed on Government agencies by women's advocates and activists (Hague & Malos, 2005). Indeed, that a book such as this one can be written from a British perspective is testament to the achievements of these groups. However, while acknowledging the efforts and substantial achievements of feminist activist groups and academics, this text does not aim to promulgate the feminist perspective and arguments beyond this acknowledgement. Rather, its principle aim is to provide an introductory overview and critical examination of the influences that have led to the provision of such programmes and the evidence regarding their effectiveness. Prior to starting this discussion however, it is necessary to examine in more detail the nature of intimate partner violence, the scale of the problem, and the likely participants in such interventions so that we can understand what it is that rehabilitation programmes are aiming to prevent, and why formal intervention may be necessary.

The Nature of 'Domestic' or 'Intimate Partner' Violence

As with all texts that examine the phenomenon of violence within intimate relationships it is necessary to define precisely the nature of the behaviours included, and to justify the terminology chosen to refer to such behaviours. This is particularly the case when considering violence in intimate relationships, as the available terminology has different meanings for different people (Burton, 2008). Moreover, modes and methods of intervention emerge directly from the manner in which we understand, conceptualize, measure and define a phenomenon, as the terms adopted typically reflect wider theoretical assumptions (Margolin & Berman, 1993). In other words, models of intervention with perpetrators – the focus of this book – vary, depending on how we describe and explain their behaviour, and what we believe to be its causes. These issues have sparked many years of debate, and consequently as this book is intended to provide an introduction to this field, they will be briefly reviewed here.

The consensus of opinion is that one definition of domestic violence is needed in order to clarify communication between agencies, and consequently, to facilitate intervention as well as to assist the development of valid aetiological theories. However, variation of definition has been flagged as an ongoing problem, both within the legal response to domestic violence (Radford, 2003) and, more broadly, within academic research examining its antecedents, nature and consequence (DeKeseredy, 2000). Of particular contention is the nature of the 'domestic' relationship(s) to be included in such definitions, as well as the characteristics of the 'violence'.

Official definitions

As might be expected, the need for a legal definition of 'domestic' violence did not present itself until society became formally aware of the problem. Legal definitions of violence had existed for over 100 years resulting primarily from the Offences against the Person Act 1861. Conversely, a statutory definition of 'domestic' did not arise until the mid-1970s (Dobash & Dobash, 1979), with the passing of the civil justice Domestic Violence and Matrimonial Proceedings Act 1976, in which 'domestic' referred to either spouses or heterosexual cohabitants (Burton, 2008). Inevitably, legal definitions have been altered in light of new understandings of the phenomenon. The 1990s saw considerable broadening of definitions. For example, within civil law, the Family Law Act 1996 included reference to 'associated persons' in order that individuals in a broader range of relationships could seek legal intervention. Burton (2008) comments, however, that individuals in long-term non-cohabiting relationships were omitted from this provision despite calls for their inclusion. More recently, the category of 'associated person' has been broadened further and now reflects a diverse array of 'domestic' arrangements and relationships, including current or former spouses, civil partners and cohabitants (either heterosexual or same sex); those who have agreed to either marry or enter a civil partnership together; those who are parents, or who have parental responsibility for a child; relatives and parties associated through adoption; and those who either were, or continue to be, engaged in a long-term intimate relationship (Reece, 2006). It is questionable whether this over-inclusiveness has resulted ultimately in the definition losing its validity owing to the inclusion of these disparate groups.

Within the criminal justice arena agencies have traditionally adopted their own bespoke definitions to suit their own individual needs resulting in rather inward looking policies. This has been due, in part, to the fact that there exists no 'domestic violence' criminal act per se (Burton, 2008; see Chapter 2). Government departments were also guilty of this practice, which resulted in confusion between agencies, and a lack of coherence within governmental and criminal justice responses to domestic violence. Particular disparity appears to have focused again on which 'domestic' relationships are included within the definitions, as well as the nature of the behaviours reflected. For example, the definition adopted by Home Office in 2003 acknowledged that the behaviours may be drawn from a range of physical, emotional and financial abuses, but restricted domestic relationships to those between current or former intimate partners (HO, 2003).

In 2005, however, the Crown Prosecution Service (CPS) emphasized the criminal nature of domestic violence (any criminal offence), while again acknowledging the breadth of behaviours (physical, sexual, psychological, emotional or financial), but the definition of 'domestic' adopted was much broader, and included current or former partners or current or former family members (CPS, 2005a). Moreover, other agencies including the Probation Service (National Probation Directorate, 2003) also included abuse in other close relationships within their definitions. The bias associated with individual agency context is apparent from these definitions, and it is perhaps not surprising that the CPS confined domestic violence to criminal acts, given its role within the criminal justice system. However, as will be discussed below (and in Chapter 2), many behaviours that may be considered abusive do not fall within current criminal law and therefore this definition fails to encompass the whole spectrum of domestic violence behaviours.

With a thrust towards more multi-agency working led by the 1997 Labour Government, however, the need for greater consistency of definitions has become apparent in order that cases of domestic violence can be accurately identified in the first place and, subsequently, so that interventions can be appropriately targeted. Most recently, in an attempt to homogenize definitions of domestic violence yet acknowledge the heterogeneity of relationships and behaviours involved, the CPS, Home Office and the Association of Chief Police Officers (ACPO) have agreed to adopt the following definition:

> Any incident of threatening behaviour, violence or abuse (psychological, physical, sexual, financial or emotional) between adults who are or have been intimate partners or family members, regardless of gender or sexuality. (Home Office, 2005)

Within this definition, an adult is considered to be anyone over the age of 18 years, and family members include: mother, father, brother, sister, son, daughter and grandparents, whether directly, or indirectly related (e.g. in laws, or step families). While this definition is useful in capturing the breadth of behaviour, and in its ability to acknowledge 'honour' based violence, it suffers owing to the range of domestic relationships included. In particular, identifying the true extent of domestic violence, traditionally understood to be violence arising within a current or former intimate relationship (Hague & Malos, 2005), is more difficult given the broader definition used, and this is now reflected in official statistics. Burton (2008) also raises the issue that a definition which does not reflect lay person perceptions may have a negative impact on the willingness of victims to report incidents if they do not identify themselves as victims thus defined. As domestic violence has the highest under-reporting rate of all crimes, in addition to the greatest level of repeat victimization (Kershaw, Nicholas & Walker, 2008), this is of particular concern, especially given the recent changes to criminal justice and legal policies aimed at increasing the number of perpetrators brought to justice (see Chapter 2).

Academic definitions and debates

Numerous terms have been used within the academic literature to refer to the phenomenon of violence committed within intimate relationships, differences between which typically reflect different weights of emphasis on either: (a) the type of intimate relationship (e.g. *spousal* violence, *wife* beating, *conjugal* violence, *marital* violence, *intimate partner* violence), or (b) the specificity and severity of behaviour (e.g. spouse *abuse*, domestic *violence*, wife *beating)*. In addition, considerable debate has centred on the role of gender in intimate partner violence and the extent to which men and women are victims and – more relevant to this book – perpetrators.

Which relationships?

Early perspectives on domestic violence were directly influenced by the characteristics of those who were first to report experiencing violence and abuse. Consequently, in the UK, definitions of domestic violence arose from the women who identified and discussed their victimization with others at the Chiswick Women's Aid hostel set up in 1971 (Dobash & Dobash, 1979; Pizzey, 1974). From their experiences, the perpetrators of their abuse were their husbands. At that time, therefore, domestic violence was viewed as reflecting violence committed by husbands against their wives.

It has been posited, however, that the use of the term 'domestic' actually disguises who the victims and perpetrators are, and this argument has propagated the development and use of a range of more specific alternatives such as 'wife abuse' or 'wife beating', even to describe violence against women in the context of non-marital, relationships (Hague & Malos, 2005). In North America the terms 'battered woman' and 'batterer' proliferate in relation to victims and perpetrators of physical violence against women, although these are not favoured terms in the UK owing to the perception that they are value laden judgements about the victim's possible role in her victimization (Hague & Malos, 2005).

Although the case for the use of highly specific terminology has been made (Dobash & Dobash, 1990), more recently, women's specialist services have called for the development of more sophisticated definitions of 'violence against women in the home' to account for the fact that such violence may be perpetrated by the full range of male associates, relatives and current or former intimate partners (Hague & Malos, 2005). It is arguable that the current definition adopted by the Home Office, ACPO and the CPS goes a considerable way to achieving this. However, while such an 'official' definition may improve the identification of victims and allocation of victim support services, it is questionable whether adopting such a broad definition for the purpose of academic research is appropriate. If we are to accept the view that domestic violence is a 'special case' of violence in general, then it is likely that violence perpetrated by a male friend is not motivated by the same underlying factors as that perpetrated by intimate partners or husbands (Gordon, 2000). Given the possibility of different aetiologies, causes, and potential modes of intervention with perpetrators of these different forms of 'domestic' violence (Gelles & Cornell, 1985, cited in DeKeseredy, 2000), adopting a broader definition would serve to increase measurement error around the concept, and possibly lead to the development of erroneous theories and intervention models.

Which behaviours?

Currently, domestic violence is understood to embrace a range of behaviours, aside from physical violence; including sexual, emotional/psychological and financial abuse. The multiplicities of behaviour that constitute domestic violence are widely acknowledged by most statutory and voluntary agencies that intervene with victims or perpetrators. Empirical research also supports the notion that different forms of violence tend to co-occur, and that it is rare for only one form of violence to be present in a domestic violence relationship. It is typically found that many individuals may engage in verbal and psychological abuse, but rarely employ physically aggressive tactics; whereas those who engage in serious acts of violence are more likely to also engage in a broader repertoire of seriously abusive behaviours (Gordon, 2000). This directly challenges the notion that psychological and verbal abuse are solely risk factors for domestic violence, but identifies them also as unique forms of abusive behaviour, which may also escalate into other forms of physical abuse (Tolman, 1989). For example, Follingstad et al. (1990) interviewed more than 200 women about their experiences of physical, verbal and psychological abuse. Patterns in the data suggested that threats of violence and destruction of property preceded episodes of physical violence. In addition, the majority of women had experienced multiple forms of abuse, including physical, verbal and emotional. Pan, Neidig and O'Leary (1994) found that, based on the self-reported use of physical and psychological aggression in the relationships of military personnel, where violence occurred, both men and women were likely to engage in a constellation of violence including minor and severe aggression and psychological aggression.

Vivian and Malone (1997) found that in contrast to husbands who reported only using verbal abuse, those who reported using minor aggression also reported using twice as much verbal abuse, and those who reported engaging in serious aggression also reported three times as much verbal abuse. Severity and frequency of abuse were also strongly associated as severely aggressive husbands used five times more moderate aggression as the minor physical abuse groups. Severity of domestic violence has also been linked to the likelihood of being stalked by an (ex) intimate partner (Logan, Shannon, Cole & Swanberg, 2007). Logan et al. (2007) found that victims of domestic violence who reported being stalked in the last year and who sought a civil protective order were significantly more likely to report experiencing verbal abuse, degradation, jealousy and control, symbolic violence, serious threats, sexual insistence, sexual violence and injury from violence in the relationship than those who did not report being stalked in the last 12 months. This would appear to confirm that domestic violence not only constitutes a broad range of abusive behaviours, but that the presence of physical violence is almost certainly accompanied by other forms of abuse and may serve as a risk factor for stalking behaviour.

Perhaps the most comprehensive definition of domestic violence presented within the clinical literature is that offered by the Duluth Domestic Abuse Intervention Project (Pence & Paymar, 1993), derived from the accounts of over 200 female victims of intimate partner violence. Although based on a 'power and control' analytical framework (see 'The Feminist Perspective' below) scholars are generally in agreement regarding its validity among clinical samples. Rather than providing a simple list of behaviours that may constitute domestic violence, the 'Power and Control Wheel' (Pence & Paymar, 1993, see Chapter 4) explains such behaviours as tools of 'intimidation and subjugation' (Dasgupta, 1999, p. 199) and emphasizes the coercive interpersonal context within which such behaviours occur. Emphasis is placed on the instrumental use of physical and sexual violence to reinforce the power of other non-physical control tactics. These include: emotional abuse, intimidation, isolation, coercion and threats, use of children, economic abuse, use of male privilege, and abuse minimization, denial and victim blaming. It is suggested that these non-physical tactics are used less systematically and serve to undermine the victim's autonomy (Pence & Paymar, 1993). As stated, this broad conceptualization of domestic violence emphasizes the role of coercion and control within violent relationships, and it is the use of such tactics that has been argued to be characteristic of domestic violence perpetrated predominantly by men.

Are men the only perpetrators?

Perhaps the most persistent and controversial argument in the partner violence field concerns the extent to which intimate partner violence is a gendered phenomenon (Johnson, 1995). There is little doubt that women can, and do, use violence within intimate relationships. However, arguments centre on the extent to which such violence is qualitatively and quantitatively the same as that used by men, and the extent to which domestic violence can therefore be considered a gender-symmetric phenomenon. Broadly, there exist two dominant perspectives within intimate partner violence research which vary in terms of their theoretical orientation, sampling methodologies and, consequently, definitions of intimate partner violence, particularly with respect to the role of gender. These can be categorized as the feminist or 'Violence against Women' and family violence perspectives.

The feminist perspective

It is generally agreed that there is no one single feminist philosophy, but according to Bograd (1988), there are four issues that are common to all feminist perspectives concerning domestic violence:

1. the explanatory utility of the constructs of gender and power;
2. the analysis of the family as a historically situated social institution;
3. the crucial importance of understanding and validating women's experiences;
4. employing scholarship for women. (Bograd, 1988, pp. 13–14)

Consistent with these underlying principles, feminist scholars initiated research examining the phenomenon of domestic violence employing qualitative research methods to obtain the first-hand experiences of victims identified through contact with statutory agencies and women's support services (Bograd, 1988). Such methods were adopted in opposition to the use of quantitative methods, which endorse the use of forced choice methodologies. This was due to the belief that such methods would lead to biased or distorted results, as they are derivatives of patriarchal social science philosophies (Yllo, 1988). The emerging research provided considerable detail of the dynamics of domestic violence as experienced by women from these 'clinical' samples:

> We didn't have the money for him to go out – that was what usually caused all the arguments. (Dobash & Dobash, 1979, p. 103)

> I have been slapped for saying something about politics, for having a different view of religion, for swearing, for crying, for wanting to have intercourse. (Dobash & Dobash, 1979, p. 104)
>
> Lewis had threatened that if I ever went to my mother's he would kill her too. (Walker, 1979, p. 103)
>
> He put one of his feet on my hips or my stomach and the other knee on my neck. He stuck his face straight at mine and said again, 'You talk too much, Joanna.' (Walker, 1979, p. 94).

These examples taken from Dobash and Dobash's (1979) Scottish study, *Violence against Wives* and Walker's (1979) North American study, *The Battered Woman*, identify the use of violence as a means of controlling wives tied closely to male expectations of the role of 'wife'. In particular, these two studies found evidence that if women infringed upon these expectations by acting out of role – in particular, challenging their husband's authority or failing to live up to his expectations, violence was more likely to occur. Their exploration of women's experiences repeatedly identified themes of male ownership and possessiveness linked directly to a lack of comfort with intimacy, male dominance and female subordination. The resulting analyses highlighted the role of patriarchal societal structures as the causes of wife abuse, both within society broadly, and also patriarchal structures in the family background of the male perpetrators. Moreover, such studies led to the understanding of domestic violence as a pattern repeated throughout relationships, and one which combined verbal, psychological and physical forms of abuse. The inability of men to acknowledge and understand the consequences of their behaviour, often resulting in their blaming the victim, minimizing or completely denying its existence was also observed (Dobash & Dobash, 1979; Martin, 1976). In addition, women's use of violence was viewed as arising solely in response to their own victimization, typically in self-defence (Saunders, 1988), or, where violence was instigated by women, this was viewed as a pre-emptive strike aimed at triggering an inevitable male attack (Bograd, 1988). Perhaps most importantly, from this perspective, the consequences of abuse for women (i.e. the erosion of autonomy and self-identity, and subjugation), are the defining feature of domestic violence, rather than the acts used by men to achieve these ends.

The family violence perspective

In contrast to the feminist perspective, researchers within the family violence perspective draw more broadly on conflict theories to explain violence (Winstok, 2007). They assert that violence is a non-legitimate tactic employed by individuals in order to settle interpersonal conflicts, and that violence within the family and between intimate partners is an extension of this. Murray Straus has been a major contributor to the field since the early 1970s and he and his colleagues define violence in terms of motive and consequences associated with specific acts, and therefore as 'an act carried out with the intention or perceived intention of causing physical pain or injury to another person' (Straus, Gelles & Steinmetz, 1980, p. 68). Housed firmly within the empiricist tradition, violence is operationalized at an act level and is most commonly measured using the Conflict Tactics Scale (CTS; Straus, 1979; revised CTS-2, Straus, Hamby, Boney-McCoy

et al., 1996) self-report questionnaire. The revised measure consists of a number of subscales, which contain items reflecting a range of physical, psychological and sexually coercive behaviours, as well as a subscale reflecting injury and another reflecting negotiation tactics. Within the measure, a distinction is made between minor and severe behaviours and injuries. A broad description of the aggression items is presented in table 1.1 below.[1]

Winstok (2007) observes that at the time the CTS was developed, it was 'politically incorrect to examine female aggression' (p. 350). Consequently, this approach drew heavy criticism by feminist scholars and activists who were working to increase awareness of violence against women. Not only did this methodology dare to question the behaviour of women, Straus and colleagues did so at a population level, and reported

Table 1.1 Broad descriptions of CTS-2 aggression items

Subscale	Items
Physical assault (minor)	• threw something • twisted arm or hair • pushed or shoved • grabbed • slapped
Physical assault (severe)	• Used knife or gun • punched or hit with something • choked • slammed partner against a wall • beat up • burned or scalded on purpose • kicked
Psychological aggression (minor)	• Insulted or swore • shouted or yelled • stomped out of the house • said something to spite partner
Psychological aggression (severe)	• Called partner fat or ugly • destroyed something belonging to my partner • accused partner of being a lousy lover • threatened to hit or throw something
Sexual coercion (minor)	• Made partner have sex without a condom • insisted on sex when partner did not want it • insisted partner had anal or oral sex
Sexual coercion (severe)	• Used force to make partner have oral or anal sex • Used force to make partner have sex • used threats to make partner have oral or anal sex • used threats to make partner have sex

[1] Respondents are required to indicate the frequency with which they and their partners used any of the tactics listed within the previous 12 months and analyses typically examine the proportion of men and women who report one or more acts in each subscale (Archer, 2000).

highly contentious findings. For example, patterns of violence identified in the 1985 Family Violence Survey (Straus & Gelles, 1990) revealed that half of the violence experienced in relationships could be considered 'mutual' – that is, used by both individuals within a dyad. A further one quarter of the violence was perpetrated only by males within the dyad, and the remaining quarter, by women within the dyad. More recent survey research has replicated these results (Kessler, Molnar, Feurer et al., 2001) while others have found that women use violence more frequently, and with a greater severity than men (Kwong, Bartholomew, & Dutton, 1999; Magdol, Moffitt, Caspi, et al 1997).

It must be noted that the use of the CTS to assess domestic violence has come under sharp attack for misidentifying the phenomenon, including poorly worded items, which not only merge different behaviours but require only one response, and for decontextualizing violent behaviours (Dobash, Dobash, Wilson & Daly, 1992). Such criticisms led to the revision of the instrument, but contention regarding its use remains. Despite this, this approach which 'equates abuse with violence' (Stark, 2006) has dominated research in this field.

In 2000, a meta-analysis of 87 studies (76 of which employed the CTS) that examined the role of gender in intimate partner violence was reported (Archer, 2000). This analysis found a small but significant effect size for gender ($d = -.05$) indicating that when act-based measures are used, women are more likely to have used physical aggression towards their partners and to have done so more frequently. In contrast, men were more likely than women to have injured their partners, but again the effect size was very small ($d = .15$). This analysis is, however, not without its critics who raise concerns regarding terminology; the bias towards non-marital samples in the primary research; and conceptual and measurement ambiguities, particularly concerning the validity of the CTS (see for example, O'Leary, 2000; White, Smith, Koss et al., 2000). Nevertheless, this research has been used to proffer the argument that women are as violent as men in intimate relationships. Consequently, for nearly 30 years, these two competing and opposing perspectives regarding the nature of domestic violence somewhat awkwardly coexisted, and the debate concerning the gender symmetry of domestic violence raged on.

A typology of domestic violence

More recently an attempt to reconcile these two perspectives has been put forward by Johnson (1995, 2006, 2008). Johnson's initial observations concluded that domestic violence is not a unitary phenomenon, and that through their use of different, but inherently biased sampling strategies, researchers from within the feminist and family violence perspectives had been exploring different forms of domestic violence. Johnson argued that the use of agency-based data (police, courts, shelters) relied on by feminist researchers was biased, due to its sampling frame, and yielded data in which domestic violence was gender biased – with males the perpetrators and females the victims. In contrast, the allegedly 'representative' population survey methods used by proponents of the family violence perspective were biased, due to sample attrition – those who refused to participate in the survey – and yielded data in which domestic violence was gender neutral, and typically mutually perpetrated.

In order to test this hypothesis, Johnson (1995) examined studies in which the CTS had been used to assess domestic violence but in agency-based samples and compared them to the findings of the general surveys detailed previously. In addition to differences in gender symmetry, it was found that the two sampling strategies also provided accounts of domestic violence that differed in terms of the frequency of per-couple incidents, escalation, severity of injuries and mutuality (Johnson, 2006). Specifically, the partner violence reported by agency samples was more frequent, more likely to escalate, more severe, less likely to be mutual, and was perpetrated predominantly, and almost exclusively, by men. Johnson likened this form of domestic violence to the accounts reported by feminist researchers in which violence is viewed as one of a number of control tactics (Pence & Paymar, 1993). This form of violence he labelled 'patriarchal, or intimate terrorism' whereas the partner violence reported by non-agency samples that was less frequent, less likely to escalate, less severe, and more likely to be mutual was labelled 'common couple violence'. In addition, the findings from Archer's (2000) meta-analysis also provided support for this taxonomy, as two studies that used act-based measures from women's refuges produced relatively high effect sizes in the male direction. However, these data were based on partner and self-report from survivors, and self-report is known to be lower than partner report, and consequently biased (Archer, 1999).

More recently, Johnson (2006, 2008) has refined this typology based on the hypothesized role of coercive control within dyadic relationships, rather than focusing on the behaviour of only one individual within a dyad. In considering the role of coercive control, Johnson (2008) settles on a quadripartite typology of domestic violence behaviours within dyads. *Intimate terrorism* consists of the use of violence to exert control over a partner, but the partner does not use such tactics in reply. *Violent resistance* occurs when the partner is violent and controlling, and the resister's violence arises in reaction to the attempt to exert control. *Mutual violent control* reflects a dyad in which both parties use violence in attempts to gain control over their partner. Finally, *situational couple violence* reflects violence used by one or both members of a dyad outside the context of control.

This proposed typology has generally been well received and acknowledged as a sensible account of the literature. As yet, however, there exists a limited empirical literature that has directly tested the underlying premises of this typology, and not all of which provides clear cut support (see for example Graham-Kevan & Archer, 2003, 2008). It is possible, however, that ongoing research designed to test the basic tenets of this typology may lead to a formal reconciliation of the feminist and family violence perspectives, and the development of more sensitive assessment and intervention strategies that account for, and address, this variation.

The Extent of Intimate Partner Violence

Obtaining an accurate estimate of the prevalence (estimates of the proportion of the population affected) or incidence (number of new cases arising within a specified timeframe) of intimate partner violence (IPV) is difficult for several reasons, and the resulting 'size' of the problem depends on both the definition of IPV, and the methods of assessment used (Gelles, 2000). Hagemann-White (2001) argues specifically that surveys sometimes adopt definitions of IPV that are too broad – in that even the most insignificant physical act of aggression is interpreted as 'violence', resulting in an inflated estimate of prevalence. Conversely, surveys may adopt a definition that is too narrow – in which only acts interpreted as indicating severe IPV, and which are less frequent, are included, leading to potential under-estimations of prevalence. Either way, it is unlikely that such operationalizations will lead to estimates of IPV that reflect the phenomena identified in qualitative studies. The extent to which such a priori definitions of 'victim' and 'violence' match the subjective experiences of respondents is, therefore, questionable. It is likely that, as previously discussed, such methods lead to an over-representation of common couple violence and an under-representation of intimate terrorism (Johnson, 1995).

Notwithstanding these limitations, estimates of the prevalence of IPV typically come from data obtained via victimization surveys, (e.g. British Crime Survey (England and Wales), US National Family Violence Survey; Netherlands National Survey of Wife Abuse; Canadian Violence Against Women Survey; Australian Women's Safety survey). A major concern with such surveys is the balance between encouraging reporting while maintaining the safety of respondents who may be potential victims (Hagemann-White, 2001). Those who experience the most severe violence are the least likely respondents in a survey. Women who are experiencing a violent relationship may either refuse to participate, or may be excluded from the survey owing to safety concerns (Walby & Myhill, 2001).

Despite these concerns, victimization surveys are deemed to be more valid assessments of prevalence than official statistics, given the high levels of non-reporting associated with IPV. For example, in 2007/08 approximately 60 per cent of the incidents of IPV reported to the British Crime Survey were not reported to the police (Kershaw, Nicholas & Walker, 2008). Indeed, it is accepted that IPV has the highest under-reporting rate of all crimes. Consequently, 'official' statistics provide a considerably less accurate picture of the prevalence of IPV. This is particularly the case in the UK, given the lack of a unique domestic violence offence. The emerging picture of the prevalence of IPV therefore rests on the willingness and ability of victims to safely report their experiences without fear of repercussions, and the quality of the survey methods employed.

International and national surveys

A recent multi-national survey conducted on behalf of the World Health Organization identified 'current' prevalence rates (experienced in the last 12 months) ranging from between 15 per cent and 71 per cent across 24,097 respondents in ten different countries, including Bangladesh, Brazil, Ethiopia, Japan, Namibia, Peru, Samoa, Serbia and Montenegro, Thailand and the United Republic of Tanzania (Garcia-Moreno, Jansen, Ellsberg et al., 2006). In this study, participants were asked to report their experiences of a range of 'acts' of physical or sexual violence, and controlling behaviours. No measure of psychological aggression was included. Respondents reported on the frequency (once, twice, a few times, many times) of experience and whether it had happened 'ever' or in the last 12 months. Despite the inclusion of the measure of controlling behaviours, partner violence was defined in terms of the experience of either physical and/or sexual violence. The lowest lifetime prevalence for *physical* partner violence of 13 per cent was recorded for Japan, while 61 per cent of women in Peru province reported having experienced some form of physical partner violence. In relation to sexual violence, 6 per cent of women in city sites in Japan and Serbia and Montenegro, and 59 per cent of women in Ethiopia province reported this type of victimization during their lifetime. Experience of controlling behaviour yielded higher prevalence rates, ranging from 21 per cent in Japan, to 90 per cent in the United Republic of Tanzania city. The results also indicated a high level of co-occurrence between these forms of abusive behaviours, with those women who experienced the broadly defined 'partner violence' more likely to also experience controlling behaviours. As the methods employed to gather data were identical across countries, the range of prevalence rates suggests that IPV is differentially normative in different cultures.

European data provide a mixed picture of the prevalence of intimate partner violence and are available for a small proportion of European countries. In 2004, Kury, Obergfell-Fuchs and Woessner identified only six national surveys conducted between 1992 and 2003, all of which differ with regard to the definition of partner violence employed, the methods with which partner violence was measured and the samples used, and the timeframe within which reports of victimization were sought (Kury et al., 2004). Based on these variations, prevalence estimates ranged from 18.7 per cent (CTS during last five years: West Germany, 1992), 16.6 per cent (CTS during last five years: East Germany, 1992), 2.4 per cent (lifetime experience of partner violence: Bavaria, 2002); 8–20 per cent depending on age (lifetime experience, female only sample: Sweden, 1999); and 12.9 per cent (CTS experience during last year: Spain, 2003).

British surveys

The systematic collection of domestic violence victimization data in England and Wales has been carried out since 1996 via the British Crime Survey (BCS). The national crime surveys of Scotland and Northern Ireland have collated data regarding the prevalence of domestic violence since 1993 and 1994, respectively (Macpherson, 2000; Northern Ireland Office, 2008). All of these surveys adopt a similar methodology for the collection of information regarding particularly sensitive crimes: that of a self-completion questionnaire rather than interview, which may be computerized. The questionnaire typically includes a modified version of the CTS, in addition to questions about victim perceptions of their experiences, and the impact that such experiences have had on their well-being.

In the first year of its use in the BCS, the results of a computer-assisted self-interviewing (CASI) questionnaire were that 4.2 per cent of women and 4.2 per cent of men reported that they had experienced intimate partner violence by a current or former partner in the last twelve months. In addition, 4.9 per cent of men and 5.9 per cent of women reported experiencing either physical assaults or frightening threats. Despite the similarity of reported levels of victimization, women were twice as likely as men to have been injured in the last year, and were more likely to have been assaulted three or more times during the same period (Mirlees-Black & Byron, 1999). Nearly one quarter (23 per cent) of women, and 15 per cent of men reported having experienced intimate partner violence at some point in their lives. At that time, intimate partner violence accounted for nearly a quarter of all violent crime.

The most recent data available at the time of writing originates from the 2007/08 BCS, which collected data from 47,000 households in England and Wales. Despite the previously identified need for a clear definition of 'domestic violence', the 2007/08 BCS reports data relating to 'intimate violence', which is then separated into partner abuse, family abuse, and sexual abuse (Povey, Coleman, Kaiza et al., 2009). According to the results of this survey, since the age of 16, 27 per cent of women and 17 per cent of men had experienced partner abuse. In the previous 12 months, 5 per cent of women and 4 per cent of men reported such victimization. In addition, 39 per cent of victims of partner abuse were repeat victims, with women more likely than men to be repeat victims (44 per cent and 32 per cent respectively).

Slightly lower figures were reported in the Scottish Crime Survey, based on data collected from approximately 5,000 households in 1999 (Macpherson, 2000). Here, of the 1,876 respondents to the self-completion questionnaire, 16 per cent of women and 6 per cent of men reported historically experiencing threats or force from a partner. These figures dropped to 6 per cent and 3 per cent respectively when reporting on experiences within the last twelve months. In Northern Ireland, of the 2,110 respondents to the self-completion questionnaire, 11 per cent had been victims of 'domestic violence' at some point in their lifetime, which represented 15 per cent of women and 8 per cent of men. Prevalence of victimization during the last 12 months was not reported (Northern Ireland Office, 2008).

Although questions regarding victim perceptions of their experience are included in the self-completion questionnaire, details of these findings are not always reported. The most detailed examination of these data is reported for the 2001 BCS (Walby & Allen, 2004), and details are also included in both the Scottish and Irish surveys. According to the 2001 BCS, when asked whether they would label the worst incident experienced as 'domestic violence', 75 per cent of women, but only 41 per cent of men stated that they would. The same question in the Irish survey found that 72 per cent of respondents believed that it had been domestic violence. The Scottish survey found that when considering their experiences of victimization over the last 12 months, 67 per cent of women and 39 per cent of men agreed that they had been victims of domestic violence. When asked whether the worst incident constituted a crime, 52 per cent of the Irish sample and 30 per cent of the Scottish sample (41 per cent women, 4 per cent men) agreed. According to the BCS, 51 per cent of female victims viewed their worst incident as a crime in contrast to 11 per cent of men.

Consistent with the concept of intimate terrorism, according to the BCS, such incidents would be labelled as domestic violence if they were more severe (resulted in injury), if the injury sustained was serious, and if they had been more frequently assaulted. Older women were more likely to label their experiences as domestic violence, and also those individuals who had sought help to deal with their victimization were more likely to perceive their experiences as domestic violence. Similar factors were also associated with perceptions of the events as a crime (Walby & Allen, 2004).

Taken together, the survey data reviewed indicates that intimate partner violence is a considerable global problem, affecting, as a conservative estimate, at least 15 per cent of women at some point in their lifetime. However, there appears to be a continuing disparity between those individuals who may be legally identified as victims of domestic violence and those who would identify themselves as such. This disparity may be associated with the under-reporting of domestic violence incidents and may also reflect a lack of awareness of the range of behaviours that can be considered to be domestic violence. The conceptual research and survey results examined suggests that those individuals who are most likely to be identified to criminal justice agencies, and consequently, court-mandated to rehabilitation programmes, are men who have engaged in either severe or repeated patterns of violence against female current or former intimate partners. Therefore, for the purpose of this book, I will use the phrase 'intimate partner violence (IPV)' to refer to the use of violent and abusive behaviours by men within current or former heterosexual intimate relationships.

Who Are 'Those Guys?'

Prior to the formal acknowledgement of IPV as a societal problem, intimate partner violence was viewed along with child abuse and sexual assault as reflecting acts committed by 'crazed sex fiends' or 'lust-murderers' (Taubmann, 1986, cited in Jennings, 1987). Similarly, perpetrators were viewed as damaged individuals, with the root of their behaviour lying in severe childhood trauma, psychopathology, brain damage and other intra-individual factors (Jennings, 1987). With the ascendance of the women's movement came an understanding of intimate partner violence as a socially learned phenomenon, which arises out of societally endorsed traditional sex roles, which serve to oppress women (Dobash & Dobash, 1979). From this perspective, such behaviours can be viewed as 'normal' rather than pathological, owing to the arguable pervasiveness of the underlying patriarchal beliefs and social structures (Bern & Bern, 1984). Indeed, Dobash and Dobash (1979) even go so far as to suggest that men who use violence in intimate relationships 'are living up to cultural prescriptions that are cherished in Western society' (p. 24). The evidence suggests however,that rather than fitting a psychiatric profile, IPV perpetrators come from all socio-economic backgrounds, ethnicities and occupational groups (Holtzworth-Munroe, Smutzler & Bates, 1997).

Despite the dominance of feminist sociological thinking in this area, interest in examining psychological and other individual factors in an attempt to identify a 'profile' of the IPV perpetrator has never waned. While it has been argued that such pursuits are misguided and serve only to propagate the myth that IPV is a function of some underlying psychopathology or addiction, and therefore is not the responsibility of individual men (Dobash & Dobash, 1992), the resulting knowledge may have important clinical implications if there is a therapeutic aim of rehabilitation groups for IPV perpetrators (this issue is discussed further in Chapters 3 and 6). In particular, this information may enable programme developers to tailor content to meet the needs of particular groups of offenders. A clearer understanding of individual risk may also be gleaned by considering a constellation of individual factors (Healey, Smith & O'Sullivan, 1998).

As IPV perpetrators have been identified in the literature on the basis of both criminal convictions, voluntary referrals to treatment programmes, and population-based screening, our understanding of the characteristics of these individuals is not unduly biased by their criminalization. Underlying the quest to identify the characteristics of IPV perpetrators is an implicit assumption that such individuals only engage in IPV – that they are specialists (Bouffard, Wright, Muftic et al., 2008). However, as already alluded to, there is considerable evidence that this is not the case, and that, as with all offender populations, IPV perpetrators represent a heterogeneous group. This is particularly the case when examining those samples identified on the basis of their criminal records. Such populations, like criminal populations in general, tend to be characterized by high levels of lifestyle instability (e.g. lack of stable employment, prior criminal convictions, substance misuse), and they are also likely to have other convictions for a range of criminal behaviours, not just those relating to IPV (Bouffard et al., 2008). Certainly, for a subsample of 'IPV offenders' they are possibly better categorized as generalized criminals/offenders who also engage in IPV (Klein & Tobin, 2008).

Indeed, the generally antisocial pattern of behaviours exhibited by this group is consistently identified within a number of IPV perpetrator typologies along with co-morbid antisocial personality disorder/psychopathy, which is not surprising given the behavioural basis of the classification schemes used. Holtzworth-Munroe and Stuart (1994), in their seminal literature review, hypothesized that such offenders would also be characterized by negative attitudes towards women, impulsivity, pro-offending attitudes, dismissive attachment style, and low empathy. These 'Generally Violent/ Antisocial (GVA) IPV perpetrators were also deemed to be most likely to have witnessed inter-parental violence or to have experienced direct victimization as a child, to use substances and to engage in the most serious and severe IPV perpetration as part of a wider repertoire of violent behaviours outside of the family context. This 'type' stands in contrast to two other subgroups: the 'Borderline/Dysphoric (BD)' and the 'Family Only (FO)' IPV types (Holtzworth-Munroe & Stuart, 1994).

Characterized by the high levels of emotion dysregulation typical of individuals presenting with borderline personality disorder (e.g. high levels of explosive anger, self-harming, fear of rejection, jealousy), the BD group were predicted to engage in moderate to severe IPV, but to be less inclined than the GVA group to engage in violence outside of an intimate relationship. The BD individuals are hypothesized to have experienced a high level of parental hostility and rejection during childhood and possible trauma responses to these experiences. In addition, such individuals express extreme dependence on, and fear of losing, their intimate partner. To a lesser extent than the GVA group, the BD group also exhibit impulsive traits, pro-violence attitudes and hostile attitudes towards women.

Finally, the FO group is deemed to have the fewest risk factors for IPV. These individuals are expected to engage in the least severe IPV and to be least likely of the three groups to engage in violence outside of the intimate relationship. In contrast to the BD and GVA groups, FO perpetrators are expected to be characterized by little or no psychopathology. It was hypothesized that the intermittent violence used by the FO group, during escalating marital conflict, arose from a combination of stress (general or relationship specific) and low-level risk factors (e.g. lack of relationship/communication skills, witnessing inter-parental violence during childhood).

Some empirical support has been found for the basic premises of this typology (Holtzworth-Munroe, Meehan, Herron et al., 2000) and typically studies have replicated either two (Chase, O'Leary & Heyman, 2001; Tweed & Dutton, 1998) or three of the subtypes (Hamberger, Lohr, Bonge et al., 1996; Langhinrichsen-Rohling, Huss & Ramsay, 2000). Taken together, these studies support the notion of the heterogeneous nature of IPV perpetrator samples, and identify clinically meaningful differences between these groups that may have implications for their response to intervention (this is discussed in greater detail in Chapters 3 and 9). Indeed, some evidence has been found to suggest that the BD and GVA groups respond differentially to different forms of group-based intervention (Saunders, 1996, discussed in Chapter 9). In addition, a recent study reported that men of the BD and GVA subtypes are more likely to fail to complete group-based interventions (Eckhardt, Holtzworth-Munroe, Norlander et al., 2008). Such findings are consistent with the broader literature that links risk to likelihood of treatment drop-out and recidivism (see Chapter 4).

The Impact of Intimate Partner Violence: The Reason to Intervene

So far we have examined the nature of IPV, determined that it is a multi-faceted and generally poorly defined phenomenon that affects the lives of millions of women around the world each year. We have also determined that, in general, men from all social groups are the most common perpetrators. However, in order to truly understand why we need to intervene in IPV, the consequences of this behaviour need to be examined.

Female victims of IPV report a broad constellation of short- and long-term 'injuries', which include physical, mental, and psychological injuries. IPV victimization is consistently associated with minor and severe physical injuries, chronic pain and, in the most serious scenarios, death (Campbell, 2002; Coker, Smith, Bethea et al., 2000; Stewart & Robinson, 1998). With some suggestion that pregnancy places women at increased risk of victimization (Jasinski, 2004), victims are at increased risk of obstetric and gynaecological injuries including miscarriage (Campbell, 2002). In addition, owing to the use of sexual control tactics in abusive relationships, victims are also at an increased risk of contracting sexually transmitted diseases (Coker et al., 2000).

A number of mental health and psychological consequences have also been identified. These include post-traumatic stress disorder, personality disorders characterized by borderline traits and dissociation, depression, anxiety, self-harm, low self-esteem (Dutton, Kaltman, Goodman et al., 2005; Sackett & Saunders, 1999; Sansone, Reddington, Sky et al., 2007; Stewart & Robinson, 1998). Interestingly, there is some evidence that it is psychological, rather than physical IPV that is more strongly associated with negative psychological and mental health outcomes for victims (Baldry, 2003; Follingstad, Rutledge, Berg et al., 1990; Lawrence, Yoon, Langer & Ro, 2009). In general, it is found that the greater the intensity of IPV, the worse the reported symptoms, suggesting a dose-response relationship (Jones, Hughes & Unterstuller, 2001).

A meta-analysis examining the role of IPV as a risk factor for mental health problems, found that women were at between 3 and 6 times increased risk of developing a range of psychological problems (Golding, 1999). Specifically, the weighted mean odds ratios for depression among victims was 3.8, for suicidality was 3.55, for post-traumatic stress disorder was 3.74, for alcohol abuse/dependence was 5.56, and for drug abuse/dependence was 5.62. However, such presentations reflect a complex interaction between the nature, duration and severity of the victimization, a woman's ability to cope with her experiences, and the extent of social support available to her (Taft, Resick, Panuzio et al., 2007). It must be noted however, that in the vast majority of research that has identified these associations, the typical research design employed is cross-sectional rather than longitudinal. It is unclear, therefore, whether such symptomatology only appears after the experience of victimization, or whether victimization occurred after the onset of symptoms. Nevertheless, the identified dose-response pattern points towards the former explanation as being most valid (Golding, 1999).

Owing to the family-based context in which IPV often occurs, women are not the only victims. According to the 1996 British Crime Survey, 29 per cent of women who reported experiencing IPV in the last year reported that their children were aware of it happening (Mirlees-Black & Byron, 1999). More recent North American data indicate that 43 per cent of households in which IPV crimes occurred included children, and that of these, 95 per cent had been exposed to IPV (Fusco & Fantuzzo, 2009). A substantial literature has examined and reviewed the evidence concerning the impact of direct, and secondary IPV victimization, on children. In general, the findings paint a picture of a range of negative developmental, social and cognitive outcomes for both boys and girls who have either witnessed IPV, or become direct victims of IPV themselves (Evans, Davies & DiLillo, 2008).

More specifically, exposure to IPV during childhood has been found to be associated with depression, anxiety, conduct problems, eating disorders, trauma symptoms, and later interpersonal and intimate relationship problems including violence, for which exposure to IPV during childhood is the most consistent risk factor (Brady, 2008; Evans et al., 2008; Grych, Jouriles, Swank et al., 2000). However, the pathways between exposure and outcome are complex and indirect (Evans et al., 2008), not least, owing to the comorbidity of physical and sexual childhood victimization, and the influence of myriad mediating and moderating factors that are rarely accounted for in the empirical literature. One prospective study which did control for child physical abuse, child neglect, general life stress, child cognitive ability and socio-economic status found that exposure to inter-parental violence during preschool years predicted conduct problems at age 16, particularly for boys, and predicted internalizing behaviours in girls at the same age (Yates, Dodds, Sroufe et al., 2003).

There is also evidence that non-physical forms of IPV exert a negative influence on child development, and that even in relationships that may be abusive, but not violent per se, the stress experienced by mothers may also negatively affect the development of their children (DePaola, Lambert, Martino et al., 1991; Lieberman, Van Horn & Ozer, 2005). This literature provides some evidence that the impact of IPV on women and children is far reaching, and can have long-term detrimental effects. Such data highlight the need to provide formal intervention in IPV so that its effects on individuals, families and society can be reduced.

Rehabilitation and Intimate Partner Violence

The terms 'rehabilitation' and 'treatment' have been taken to mean different things within the criminal justice system, depending on the underlying penal philosophy advocated at the time (Bowen, Brown & Gilchrist, 2002; Robinson & Crow, 2009). Consequently, the term treatment has been used to describe a mode of intervention based on an authoritarian medical model; the method by which offenders are dealt with by the criminal justice system and, more commonly, an approach to dealing with crime that is placed in contrast to retribution and punishment (Crow, 2001). For the purpose of this book, however, the term rehabilitation is taken to refer to the practice of crime prevention through directly challenging the economic, social or personal factors believed to be its causes (Hollin, 2001).

Interventions aimed at preventing crime, in this case intimate partner violence, have been conceptualized as operating on one of three levels: primary, secondary and tertiary prevention (Guerra, Tolan & Hammond, 1994). Primary prevention, sometimes referred to as developmental prevention (McGuire, 2001), aims to prevent the initiation or onset of partner violence. Such endeavours may include public awareness campaigns; policy changes; marital counselling; school-based interventions, and parenting classes (World Health Organization, 2002). secondary prevention targets identified 'at risk' groups with a view to early detection and intervention (McGuire, 2001). Interventions based at this level may focus on those with pre-existing behavioural problems and/or recently identified partner violence, and may include the provision of information regarding support services and counselling for perpetrators. Tertiary prevention is aimed at those offenders who have been convicted for partner violence, with the over-arching aim of reducing rates of reoffending (Gendreau & Andrews, 1990).

Since the mid-1990s, the British government has passed a range of criminal and civil justice legislation, and implemented procedural changes designed specifically to help victims of IPV bring their abusers to account. To this end, in 2006, the Sentencing Guidelines Council recommended that where appropriate in cases of IPV, custodial sentences should be imposed. However, it was also recognized that in some instances custody would be inappropriate. These cases were identified as those in which the use of violence was intermittent and did not reflect an entrenched pattern of behaviour. In addition, consideration of the intentions of the victim to remain in a relationship with the perpetrator was acknowledged, such that in 'low risk' relationships where the victim wishes to maintain a relationship with the perpetrator, judges are within their rights to pass a community sentence with a condition for the perpetrator to attend a rehabilitation programme.

Although programmes for IPV perpetrators have been offered since the 1970s in the voluntary sector (see Chapter 4), it is only since the early years of the twenty-first century that rehabilitation programmes for male IPV perpetrators have sat centrally within the criminal justice response. This reflects broader changes to government policy, which has endorsed the development, standardization and accreditation, of offending behaviour programmes for many types of offence. This move has been fuelled by increasing evidence that some approaches to offender rehabilitation can be effective in reducing reoffending (see Chapter 4), although the evidence for the effectiveness of programmes for male perpetrators of IPV is less than conclusive (this is discussed further in Chapter 8).

Conclusion

The purpose of this first chapter has been to provide an overview of some of the key debates regarding issues of definition that are central to research and policy in this area. It should be clear from this discussion that our understanding of what constitutes IPV is intrinsically linked to the theoretical perspective adopted, as theory guides the methods used to collect data, as well as their interpretation. It should also be clear that the lack of adherence to consistent definitions and methodologies has led to a huge range in the estimates of prevalence of IPV around the world. Regardless of the methods employed, however, there is consensus in the view that all estimates are likely under-representations of the real extent of IPV. There is growing consensus also that IPV constitutes a range of behaviours of differing severity and impact, motivated by different factors either within the individual or within the couple, and that those individuals who come to the attention of criminal justice agencies are likely to be male, and to use violence as a means of control.

The remainder of this book examines in more depth the move towards offering rehabilitation programmes for male IPV perpetrators in the UK, drawing on the international literature where appropriate. Chapter 2 examines the recent legislative change in this area which has culminated in domestic violence perpetrator programmes (DVPPs) being a central component of the criminal justice response to IPV. This is examined in the context of case attrition and reviews the limited literature that has attempted to examine the effectiveness of these changes. Chapter 3 provides an overview and critique of current theories of IPV in order to set the theoretical context for the book. In Chapter 4, attention turns to the history of DVPPs and how UK developments have been influenced by international progress, including the development of accredited programmes. Chapters 5 and 6 examine current UK criminal justice based practice, including risk assessment, and the links between risk and rehabilitation. A critical review of evaluation methodology is given in Chapter 7, before the results of international and national outcome evaluation studies are examined in Chapter 8. A broader evaluation model which emphasizes consideration of the process of intervention is provided in Chapter 9. Finally, Chapter 10 provides a point of consolidation and future directions for intervening in domestic violence.

2

Changes to the Criminal Justice Response to Partner Violence

Alongside the identification of partner violence as a social problem in the 1970s, feminists started to campaign for the criminalization of partner violence (Hester, 2006). Such campaigning has achieved positive outcomes since the late 1980s with the implementation of a range of policy initiatives aimed at developing criminal justice responses to partner violence (Harwin, 2006). In addition, supplementary procedural changes within the criminal justice system have been implemented with two main objectives: to move toward a multi-agency coordinated response to partner violence, and to reduce the level of case attrition (withdrawal) in criminal prosecutions for partner violence (S. Edwards, 2000).

The aim of this chapter is to provide an overview of these procedural and legislative changes within the criminal justice system as they impact on the prosecution of partner violence offenders. Readers interested in civil justice developments, and criminal justice developments aimed at supporting victims and/or witnesses through the process are pointed in the direction of Hague and Malos (2005) or Burton (2008) for authoritative and comprehensive examination of these issues. This chapter first provide an outline of the problem of attrition in the prosecution of cases of intimate partner violence. This will lead into an overview of change across the sector including changes to the detection, prosecution, and sentencing policies and procedures. The final part of the chapter will critically examine the evidence regarding the impact of these changes on the prosecution of cases, and case attrition.

The Rehabilitation of Partner-Violent Men, by Erica Bowen

Attrition in the Prosecution of Partner Violence Cases

Not all crimes result in a successful prosecution, and this is particularly the case in the prosecution of intimate partner violence, despite the comparative ease with which the perpetrator can be identified (HMCPSI & HMIC, 2004). Early data indicated that only 2.2 per cent of over 700 partner violence cases reported to the police in London, resulted in successful prosecution (S.S.M. Edwards, 1986). Historically, both in the UK and internationally, the response to incidents of partner violence by criminal justice agencies has come under justifiably sharp attack, owing to the failure to report incidents of partner violence, to arrest male perpetrators, and to treat domestic violence as a less serious crime than non-domestic violence (Dobash & Dobash, 1979; Paterson, 1979; Walker, 1979).

The possibility of a case being withdrawn from the criminal justice process is present at every stage of engagement with criminal justice agencies, including: the incidents to which the police are called, potential crime reports, crime reports, arrests, charges, and convictions (HMCPSI & HMIC, 2004). In addition, there are factors peculiar to the interpersonal context of violence within relationships that exert additional influence on a victim's ability and/or inclination to cooperate with the process. In *Violence at home: Joint thematic inspection of the investigation and prosecution of cases involving domestic violence*' (HMCPSI & HMIC, 2004) the following issues are highlighted:

> ... concerns about the consequences of reporting where the victim is financially dependent upon the perpetrator; ... the underlying fear that contact with the police and social services..exposes them to the risk of their children being removed. Others ... believe that the end result will not be worth the cost to them. (p. 24)

This final point, relating to the victim's reluctance to begin the process is important as domestic violence has higher under-reporting rates than any other crime (HMCPSI & HMIC, 2004). Indeed, it is at the point of reporting that the greatest proportion of cases are lost. Early estimates indicated that well over 90 per cent of incidents were never reported to the police (R.E. Dobash & Dobash, 1979). It is widely documented that victim help-seeking behaviour typically involves the police as a last resort, with friends, family, health care professionals and solicitors more likely to be made aware of intimate partner violence (Morris & Gelsthorpe, 2000). Somewhat dated figures estimate that, on average, 35 incidents of domestic violence occur prior to the police being notified (ACPO, 1996, cited in CPSI, 1998), illustrating that the rate of under-reporting of domestic violence incidents, and lack of victim confidence in the criminal justice process, is a considerable problem if the criminalization of domestic violence is to serve to protect victims.

Policing partner violence

In the United Kingdom, prior to 1970 it was very rare for police to use their powers of arrest in incidents of partner violence, owing to the widely held belief that violence in the home was a private issue and, consequently, a civil rather than criminal matter, which was outside of their remit (Grace, 1995; Hague & Wilson, 2000). Moreover, domestic violence was typically perceived as being less serious than non-domestic violence, and therefore required a less interventionist approach to policing (Morley & Mullender, 1994). The conclusion of research conducted in the UK in the 1980s was that the police were generally very reluctant to become involved in domestic violence incidents; and when they did, typically attempted reconciliation and occasionally sided with the aggressor who was rarely arrested even when serious injury had resulted from their actions (S.S.M. Edwards, 1989; Pahl, 1985). As Morley and Mullender (1994) note:

> legal criteria (whether an offence had been committed) were frequently superseded by 'moral' criteria (often a suspicion that the woman was to blame for the violence). (p. 14)

In addition to general reluctance, the police were found to be slow to respond to domestic incidents, and poor record keeping practices prevented an accurate picture of domestic violence from being formed (Edwards, 1986). It is perhaps unsurprising, given this evidence, that victim perceptions of the police response to domestic violence has been less than favourable. Indeed, although the police are one of the most frequently contacted agencies during the course of a domestic violence incident, they were perceived by victims to be one of the least helpful (e.g. Dobash & Dobash, 1979). Tuck (1992) attributed the difficulties in dealing effectively with domestic violence experienced by the police to the overarching police culture. According to Tuck (1992):

> The police tend to be a male-dominated, action oriented organization who like decisions to be clear cut and problems to have a solution. (p. 11)

As Saunders and Size (1986) note, incidents of domestic violence are characterized by complex interpersonal dynamics and are for the police, among the most complex, dangerous and unpredictable cases to be involved in, the solutions to which being rarely straightforward.

Aside from victim reluctance to involve the police in domestic violence incidents, so-called 'victim-screening' (Buzawa & Buzawa, 2003), is evident – that is, certain police practices which serve to screen out incidents once they are reported. For example, a UK study found that once called to attend a domestic violence incident, police would listen outside the house to which they were called. If no noise was audible from outside, the incident would be recorded as 'no call for police action'. It was estimated that 60 per cent of domestic violence incidents were screened out through this practice (Sheptyki, 1991). Given both victim reluctance to call the police, and potential police screening-out strategies, it is perhaps not surprising, therefore, that the rate of arrest resulting from domestic violence incidents has been found to be lower than 10 per cent (e.g. 7.7%; Holmes, 1993).

Factors influencing arrest in intimate partner violence

The decision to intervene, arrest, caution and/or charge a perpetrator of domestic violence is down to the discretion of the police officer who attends the incident (Hester,

Pearson & Harwin, 2007) and reflects both subjective appraisals of events as well as objective evidence (where available). Although mandatory arrest laws have been implemented in many North American states since the 1980s, it does not follow that all offences result in arrest (Henning & Feder, 2005). Despite the potential availability of objective evidence, research suggests that such decisions have traditionally been unduly influenced by the subjective perceptions of events, victims and perpetrators. Consequently, a considerable number of studies have examined the factors associated with an increased likelihood of the police arresting perpetrators of domestic violence (see Buzawa & Buzawa, 2003 for an authoritative review of this literature).

Central to early feminist arguments for greater police intervention was the observation that the police exhibited biased judgement in their appraisals of domestic violence incidents. Indeed, there is evidence that arrest is more likely to occur if police officers believed that victims had acted 'appropriately' (E.S. Buzawa & Buzawa, 1993). Feder (1998) also found that if officers held attitudes that were biased against helping victims of domestic violence, then arrest was significantly less likely to occur. Buzawa and Buzawa (2003) note, however, that it is the role of the police to make appraisals of these typically ambiguous situations, and that the police are no more immune to biased information processing than anyone else. When determining who is, and who is not a victim, it is necessary to consider the behaviour and demeanour of both parties. On this basis, it has been found that at incidents where the victim is visibly upset, arrest is more likely to occur. Indeed, if the victim was seen to 'tremble' this was more likely to increase the odds of arrest occurring than if the victim was injured (E. Buzawa & Hotaling, 2000).

The extent to which a victim is perceived as 'cooperative' has also been found to influence the likelihood of arrest (Berk & Loseke, 1981; Buzawa & Austin, 1993; Ferraro, 1989; Smith, 1987). Buzawa and Buzawa (2003) note that victims of domestic violence are typically viewed by police as 'fickle' (p. 149) owing to the likelihood of their retracting their complaint following reconciliation with their violent partner. Research has found, however, that police perceptions of cooperation often actually reflect other situational variables (A.L. Robinson & Chandek, 2000). Such variables include: whether the victim has consumed alcohol or is perceived to be under the influence or alcohol, or intoxicated; whether the victim is abusive or disrespectful to officers. Under such circumstances the likelihood of arrest is reduced (Berk & Loseke, 1981; E.S. Buzawa & Buzawa, 1993; Ferraro, 1989; Ford, 1993; Smith, 1987). If, on the other hand, both parties are present and the victim makes an allegation of assault, signs an arrest warrant, or simply requests that an arrest be made, then it is more likely to occur (Berk & Loseke, 1981; Buzawa & Austin, 1993; Worden & Pollitz, 1984).

Returning to the potential influence of victim injury, the available data provide equivocal evidence. In some studies the presence of injury or more serious injury increases the likelihood of an arrest being made (e.g. Buzawa & Austin 1993; Ferraro, 1989; Hotaling & Buzawa, 2001). In contrast, other studies find no such association (e.g. Berk & Loseke, 1981; Feder, 1998; Worden & Pollitz, 1984). Indirect evidence to suggest that victim injury may indirectly influence arrest decisions comes from Berk & Loseke's (1981) finding that if a victim called the police they were less likely to make an arrest. These findings were interpreted as suggesting that the ability to call was perceived as a proxy indicator of a lack of serious injury, which the police took to indicate that the incident was not serious and, therefore, did not warrant arrest. However, these findings were not replicated by Worden and Pollitz (1984).

Other factors associated with police appraisals of risk or incident seriousness and their potential influence on arrest decisions have also been examined. As might be expected, if an incident is characterized by features thought to increase the risk of serious outcomes, arrest is more likely to occur (Buzawa & Buzawa, 2003). This has been found to be the case in incidents where weapons are used (Kane, 1999), children are present (Buzawa & Austin, 1993) and the perpetrator is in violation of a court order (Holmes, 1993).

Finally, early studies found relatively consistent evidence that the nature of the relationship between victim and perpetrator influenced the decision to make an arrest. In particular, if offenders were married to their victim the likelihood of arrest was reduced (Dobash & Dobash, 1979; Ferraro, 1989; Martin, 1976; Worden & Pollitz, 1984). In some studies, being married and cohabiting reduced the likelihood of arrest (Worden & Pollitz, 1984), whereas in other studies, cohabiting increased the likelihood of arrest (Buzawa & Austin, 1993). It seems that an ongoing relationship between the parties involved has been interpreted by officers as reflecting an increased likelihood of the victim withdrawing her complaint, and thus reducing the likelihood of achieving a prosecution, thereby leading the police to be more reluctant to make an arrest in the first place (Buzawa & Buzawa, 2003).

Prosecuting partner violence

Early international data suggested that partner violence offences which resulted in arrest led to prosecution in only 10 per cent of cases (Ford, 1993). Prosecutors appeared reluctant to proceed with cases on the basis that victims were likely to withdraw their support and, consequently, were unreliable witnesses, that domestic violence was a private matter, and the view that incarceration may be detrimental to families if the perpetrator was the main breadwinner (Ford, 1993). However, the findings that cases of domestic violence are rarely prosecuted has recently been challenged (Garner & Maxwell, 2009). Garner and Maxwell reviewed 135 international reports of conviction rates for domestic violence and found that approximately one-third of offences reported to the police result in a prosecution. Nonetheless, there is inconsistent support for the protective impact of conviction in cases of domestic violence (Hart, 1993; Ventura & Davis, 2005).

Factors influencing the decision to prosecute partner violence cases

In contrast to the glut of studies regarding the policing of partner violence, the literature that has examined the prosecution of partner violence is, by comparison, rather limited (Hartley, 2001; Henning & Feder, 2005). Hartley (2001) observes that the literature has focused primarily on four areas: obstacles to prosecution, victim cooperation/non-cooperation, juror knowledge of domestic violence and the role of prosecution in preventing future violence (p. 510). Henning and Feder (2005) additionally found two studies that examined the factors associated with trial verdicts in domestic violence cases. Of interest here are studies that have examined barriers to prosecution and victim cooperation, as these are of most relevance in understanding attrition.

To date, researchers have been unable to consistently identify predictors of prosecution of domestic violence cases (Henning & Feder, 2005) when victim, defendant and offence-related factors are considered. For example, the majority of studies have found no association between relationship type and the decision to prosecute (Davis, Smith & Taylor, 2000; Henning & Feder, 2005; Hirschel & Hutchinson, 2001; Kingsnorth, Macintosh, Berdahl et al., 2001; Schmidt & Steury, 1989) and those studies that have identified associations provide conflicting results (Dawson & Dinovitzer, 2000; Kingsnorth, Macintosh & Sutherland, 2002). For example, Dawson and Dinovitzer (2000) found that if the couple were dating, prosecution was less likely to result. In contrast, Kingsnorth et al. (2002) found that if the couple were married, but not cohabiting, the likelihood of prosecution was also reduced. No relationship characteristics have been found to increase the likelihood of prosecution.

Only one study found that if the victim of the alleged assault was under the influence of alcohol, or deemed to be intoxicated at the time, the likelihood of prosecution was reduced (Davis et al., 2000). No other study found any association between these variables. Two studies have examined the relationship between the victim also being arrested at the scene and later prosecution (Kingsnorth et al., 2001, 2002). Kingsnorth et al. (2001) identified no such relationship, whereas the victim being arrested was associated with a reduction in the likelihood of the perpetrator being prosecuted in the later study by Kingsnorth and colleagues. Finally, there is no evidence to suggest that the likelihood of prosecution is significantly affected by either the victim's ethnicity (Henning & Feder, 2005; Hirschel & Hutchinson, 2001; Kingsnorth et al., 2001, 2002), or age (Dawson & Dinovitzer, 2000; Hirschel & Hutchinson, 2001).

Examination of the potential role of perpetrator (defendant) characteristics in prosecutorial decision making has yielded similarly equivocal findings. For example, whereas Schmidt and Steury (1989) found that if a defendant is unemployed, the likelihood of prosecution increased significantly, the opposite was found by Hirschel and Hutchinson (2001). However, Henning and Feder (2005) found evidence that socio-economic status (of which employment is one indicator) was associated with prosecution, with those defendants of a higher socio-economic status less likely to face prosecution. Once again, the weight of evidence suggests that the likelihood of prosecution appears not to be associated with defendant race (Hirschel & Hutchinson, 2001; Kingsnorth et al., 2001, 2002) or age (Dawson & Dinovitzer, 2000), although Henning and Feder (2005) found that if a defendant was Caucasian and older, they were less likely to face prosecution.

The role of risk (as assessed by prior arrest/incarceration/domestic violence) has also been examined, again yielding less than straightforward results. For example, there is some evidence that prior conviction increases the likelihood of prosecution (Schmidt & Steury, 1989). However, this is not always the case, with some studies finding no significant association (Dawson & Dinovitzer, 2000; Henning & Feder, 2005; Kingsnorth et al., 2001). Moreover, in some studies, prior arrests for domestic violence or known history of domestic violence have been found to increase the likelihood of prosecution (Davis et al., 2000; Martin, 1994) but not in the majority of studies (Dawson & Dinovitzer, 2000; Henning & Feder, 2005; Hirschel & Hutchinson, 2001; Kingsnorth et al., 2001, 2002). Only one study has found that prior arrests for non-domestic violence offences increases the likelihood of prosecution for domestic violence (Kingsnorth et al., 2002). Slightly more consistent evidence exists to suggest that if the defendant was either under the influence of alcohol, or was perceived to be intoxicated at the time of the offence, the likelihood of prosecution increases (Henning & Feder, 2005; Kingsnorth et al., 2001; Martin, 1994; Schmidt & Steury, 1989). However, Hirschel and Hutchinson (2001) failed to identify such an association.

Several factors relating to the potential severity of the incident have been examined. In the majority of studies, injury to the victim and/or severity of injury is associated with an increased likelihood that the case will be prosecuted (Henning & Feder, 2005; Hirschel & Hutchinson, 2001; Kingsnorth et al., 2001, 2002; Schmidt & Steury, 1989; Ventura & Davis, 2005; Worrall, Ross & McCord, 2006). However, some studies identified no association between severity of victim injury and the decision to prosecute (Davis et al., 2000; Dawson & Dinovitzer, 2000), and furthermore, Martin (1994) found that the more serious the injury to the victim, the *less* likely prosecution was to follow. A minority of studies have examined whether the presence of weapons affects decisions to prosecute, and while two studies found that the use of weapons increased the likelihood of prosecution (Henning & Feder, 2005; Schmidt & Steury, 1989), Davis et al. (2000) found that the presence of weapons exerted no influence on such decisions.

Studies have also considered the potential influence of additional forms of evidence and case characteristics on prosecutorial decisions. Factors considered include the availability of non-witness dependent evidence (e.g. photographic evidence, eyewitnesses, 911/999 tapes), in addition to the extent to which victims are cooperative and supportive of police action. Once again, the findings in relation to these factors are inconsistent. The evidence suggests that the availability of non-witness dependent evidence only exerts a marginal influence on the decision to prosecute with only two studies identifying a positive association between the presence and/or availability of independent eyewitnesses and decisions to prosecute (Kingsnorth et al., 2001, 2002). Moreover, of those studies that examined the availability of photographic or audio evidence (Dawson & Dinovitzer, 2000; Kingsnorth et al., 2001), neither found any associations with the decision to prosecute. There is tentative evidence for the role of victim evidence in the decision to prosecute, which suggests that the provision of video evidence (Dawson & Dinovitzer, 2000), the victim requesting that the defendant be arrested (Hirschel & Hutchinson, 2001; Kingsnorth et al., 2001) and the victim's cooperation with authorities (Dawson & Dinovitzer, 2000; Kingsnorth et al., 2001) are likely to increase the chance of prosecution.

Factors influencing victim support of prosecution

It is interesting that the available evidence reviewed above provides only tentative evidence for the role of victim support in the decision to prosecute cases, particularly in light of the reported importance of this factor in the general literature (Kingsnorth & Macintosh, 2004). Edwards (1986) for example found that the 80 per cent of cases dropped by the CPS were dropped as a result of either of two factors: the victim being unwilling to appear as a witness, or her lack of support for the prosecution. Dwyer (1995) reports that until 1978, victims of domestic violence could be compelled to testify against their abuser. Case law arising from *Hoskyn v. Metropolitan Police Commissioner* overturned this position. However, in 1984 the Police and Criminal Evidence Act reinstituted the common law practice of compelling wives to act as witnesses (S.S.M. Edwards, 1985). In practice, however, prosecutors have been unwilling to use reluctant and/or potentially hostile witnesses despite being permitted to pressurise victims of domestic violence to appear (Tuck, 1992). Therefore, victim willingness to provide testimony remained very relevant to prosecution decisions. Despite the importance of victim evidence, research has focused more extensively on trying to understand factors associated with victims' support for prosecution more generally, rather than their willingness to provide testimony. As Bennett, Goodman and Dutton (1999) state, understanding the factors associated with a victim's decisions to withdraw is important if we are to value victims' needs within the criminal justice process. Moreover, victims have been found to withdraw in nearly half the cases that are initiated (Rebovich, 1996). Therefore, a criminal justice response aiming to increase prosecutions needs to account for these factors in any changes that are made.

Research has identified a number of reasons as to why victims may choose to withdraw their support for the prosecution of their (ex) partner. In a North American context, Ford (1991) found that victims would often call the police in order to help them manage the violence experienced at one occasion but, after this goal is satisfied, drop the charges against the perpetrator. In addition, Bennett et al. (1999) identified a further four reasons provided by victims to account for their withdrawal of support. These included:

- misperceptions/ignorance about the court process;
- frustration with the complexity of court process and the length of time taken for cases to conclude;
- fear about their own, and their children's, safety during the case; and
- disagreement with imprisonment as the goal when many have children by the offender and/or believe that their partners need rehabilitation.

The results of a quantitative study by the same team of researchers found that the level of social support, severity of violence experienced and having children in common with the defendant influenced victims' cooperation with prosecution (Goodman, Bennett & Dutton, 1999). Specifically, the more people that victims could call on in order to oversee practical issues such as childcare, the more likely they were to cooperate with prosecution. In addition, victims were significantly more likely to cooperate if they had experienced more severe violence, and if they had children with their abuser – a factor which led to a fourfold increase in the likelihood of cooperation.

Similar themes have appeared in British research. For example, Cretney and Davis (1997) found that a substantial proportion of victims had hoped that the outcome of the case would lead to the defendant gaining access to some form of intervention to help them control their behaviour. In her examination of case attrition for domestic violence, Hoyle (2000) identified three reasons given by victims for their withdrawal from prosecution, which included: not wanting to break up existing family bonds (perceived as an inevitable outcome of prosecution); fear of retaliation, and the perception that the effort and risks associated with pursuing prosecution were not justified, given the sentencing practices at that time, which resulted most frequently in domestic violence offenders receiving a fine. An evaluation of a specialist domestic violence court (see p. ••, this chapter) in Wolverhampton found additional support for the validity of these reasons given by victims. Issues of greatest concern to the victims interviewed included, living in fear of the offender, problems regarding the offender's access to children, and finding a safe place to live.

Summary

In summary, it is evident that despite the apparent availability of the perpetrator in domestic violence cases, the likelihood of an incident leading to prosecution is small. Moreover, the likelihood of either arrest or prosecution appears to be potentially influenced by a wide range of factors. Some of these can be considered legal factors – that is, those factors arising from policy, or situational characteristics with direct relevance to the law (e.g. presence of weapons), while others reflect extra-legal factors and tend to reflect subjective biases (e.g. race, relationship status). However, the evidence suggests that the factors that increased the likelihood of arrest either reflected objective indicators of offence seriousness, or reflected the requests and behaviours of victims.

A problem arises, however, with the apparent consensus that police perceptions of victims as those likely to drop charges leads to a decrease in the likelihood of arrest. This perhaps reflects a fundamental mismatch between the goals of police and victims. As Tuck (1992) notes, the police goals of arrest are to secure a conviction, the goal for victims, in contrast, can range from gaining immediate, short-term control of a set of circumstances, to potentially removing the perpetrator from their life via prosecution (Ford, 2003). Henning and Feder (2005) observe, however, that in contrast to research conducted prior to the adoption of mandatory arrest policies, later studies indicate that more weight is placed on legal factors when the decision to arrest is made.

That many of the findings examined provide only equivocal evidence for the influence of the range of factors identified, perhaps reflects the wide range of legal practices within and between countries and jurisdictions, and also policy change across time. Consequently, the ability to draw firm conclusions regarding the role of these factors is somewhat impeded. However, that biases in decision making, and the response to domestic violence have been found at all, is problematic and indicates that clear policies are required in order to provide a response to domestic violence that best serves victims.

A Changing National Policy Context

In the late 1990s, the British Government formally renounced the acceptability of violence within intimate relationships through their 'Living without fear' campaign. This aimed to target the societal attitudes believed to endorse, legitimize and perpetuate intimate partner violence. The need for multi-agency working around domestic violence was then acknowledged in 2000 *in Domestic Violence: Break the chain multi-agency guidance for addressing domestic violence*, which detailed exemplars of good practice in the field. The 'Living without fear' initiative detailed three strands of practice: support and protection, justice and preventing violence, all of which have been maintained as the bedrock of government policy for the last ten years (HMCPSI & HMIC, 2004). In 2003, the Government produced a consultation paper *Safety and Justice*, in which its strategic approach to tackling domestic violence was described. In 2005, the *National Report* (Home Office, 2005) identified five outcomes that were to be achieved by Government. These included:

- reducing the prevalence of domestic violence, particularly in high incidence areas and /or communities;
- increasing the rate that domestic violence is reported;
- increasing the rate of reported domestic violence offences that are brought to justice;
- ensuring victims of domestic violence receive adequate protection and support;
- reducing the number of domestic homicides. (p. 25)

The pursuit of these targets have, in combination with the above-mentioned policies, fed into the changing criminal law and policies of the police, crown prosecution and court services during the last decade.

Partner Violence within the Criminal Law

During the period of social change that led to the expanding provision of refuges for women escaping violent relationships, civil and criminal legal remedies were available to those who experienced assault as defined predominantly by the Offences against the Person Act 1861. Indeed, this remains the case today (HMCS, 2007). Chapter 1 showed that domestic violence is rarely defined solely in terms of physical aggression. Consequently, there are a range of alternative behaviours that may constitute domestic violence, not all of which can be categorized as illegal acts. Some of these have been formally recognized, such as the case-law definition of actual bodily harm (ABH) to include shock and nervous disorders, thus acknowledging the more psychological consequences of domestic violence. Table 2.1 contains some examples of behaviours that constitute domestic violence that *may* be considered as criminal offences, and the potential relevant offence.

Table 2.1. Examples of some of the behaviours that can occur in cases of domestic violence and which MIGHT amount to a criminal offence (reproduced with permission from the CPS, 2009)

Behaviours	Possible offences
Pressuring a victim/witness to 'drop the case' or to not give evidence	Witness intimidation, obstructing the course of justice, conspiracy to pervert the course of justice
Physical violence, with or without weapons, including punching, slapping, pushing, kicking, headbutting, and hairpulling	Common assault, actual/grievous bodily harm, wounding, attempted murder
Violence resulting in death	Murder, manslaughter
Violence resulting in miscarriage	Child destruction, procuring a miscarriage or abortion
Choking, strangling, suffocating	Common assault, actual/grievous bodily harm, attempting to choke, strangle or suffocate
Spitting at a person	Common assault
Threatening with an article used as a weapon e.g. a knife, tool, telephone, chair	Common assault, actual/grievous bodily harm, wounding, criminal damage, affray, threatening behaviour
Throwing articles e.g. crockery, even if they miss their target	Common assault, actual bodily harm, criminal damage, affray, threatening behaviour
Tying someone up	Common assault, actual bodily harm, false imprisonment
Threatening to kill someone	Threats to kill, harassment
Threats to cause injury	Common assault, affray, threatening behaviour
Threats to seriously damage or undermine social status	Harassment, blackmail
Damaging or destroying property or threatening to damage or destroy property	Criminal damage, threatening to cause criminal damage, harassment
Harming or threatening to harm a pet	Criminal damage, threatening to cause criminal damage, cruelty to animals, harassment
Locking someone in a room or house or preventing them from leaving	False imprisonment, harassment
Preventing someone from visiting relatives or friends	False imprisonment, kidnapping, harassment

(Continued)

Table 2.1. (*Continued*)

Behaviours	Possible offences
Preventing someone from seeking aid e.g. medical attention	False imprisonment, actual bodily harm
Preventing someone from dressing as they choose or forcing them to wear particular make-up, jewellery and hairstyles	Actual bodily harm, harassment
Racial abuse	Racially aggravated threatening behaviour, disorderly conduct or harassment
'Outing' e.g. sexual orientation or HIV status	Harassment, actual bodily harm, blackmail
Enforced financial dependence or unreasonably depriving someone of money	Harassment
Dowry abuse	Blackmail, harassment, common assault, actual/grievous bodily harm
Unreasonable financial demands	Blackmail, harassment
Forced marriage	Kidnap blackmail, false imprisonment, common assault, actual/grievous bodily harm, rape, indecent assault
Enforced sexual activity	Rape, indecent assault, harassment
Persistent verbal abuse e.g. constant unreasonable criticism	Harassment, actual bodily harm
Offensive/obscene menacing telephone calls, text messages or letters	Improper use of public telecommunication systems, malicious communications, actual/grievous bodily harm, harassment
Excessive contact e.g. numerous telephone calls to check someone's whereabouts	Harassment, false imprisonment
Secret or enforced administration of drugs	Common assault, actual bodily harm., grievous bodily harm, administering poison
Neglecting, abandoning or ill-treating a child	Child cruelty
So-called 'honour crimes'	Murder, aiding and abetting suicide
Female circumcision	Female genital mutilation
Forced entry into a house	Using violence to secure entry

Table 2.2 Aggravating factors for domestic violence

Factor	Comment
Abuse of trust and/or power	Trust is understood to mean 'a mutual expectation of conduct that shows consideration, honesty, care and responsibility' (s3.3 p. 4). It is the abuse of trust or power where domestic violence behaviours that are not in and of themselves criminal, impact on the potential sentence offered. Specifically, the guidance states that an abuse of trust may include either direct violence or emotional abuse. In addition, an abuse of power refers to the restriction of another's autonomy through any form of abusive behaviour, and can include psychological, financial, sexual, emotional and physical abuse (p. 4).
Vulnerable victim	Vulnerability is defined as reflecting a potential range of factors including, but not limited to, for example: race, religion, language, financial, age, intellectual ability, recent/current pregnancy. In circumstances where these factors have been exploited by an offender, including preventing the victim from seeking help, a more severe sentence should be handed down.
Use of child contact arrangements	If a man through, child contact arrangements with an estranged partner, instigates abusive behaviours, this is deemed to be an aggravating factor.
Proven history of threats or violent by the defendant in domestic settings	The guidelines stipulate that there should be an appraisal of the cumulative impact of victimization experiences including threats over an extended period of time, particularly where there is sufficient prior evidence that such offences occurred. If an offender has a prior criminal record for domestic violence offences this is viewed as a statutory aggravating factor as per the Criminal Justice Act 2003.
History of disobedience to the court	If the offender has a history of failing to adhere to prior sentences, including breaches of orders (e.g. restraining orders) imposed with a view to increasing the safety of a victim, which have resulted in increased risk to the victim and anxiety or distress, this is also viewed as an aggravating factor. If the alleged offence constitutes a breach of a non-molestation order, breach of a sentence handed down for a similar prior offence (e.g. conditional discharge), or a breach of a restraining order, then this too increases the severity of the offence.
Victim forced to leave home	Finally, if as a result of the alleged offence, the victim has been forced to leave her home, this would be viewed as an aggravating factor.

What should be apparent from tables 2.1 and 2.2 is that nowhere in criminal law is an act defined as 'domestic violence' per se. This is in spite of ongoing pressure to isolate domestic violence as a unique offence, due to the characteristics of the relationship between victim and perpetrator and the systematic nature of the abuse, which together serve to restrict the options available to victims (Tadros, 2005). An offender cannot be prosecuted for 'domestic violence' per se, but instead for a range of criminal behaviours that occur within an intimate relationship. Consequently, as not all abusive behaviours constitute illegal behaviours, many perpetrators can never be held accountable for their behaviour by criminal law.

Changes to criminal law

Since the mid-1990s, several notable criminal laws have been passed that have direct implications for the handling and prosecuting of domestic violence.

Criminal Justice and Public Order Act 1994 s.142

It was through the statutory amendment to the Sexual Offences Act provided by s.142 that rape within marriage became a criminal offence. Prior to this it was assumed in law that by virtue of marriage, wives automatically consented to all sexual advances by their husbands (Burton, 2008).

Protection from Harassment Act 1997 (criminal)

Although originally implemented to target stalkers, the main advantage of this act is its availability to those who have not lived with their abusive partner, nor had children with them (HMCS, 2007). There is considerable evidence that victims of domestic violence are likely to be victims of stalking. For example, Wallis (1996) found that in relation to the most serious incidents of stalking, in nearly 40 per cent of cases, the perpetrators were men who targeted either their ex-partners or someone with whom their ex-partners had subsequently had a relationship with. These figures are similar to those reported in the BCS (Walby & Allen, 2004), in which 37 per cent of the victims of aggravated stalking (that which featured additional violence), identified their current or former intimate partner as the perpetrator. This is slightly higher than the 34 per cent reported for perpetrators of non-aggravated stalking (Budd, Mattinson & Myhill, 2000).

Criminal proceedings under the Protection from Harassment Act 1997 can result in both a conviction and a restraining order, which can prohibit an offender from a wide range of conduct. Two offences arose from the Act: harassment (under section 2) and fear of violence (under section 4; see table 2.2 for offence definitions). The police can arrest anyone they suspect of committing either offence and do not need a warrant to do so. Separate incidents do not need to be of the same type of behaviour in order to constitute a 'course of conduct'.

The Crime and Disorder Act 1998

This act underpins multi-agency working at a local level in order to tackle crime. This is achieved through the implementation of regional community safety strategies, which should specifically target domestic violence and which are held accountable through the audit process (Home Office, 2000). Such crime and disorder reduction partnerships bring together the police with additional agencies including health services (compelled to act through primary care trusts in the 2004 update of this act), housing associations, specialist domestic violence services and other statutory and voluntary sector organizations, in order to provide an inter-agency response to domestic violence. Each local authority was compelled under the Act to identify the level of domestic violence in their region and to devise strategies to deal with it.

Domestic Violence, Crime and Victims Act 2004

The Domestic Violence Crime and Victims Act, developed as a bill addressing some of the proposals set out in the *Safety and Justice* consultation paper, was passed into law at the end of 2004. Some elements of the Act are intended to improve both civil and criminal justice responses to domestic violence. It includes, but is not limited to the following components that impact on the criminal justice response:

- Breach of non-molestation orders (a civil court order) is made an automatic criminal offence,
- There is a new offence of allowing the death of a child or vulnerable adult.
- Common assault is made an arrestable offence – that is, police can now arrest for common assault without a warrant. However, from January 2006, the police have had a single power of arrest under the Serious and Organised Crime and Police Act 2005, which repeals this clause
- From July 2007, section 12 of the Domestic Violence, Crime and Victims Act 2004 amends section 5 of the Protection from Harassment Act 1997 and inserts a new section 5a to give courts wider powers to impose restraining orders when sentencing for any offence. Prior to this, restraining orders were only available when an offender was convicted under sections 2 or 4 of the Protection of Harassment Act 1997. Under the Domestic Violence, Crime and Victims Act 2004 this has changed to allow courts to impose restraining orders where the defendant has been tried or acquitted. This move is designed to deal with a situation where a criminal case ends in acquittal but it is evident from the circumstances of the case that ongoing protection is required for the victim (HMCS, 2007).

This Act has been broadly welcomed by many agencies that are involved in providing services to domestic violence victims, and represents a substantial overhaul of legislation, which, for the first time, is directed specifically at domestic violence as a crime. However, the Act has been criticized for its narrow focus and the emphasis placed on criminal justice agencies with the role of extended multi-agency working somewhat marginalized (Hague & Malos, 2005).

Changes to the policing of partner-violence

Changes to the policing of partner violence in the UK have mirrored those observed in the USA. In the late 1980s, the general approach to partner violence incidents in the USA moved from one of indifference to one of control (Mederer & Gelles, 1989), based in part on the feminist critique of policing practices detailed earlier in this chapter, and the results of the first study into the effectiveness of arrest as a deterrent in domestic violence incidents (Sherman & Berk, 1984). In the Minneapolis Police Experiment, 'misdemeanour' domestic violence incidents were randomly assigned to one of three experimental conditions: separation, advice/mediation or arrest. Interviews were then conducted with victims and perpetrators during a six-month follow-up period. In addition, official records detailing any subsequent domestic violence incidents were also collated. Sherman and Berk (1984) found that when the perpetrator was arrested the rate of recidivism was only 10 per cent in contrast to 19 per cent for the advice and mediation group, and 24 per cent for the separation group. These results led to the adoption of presumptive arrest interventions by a large number of urban police forces (Mederer & Gelles, 1989) and formed the basis of recommendations for the criminalization of domestic violence, and appropriate criminal justice responses in the USA (Attorney General Task Force on Family Violence, 1984, cited in Mederer & Gelles, 1989). However, it must be noted, that more recently there have been six replication studies of the Minneapolis experiment. Of these, only two replicated the findings (Sherman, 1993).

During this same period in the UK, the criticisms of policing were also beginning to have an impact on policy. Indeed, the police were the first criminal justice agency to tackle the need to improve their response to domestic violence (Morley & Mullender, 1994). For example, in 1986, a Home Office Circular (69/1986) called for a review of police officers' training and record keeping with regard to domestic violence. The circular also highlighted the need to safeguard victims and children at the scene of domestic violence incidents, and for officers to provide victims with appropriate information and, if necessary, take them to a refuge and liaise with associated support services. While this circular importantly linked police practice to the risk management of victims and children, it fell short of acknowledging and addressing the widely held criticisms of police practice at that time regarding the police attitudes towards domestic violence. It took a further four years before the criminalization of domestic violence was officially documented.

Home Office Circular 60/1990 represented a significant change to national policy with regard to the policing of domestic violence in England and Wales, and parallel circulars were issued in Scotland and Northern Ireland (Morley & Mullender, 1994). Several recommendations concerning police practice were made. These included the adoption of a more interventionist, pro-arrest, pro-prosecution approach (Hague & Malos, 2005) in which domestic violence was treated as seriously as non-domestic violence; the arrest of perpetrators was emphasized, but the safety of women and children was prioritized above this. To this end, the police were required to produce information leaflets for victims, to arrange for medical assistance if needed and to escort victims to a place of safety if requested. The police were warned about the dangers of attempting to reconcile parties involved in domestic violence incidents and were instructed to interview victims and perpetrators separately. Police forces were also encouraged to either set up dedicated domestic violence units, or to appoint specialist officers to liaise with other agencies in the case of domestic violence. Forces were also required to produce policy documents detailing their procedures for handling domestic violence cases. Circular 19/2000 provided additional guidance building on this original circular, framed within more recent legislation. The linking of the police response with other domestic violence agencies alluded to in Circular 60/1990 was more formally reported in the Home Office document *Domestic violence: Break the chain multi-agency guidance for addressing domestic violence*, which provided detailed advice on a partnership approach to the policing of domestic violence (Applegate, 2006). Explicit guidance for the investigation of domestic violence cases, and cases of stalking has been produced by the Association for Chief Police Officers (ACPO, 2008, 2009). Step-by-step comprehensive procedures are outlined in this document for all officers involved in the investigation and prosecution of domestic violence cases with clear guidelines for the handling of information, consideration of victim safety, and their role within a multi-agency context.

Changes to Crown Prosecution Service (CPS) policy

It has been acknowledged by the CPS that, historically, incidents of domestic violence have not been perceived to be as serious as those of non-domestic violence, nor have they been treated as such when it comes to the sentencing of such offences (CPSI, 1998). Indeed, Cretney & Davis (1997) found evidence that the reduction of charges from s.47 (ABH) to s.39 (Common Assault) was commonplace and that for initial charges of ABH, domestic violence offences were more likely to result in the charge being withdrawn, increased rates of bind over and a relative paucity of sustained serious charges (s.47 or above). Reducing s.47 offences to s.39 offences means that such offences are dealt with summarily, via magistrates' courts. Such practice was viewed as having three advantages: speed of processing, greater certainty of the outcome of prosecution and cost reduction. That processing via magistrates' courts reduces the overall speed with which the offence is dealt with was viewed positively as it reduced the period of uncertainty for the victim, and allowed the CPS to make the most from the victim's original commitment to prosecution. However, such sentencing practices minimize the severity of domestic violence both to the victim and society, and implicitly reinforces such behaviour by failing to administer appropriate punishment.

A review of CPS decision making in cases of domestic violence was undertaken in 1998 (HMCPSI, 1998). The inspectorate reported that, in the majority of cases, the correct decisions were being made. However, a number of notable concerns were also raised. These included that in a number of cases that were dropped, owing to the victim no longer wishing to give evidence, there had been sufficient evidence to continue with the case. In addition, in a number of cases, decisions to prosecute and terminate had been made without key personnel having access to important relevant information. The use of relevant contextual background information was found to be inconsistent despite its acknowledged utility. It was found that in over 75 per cent of cases in which the victim withdrew, the case was dropped without any pursuit of alternative courses of action, despite evidence that, when used, alternative courses of action led to successful prosecutions in all instances. The recommendations that emerged from this inspection included the use of special measures for victims in order to increase their safety and support the provision of evidence; the acquisition of all relevant background information; seeking appropriate background regarding the withdrawal of victim support including whether such decisions were coerced, and the use of alternative, 'victimless' prosecution strategies, where appropriate (HMCPSI, 1998).

In 2001, the CPS policy for prosecuting cases of domestic violence was amended in light of the Human Rights Act 1998, the revised Code for Crown Prosecutors and the Youth Justice and Criminal Evidence Act 1999. In addition, the Criminal Justice Act 2003 gave the CPS a greater level of responsibility in deciding whether suspects should be charged, and what offences they should be charged with (HMCS, 2007). The revised CPS policy adopted many of the recommendations that emerged from the earlier inspection of CPS practice. In particular, the policy placed an emphasis on the victim's priorities, including safety, support and information so that throughout the prosecution process the victim's safety and that of any children or any other person involved, is prioritized. In addition, the policy emphasized joined-up working between the CPS and police in order to keep the victim informed of information pertinent to the case and/or her safety. When making key decisions, prosecutors were to be made fully aware of the victim's circumstances, including the existence of relevant civil orders. The construction of cases without relying solely on evidence given by the witness was also mandated. In addition, victims were no longer required to attend court to provide reasons for their withdrawal from the case, as had previously been practice. A programme of staff training was also announced, along with the provision of domestic violence coordinators in each of the 42 CPS areas.

The CPS policy was subsequently amended in 2005 and again in 2009. The 2005 amendments reflected the Government's National Delivery Plan. Consequently, the policy highlighted the importance of working sensitively with victims, while acknowledging that owing to the relationship dynamics involved, domestic violence is nearly always an aggravated offence (CPS, 2005). The 2009 amendments reflected broader changes to the court system (see later, this chapter) and legislation, including: statutory charging; the training of CPS staff; implementation of special measures for witnesses and victims; specialist domestic violence court services; independent domestic violence advisers (IDVAs); multi-agency risk assessment conferences (MARACs); the Code of Practice for Victims of Crime; the Prosecutors' Pledge; and the introduction of Witness Care Units. Consequently, the guidance restates the importance of victim safety and appropriate information sharing and multi-agency engagement. It also reinforces the requirements to charge where sufficient evidence is available, and to continue with prosecutions in instances where the victim withdraws, only after full consideration of the potential risk associated with such decisions. CPS policy also allows for fully trained staff to conduct the case in order to provide a more informed service to victims.

The decision to prosecute follows the Full Code Test which has two elements – the Evidential Test, and the Public Interest Test. According to the Evidential Test there must be sufficient evidence of a crime to provide 'a realistic prospect of conviction' (HMCS, 2007, p. 25). It is not the case that should a victim withdraw their support for the prosecution then the case is automatically discontinued, as it is possible that prosecution may still occur if there is additional evidence which meets these criteria. In cases where public interest necessitates a prosecution, if for example, there are escalating levels of violence, the victim is extremely vulnerable, or there are children involved, a witness may be compelled to attend court. Should the victim withdraw her support, the police, acting on instruction from the CPS, will take a statement from the victim explaining the reasons for withdrawing her support, confirming whether the original statement was true, and asking whether she has been coerced into withdrawing (HMCS, 2007).

The Public Interest Test is only considered once the criteria for the Evidential Test have been met. Relevant public interest factors include the extent to which the offence was premeditated, whether the offence was committed in the presence of, or in close proximity to, a child, or where there are grounds for believing that the offence is likely to be repeated. In addition, when considering whether prosecution is in the public interest, it is also necessary to consider the potential impact of prosecuting or not, on the victim and family (CPS, 2005). In instances where the decision is taken to prosecute, despite the victim withdrawing her support, the CPS will consider whether to apply to the court for the victim statement to be submitted without her having to give evidence in court. This is typically, however, only allowed in special circumstances, such as when the victim cannot be found. In addition, it might be possible to include the victim as a witness through the use of special measures afforded to vulnerable witnesses or the victim may be compelled to attend and give evidence. Such decisions will be made after consultation with the police in order to determine the potential impact on risk to the victim and any children involved.

Changes to sentencing guidelines

The manner in which an offence is sentenced is one way of indicating how seriously a particular category of crime is taken (Cretney & Davis, 1997). At the end of the 1980s, Edwards (1989) argued, based on data from the 1984/85 London Policing Study, that the sentencing of domestic violence cases propagated the myth that such offences are trivial and, in the main, non-criminal. More recently, however, the task of reinforcing the message that domestic violence is a crime to be taken as seriously as non-domestic violence crimes, has been supported by changes to the sentencing guidelines for rape and domestic violence.

Rape

Although rape within marriage was formally acknowledged by the law in 1994, in practice, rape within relationships was perceived as less serious than 'stranger rape' and the relationship between defendant and victim was often perceived as a mitigating rather than aggravating factor. This issue was directly addressed by the 2002 revision to the sentencing guidelines (SGC, 2002). The guidelines argue that while there may exist a greater level of fear in stranger rapes, the abuse of trust within marital or relationship rapes renders the offence of equal seriousness. Indeed, there is evidence that the impact on victims of relationship or marital rape is more devastating than that experienced by victims of stranger rape (Finkelhor & Yllo, 1985). The new guidelines, therefore, state that rape by a defendant known to the victim should be treated no less seriously than rape committed by a stranger, and that sentencing should proceed as in the cases of stranger rape, and should account for the presence of both aggravating and mitigating factors (HMCPSI & HMIC, 2004).

Domestic violence

In 2006, definitive guidance for the prosecution of domestic violence offences was finally produced by the Sentencing Guidelines Council to which all courts in England and Wales should adhere (Criminal Justice Act 2003 s.172). This document clearly stated that offences committed within a 'domestic' setting should be considered, at a minimum, to be as serious as those committed in a non-domestic setting. Moreover, it is suggested that those offences committed within a domestic setting should actually be perceived as aggravated offences as the context within which they occur is likely to be characterized by factors that increase the seriousness of the offending. Explicit within the guidelines are the aggravating and mitigating factors to be considered at the point of sentencing.

Aggravating factors

The 2006 guidelines identify a number of specific aggravating characteristics of criminal acts within a domestic context, the presence of which is likely to lead to an increase in the appraisal of offence seriousness, and consequently the potential range of sentences available. The factors identified in table 2.2 are to be considered in addition to standard aggravating factors applicable to all other offence categories.

Burton (2008) notes that the inclusion of 'psychological bullying' as potential provocation may prove to be problematic for the courts unless dealt with sensitively as it is likely that such a criterion may open up criticisms for allowing relatively minor incidents of 'alleged nagging' to constitute sufficient provocation for serious domestic violence.

Mitigating factors

The two factors offered as mitigation against the severity of an offence are both highly controversial within the context of domestic violence. The first mitigating factor – positive good character – is offered as a potential mitigating factor in all sentencing, regardless of the nature of the offence. Within the domestic violence context, however, this is particularly germane due to the observation that male domestic violence perpetrators can, in some instances, present themselves as of good character to those outside of their intimate relationships (WNC, 2004). This is acknowledged within the guidelines and, in order to minimize the impact of such abilities, it is recommended that any evidence of good behaviour in external contexts should not be taken to be relevant in cases where there is an established pattern of domestic violence behaviour. However, when the court can be satisfied that the alleged offence represents a single solitary act, positive good character evidence may be considered relevant to sentencing.

The second mitigating factor – provocation – is equally contentious, owing to claims that criminal justice agencies have in the past regularly accepted extremely trivial departures from stereotypical 'appropriate wife behaviour' as 'provocation' (S. Edwards, 1987). The sentencing guidelines, however, seek to clarify this position by stating that provocation occurs only in instances in which the context of the alleged offence included either actual or anticipated physical or psychological abuse by the alleged victim. The guidelines also make clear that there must be sufficient evidence of this being a factual antecedent of the alleged incident in order for the charge of provocation to be accepted as a mitigating factor. Moreover, it is stated that such a charge of mitigation is more likely to be accepted if the provocation has occurred over an extended period.

While it is a general principle in cases of violent offences that the sentence is determined by the seriousness of the offence, without influence of the victim's wishes, and the sentencing guidelines specifically argue that this is the case in instances of domestic violence offending, it is also acknowledged that there may be circumstances where the victim's wishes should be considered. Specifically, if both parties within the relationship express the wish for the relationship to continue, and the court is confident that such a wish is genuine, not coerced by either party, and will not result in exposing the victim to increased risk of future victimization, then the court may mitigate the sentence. A second consideration which may mitigate the sentence is that of the potential impact of sentencing on the children within the relationship. Such deliberations must include a consideration of the risk to children of future domestic violence, balanced with the potential disruption of having a parent withdrawn from their family unit (SGC, 2002).

Little specific detail is provided in the guidelines regarding the nature of sentences to be imposed (Burton, 2008). However, it is noted that those offences involving violence more severe than those that warrant charges of common assault or actual bodily harm will typically warrant a custodial sentence (SGC, 2006). However, in circumstances where it is likely the resulting custodial sentence will be short, the court has the power to consider passing a lesser sentence. Such a sentence might be a community sentence with the provision for the offender to attend a domestic violence perpetrator programme. Consequently, this is the first time that the provision of perpetrator programmes is acknowledged formally through sentencing guidelines. A major caveat to this decision is that it can only be taken if the court is convinced that it is possible for the offender to be rehabilitated and genuinely wishes to change his behaviour. It is acknowledged however, that if there is a proven history of abuse, this condition is unlikely to be met. This caveat is important when considering referrals to programmes as it is unlikely that many of the offenders for whom such a sentence is deemed appropriate will not have previous histories of domestic violence. What is likely however is that such histories will not be formally 'known' or 'accepted' – i.e. there may be no record of incidents in previous relationships, and the current victim may also not be aware of previous victims and/or may never have contacted criminal justice agencies before. Moreover, such sentencing requires that a sufficiently detailed assessment is conducted through which the suitability of the individual offender for a programme is adequately determined given the widely acknowledged unreliability of self report, and the tendency for minimization, denial and victim blaming by domestic violence offenders (R. Dobash, Cavanagh, Dobash et al., 2000). Referral criteria for programmes are discussed in considerably more detail in Chapter 6.

Changes to the Court System

The need to make changes to the manner in which courts deal with cases of domestic violence has only recently been formally acknowledged. In 2002, the British Government recognized the potential to introduce specialism within the criminal court system in their White Paper *Justice for All* (A. Robinson & Cook, 2006). Within this paper, the Government set out its plans to investigate the potential benefits of clustering domestic violence cases within one court. These proposals, specific to domestic violence, were set against broader proposals for reshaping the criminal justice system in England and Wales, in order that it adopt a victim centred approach. Additional pressure to engage more directly with victims and witnesses throughout the prosecution of cases arose from the publication of the framework paper *Narrowing the Justice Gap* (2002), which provided evidence that offenders were brought to justice in only approximately 20 per cent of crime reported to the police. Such engagement is particularly important in domestic violence cases where the victim is often the only witness to the crime. The following year, the Criminal Justice Service published *No Witness – No Justice* (2003), which advanced a new protocol for information sharing with victims and witnesses alongside the provision for the separation of prosecution and defence witnesses at court. The aim of this paper was to provide practice guidelines aimed at facilitating the provision of evidence by witnesses and/or victims through providing information, support and protection. These principles were then re-emphasized in the 2003 Home Office strategy for improving services for victims and witnesses.

Specialist domestic violence courts (SDVCs)

In response to the widely acknowledged problems associated with the prosecution of domestic violence cases, courts have increasingly adopted a more specialized service. The specialization of courts in the criminal justice system is not a new concept (Walsh, 2001), and specialized domestic violence courts have been adopted internationally (USA, Canada, Australia) since the first was set up in the early 1980s in Cook County, Illinois (Eley, 2005). The American Bar Association (1996, cited in Eley, 2005) explains that with reference to courts:

> specialization usually signifies that a court has limited and frequently exclusive, jurisdiction in one or more specific fields of law. Specialized courts are typically defined as tribunals of narrowly focused jurisdiction to which all cases that fall within that jurisdiction are routed.

The courts that were initially set up in the USA and Canada adopted different models for dealing with cases – some handled both criminal and civil cases, others reserved a specific session to deal with criminal matters. Aside from improving the court process for victims of domestic violence, courts often served to promote specific approaches to domestic violence: 'problem solving' or 'therapeutic jurisprudence' (Cook, Burton, Robinson et al., 2004). Such approaches focus on the extent to which the legal process promotes the psychological and physiological well-being of those it affects (Hester, Westmarland, Pearce et al., 2008). Consequently, rather than simply deciding guilt, this approach aims to understand the root causes of the problem, and achieves this through the judge working as part of a multi-agency partnership in order that a multi-disciplinary and holistic approach is taken to understand the problem. Typical models include support for victims, treatment for perpetrators in combination with judicial monitoring in order to hold offenders accountable, and access to multiple services (Hartley, 2003). Such approaches have been adopted in Australia, New Zealand and Spain (Stewart, 2005).

In the UK, the first part-time specialized cluster court was set up in Leeds in 1999 (Walsh, 2001). This was followed in 2002 by courts in Cardiff, Wolverhampton, west London and Derby, and in Croydon and Caerphilly in 2004 (Hester, Pearce & Westmarland, 2008). As is characteristic of many innovations in the response to domestic violence, the initial development of such courts reflected a perceived need in the community rather than statutory mandate. Indeed the Department for Constitutional Affairs (DCA, 2006) argues that SDVCs should be thought of as systems rather than as modified court processes. Although the court process is central to SDVCs, the early identification of domestic violence via ancillary agencies (e.g. health, education, local authority, criminal justice, voluntary) is also a key element. The SDVC, therefore, represents, a coordinated community response in which civil and criminal justice interventions are combined, victim safety is increased, and perpetrators are held accountable for their behaviour through a multi-agency response.

Three specialist courts were examined by HMCPSI and HMIC in their joint inspection. As a result, it was suggested that the main benefits of such courts were the professionalism of prosecutors, the efficient flow of information, and the support available to victims. In addition, the presence of a police officer was perceived to be a positive factor, given the protection and support offered to victims and the improved efficiency of prosecutions (HMCPSI & HMIC, 2004). Court users reported that, owing to the specialist nature of the court, they felt that domestic violence was taken seriously with sentences that reflected this. The resulting inspection report called for the systematic evaluation of such courts in order to increase the evidence base and confidence in any initial conclusions. Cook, Burton, Robinson and Vallely completed this research in 2004.

The SDVC evaluation (Cook et al., 2004) examined the process and outcomes of cases heard at specialist courts in Cardiff, Derby, west London, Leeds and Wolverhampton. The evaluation consisted of mixed methods: interviews with key agency representatives; examination of relevant documentation (reports and prior evaluations); examination of CPS files and site visits. In terms of the type of domestic violence incidents that reached court, the majority of cases were charged as either s.39 Common Assault, or s.47 Actual Bodily Harm, committed by male perpetrators against female victims with whom their relationship featured a pattern of prior domestic violence, and who had been injured in the index offence.

Although the study identified several concerns with elements of the criminal justice process (e.g. missed opportunities for evidence gathering by the police) several benefits of the SDVC system were identified. These included:

- the perception that cases were expedited;
- improvements in bail condition decisions;
- high levels of victim satisfaction with support and information sharing;
- evidence that victim support increased victim engagement with criminal justice process;
- victim satisfaction from the message sent to all parties that domestic violence was being taken seriously, and the support offered throughout the process.

It is interesting to note, however, that despite these positive features, half of the victims retracted at some point during the process, typically just after one month into proceedings. While the authors acknowledge that victim retraction is not a feasible outcome measure of effectiveness for SDVCs owing to the possible pressures experienced by victims to retract, this finding questions the suitability of a purely criminal justice response to domestic violence. This therefore suggests that although the Government may be set on increasing the number of prosecutions for domestic violence, this may not be what victims actually want in all cases. Those victims who retracted were typically engaged in an ongoing cohabiting relationship with the defendant, and were more likely to have been injured in the index offence. Indeed, despite some victims requesting 'help' for their partners, it seems that the opportunity to offer help through Community Rehabilitation Orders was not taken up in the majority of cases as sentences were typically fines or other monetary penalties (Cook et al., 2004). However, the authors concluded that the SDVC process as a whole offered substantial benefits to victims and society and recommended the development of SDCV systems across the country.

The Specialist Domestic Violence Court (SDVC) system in England and Wales

The consequences of this evaluation have been far reaching with the Government pledging the development of regional domestic violence courts. This national system was initiated in 2006 (HMCS, 2008). The Specialist Domestic Violence Court (SDVC) system is a specialized method of dealing with domestic violence cases in the Magistrates' Courts. Specialist criminal domestic violence courts operate either by:

- Clustering: all domestic violence cases are grouped into one court session to deal with a range of matters – bail variation, pleas, pre-trial interviews, pre-sentence reports and sentencing. Some cluster courts also hear trials in specific domestic violence sessions.

Or:

- Fast-tracking: priority is given to domestic violence cases by allocating specific sessions of the court list (e.g. 1 in 4 court slots allocated to domestic violence for further hearings/trials (HMCS, 2007). According to the DCA (2006) SDVC systems should share the following core components, and close coordination of these components is deemed vital to the success of the SDVC system:

- multi-agency partnerships;
- Multi-Agency Risk Assessment Conference (MARAC) and Multi Agency Public Protection Arrangements – coordination between existing public protection arrangements;
- identification of cases – within any/all public organizations (e.g. education, health, housing, criminal justice, civil justice agencies);
- specialist domestic violence support services;
- trained and dedicated criminal justice staff;
- domestic violence cases either clustered or fast-tracked;
- equality and diversity issues – good practice in relation to gender, sexuality, ethnicity and disability;
- data collection and monitoring;
- court facilities – separate entrance/exits or making special provisions; separate waiting facilities for victims and defendants;
- children's services;
- community-based perpetrator programmes.

Integrated domestic violence courts

The first integrated domestic violence court (IDVC) was set up in Croydon, London. In contrast to the cluster or fast-track specialist courts, the IDVC brings together cases of domestic violence that have criminal components and concurrent Children Act or civil injunction proceedings (Hester et al., 2008). Therefore, both criminal and family matters relating to one family, and where domestic violence is a factor, are heard before the same judge, wherever possible. According to the Department for Constitutional Affairs Resource Manual (DCS, 2006) the aims of the IDVC are to:

- ensure that all cases are dealt with justly;
- ensure that the safety of survivors of domestic violence/abuse and their children are considered and addressed by the court at every stage;
- hold perpetrators of domestic violence/abuse accountable to the court for their actions and to monitor their compliance with court orders;
- provide an efficient and expeditious response to criminal and family domestic violence proceedings;
- increase the amount and quality of information available to the court to enable effective decision making by the court at all stages;
- demonstrate that domestic violence is taken seriously by the court;
- increase the confidence in and use of the courts by those experiencing domestic violence
- achieve this as part of a coordinated partnership response;
- share information about the workings and impact of the pilot court at a national level.

Specifically, the criminal case is completed to the point of conviction or acquittal before the family case is heard by the same judge. It is hoped that by combining criminal and civil approaches the processing of cases will be expedited and benefit from transparency of information sharing (Hester et al., 2008). It must be noted however that not all domestic violence cases may be eligible to be heard at IDVC as these procedures are only available at magistrate court level. Therefore any criminal component which is sent to Crown Court becomes automatically excluded from IDVC (Hester et al., 2008).

Summary

Since the beginning of the twenty-first century, substantial changes have been made to the criminal justice response to domestic violence, from addressing some of the potential gaps in criminal law provision, to the manner in which the police, crown prosecution and court services investigate and prosecute incidents. Such changes have been made in order to place the victim at the centre of this response and, consequently, to provide a more sensitive and risk-aware service.

So Have These Changes Improved the Response to Partner Violence in the UK?

In order for change within the criminal justice system to be identified, it would have been necessary for a systematic programme of research to be conducted before and after the implementation of policy change, or at the very least for the processing of domestic violence cases to have been systematically recorded throughout this period. This alas, is not the position in the UK. Consequently, in order to determine the extent of change we have to rely on the findings of a few studies that have assessed the impact of discrete elements of policy change. These have focused primarily on the police response and the development of specialized domestic violence courts.

The impact on reporting incidents of partner violence

As stated in the introduction to this chapter, the raft of legislative and policy change that has been implemented since the mid-1990s has focused on one real goal – to increase the number of cases of domestic violence brought to justice. It has already been reported that the point where the greatest proportion of cases are 'lost' is the point at which victims decide whether or not to involve criminal justice agencies. Early data suggested that only 2 per cent of cases were actually reported to the police (Dobash & Dobash, 1979). Consequently, any reported increase on this number would possibly indicate an impact of policy change, and changes in victim's perceptions of the potential utility and benefit of criminal justice agency involvement.

In recent times, data concerning the incidence and reporting of domestic violence incidents has been collated via the BCS – a nationally representative, self-report victim survey. Data pertaining specifically to the reporting of domestic violence cases has been available via this method since 1981. The 2007/08 report (Kershaw, Nicholas & Walker, 2008) indicates that during this period the percentage of victims of domestic violence who reported incidents to the police rose substantially. For example in 1981, only 19.6 per cent of cases were reported, whereas in the 2006/07 year this had risen to 44.7 per cent. Most recently (2007/08), this figure has declined to 39.7 per cent, but still represents a twofold increase in the percentage of victims reporting to the police. It must be noted, however, that throughout the same period, the rates of domestic violence reported within the BCS have also dropped considerably.

On the face of it, these figures may present an encouraging picture regarding the reporting of domestic violence. However, these data need to be interpreted with caution as it is not possible to determine which percentage of victims reported intimate partner violence, given the broad definition of domestic violence now currently used by the Home Office, as this includes violent and abusive behaviours by anyone within a household. It is interesting to note, however, that the trends in these data seem to follow trends in data that suggest that public confidence has increased in both the police and the criminal justice system (Kershaw et al., 2008). However, a disparity between these trends appears when the results relating to those individuals who had experienced crime in the last 12 months are examined. Conversely, these data suggest that those individuals, who were either a victim or a witness of crime, were less likely to have high levels of confidence in the criminal justice system, and less likely to rate the police highly, than compared to those who had not experienced crime. It is not possible to determine the associations between public perceptions and reporting of domestic violence incidents specifically, but these data perhaps indicate that victim reporting may reflect the need to control a situation rather than broader attitudes about police and criminal justice system efficacy.

The impact on policing

Since the implementation of Home Office Circulars 60/1990 and 19/2000, a small number of disparate studies have examined their effects on police practice and, more recently, the implementation of recommendations arising from the Domestic Violence Crime and Victims Act 2004, has been published (Hester, Westmarland, Pearce et al., 2008). However, prior to 1991, as the police were not required to identify and record domestic violence cases separately from other cases, true evaluation of the impact of this circular is impossible (Grace, 1995). Most notably, Grace (1995) conducted an early survey and evaluation of the implementation of the first of these, collecting data from September 1992. Of the 41 (out of 42) police forces to participate in the survey, it was found that all but three had developed policy documents, the majority of which only existed as a direct response to the circular. Only five forces had domestic violence units which were dedicated solely to dealing with domestic violence (nearly half had units that were less specialized). The vast majority (39) of forces stated that they worked within a multi-agency context, although this usually meant that they referred victims to support services and that they rarely engaged with other agencies outside of this function. The majority (33) of forces reported adequate mechanisms for recording and monitoring domestic violence incidents. The majority of forces provided an information leaflet for victims, although in some instances external agencies had prepared them. The notification of victims of court dates and release dates for perpetrators were very rare. In part, this was due to poor communication between agencies as the police forces were not typically informed by prisons of release dates. In general, and somewhat worryingly, forces believed that training was adequate.

More detailed examination of the processing of domestic violence cases within five police forces identified a mixed response to the circular. For example, more than half of operational officers reported not receiving any additional guidelines for dealing with domestic violence, and a third had not heard of the circular. Despite the pro-arrest ethos of the circular, which was acknowledged by the majority of officers, alternative priorities such as victim safety took precedence at domestic violence incidents, and decisions to arrest reflected whether the victim would support this action. Contrary to the survey results, more detailed analysis failed to identify systematic recording practices.

Though committed to their work, domestic violence officers appeared to exert little influence as they were often marginalized, which in some cases resulted in poor communication between officers with regard to the processing of cases. Although victims reported positive interactions with specialist officers, this was often not the case with other members of the police force. In addition, victims perceived that courts dealt unfairly with their cases because of an underlying belief that domestic violence was not perceived as a serious crime.

Overall, it seems that in the early 1990s, the main recommendations of Circular 60/1990 had been acknowledged in policy, but not implemented in practice by the majority of police forces in the UK. In particular, Grace (1995) highlighted persisting flaws in the monitoring and recording of incidents; insufficient emphasis placed on getting cases to court; insufficient adoption of specialist domestic violence officers; poor integration of these officers within the general police force, and greater inter-agency cooperation, as areas requiring attention.

Picking up on issues regarding internal force structures that Grace (1995) had highlighted, Plotnikoff and Woolfson (1998) further examined how variation in internal structures affected the police response to domestic violence, with particular focus on the role of domestic violence officers, information management, monitoring and training. Adopting a very similar methodology to that of Grace – a national survey of police forces, followed by in-depth analysis of five forces, continuing variation in practice was again identified five years later. Significant variations in definitions of domestic violence were found in policy documents with regard to the specificity of relationship identified, the range of behaviours included and the range of offences recorded as domestic violence, with only one force making reference to repeat victimization within their definition. Consequently the ability to compare performance across forces was, and continues to be, impeded. There also appeared to be some lag between changes in criminal law and updating of policy documents, although 90 per cent of policy documents did reflect the pro-arrest approach requested by Circular 60/1990.

In contrast to Grace's findings, 36 forces had appointed specialist domestic violence officers (DVOs), half of which were based in specialist units. However, there appeared to be considerable variation between forces with regard to the remit of the role of DVOs, and this was not always made explicit. What emerged was a picture of the DVO role as one which was unclear, undervalued by colleagues and included high levels of stress and increased workload within a context of typically unsatisfactory line management.

In relation to the police response examined through information management systems, a small number of notable instances of inappropriate procedure were identified. These included the mishandling of calls within the command and control systems; inconsistent coding of domestic violence incidents; inaccurate tagging of incidents for the attention of DVOS; inconsistent provision of historical information regarding domestic violence to patrol officers, and insufficient information-sharing regarding domestic violence incidents. In addition, there appeared to be considerable uncertainty about what was done with information collated in relation to the number of domestic violence incidents, which suggested that while monitoring may occur, the resulting information is ineffectively used to develop service provision. Finally, it was observed that the majority of forces did not have a coherent training plan regarding domestic violence, despite the emphasis placed on domestic violence within policy.

Taken together, these results suggest that nearly a decade after the publication of Circular 60/1990 which aimed to homogenize police practice in relation to domestic violence, considerable variation in the interpretation of its recommendations, and adherence to good practice guidelines was evident. Unfortunately, similar inconsistencies have also been identified more recently. The most recent review of police practice (HMCIP and HMIC, 2004) found that considerable effort had been made to change the police response to domestic violence incidents and to increase the seriousness with which they are perceived. However, it was also noted that paper policies did not always translate into good practice, with regional variations in the guidance issued being observed. In addition, evidence indicates that there exist quite dramatic regional variations in arrest rates, despite these alleged changes to police practice. For example, Cook et al. (2004) reported that only 10 per cent of incidents resulted in arrest in Derby, while in Leeds, one-third of incidents resulted in arrest. Hester (2006) reported that 26 per cent of incidents in Northumbria resulted in arrest, and similar figures were reported by Hester and Westmarland (2005) when examining data from Bradford. Overall these data suggest that ongoing effort is needed to provide a more uniform police response to domestic violence.

The effects of CPS policy and specialist domestic violence courts

In 2008, a Home Affairs Select Committee reported on the response to domestic violence. According to this report (HASC, 2008), the CPS has set targets for the number of unsuccessful prosecutions of domestic violence at 30 per cent. Figures provided by the CPS for the report indicate that in 2004, of the 34,893 domestic violence cases dealt with, 45 per cent were not successfully prosecuted. In contrast, in 2008, of the 14, 966 cases dealt with up to that point, 67 per cent had been successfully prosecuted. In areas that were serviced by a specialist court, this rate was 70 per cent. Indeed, a review of the first 23 specialist courts found that 10 of these achieved over 70 per cent successful prosecutions and had the least number of cases discontinued where no evidence was being offered (HMCS, 2008). In addition, in the 11 SDVC areas for which data were available, over 80 per cent of domestic violence incidents had resulted in arrest. Those SDVCs that were most successful in bringing perpetrators to justice shared several specific characteristics. These were:

- strong multi-agency partnerships;
- effective systems for the identification of cases;
- IDVAs with a focus on supporting victims at court;
- good training and dedicated staff;
- clustered court listing or a combination of cluster and fast-track court listings;
- criminal justice perpetrator programmes. (HMCS, 2008, p. 41)

As previously discussed, the CPS has adopted powers to continue with prosecutions after victims have withdrawn their support. Data obtained in December 2006 indicate that the proportion of victims who retracted their statement had fallen from 37 per cent in 2002, to 28 per cent in 2006 (HASC, 2008). In 2006, of 868 cases in which the victim retracted, the CPS continued with prosecution in 421 (49%) of cases, based on the use of alternative evidence (999 tapes, photographs, other witness evidence) – an increase from the 36 per cent in 2005, 40 per cent in 2004, 27 per cent in 2003 and 19 per cent in 2002 (HASC, 2008).

These data provide some indication that the inclusion of measures aimed at supporting victims through the criminal justice process just may be having a positive impact on the number of cases continued through this process. In addition, it seems that the CPS is now more willing to continue with 'victimless' prosecutions. These data also provide tentative evidence that successful prosecutions are more likely to occur in SDVCS. Such data seems consistent with the benefits identified from the pilot court evaluation (Cook et al., 2004). More recently, the IDVC based in Croydon was subject to preliminary evaluation. Despite initial expectations that at least 75 cases would be heard at the court during the 18-month study period, only five cases were heard during the first 12 months. Consequently, the evaluation conducted by Hester, Pearce and Westmarland (2008) was unable to examine whether the court fulfilled its role. The reasons behind such a low caseload were not clear, and possibly reflected inadequate flagging of domestic violence cases, suggesting that the identification of those eligible to be heard at the court (those with both criminal and civil justice components) was flawed.

Alternatively, it is possible that the actual relevant caseload is considerably lower than estimates had suggested. The two victims who were interviewed after their cases were heard expressed additional concerns. Although generally happy with the manner in which domestic violence had been dealt with, both victims reported being made to feel as though they just had to move on, without the dynamics of domestic violence or its potential impact on their children being completely understood by the judge. This raises concerns regarding the understanding and appraisal of risk within the family that arises from domestic violence.

In general, therefore, it would appear that there is insufficient data available to determine the impact of CPS policy change and the implementation of domestic violence courts. While the data presented thus far would seem to indicate that changes to policy and court practice have had a positive impact on the number of successful convictions, the Home Affairs Select Committee caution against such an interpretation, as these figures taken independently of data relating to the number of incidents, arrest, charges or cautions, say little about the overall response to domestic violence.

The Overall Impact on Attrition

Ultimately, the changes that have been detailed and examined so far have been implemented with a view to improving the overall criminal justice response to domestic violence. The improvement is associated with the goal of increasing the reporting of domestic violence incidents in the first place, maintaining victim support for prosecutions, and gaining an increase in the number of perpetrators brought to justice. The piecemeal evidence reviewed thus far provides questionable evidence about the effect of recent policy change. However, as the Home Affairs Select Committee observed, systematic data is needed at all stages of the criminal justice response in order to monitor whether or not such practice is indeed resulting in an improved service for victims of domestic violence. To date, surprisingly, only one academic study has obtained such data.

Hester (2005) provides a detailed account of attrition in domestic violence cases based on research conducted across the Northumbria Police Force area during three one-month periods between 2001 and 2003. Overall, it was found that 4 per cent of the 869 incidents recorded by the police during this period resulted in a conviction. Just over one quarter of all incidents resulted in an arrest, of which just over one quarter were charged. Just over half of those charged were convicted, with 13 per cent resulting in custodial sentences.

When key personnel were interviewed about their perception of the main issues surrounding attrition, the role of the victim was highlighted. In particular, police officers and criminal justice agencies expressed ongoing frustration with the withdrawal of victim support and stated that this was the major factor in attrition. Conversely, victims and staff from a range of agencies also highlighted the role of criminal justice agencies and the police, stating that some cases were not pursued to the full extent possible. It seems, therefore, that despite the overhaul of guidance and policy regarding the investigation and prosecution of domestic violence cases, little has changed in practice. Indeed, Hester herself acknowledges that the rates of attrition reported in her 2005 study are 'depressingly similar' to those reported nearly a decade earlier by Hoyle (1998) in relation to Thames Valley.

Conclusion

Traditionally, the criminal justice response to domestic violence has been criticized, owing to the overarching attitude that domestic violence was a less serious, yet more complex crime than non-domestic violence, and consequently did not require an interventionist approach. Over time, however, this has been challenged, and has resulted in changes not only to the criminal law, but also to how the police, CPS and the courts approach cases of domestic violence – on paper at least. The evidence suggests that adherence to policy change has been problematic, particularly for the police, with regional variations in the police response identified. It is too soon, however, to determine the impact of the changes to CPS and court procedures and, consequently, future evaluations of practice are awaited in anticipation. The limited evidence examining attrition would suggest that, unfortunately, despite extensive changes to policy, practice has changed little since the late 1990s. Recent publicity would certainly support the notion that gaps in the criminal justice response to domestic violence remain. For example, in May 2009 Refuge (a national victim support organization) announced that it would be suing Greater Manchester Police over the alleged mishandling of the case of Sabina Akhtar who died after being stabbed through the heart by her husband, despite repeatedly informing the police of ongoing abuse in the two months prior to her death.

But what does this change mean in relation to perpetrator programmes? It is the provision and nature of these programmes that is the central focus of this book. The recently amended sentencing guidelines make direct reference to the potential suitability of programmes within a community sentence in some cases, where both parties wish to remain together and the risk is perceived to be low. In addition, examination of the specialist court service flagged the availability of perpetrator programmes as a feature of those court systems that had the highest successful prosecution rates. Consequently, such programmes are now perceived as a legitimate sentencing option by criminal justice agencies. As the specialist court system continues to expand, it is more likely that an increasing number of offenders will be referred to attend community-based domestic violence perpetrator programmes. Nevertheless, it is interesting that this is the situation we now find ourselves in, given that the evidence for the effectiveness of these programmes is still in question (see Chapter 7), and the development and provision of these programmes has not been without controversy.

3

Theories of Intimate Partner Violence

It was observed in Chapter 1 that the way in which intimate partner violence (IPV) is measured, defined, and consequently responded to, is directly linked to the theoretical perspective adopted. Therefore, prior to discussing the history of rehabilitation programmes for male IPV perpetrators in Chapter 4, this chapter provides a critical evaluation of the major theoretical accounts of this behaviour. In order to effectively evaluate the qualities of a theory, it is necessary to identify its required components. In general, an adequate theoretical account of behaviour will generate hypotheses that can be tested empirically. In addition, a theory will account for a large number of observations (Hergenhahn, 1982). It has been argued by some that when it comes to explaining IPV we are yet to develop an adequate theoretical account that fulfils both of these criteria (Bell & Naugle, 2008; Polaschek, 2006; Woodin & O'Leary, 2009). Therefore, if, as has been asserted, current theories of IPV are fundamentally flawed in their explanatory power, it is likely that interventions forged on these theoretical foundations, may also be fundamentally flawed.

Polaschek (2006) observes that theories of IPV vary with regard to the number of factors proposed as causal explanations of behaviour. Specifically, theories of IPV tend to either focus on the role of single factors, or incorporate a multifactorial analysis. Single factor theories also vary in respect of the adequacy of the explanation offered. Good single-factor theories are identified by Ward, Polaschek and Beech (2005) as those which elucidate the structures and processes associated with a particular factor, that is viewed as having an etiological role in IPV, alongside the operation of other individual factors. Less competent single factor theories tend to be promoted as complete etiological explanations, but typically lack sufficient detail about how the particular

The Rehabilitation of Partner-Violent Men, by Erica Bowen

factor in question works to increase an individual's risk of IPV. Multifactorial approaches, in contrast, attempt to explain the variation in motives associated with the use of IPV, and explain such motives in terms of the variations in the interactions between multiple factors that are variously associated with an individual's IPV behaviour. Numerous theoretical accounts of IPV have been developed and reflect socio-cultural, interpersonal and intrapersonal explanations. This chapter critically examine theories at each level of explanation before examining the one multifactor model that has influenced current approaches to intervention for IPV perpetrators. Specifically, socio-cultural, social learning, family systems, personality disorder, anger and hostility, attachment, and alcohol and drug use theories of IPV will be explored prior to the nested ecological model.

Socio-Cultural Theories

A range of feminist theories are encapsulated within the 'socio-cultural' category. At their most basic, feminist theories assert that IPV arises from gender inequality (Yodanis, 2004). However, several explanatory factors are encompassed within feminist theories, including gender roles, gender inequality, power and control, and patriarchy (Woodin & O'Leary, 2009). Common to all perspectives is the aim to understand why, at a societal level, men use violence against women (Schechter, 1982).

Gender roles and inequality

According to gender role theory (O'Neil, 1981), individuals behave in ways appropriate to their beliefs regarding what constitutes behaviour that is appropriate to their gender identification. Consequently, as aggression is endorsed by male cultural norms, individuals who have a strong masculine gender identity will be more likely to engage in aggressive behaviour. In particular, it is suggested that men who hold conservative gender role ideals concerning providing for one's family, may be more likely to perpetrate violence if it is perceived that these norms are being violated (Kwesiga, Bell, Pattie et al., 2007).

There exists some empirical evidence to support the idea that when threats to masculinity or masculine ideals are perceived, men who are susceptible to gender role stress report negative attributions and negative affect and are also found to endorse verbal aggression in response to hypothetical scenarios involving partner behaviour (Woodin & O'Leary, 2009). When partner behaviour is relevant to masculinity (e.g. flirting, cancelling a date), or threatens the man's authority, these effects are particularly strong (Franchina, Eisler & Moore, 2001). Additionally, it has been found that in contrast to maritally-distressed but non-violent men, men who have a history of marital violence are more likely to attribute negative intentions to wives' behaviour depicted in vignettes. This was particularly the case when the scenarios depicted involved jealousy or rejection (Holtzworth-Munroe & Hutchinson, 1993).

In addition to conformity to gender role stereotypes, it has been suggested that conflict with the ability to achieve this may also play a role in IPV perpetration.

According to gender role conflict theories, socially constructed gender roles can have detrimental consequences for individuals, owing to the pressure that results from trying to conform to societal gender role expectations (Mahalik, Cournoyer, DeFranc et al., 1998). Indeed, there is some evidence that men who experience excessive conflict are more likely to report depression, anxiety anger and passive-aggressiveness (Hayes & Mahalik, 2000; Mahalik et al., 1998). Consequently, it seems that such conflict might be better perceived as a risk marker for IPV through which individual men may be at increased risk of engaging in behaviours that are known to increase the likelihood of IPV, rather than as a direct cause of IPV per se.

Of particular relevance to the study of IPV perpetration is the role of gender-related belief systems. A differentiation has been made between instrumental and expressive belief systems. Traditional conceptualizations of masculinity emphasize instrumental beliefs – the desire to manipulate objects, the environment, or social situations to achieve goals (Woodin & O'Leary, 2009, p. 43), whereas femininity is traditionally viewed as emphasizing expressive beliefs – the desire to regulate emotions and sustain interpersonal relationships (Gill, Stockard, Johnson & Williams, 1987, cited in Woodin & O'Leary, 2009). It has been found that the endorsement of instrumental beliefs is associated with the use of violence by men and women in intimate and non-intimate contexts (Archer & Graham-Kevan, 2003; Archer & Haigh, 1997).

Evidence for the role of attitudes that endorse traditional gender role stereotypes and ideals in IPV is mixed. Jenkins and Aubé (2002) found a relationship between endorsing a conceptualization of masculinity characterized by control, hostility and self-absorption and both physical and psychological violence, with the relationship differing for men and women. For men, such beliefs were associated with the use of psychological aggression only, whereas for women, such a conceptualization of masculinity was associated with the use of both physical and psychological aggression towards their partners. Consistent with this, a meta-analysis conducted by Sugarman and Frankel (1996), across 29 studies, found that holding traditional gender role beliefs was not associated with physical IPV. Conversely, attitudes supporting the use of violence in relationships were found to differentiate men who were violent in intimate relationships from those who were not and yielded the largest effect size of all characteristics examined. It is interesting to note, however, the finding that rather than endorsing traditional beliefs, a lack of either masculine or feminine gender schemas was most likely to be exhibited by violent men. In order to explain this, it was suggested that violent men might use violence because they believed that this constituted 'proper' male behaviour. The difficulty in interpreting these results, however, arises from the fact that the majority of studies examined within the meta-analysis employed cross-sectional designs. Consequently, rather than suggesting that pro-violence attitudes may increase the risk for IPV, it is equally plausible that such attitudes arise as a consequence of the behaviour, and serve merely as post-hoc justifications.

Power and control

Feminist theorists argue that in addition to the influence of societal gender role expectations, IPV arises out of a broader societal system of male dominance and privilege

(Woodin & O'Leary, 2009). Chapter 1 examined the feminist conceptualization of IPV as reflecting the male need, alongside societal endorsement, to control and dominate their female partners. This conceptualization forms the basis of feminist treatment models in which the Power and Control Wheel (Pence & Paymar, 1993) which is used to define IPV as including a range of non-violent, but psychologically, emotionally and financially coercive behaviours, is a central component. However, inconsistent evidence for the relevance of power and control related behaviours have been found. Dutton and Starzomski (1997) compared 89 men who were within the first three weeks of a 16-week perpetrator programme, with 18 non-violent controls (small sample is due to the number of wives involved) on behaviours within the Power and Control Wheel as reported by their wives. It was found that, in contrast to the non-violent men, the violent men scored significantly higher on intimidation, emotional abuse, minimization/denial/blaming and economic abuse. However, no difference was reported for coercion, isolation or male privilege and, controversially, the non-violent group were reported to be significantly more likely to use their children to control their partners. In addition, Umberson, Anderson, Glick and Shapiro (1998) failed to find any differences in perceptions of personal control in a population sample associated with the use of violence in relationships.

Goode (1971) from arguably more a resource theory than feminist theoretical position (Ronfeldt, Kimerling & Arias, 1998), posited that men who did not hold power, because they had a lower income, lower educational attainment or lower occupational status than their wives, would use violence as a means to achieve a sense of power and potency in the relationship. Although there is evidence that links IPV to socio-economic status (SES) in absolute terms, with higher rates of IPV reported in lower SES partnerships (see Holtzworth-Munroe, Smutzler & Bates, 1997, for a review), there is also some evidence to support the relevance of relative SES within partnerships. These findings support Goode's position. For example, Anderson (1997) found that the proportion of the family income that comprised women's income was related to the likelihood of IPV. Specifically, the women whose contribution made up less than 31 per cent of the total family income were least likely to report IPV, whereas women whose income comprised 70 per cent or more of the total were five times more likely to report IPV.

Perceptions of power inequality have also been found to be associated with IPV. For example, Babcock, Waltz, Jacobson and Gottman (1993) found that greater differences in education and decision making, where wives had achieved higher educational attainment or took greater decision-making responsibility, were associated with higher rates of violence perpetrated by their husbands. Similar findings were reported by Leonard and Senchak, (1996), who found that if newlywed men perceived themselves as having less power relative to that held by their wives, they were more likely to report being in a relationship characterized by destructive marital conflict, and consequently reported using physical violence against their wives. This suggests that the relationship between perceived power and violence was mediated by marital conflict styles. Furthermore, Sagrestano, Heavey and Christensen (1999) found that men with less perceived power were more likely to use violence, whereas women with greater levels of perceived power were more likely to report using both verbal and physical violence in intimate relationships. In an extension to this work, Ronfeldt et al. (1998) examined the role of both perceived relationship power, and satisfaction with relationship power in self-reported IPV in a college sample. It was found that satisfaction with, rather than perceptions of, power predicted men's use of violence against their intimate partner.

Patriarchy

Power imbalance between genders at the societal level has also been theorized by feminist scholars to be a causal agent in IPV. According to feminist theory, in societies where men control the range of resources through which women's societal status is crafted (e.g. economic, educational and political), institutions which endorse the subordination of women and which legitimize male dominance will flourish (Dobash & Dobash, 1979). From this perspective, violence is viewed as a patriarchal mechanism of female subordination.

Population level data provide some evidence to support this theory, although the association is not necessarily straightforward. For example, it has been found in North America that states characterized by lower levels of female equality report higher rates of physical and sexual assaults by men against women (e.g. Baron & Straus, 1989). Higher rates of sexual assaults against women are also reported in countries with less equality of occupation and education (Yodanis, 2004). In addition, Archer (2006) found that across 52 countries, cultures characterized by lower levels of gender equality and individualism and greater endorsement of sexist attitudes and pro-IPV attitudes had the highest rates of IPV.

A direct challenge to the patriarchal theory of IPV comes from a study conducted by Yllo and Straus (1990). Yllo and Straus (1990, cited in Dutton, 1994) examined the association between Conflict Tactics Scale reports and economic, political, legal and educational indicators of structural inequality towards women across US states. The extent to which residents believed that husbands should have dominance over wives in relation to family decision making was also assessed. Contrary to expectations, it was found that in states characterized by the highest and lowest status of women, the rates of self-reported IPV by men were highest, indicating a curvilinear association. In addition, no significant association between inequality and patriarchal normative beliefs was found.

Criticisms of Socio-Cultural Theories

Hunnicutt (2009) notes that although the feminist understanding of IPV has dominated research and policy through the influence of social action, in general, feminist theories of IPV have been under-developed. Flavin (2001) observes that feminist approaches have been more successful in criticising the approaches of others, rather than in developing gendered theoretical accounts of crime. Indeed, Fox (1993) argued that out of all the components of gender inequality, violence against women was the most poorly theorized. Hunnicutt identifies five core criticisms of the use of 'patriarchy' to explain IPV:

- the over-simplification of power-relations;
- the implicit 'false universalism' associated with the term patriarchy;
- the consequence that individual differences within the population of men are ignored;
- the inability of patriarchy to account for violence by women;
- the lack of power when explaining the behaviour of a minority of men within a patriarchal society. (Hunnicutt, 2009, p. 554)

Dutton and colleagues (Dutton, 1994, 1995; Dutton & Corvo, 2006, 2007; Dutton & Nicholls, 2005) have launched a prolonged and scathing attack on feminist conceptualizations and explanations of IPV, the complete detail of which is outside of the scope of this chapter. The main tenets of these criticisms, however, are based on the following observations:

- evidence that IPV perpetration is associated with a much broader range of situational, psychological, interpersonal and contextual factors than simply indices of patriarchy (see Chapter 5 for an overview of risk factors for IPV);
- the inability of feminist accounts to explain female initiated IPV, and the similar rates of violence used by men and women in relationships;
- evidence concerning the developmental etiology of IPV which questions the role of sex-role beliefs (e.g. Magdol, Moffitt, Caspi et al., 1997);
- inconsistent evidence of an association between indices of patriarchy and IPV perpetration: for example, only a minority of couples are male dominated (Coleman & Straus, 1986); abusiveness is higher in lesbian than heterosexual relationships (Lie, Schilit, Bush et al., 1991); and insufficient evidence that patriarchal cultures are indeed characterized by higher rates of IPV than non-patriarchal cultures (e.g. Sorenson & Telles, 1991);
- the fact that only a minority of men are ever violent within intimate relationships (e.g. Kennedy & Dutton, 1989).

As Polaschek (2006) notes, the greatest weakness of the feminist account of IPV, as evidenced by these criticisms, is its inability to account for the diversity of research findings that have emerged regarding the nature and prevalence of violence in intimate relationships. Despite this, the feminist ideology remains the single most influential theory in relation to the development of intervention programmes (see Chapters 4 and 6).

Social Learning Theory

Central to social learning theory (SLT; Bandura, 1977) explanations of IPV is the notion that violent and abusive behaviours and pro-violence beliefs are learned during childhood either through the direct experience or observation of these behaviours and attitudes modelled by others. The likelihood that such behaviours will then be exhibited is contingent upon the actual or observed reinforcement of these behaviours. Woodin and O'Leary (2009) note that behavioural learning is deemed not only to occur through processes of both classical and operant conditioning, but also through cognitive mediational processes (p. 46). At its most basic then, an SLT account of IPV predicts that violence between parents observed by their children leads their children to use violence in intimate relationships – the so-called intergenerational transmission of violence. This is the most widely tested assumption of the SLT account of IPV. Despite the intuitive appeal of this explanation, the actual empirical evidence that examines this association provides equivocal evidence that such a link exists.

Stith, Rosen, Middleton et al. (2000) conducted a meta-analysis of 39 studies that examined the association between either witnessing, experiencing, or both experiencing and witnessing violence in childhood (i.e. interparental violence and/or child abuse), and receiving or perpetrating physical violence during adulthood. The composite sample exceeded 12,900 participants. The overall effect size was small yet statistically significant ($r = .18$, $p < .001$). Differential associations were found, depending on whether witnessing interparental violence or child abuse was examined, and differences relating to participant sex, and sample setting (community/clinical) were also found. For example, experiencing child abuse yielded a slightly smaller effect size than witnessing interparental violence when perpetration was considered ($r = .16$ vs $r = .18$, respectively). Overall, effect sizes were larger for males than females ($r = .21$ vs $r = .11$ respectively), and for studies conducted using clinical rather than community based samples ($r = .30$ vs $r = .12$ respectively). Similar findings with regard to sex and setting were reported when the studies were examined, based on whether child abuse or witnessing interparental violence were examined. When IPV victimization was considered as the outcome, a different pattern of results emerged, although once again the overall effect size was small ($r = .17$). In this instance, experiencing child abuse yielded a slightly higher effect size than witnessing interparental violence ($r = .19$ vs $r = .14$ respectively). Sex differences were once again identified but in the opposite direction to those associated with perpetration, with a larger effect size obtained for females than males ($r = .18$ vs. $r = .09$). Once again, the setting also impacted upon effect sizes with a larger effect size for clinical than community samples ($r = .24$ vs $r = .15$ respectively).

Taken together, these results indicate that whilet exposure to violent models during childhood is associated with an increased likelihood of experiencing IPV during adulthood, as either a victim or a perpetrator, the association is weak, and owing to the small proportion of variance explained, other variables are likely to play a role in the intergenerational transmission of violence. The authors point to a number of weaknesses in the design of the meta-analysis, the most problematic of which was the reliance on retrospective accounts of both exposure (witnessing interparental violence or experiencing child abuse) and outcome (IPV experience). Indeed, prospective longitudinal studies suggest that this association may be even weaker than the results of Stith et al.'s (2000) meta-analysis might indicate, and is likely to be indirect.

Simons, Lin and Gordon (1998) conducted a prospective study of 113 adolescent boys, with data collected when the children were in the 7th, 8th, 9th 10th and 12th grades. Parents reported on their use of corporal punishment, their experiences of spousal violence, and their parenting style in the first three waves of data collection. At these same points the adolescents provided self-report estimates of involvement in delinquent behaviour. In the final two data collection waves, self-report dating violence data were obtained from the adolescents. No evidence to support the intergenerational transmission of violence was found based on witnessing interparental violence. Instead, low parental support and involvement predicted involvement in delinquent behaviour and drug use, which in turn, predicted dating violence. In addition, the use of corporal punishment predicted dating violence, but not delinquent behaviour.

In a 20-year prospective study of 582 youths and their mothers, Ehrensaft, Cohen, Brown et al. (2003) examined the prospective role of childhood disruptive behaviour disorders, childhood neglect and abuse, parenting practices, and interparental violence as risk factors for adult IPV. It was found that a diagnosis of childhood conduct disorder was the single most important risk factor for IPV, increasing the odds of it occurring by seven times. However, exposure to interparental violence and childhood abuse both remained significant predictors, even when childhood conduct disorder was entered as a predictor in the model, although conduct disorder partially mediated the effect of child abuse.

Fergusson, Boden and Horwood (2006) included a comprehensive range of family-based risk factors including family socio-economic background, family functioning (alcoholism, drug use, criminality, parenting styles), and child abuse, in addition to the presence of childhood behavioural problems, in their prospective study of the Christchurch birth cohort. It was found that exposure to interparental violence was *not* associated with increased rates of physical IPV at age 25 although, prior to controlling for family-based risk factors, an association with psychological IPV was found. This however, became non-significant once family-based risk was controlled. A similar pattern of results for IPV victimization was also found. When predicting physical IPV perpetration it was found that childhood sexual abuse, maternal age and family standard of living were significant mediators of the intergenerational transmission of violence.

The results of these and other prospective longitudinal studies (e.g. Capaldi & Clark, 1998; Lussier, Farrington & Moffitt, 2009; Magdol, Moffitt, Caspi et al., 1997; White & Widom, 2003) confirm that the relationship between exposure to violent models during childhood and adult IPV is weak, and is mediated by a range of additional factors, most notably childhood conduct disorder and anti-social personality traits. This is consistent with an expanded social learning theory model (O'Leary, 1988).

As noted, the modelling component of the SLT explanation of IPV has received the greatest empirical examination. However, Woodin and O'Leary (2009) argue that the hypothesized role of cognitive mediators (e.g. attitudes towards violence) is also important. Indeed, it is at the point of cognitive mediators where social learning and feminist theories overlap, as both predict that pro-violence attitudes will be associated with IPV, and mediate the intergenerational transmission of violence (Markowitz, 2001). Some evidence has been found to support this hypothesis (e.g. Markowitz, 2001; Reitzel-Jaffe & Wolfe, 2001; Stith & Farley, 1993). Additional cognitive mediators have also been identified, including conflict resolution skills (Choice, Lamke & Pitman, 1995), emotion dysregulation (Dankoski, Kelley, Thomas et al., 2006) and social information processing deficits (Dodge, Bates & Pettit, 1990).

Dutton (1999) acknowledges that SLT provides a relatively expansive account of how violence is learned and imitated as well as the external factors that lead to violence being learned. However, it is argued that there is a range of internal triggers for violence which are not accounted for through an SLT approach (e.g. dysphoric states, insecure attachment styles, attributional styles).

The evidence concerning the utility of SLT in explaining IPV indicates that experiencing violence during childhood, whether directly or indirectly, may increase the likelihood of experiencing IPV during adulthood, but this is an imprecise and weak association that is attenuated or amplified by a range of additional mediating characteristics. Indeed, in a recent review, Delsol and Margolin (2004) concluded that approximately 60 per cent of maritally violent men report experiencing family of origin violence. Consequently, it is not a given that witnessing violence leads to violence. Polaschek (2006) notes that there are three main implications of SLT for treatment:

- Violent behaviour and associated cognitions are likely to be well established by the time an individual reaches adulthood.
- Alternatives to violence can be learned as appropriate responses to preceding risk factors.
- IPV perpetrators are likely to have a range of deficits that will also require some form of treatment (e.g. problem solving, p. 119).

Along with feminist theories, SLT has been a major influence on the skills-based components of treatment programmes, and many current programmes combine feminist ideology with cognitive-behavioural skills training to a greater or lesser degree (see Chapter 6).

Family Systems Theory

Among the most controversial theoretical approaches to explaining IPV is the diverse array of family systems theories (Polaschek, 2006). From this perspective, rather than arising from within the individual, IPV is viewed as arising from within the family system (Lane & Russell, 1989). This is viewed as a dynamic group of perpetually interacting individuals (Cunningham, Jaffe, Baker et al.,1998). Aggressive actions by one family member are viewed as causing reactions by other family members, which then feed back and affect the likelihood of future violence. Thus, it is the family system, or subsystem (couple, parent–child dyad) that maintains violence through, 'the roles, relations, and feedback mechanisms that regulate and stabilise the system' (Cunningham et al., 1998, p. 10). Consequently, this approach adopts a non-blaming ethos (Lane & Russell, 1989), which is the crux of the controversy surrounding this approach.

The regulatory mechanisms identified in family systems theory are deemed to be patterns of interaction and causal attributions (Lane & Russell, 1989). Geffner, Mantooth,

Franks and Rao (1989) suggest that communication in abusive families often lacks clarity, is inconsistent and overtly hostile and critical of family members. Indeed, it has been suggested that it is patterns of inter-relating within couples, rather than demographic or intrapersonal features that more precisely distinguish aggressive from non-aggressive relationships (Stets, 1992). Several interpersonal correlates of relationship aggression have been identified in the literature that supports the basic premise of systems theory. For example, Cordova, Jacobson, Gottman, Rushe and Cox (1993) examined interaction patterns among violent, non-violent distressed and happily married couples. Relative to the two non-violent groups, violent couples were significantly more likely to engage in negative reciprocity, and were more aversive and hostile. Babcock, Waltz, Jacobson and Gottman (1993) found that in contrast to distressed *non-violent* and happily married couples, violent couples were more likely to engage in husband-demand/wife withdraw interaction pattern. Feldman and Ridley (2000) replicated this finding in a study of 251 men. It was also found that violent relationships were characterized by higher levels of unilateral verbal aggression, mutual verbal aggression, less constructive relative to destructive communication, and less mutual problem solving. On the basis of these and other data, Cahn and Lloyd (1996) have argued that IPV should be conceptualized as a communicative act. Despite the apparent support for the role of communication and interaction within IPV, the majority of studies that have examined these issues have adopted a purely cross-sectional design. Consequently, it is unknown whether such interaction and communication patterns serve as antecedents or consequences of violence within relationships (Polaschek, 2006).

Systems theory-based couples interventions for IPV have been developed, and are deemed appropriate in relationships where mutual violence has existed but the members of the dyad wish to remain together (Lane & Russell, 1989). However, there has been a backlash against such approaches led by feminist scholars and advocates who are disturbed by the no-blame ethos of these approaches, and fears that conjoint counselling does nothing but increase the risk of violence to women (Cunningham et al., 1998). Indeed, such is the wave of discontent surrounding this approach that current state guidelines expressly prohibit the model from being adopted (see Chapter 5).

Attachment Theory

Attachment theory is a well developed theory of early development, which focuses on the formation of early relationships, and the implications of relationship formation on later childhood and adult functioning. In particular, the attachment model proposes the need for infants to have a secure base in the form of one or more preferred caregivers, from which they can safely explore the world, and to which they can return for safety if required (Bowlby, 1980). During healthy development, attachment behaviours such as crying, clinging and seeking contact lead to the development of attachments or emotional bonds between the child and parent (Goodwin, 2003), and serve to attain proximity to the caregiver in times of fear, anxiety and stress. This so-called attachment behaviour is viewed as parallel to imprinting in non-human mammals, and there is deemed to be survival value in attachment behaviour as it is rooted in an evolutionarily-rewarded method of protecting offspring from predators (Corvo, 2006).

It is proposed that the pattern of interactions with this secure base determine the child's emotional development, their beliefs and perceptions of themselves, their ability to develop and maintain relationships with other people, and their perceptions of the world around them (Bowlby, 1980). These are developed through an internal working model – that is, an internal mental representation, prototype or schema which reflects the child's set of assumptions relating to each domain. Consequently, if a child's interactions with their secure base are predictable, warm and supportive and responsive to their needs, the individual develops a positive sense of self and a view of themselves as both loveable and worthy of being loved, and secure models for interpersonal relationships. If however, the child's interactions with their secure base are unpredictable, unresponsive, neglectful or abusing, the individual is more likely to develop insecure models for interpersonal relationships, a negative sense of self and a view of themselves as unlovable and not worthy of being loved. These individuals become either preoccupied by, or dismissing of close relationships (Ainsworth, Blehar, Waters et al., 1978). Ultimately then, the parent–child relationship becomes a prototype for adult intimate relationships (Bowlby, 1958). It is proposed that such models are in general, stable throughout the lifespan, although they can be modified by new interpersonal experiences (Bowlby, 1988).

Bowlby (1984) proposed that child abuse and IPV were expressions of similar underlying processes, as both involve the relationships that are centrally important to attachment theory (parent–child, intimate partner), and both are concerned with reproduction and survival of the young. Consequently, it is hypothesized that both are influenced by genetic and evolutionary forces, and that family violence in its broadest conceptualization may be a distorted version of behaviour that was once evolutionarily adaptive. The disordered attachment styles that arise between parents and children can continue across generations. IPV is viewed as arising from similarly disordered attachment styles.

Romantic attachment patterns have been proposed to hold particular promise in the study of domestic violence (Lawson, Barnes, Madkins et al., 2006), as attachment regulates proximity and distance in intimate relationships (Hazan & Shaver, 1987). Attachment theory therefore appears well placed to be able to explain the apparent contradictions between intimacy and violence (Roberts & Noller, 1998). Moreover, by adopting an individual difference perspective as represented by attachment theory (Ainsworth, 1991), it is possible that we may gain greater understanding of the factors that lead some, but not all, men to be violent in intimate relationships, and more controversially it may also explain the violence used by women in intimate relationships (Gormley, 2005).

Although both child and adult attachment styles are described along a dimension from secure to insecure, four adult attachment styles have been identified (Bartholomew & Horowitz, 1991). These reflect two underlying dimensions – positivity of self, and positivity of other. Individuals who view both themselves and others in a positive light – the secure attachment style – are theorized to be comfortable with intimacy and are also autonomous in intimate relationships. Those who view themselves in a positive light, yet view others negatively – the dismissing attachment style – are compulsively self-reliant and typically minimize the importance of intimate relationships. Individuals who view themselves negatively, but others positively – the preoccupied attachment style – exhibit high levels of dependency on others, and are preoccupied with the importance of intimate relationships from which they gain a sense of self-esteem. Finally, individuals who view both themselves and others negatively – the fearful attachment style – are afraid of rejection which then manifests itself as a fear of intimacy. Consequently, these individuals avoid social interactions and intimate relationships.

A growing body of literature has developed the application of attachment theory to IPV, and empirical research exists which provides some support for its relevance. It has been theorized by Dutton (1995, 1998, 1999) and Feeny (1999) that adult partner violence reflects insecure attachment styles developed during childhood, and is associated with abandonment anxiety and anger. Dutton argued specifically that insecure attachment styles resulted from the increased rate of trauma experienced in childhood by one particular subgroup of domestically violent men as a result of family violence. In situations of perceived abandonment, anger may function as an attachment behaviour and when unresolved may lead, in extreme case,s to the use of violence in order to retain proximity to the attachment figure (Bowlby, 1988). Indeed, there is considerable evidence that IPV men are more likely to be characterized by insecure than secure attachment styles (e.g. Dutton, Saunders, Starzomski et al., 1994; Babcock, Jacobson, Gottman et al., 2000).

In addition, several personality constructs and styles of interpersonal functioning, consistent with insecure attachment characteristics, have also been found to be prevalent in samples of IPV perpetrators. For example, Dutton et al. (1994) found that fearful attachment styles were related to anger, jealousy and trauma symptoms. Murphy, Meyer & O'Leary (1994) found that maritally violent men reported higher levels of interpersonal dependency, dependency on their intimate partner, and lower self esteem than did maritally distressed but non-violent, and maritally satisfied and non-violent men. Holtzworth-Munroe, Stuart & Hutchinson (1997) found violent men to be more likely characterized by preoccupied and disorganized attachment patterns, jealousy and higher levels of dependency on their wives than non-violent men. Studies have also identified that insecurely attached violent men are also more likely to engage in controlling behaviours, and that this combination predicts the frequency and severity of violence used (e.g. Mauricio & Gormley, 2001). Although attachment theory appears to make a valuable contribution to understanding the origins of interpersonal behaviours within relationships, intervention models based on this approach are yet to become fully established (Healey, Smith & O'Sullivan, 1998, see Chapter 9).

Personality Disorder and IPV

Since the mid-1980s, researchers have attempted to identify common psychological and personality profiles of IPV perpetrators (e.g. Hamberger & Hastings, 1986; Chambers & Wilson, 2007; Hines, 2008; Ross & Babcock, 2009). This research indicates that several types of psychopathology or personality traits, particularly those that characterize anti-social and borderline personality disorders, are over-represented within this population and are consistent correlates of IPV. Additionally, there is some longitudinal evidence that such characteristics may act as risk factors for IPV. For instance, childhood conduct disorder, a prerequisite of adult anti-social personality disorder, which is characterized by social skills deficits, bullying and violent and aggressive behaviour, has been found to be an important predictor of later adult IPV (Capaldi & Clark, 1998; Ehrensaft et al., 2003; White & Widom, 2003). In addition, anti-social characteristics in early adulthood increase the risk of IPV for men and women, and also increase the risk of severe IPV for young men (Capaldi & Owen, 2001; Magdol et al., 1997).

Ehrensaft, Cohen and Johnson (2006) observe that while there appears to be a consensus of opinion regarding the role of anti-social personality traits in IPV, there is less agreement concerning the role of other forms of personality pathology. Moreover, while personality traits represent consistently identified correlates of IPV, little is understood about the developmental origins of such an association. Arguably, however, a more coherent theoretical framework surrounds the potential role of borderline personality traits in IPV. Dutton (1998, 1999) proposes that early trauma experiences in the form of witnessing interparental violence, shaming by a parent and insecure attachment styles may lead to the development of an 'abusive personality', characterized predominantly by borderline personality organization, which in turn leads to the use of violent and abusive behaviours in intimate relationships. Features of borderline personality organization include unstable interpersonal relationships, self-harming, excessive anger responses and behavioural impulsivity (American Psychiatric Association (APA), 1994). Individuals with such traits are less able to regulate their emotional responses in the face of perceived threat, and may be more likely to respond impulsively and aggressively to interpersonal confrontation. Mauricio, Tein and Lopez (2007) found that borderline personality disorder mediated the link between anxious attachment and the use of physical violence.

Empirical investigations have also identified associations between IPV and other personality disorder traits, including schizoid and paranoid traits (Hamberger, Lohr & Gottlieb, 2000). Moreover, some overlap between anti-social and borderline traits has also been identified (Holtzworth-Munroe et al., 2003). Consequently, Ehrensaft et al., (2006) examined whether the DSM-IV (APA, 1994) personality disorder clusters were a more cohesive explanatory framework within which to consider the role of personality disorders in IPV. Using a 20-year prospective longitudinal study, the question of whether personality disorder mediated the intergenerational transmission of violence was addressed. That is, are individuals who experience family violence during childhood at an increased risk of adult IPV because they are more likely to develop a disordered personality? It was found that cluster A personality disorders (paranoid, schizoid, schizotypal) and cluster B personality disorders (borderline, narcissistic, anti-social, histrionic) but not cluster C disorders (dependent, avoidant, obsessive-compulsive) at age 22 increased the likelihood of perpetrating IPV at age 31. In addition, both cluster A and B disorders partially mediated the intergenerational transmission of violence, although witnessing interparental violence and harsh parenting practices remained significant independent predictors. Interestingly, cluster C disorders seemed to exert a protective effect by reducing the likelihood of IPV.

When anti-social personality was entered into the model, the intergenerational transmission effect disappeared, suggesting that the effect of exposure to family violence was due to its relationship with the development of anti-social traits. Even with anti-social personality in the model, cluster A and cluster C mediating results remained the same. However, the effect of cluster B symptoms became non-significant, indicating some overlap with anti-social traits. These data indicate not only the shared etiological factors between anti-social personality disorder traits and IPV, but also indicate that a range of other pathological personality traits play a role in IPV. Consistent with previous research, these include the traits of suspiciousness, jealousy, hostility, hypervigilance to threats, and controlling and combative behaviours consistent with paranoid personality disorder.

Associations between personality heterogeneity and violence heterogeneity has also been documented. For example, Ross and Babcock (2009) found that partner violent men diagnosed with borderline personality disorder used violence more reactively – that is, their violence was impulsive and motivated by emotion. In contrast, partner violent men diagnosed with anti-social personality disorder tended to use violence both reactively and proactively – that is, their use of violence was also goal directed, without provocation and not motivated by anger.

These data taken together indicate that personality disorders may indeed function as risk factors for later IPV, and may also determine the nature of the violence adopted by those who use violence in intimate relationships. By understanding that personality disorders feature highly within clinical populations of IPV men, clinicians may be better placed to screen for such traits, particularly those which are known to be difficult to change, and then to tailor treatments appropriately. Such factors may be considered as responsivity issues (Andrews & Bonta, 2006, see Chapter 4) and therefore need to be evaluated during the process of treatment design and implementation. The findings that these traits are associated with the nature of violence used, and the motivations for violence, indicate that treatment programmes need to be sensitive to the range of motives for violence, rather than applying a single analysis to the problem.

Anger and Hostility Models of IPV

Hostility is typically conceptualized as an attitudinal construct characterized by cynicism (believing that others are motivated by selfish goals), mistrust (believing that others are intentionally harming and provoking), and denigration (believing others to be dishonest, ugly and mean (Miller, Smith, Turner et al. 1996). In contrast, anger is assumed to be a product of the hostile cognitive set, which is also assumed to motivate aggressive behaviour (Spielberger, 1988). Anger is acknowledged to consist of myriad physiological, cognitive, affective and behavioural changes that are all experienced simultaneously (Berkowitz, 1993).

The potential role of anger as a risk factor, or indeed potential cause of IPV, is a controversial concept, particularly as feminist theorists have argued adamantly that IPV is not simply a matter of poor anger control, but reflects a range of tactics employed to control their partners (Dobash & Dobash, 1979). Despite their reluctance to consider the role of anger in IPV, a considerable corpus of empirical evidence has suggested that IPV perpetrators exhibit elevated levels of both anger and hostility. However, it is unlikely that anger directly leads to aggression, but that a predisposition towards anger causes changes to cognition, arousal and affect that then increase the likelihood of aggressive behaviour occurring in particular circumstances (Anderson & Bushman, 2002).

In their meta-analysis of 28 studies examining anger and hostility in samples of IPV men and non-violent controls, Norlander and Eckhardt (2005) identified a moderate composite effect size of $d = 0.51$. When examined separately, the effect size for anger was found to be $d = 0.47$ and for hostility $d = 0.58$, with the effect size for hostility being significantly higher than that for anger. Anger and hostility were also found to differentiate violent from non-violent maritally distressed men with higher reported levels in IPV men. In addition, relative to men who reported low to moderate severity IPV, those who reported moderate to high severity IPV consistently reported moderately higher levels of anger and hostility. No significant effects of assessment method were identified.

While this meta-analysis provides substantial evidence that there is a statistical association between reported levels of anger and hostility, and that this relationship is greater for hostility than anger, the literature currently fails to elucidate the precise mechanisms by which these associations occur (Woodin & O'Leary, 2009). It remains the case, however, that although current treatment methods include an anger management component (see Chapter 6), pure anger management approaches to intervention with IPV perpetrators have been heavily criticized for providing perpetrators with an excuse, rather than a reason for their abusive and violent behaviour (e.g. Gondolf & Russell, 1985). The current evidence suggests that until a clearer theoretical framework exists to more fully understand the role of anger and hostility in IPV, this is possibly a sensible view to adopt.

Alcohol and Drug Models of IPV

There is substantial evidence of a statistical association between alcohol consumption and rates of IPV. In a meta-analysis of five studies, effect sizes were found to range from $r = 0.28 - 0.58$, indicating small to large associations (Schumacher, Feldbau-Kohn, Slep et al., 2001). In a relatively recent British survey of 2,027 adults, of the 20 per cent that reported partner aggression, alcohol was implicated in up to 40 per cent of incidents. The presence of alcohol was also associated with increased aggression severity, anger severity and fear (Graham, Plant & Plant, 2004). Empirical evidence also indicates that alcohol use is a situational risk factor that increases the likelihood that a female partner will be injured (e.g. Thompson & Kingree, 2006). In addition, the prevalence of male-to-female aggression among alcoholic samples is four to six times higher than among non-substance using controls (e.g. Murphy & O'Farrell, 1994). Moreover, among alcoholic men, the amount of alcohol consumed has been found to be higher directly prior to violent, rather than non-violent, conflict (e.g. Murphy, Winters, O'Farrall et al., 2005).

Currently, three main theoretical perspectives attempt to account for this observed association between alcohol and IPV: the spurious model, the proximal effects model, and the indirect effects model (Fals-Stewart, 2003). According to the spurious model, it is suggested that any observed relationships between alcohol consumption and violence are an artefact of their relationships with a confounding variable. In other words, that such a relationship is observed merely reflects the fact that both alcohol consumption and the use of violence are associated with a third variable, for example anti-social personality traits, age, socio-economic status (Fals-Stewart, 2003). The indirect effects model suggests that IPV arises out of the breakdown of relationships fuelled by the alcohol misuse of one or both of the members of the dyad (Fals-Stewart, Golden & Schumacher, 2003). Consequently, the alcohol exerts its effects on IPV via its impact on relationship satisfaction and conflict. In contrast, according to proponents of the proximal effects model, it is the acute psychopharmacological effects of alcohol (Chermack & Taylor, 1995), or the expectancies associated with alcohol consumption (Critchlow, 1983) that facilitates aggression and IPV.

In a review of the available evidence, Klostermann and Fals-Stewart (2006) identify a number of studies, the findings of which directly challenge the basis of the spurious model, with the relationship between alcohol consumption and IPV persisting after controlling for factors including age, socio-economic status, and general hostility (e.g. Leonard & Senchak, 1996; Pan, Neidig & O'Leary, 1994). In addition, studies typically find that when relationship satisfaction variables are controlled, the association between alcohol use and IPV remains, thus challenging the indirect effects model (e.g. McKenry, Julian & Gravazzi, 1995).

In support of the proximal effects model Fals-Stewart (2003) found, using a daily diary study approach, that male-to-female physical IPV was more likely on days that the male partners consumed alcohol than on days when they remained sober, even when relationship discord and alcohol severity were controlled. In a further study, which adopted a similar methodology but included the consideration of psychoactive substances alongside alcohol, Fals-Stewart et al. (2003) found that IPV increased on days when either alcohol or cocaine were used.

The links between alcohol use and IPV are the most widely researched when the role of substance use in IPV is considered. However, as this previous study indicates, there is some evidence to suggest that other drugs, aside from alcohol, may also play a role in IPV. Interestingly, Fals-Stewart et al. (2003) found that there was no association between the use of cannabis or opiates and IPV. Moore and Stuart (2004) examined the effects of illicit substance use as well as alcohol, on IPV in a sample of men who were referred to a treatment programme for IPV. In their sample of 151 perpetrators, 53 per cent reported past year marijuana use, 23.8 per cent past year cocaine use, more than 10 per cent reported past year use of hallucinogens and sedatives, and more than 5 per cent reported using stimulants or opiates within the last 12 months. It was found, relative to non-users, that those who reported drug use were more likely to report using and receiving IPV. In addition, after controlling for alcohol consumption, substance use predicted psychological abuse perpetration, with a trend identified for physical abuse perpetration. When substance use was controlled for, alcohol use predicted sexual coercion.

The evidence reviewed indicates that alcohol and substance use and abuse are associated with the use and severity of IPV, and that alcohol consumption in particular may act as a proximal risk factor for IPV (Murphy et al., 2005). While there is insufficient evidence to indicate a causal link, it is clear that such difficulties pose problems for individuals in mainstream rehabilitation programmes that do not address these underlying issues. Alcohol and substance use issues therefore should be considered, like personality traits, as responsivity issues that might impact on an individual's ability to attend to, and benefit from, mainstream IPV intervention attempts (Tolman & Bennett, 1990; Ting, Jordan-Green, Murphy & Pitts, 2009).

Summary of single factor theories of IPV

It is evident from the theories reviewed that each examines explanatory variables that operate at different analytical levels, from the socio-cultural to the interpersonal and intra-individual. As Woodin and O'Leary (2009) note, these theories, although competing, are not necessarily mutually exclusive, and much of the supporting evidence reviewed adopts a multivariate approach whereby other correlates are considered and/or controlled. Moreover, many of these single factor theories adopt components of competing theories in order to explain IPV more fully. Consequently, it is typically acknowledged that IPV arises out of the interplay of a range of risk factors and risk markers that interact with one another. Moreover, it is understood that more complex multivariate models are required to further our understanding of the phenomena. One such multifactor explanatory framework has directly influenced current practice in the UK (see Chapter 5), and hence it will be discussed next in this chapter.

Nested Ecological Theory

The ecological framework attempts to consider the complex interplay between ecological systems and the way the interaction of factors within these different systems leads to IPV (Edleson & Tolman, 1992). Drawing upon Bronfenbrenner's (1979) ecological developmental model, Dutton (1985) was the first to apply such an approach to understanding the interplay of risk factors for IPV. Edleson and Tolman (1992) have applied an ecological analysis to intervention with perpetrators of IPV. Within these approaches, risk factors and approaches to intervention are viewed as occurring within different ecological systems. These systems are consistently identified as including the macrosystem, the exosystem, and the microsystem. Dutton (1985) includes an ontogenetic system after the microsystem, whilst Edleson and Tolman (1992) include both a mesosystem in between the micro- and exosystems, and in addition include the chronosystem.

Macrosystem

The macrosystem represents the broadest level of analysis, which reflects socio-cultural influences including factors that maintain gender inequality, gender role norms and pro-violence societal norms. These influences may include ethnic group and social class (Edleson & Tolman, 1992).

Mesosystem
This describes the connections between microsystems in an individual's environment and includes links to social institutions. Such connections may include those between the extended family, peer group, and child's school. Social institutions may include links with social services, police and courts. It is at this level that the dominant community-based interventions for IPV operate (Edleson & Tolman, 1992; see Chapter 6).

Exosystem
According to Dutton (1985), the exosystem represents the linkages between the family and the broader culture, and might include the level of integration within a community. Edleson and Tolman (1992), however, suggest that this level consists of interactions within relationships that exert an indirect influence on the behaviour of the individual violent man. Such interactions may include community justice responses that draw upon multi-agency partnership strategies that reflect the range of micro-systems, which through strategy, may indirectly influence the individual's behaviour.

Microsystem
Dutton (1985) proposes that the microsystem consists of the risk factors for IPV that arise from the characteristics of families and individuals. Such factors may include the interaction between intimacy and independence within a dyad, and the individual's predisposition towards jealousy and/or control, which leads to violent responses in relation to perceived abandonment. Edleson and Tolman (1992) identify factors arising from the interactions within any given setting in which the individual is an active participant, as well as the meanings assigned by the individual to such interactions. Examples of relevant microsystems include social group membership such as the church, the family, and the neighbourhood.

Ontogenetic system
This consists of risk factors that arise from within the individual as a function of physiology, cognitions, learned behavioural responses or predispositions, and emotional responses, which serve to increase or decrease the likelihood of violence occurring (Dutton, 1985).

Chronosystem
Edleson and Tolman (1992) point to the importance of acknowledging the individual's developmental history when trying to understand and intervene in IPV. So it is therefore acknowledged that some of the factors within this system overlap with those identified in Dutton's ontogenetic system above. However, in addition to these, the historical development of the broader ecological systems is also acknowledged by Edleson and Tolman.

The basic premise of ecological explanations is that each level within the ecology interacts with the systems closest to them. Consequently, the impact of factors at the broadest ecological level, the macrosystem, may exert an influence on the individual at the ontogenetic level, but this influence is expected to be indirect, and mediated by factors within the intervening ecological systems (Dutton, 1995b). Partially consistent with this expectation are the findings of a meta-analysis of risk factors for IPV perpetration conducted by Stith, Smith, Penn et al. (2004), who employed the ecological model as an organizational and analytical framework for their analysis. They found that the smallest effect sizes were obtained for factors within the exosystem, which were those most distal in the model employed. However, factors within the microsystem and ontogenetic system could not be clearly differentiated by their effect sizes. For example, the most important risk factors based on effect size were emotional/verbal abuse, forced sex and marital satisfaction (all microsystem variables), and illicit drug use, pro-violence attitudes and traditional sex-role ideology (all ontogenetic variables).

Summary and Conclusions

Chapter 1 presented evidence that highlighted the heterogeneity and complexity of IPV as a phenomenon. Bell and Naugle (2008) identify the inability of current theoretical frameworks to explain this complexity as their most serious limitation. Indeed, the majority of the theories examined focus on the role of a limited number of variables that are hypothesized to share a causal relationship with IPV, even if sufficient empirical evidence to support these claims is yet to amass. At the start of this chapter the features of good theories were described, among which was the ability to account for a large number of observations. However, many, if not all, of the current single factor theories appear to fall short of being able to explain apparently contradictory findings (Bell & Naugle, 2008). It is the case that not all IPV perpetrators are characterized by pro-violence attitudes, patriarchal attitudes, have witnessed interparental violence or other violent models, have deficient interpersonal communication styles, insecure attachment styles or have pathological personality traits, report elevated anger responses and latent hostility, or use violence within the context of alcohol or drug use or addiction. Consequently, there has been a move towards the development of multi-factor models. As illustrated through the nested ecological model described, these offer some promise in terms of understanding the interaction of influences on individual behaviour, as well as a means of conceptualizing intervention attempts.

4

The Development of Group-Based Programmes for Male Domestic Violence Perpetrators

The provision of 'therapeutic' rehabilitation programmes, either within or outside broader criminal justice interventions has a relatively recent history, particularly in the UK (Hester, Pearson & Harwin, 2007). In 2005, the National Probation Service and HM Prison Service rolled out a portfolio of 'accredited' rehabilitation programmes for male perpetrators of IPV. However, the idea of providing such therapeutic intervention programmes remains controversial. Women's advocates, in particular, are sceptical about the need and potential success of such programmes, partly on account of the competition between perpetrator, victim and child services for any available funding, and, in part, because of the less than conclusive evidence regarding their effectiveness (see Chapter 8) (Hague & Malos, 2005; Schechter, 1982). In addition, understanding IPV as a by-product of entrenched patriarchal social structures and cultural norms requires a societal-level intervention, and advocates of this perspective are less than convinced about the potential effectiveness of comparatively small-scale interventions with only a minority of violent men in eliciting broader societal change (Hague & Malos, 2005).

As identified in Chapter 2, the vast majority of cases of IPV go unreported, and fewer still result in a conviction that might carry with it the possibility of attending such a programme. So, considering the influence that the feminist movement has had, particularly in the UK, and the associated pessimism regarding the effectiveness of programmes, how did we come to provide group-based rehabilitation programmes for male IPV perpetrators within the criminal justice system? This chapter examines the broad penal and social factors that have contributed to the current context, whereby

The Rehabilitation of Partner-Violent Men, by Erica Bowen

group-based interventions for IPV offenders are central to the government's multi-agency response to domestic violence.

Changing Perspectives on the Causes of IPV and Approaches to Intervention

In the 1950s and 1960s, positivist thought dominated the criminal justice responses to crime and emphasized the role of individual characteristics in criminal behaviour (Hollin & Palmer, 2006). In addition, the associated treatment model propagated the view that the causes of crime were knowable, and could therefore be identified and addressed, resulting in an overall reduction in crime (Robinson & Crow, 2009). At this time, IPV was viewed as neither an important, nor substantial social problem (Hanson, 2002). At the same time, theoretical perspectives on IPV also emphasized the role of individual characteristics as its causes, and IPV was viewed as the behaviour of the 'sick' (Bern & Bern, 1984). Traditionally, men's violence against women was viewed as a feature of either physiological or intra-psychic factors (Thorne-Finch, 1992). Consequently, in the rare instances when treatment was available (and this was rarely as part of a criminal justice response), it focused on altering physiological or psychological features of the individual. It must be emphasized that these treatments were not developed specifically for IPV, but reflected an extension of theories of general aggression and/or violence to account for IPV.

Thorne-Finch (1992) identifies two main physiological treatments that have been used to treat male violence – stereotaxic surgery and testosterone reduction. Stereotaxic surgery involves the surgical altering of the brain, in areas or structures identified to have a functional role in the individual's aggressive and/or violent behaviour. In particular, this form of surgery was targeted at the hippocampus, amygdala and hypothalamus – all regions associated with the regulation and experience of emotion. Although case examples of such surgery used to treat men who are violent to their wives are available in the literature (Averill, 1982), such treatments were rarely used, owing to the lack of consenting patients, and potential significant side effects including epilepsy (Thorne-Finch, 1992).

Based on two theoretical assumptions, that (a) elevated levels of testosterone are linked to an increase in aggressive behaviour when met with the appropriate social context, and that (b) testosterone levels are associated with sexual aggression (this is also associated with violence against women), testosterone reduction treatment has been offered in two forms to address men's violence: castration, and hormone therapy (Thorne-Finch, 1992). In particular, it is assumed that violence against women is a function of sexual aggression, and therefore testosterone reduction should lead to a reduction in violence against women as a consequence of a reduction in sexual activity (Thorne-Finch, 1992). While castration has been found to have some therapeutic effect in sexual offenders (Schmucker & Losel, 2008), there is little data to support its use as a treatment for intimate partner violence. In addition, while there is some evidence to support a weak link between testosterone levels and aggression in general (Book, Starzyk

& Quinsey, 2001), and intimate partner violence specifically (McKenry, Julian & Gavazzi, 1995), the alleged mediating role of sexual aggression is not substantiated. Consequently, early treatments offered on the basis of physiological risk factors were marred by insufficiently validated theoretical assumptions.

During the 1970s, the formal response to IPV changed from being victim to perpetrator focused. Although shelters were being set up to help women victims to leave their abusive partners, victims were also viewed as responsible for the violence that they suffered (Dobash & Dobash, 1992). The increased public awareness of IPV raised by the women's movement in the 1960s and 1970s brought with it a labelling of both female victims *and* their abusers as deviant, and as somehow deficient (Schechter, 1982). The initial attempts to address the problem of IPV as victim oriented often adorned female victims with psychiatric classifications, particularly owing to a lack of understanding regarding the context and dynamics which impede women's ability to leave abusive relationships. Women's personalities were viewed as the cause of men's abusiveness, and consequently as the avenue for intervention (Dobash & Dobash, 1992).

The Inception of Men's Programmes

During the late 1970s, it became apparent that women's shelters could only provide a partial solution to the problem of IPV, and that in order to address the issue more directly, work had to be undertaken with the perpetrators themselves). Considering the contention surrounding the provision of rehabilitation programmes for male IPV perpetrators, particularly among women's advocates, it is somewhat ironic that these interventions emerged directly out of the women's shelter movement (Jennings, 1987). Women's support and treatment services became points of contact for men wanting to end their abusive behaviour, and consequently, the development of counselling groups and services for male perpetrators were initially provided outside of the criminal justice sector. For example, in the UK, the Chiswick shelter that formed the cornerstone of Women's Aid, was also the first to offer services to abusive men under the guise of the 'Men's Aid House' in 1976. The Men's Aid House provided group-based counselling for separated men and couples. This service survived for a truncated period of two years, at which point a lack of funding led to its closure (Deschner, 1984).

Similarly, and at about the same time in North America, it was a women's support service that first developed a systematic treatment programme for male perpetrators. The Victim's Information Bureau of Suffolk County began to offer couples therapy after acknowledging that a substantial majority of the women who sought help ultimately returned to their abusive partner (Jennings, 1987). This service lasted from 1976 to 1980. In 1977 and 1978, 'Emerge' in Boston and RAVEN (Rape and Violence End Now) became the first agencies devoted to providing counselling to male perpetrators of IPV. Emerge was set up again primarily in response to the perceived need reported by local women's shelters in the Boston area (Jennings, 1987). At the time of their inception both of these programmes were met with considerable hostility by women's advocates. However, by adopting a pro-feminist approach, whereby the protection of women is seen as the first priority, both programmes were directly accountable to the feminist shelter movement (Ritmeester, 1993). Such approaches emphasized a feminist understanding of IPV as rooted within the patriarchal structure of society, and the RAVEN programme even attempted to appeal to the wider male population and encourage them to engage in non-sexist practices. These included, among other activities: confronting sexist jokes and advertisements; educating men about responsibility for birth control; raising money for rape crisis centres and/or women's shelters (Ritmeester, 1993, p. 177).

Programmes such as these were not accepted without resistance. In particular, those offering support to voluntary referrals were often subject to very low numbers due to the unwillingness of men to acknowledge their behaviour and seek help. Moreover, tension from within the shelter movement itself, particularly from those who perceived the provision of men's programmes as a threat and competition for scarce resources, led to mistrust between groups of service providers (Schechter, 1982). The lack of evidence to support the effectiveness of men's programmes at this time also fuelled the doubts of those within the shelter movement. On an ideological level, the women's movement was in conflict regarding its views on offering services to men. One perspective perceived there to be some potential in treating IPV therapeutically, on the basis that IPV was a disorder of power. In contrast, some viewed the provision of counselling services as detrimental to the movement as a whole, because to the diversion of resources. Finally, some believed that assisting male perpetrators of IPV was an inappropriate endeavour for feminists (Schechter, 1982). The underlying mistrust of men's programmes has manifested itself in attempts to control their provision (Shupe et al., 1987). For instance, feminist guidelines for the funding of men's programmes developed in collaboration with counsellors from the EMERGE programme specified that such programmes should only be funded in communities where a women's shelter already existed. In addition, shelters should be prioritized for funding over and above men's programmes, and men's programmes should share the feminist ideology espoused by shelters (Shupe et al., 1987). The impact of these specifications can still be felt today in the mandatory state standards for men's programmes adopted throughout North America, and in practice guidelines for British programmes (see Chapter 6 for further details).

'Nothing Works'

In the mid-1970s, at the same time that the problem of IPV was formally recognized, and the first rehabilitation programmes designed to eliminate IPV were developed, an international debate was initiated concerning the effectiveness of tertiary level interventions (McGuire, 2001). At that time, the idea that sentences had to be 'accountable' (i.e. achieve their aims), was new (Brody, 1976). This followed an extensive period from the early eighteenth century, during which time sentencing philosophies were retributive, in that the sentence simply had to fit the crime (Robinson & Crow, 2009). During this period, sentences primarily served as a function of punishment and incarceration in prison, although offenders were also more permanently removed from society either through transportation, banishment and execution (Brody, 1976). The eighteen century Enlightenment brought with it greater concern for the humanitarian needs and individual human rights of those incarcerated. In addition, the development of modern psychology (which provided insights into the origins of human behaviour), and a need for non-custodial, cost-effective, alternative sentences because of escalating prison overcrowding after the Second World War, these three factors provided the impetus for the development of non-retributive sentencing options (Brody, 1976), of which community sentences were part.

In the mid-1970s the notion of keeping offenders out of prison was well accepted, and the role of non-custodial sentences and the probation service were emphasized in this endeavour. However, up to this point, despite there existing general optimism about the potential of non-custodial sentencing, there was equivocal evidence regarding the ability of the probation service to rehabilitate offenders effectively (Mair, 1997). To address the question of how far different sentencing options were successful in achieving their aims, comprehensive reviews of the then extant literature were conducted in Europe and North America at roughly the same time (McGuire, 2001). The result was that the original ambivalence concerning the effectiveness of rehabilitation, shifted to outright pessimism after the publication of Martinson's (1974) misinterpreted review of 231 studies, which examined the rehabilitative potential of a range of programmes conducted across a range of non-custodial and custodial settings.

While taken as evidence that 'Nothing works' in offender rehabilitation, the actual review concluded that it was possible for some programmes to exert positive effects on offending behaviour, but that major methodological flaws in the original research precluded such a conclusion. Moreover, Palmer (1975) noted that Martinson referred to some beneficial effects of intensive supervision and individual psychotherapy for subsamples of offenders who were deemed to be amenable, pro-social, or of medium risk. Similarly, in 1976 Brody's review of 65 studies published since 1970 (none of which were represented in Martinson's earlier review, owing to a considerable publication lag), concluded that the vast majority of studies failed to find significant effects of sentencing options on recidivism. Again, methodological flaws concerning the lack of comparability between samples, and variations in outcome measures are cited as confounding factors. However, Brody highlights the importance of interaction effects between offender and sentence characteristics, in that 'different types of offenders respond in different ways to the various treatments applied to them' (p. 41). Despite this, the overarching conclusion of this and other reviews published around the same time (Lipton, Martinson & Wilkes, 1975), was that there was little evidence that correctional interventions had any significant positive effect on offending behaviour.

The repercussions of the 'nothing works' dogma dominated correction policies in North America and Britain for the best part of two decades after the publication of Martinson's notorious review. This was the case despite the interim publication of research that suggested that some interventions were, in fact, effective (Palmer, 1975; Quay, 1977). That such contradictory evidence was so swiftly dismissed in deference to the 'nothing works' doctrine has been attributed to the dominant political forces at the time (Hollin, 1999).

The Expansion of Men's Programmes

Despite their meagre beginnings and the challenges presented, the 1980s and 1990s saw a proliferation of counselling services for male IPV perpetrators develop in the USA, although such programmes were slower to emerge in the UK. For example, surveys conducted in the early 1980s identified hundreds of group treatment programmes for male IPV perpetrators throughout North America (Feazell, Mayers & Deschner, 1984; Pirog-Good & Stets-Kealey, 1985). These represented a broad array of therapeutic perspectives that varied in terms of whether the individual man, couple or family were the unit of intervention, and also the theoretical approach taken to addressing IPV behaviours (Edleson & Tolman, 1992). In general, such developments were not systematic, and reflected the increasing ad hoc provision of counselling services, set up by therapists who began to acknowledge the need for interventions of this kind. Adams (1988) argues that the early approaches to intervention with male IPV perpetrators represented five main therapeutic models: insight, ventilation, interaction, cognitive behavioural and pro-feminist models.

The insight model describes an individual psychodynamic approach, which focuses on understanding underlying psychological contributors to violence. These may include (although are not limited to) poor impulse control, fear of intimacy, dependency, fear of abandonment, depression and the long-lasting effects of childhood trauma (Adams, 1988). From this perspective, IPV perpetrators are characterized in terms similar to those of Holtzworth-Munroe and Stuart's (1994) dysphoric/borderline type (see Chapter 1). Violence is viewed as occurring in response to real or perceived threats, and the underlying emotional deficits are viewed as consequences of earlier negative childhood experiences within the family and peer group. Consequently, the overarching aim of this approach is to enable IPV perpetrators to achieve insight into how their current behaviour has been influenced by these past experiences, with a view to learning more appropriate methods of responding within current relationships. In addition, it is expected that through gaining insight, violent men will develop a more positive self-image, which will then lead to a reduction of violent behaviour (Adams, 1988).

The ventilation model, by contrast, conceptualizes IPV as being an artefact of suppressed anger and emotional repression. Popular during the 1960s, this model was ensconced within (among other therapeutic approaches) Gestalt Therapy, and advocated the open expression of anger, in order to void oneself of emotional repression and facilitate communication (Rubin, 1970, cited in Adams, 1988). The suppression of anger was feared to lead to uncontrollable outbursts, or to become internalized and presented as other physical symptoms such as depression. Treatment models based on this approach promote the inclusion of couples as the target for intervention (Adams, 1988).

Another approach that emphasizes the treatment of both individuals within an intimate relationship is the interaction model. Based on systems theory, this approach views IPV as an artefact of 'interpersonal transactions' (Neidig, 1984) in which violence arises out of the interacting behaviours of two or more people within a family. Such interactions are typically viewed as incorporating deficient communication patterns. The overarching goal of therapy cast from this perspective is to enable each partner to identify their role in an ongoing circular interplay of deficient communication that incorporates violence at points (Adams, 1988). From this perspective, both partners are equally culpable for the use of violence by one or both of them.

According to the cognitive behavioural model, violence is a behaviour that is learned, and consequently, non-violent alternative behaviours can also be learned (Ganley, 1981). Violence is viewed as reflecting a range of social skills deficits. Within this model it is violence itself which is the primary focus rather than associated emotional repression or poor communication patterns. Violence is conceptualized within a social-learning framework as self-reinforcing and functional. Through the use of violence the perpetrator experiences a sense of physiological relief associated with reduced tension, as well as achieving a behavioural goal (to resolve an aversive set of circumstances, e.g. an argument). Psycho-educational models based on this approach therefore aim to raise awareness of the functional aspects of violent and abusive behaviours, as well as their self-defeating consequences. In addition, such approaches teach non-violent alternative behaviours and incorporate social problem solving training, communication and negotiation skills training.

The final model, the pro-feminist model examined in Chapter 1, conceptualizes intimate partner violence as, primarily, an instrument of control, which is used purposefully to create and maintain a power imbalance between members of an intimate dyad (Adams, 1988). Intervention models based on this approach directly challenge attempts to control female partners through the use of physical and nonphysical abuse. Pro-feminist models are sympathetic to the need to educate violent men in communication and assertiveness skills but, in addition, view education concerning patriarchal attitudes and sex-role socialization as equally, if not more, important (Adams, 1988). As with the cognitive behavioural model, violence is viewed as the sole responsibility of the men who perpetrate it and, consequently, intervention takes place with men only and typically in groups.

It is these last two models that have had the most enduring impact in the field of rehabilitation of IPV perpetrators, and both currently influence models adopted nationally and internationally. The specific models adopted and currently implemented in the UK are described and discussed in more detail in Chapter 6. Arguably, it is the group-based pro-feminist treatment model which has had the greatest influence in this area, particularly the model developed by the Domestic Abuse Intervention Project, in Duluth, Minnesota.

The Duluth model: a change of emphasis

Rather than lone agencies developing ad hoc interventions for male perpetrators that stood in isolation from other social support and criminal justice agencies, the Duluth model was initially based on the collaboration of nine agencies (Pence & Paymar, 1993). Initiated in 1981, the Domestic Abuse Intervention Project (DAIP) brought together police, county jail, prosecutor's office, shelter, county court, probation department and three mental health agencies, who adopted written guidelines, procedures and policies concerning their response to domestic violence. Through this agreement, all agencies, apart from shelter, allowed DAIP access to records regarding incidents of domestic violence and engagement with services by perpetrators.

Through the workings of this inter-agency model, a fundamental shift in emphasis occurred whereby all agencies agreed that the behaviour used was the responsibility of the person using it. Consequently, decisions to arrest were made on the basis of the evidence of assault rather than in response to the wishes of the victim, or the potential role that the victim may have played in the incident. In addition, perpetrators were held in jail after booking, in order to allow for the judicial review of release conditions. A victim's request to drop a case was reinterpreted as a sign of vulnerability rather than safety. In addition, judges would not order a victim to attend counselling with her abusive partner, and therapists would not provide marital counselling to couples when violence was present in the relationship. A further change of emphasis was that the agencies involved agreed that their contact with IPV perpetrators should be part of a community effort to address IPV. The primary function of the DAIP is one of monitor – ensuring that perpetrators comply with court orders, and that agencies comply with the inter-agency agreement. Consequently, the perpetrator is held accountable for their behaviour by a range of community agencies.

Nested within this community-based intervention, is a group-based perpetrator programme provided to offenders who are court-mandated to the DAIP. Therefore, offenders are court-mandated to the wider monitoring system of which the group-based programme is part, rather than being court mandated to the group-based programme as a stand-alone component of a court order, which may or may not be supported by other community agencies. The intervention initially consisted of two components, group-based anger-management counselling for 12, weekly sessions, followed by weekly attendance at 12 Batterers' Anonymous meetings. In 1984, however, the intervention approach was changed to a group-based educational and counselling approach based on pro-feminist assumptions that focused on the use of violence as a means to control (Pence & Paymar, 1993). Attendance and compliance was stringently monitored, and should a perpetrator miss three meetings he is returned to court, which may, depending on the circumstances, result in a jail sentence, or him being mandated to complete the second phase of the intervention.

The overarching aims of the Duluth men's programme are to:

1 help perpetrators to understand their use of violence as a means to control;
2 increase the perpetrator's understanding of the socio-cultural influences on his behaviour and their causal role;
3 increase the perpetrator's willingness to change through increasing his awareness of the negative consequences of his behaviour;
4 encourage the perpetrator to be accountable to the victims of his behaviour through the acknowledgement of his behaviour and acceptance of responsibility for it;
5 provide non-controlling and *non-violent* ways of relating to women.

As already noted in Chapter 1, a large proportion of male IPV perpetrators will have had direct experience of family violence as a child, either as a witness of interparental violence or as a victim of physical and/or sexual abuse. Although the authors of the Duluth model acknowledge this, rather than being viewed as a potential explanation of IPV, such experiences as part of their socialization are viewed as having 'dehumanised' them (Pence and Paymar, 1993, p. 4). Such factors, including poor impulse control, interpersonal insecurity, drug addiction, alcohol use and jealousy, are viewed as contributors to, or modifiers of, abusive behaviours and also as inhibitors to meaningful change, but are not viewed as causes. Consequently, the model focuses on making the individual accountable for the behavioural choices they have made (i.e. using abusive behaviours), raising their awareness of the socialization factors that may have influenced these decisions, and teaching alternative, more egalitarian behaviours. Central to the Duluth philosophy are the Power and Control Wheel and the Equality Wheel (see figure 4.1).

The power and control wheel represents the overarching definition of domestic violence employed by the programme. the equality wheel presents a model of the qualities of an egalitarian relationship. Each of the segments contains details of a feature of egalitarian relationships that will be examined in depth across a three-week period of the course. The power and control wheel is used to facilitate the identification of abusive tactics employed, which undermine the achievement of an egalitarian relationship. Within group sessions a range of approaches are adopted, including role-play, videotaped vignettes, discussions and the didactic presentation of material. A key tool employed is that of the control log.

The control log provides perpetrators with an avenue for analysing the intentions and beliefs behind their use of abusive behaviours, as well as for identifying alternative behaviours. Drawing on their own experiences in between the group sessions, men are asked to identify the behaviours they engaged in that constituted an abusive act. They are then required to identify the intentions and beliefs that supported their choice of behaviour, the feelings that motivated the abusive actions, the methods of minimization/denial/victim blaming used and the consequences of their actions for themselves, their (ex) partner, and other people present. Perpetrators are also required to reflect on how their use of violence in the past impacted on the situation described, before identifying possible non-abusive alternative behaviours. The aim of using such a log is to maintain the focus of the intervention on the perpetrator's current behaviour, rather than engaging them in a discussion about their prior experiences and other factors that could lead through collusion to the minimization and justification of their behaviour. Consequently, the control log serves as a mechanism through which to confront perpetrators with the nature and consequences of their behaviours.

Group tutors have several roles, which include those of monitor, facilitator and teacher. The tutors are responsible for monitoring attendance and compliance in conjunction with the other agencies, with clear lines of accountability and reporting. Tutors also have to maintain the group process in order to facilitate change (group process is examined in more detail later in this chapter), and maintain the focus on challenging the abusive behaviours of the perpetrators without engaging in collusion. In addition,

Power and Control Wheel Sector Description		**Equality Wheel Sector Description**
Using coercion and threats Threatening to leave her, to commit suicide; making her drop charges; making her do illegal things	→	Negotiation and fairness Being willing to compromise; accepting change
Using intimidation Making her afraid by using looks, actions, gestures; smashing things; abusing pets	→	Non-threatening behaviour Talking and acting so that she feels safe expressing herself
Using emotional abuse Putting her down; calling her names; making her think she's crazy; making her feel guilty	→	Respect Listening to her non-judgmentally; valuing opinions
Using isolation Controlling what she does, where she goes and who she sees; using jealousy to justify actions	→	Trust and support Supporting her goals in life; respecting her right to her own friends and opinions
Minimizing, denying and blaming Making light of the abuse; not taking her concerns seriously; shifting responsibility for abusive behaviour	→	Honesty and accountability Accepting responsibility for self; admitting being wrong
Using children Making her feel guilty about the children; using visitation to harass her; threatening to remove the children	→	Responsible parenting Sharing parental responsibilities; being a positive non-violent role model
Using male privilege Treating her like a servant; making all the big decisions; being the one to define men's and women's roles	→	Shared responsibility Making family decisions together
Using economic abuse Preventing her from getting a job; making her ask for money; taking her money	→	Economic partnership Making money decisions together; making sure both partners benefit from financial arrangements

Figure 4.1 Sectors from the Power and Control Wheel and the equivalent non-abusive alternatives from the Equality Wheel with examples (adapted from Pence & Paymar, 1993)

tutors have to provide perpetrators with new skills with which to replace their existing abusive behaviours, as well as ensuring that the group itself is an appropriate place for these new skills to be practised.

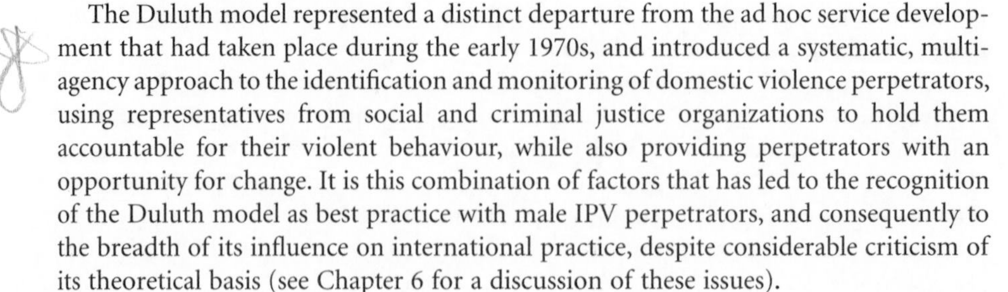

The Duluth model represented a distinct departure from the ad hoc service development that had taken place during the early 1970s, and introduced a systematic, multi-agency approach to the identification and monitoring of domestic violence perpetrators, using representatives from social and criminal justice organizations to hold them accountable for their violent behaviour, while also providing perpetrators with an opportunity for change. It is this combination of factors that has led to the recognition of the Duluth model as best practice with male IPV perpetrators, and consequently to the breadth of its influence on international practice, despite considerable criticism of its theoretical basis (see Chapter 6 for a discussion of these issues).

Evidence that Something Works

Despite the widespread impact of the 'Nothing Works' message, some practitioners, academics and government officials failed to be dissuaded from developing and evaluating rehabilitation programmes for offenders, particularly in Canada (Vennard, Sugg & Hedderman, 1997). Moreover, a small number of studies were published, which directly challenged this view and claimed that some approaches to offender rehabilitation do indeed work (Palmer, 1975; Quay, 1977; Romig, 1978). Indeed, the research conducted during the late 1970s and 1980s underpinned an international step-change in attitudes towards rehabilitation, and formed the basis of a renaissance of the rehabilitative ideal in the early 1990s.

A particularly influential literature review was published in 1979. Gendreau and Ross (1979) examined the results of 95 diverse studies, published between 1973 and 1978, employing at least a quasi-experimental methodology (see Chapter 6 for a discussion of evaluation methodology), and reported some statistical analyses of the data, along with a follow-up period of at least six months. The results of the review indicated that, in the vast majority of cases (nearly nine out of every 10 studies), positive effects were observed. Moreover, consistent with Brody's earlier commentary, Gendreau and Ross highlighted the importance of interaction effects as evidence that under some circumstances, some offenders benefited from some forms of intervention.

In addition, Gendreau and Ross made some key observations that formed the bedrock of the future systematic development of offending behaviour programmes. It was noted that small treatment effects were obtained if offenders had been subject to modes of intervention that relied only upon a single technique, and that those which were multi-modal yielded greater effects. Additionally, concerns regarding the relevance of treatment dosage were raised, supported by evidence that more intense interventions led to better outcomes. Community-based programmes were cited as more effective than institutional ones, particularly if they were well embedded within the community.

Despite the apparently positive conclusions drawn from Gendreau and Ross' review, there are issues concerning the validity of the conclusions, based upon the method of review employed. The narrative review approach adopted has several strengths, primarily that it can enable examination of some of the more complex and subtle features of primary research, particularly when the topic under scrutiny is diverse (Lipsey & Wilson, 2001). However, this approach leads to qualitative rather than quantitative appraisals of the research, and consequently any conclusions are likely to be influenced by the underlying beliefs and attitudes of those conducting the review (McGuire & Priestley, 1995). Such concerns led researchers in the 1980s to employ the comparatively new technique of 'meta-analysis' to re-examine the corrections evaluation literature.

Meta-analysis is a quantitative approach to literature reviewing, in which treatment-control differences across studies are standardized, and an overall effect size is computed (Lipsey & Wilson, 2001). By taking this approach, studies that have small samples can be integrated, and effect sizes calculated on the larger, aggregate sample (Lösel,

1995). While this approach has the appeal of reducing the bias of interpretation and the computation of a perceived 'objective' measure of effectiveness, meta-analysis is not in itself a panacea, and has its critics. One of the main concerns with meta-analysis is that the results are only as good as the literature from which they are drawn (Lipsey & Wilson, 2001). Of particular concern are methodological variations across studies and the coherence of the studies incorporated (i.e. the extent to which the focus of the research is similar across studies). However, it is possible to include within the analysis, examination of mediating and moderating factors and other sources of variance across studies and populations (Lipsey & Wilson, 2001; this technique is discussed in greater detail in Chapter 6).

The first meta-analytic study of the effectiveness of correctional treatment was conducted by Garrett (1985), and examined the effectiveness of residential or community-based correctional treatments for juvenile offenders. The analysis included studies published between 1963 and 1983 that incorporated some form of comparison group, and employed samples of adjudicated juveniles (younger than 21 years of age). Such parameters resulted in a pool of 111 studies, and an aggregate sample in excess of 13,000. Nearly half of the studies (48%) did not employ particularly rigorous study designs (e.g. convenience sample, pre-post, no control group). A range of outcome measures were evident across studies (e.g. psychological adjustment, institutional adjustment, recidivism, vocational adjustment, academic adjustment, community adjustment). Overall, a global effect size of +.37 was calculated, indicating that, in contrast to the non-treated group, juveniles who received any form of treatment were performing at the 64th percentile (in contrast to the non-treated groups at the 50th percentile) (Garrett, 1985). In addition, particular evidence was found for the effectiveness of cognitive behavioural interventions, even when variations in methodological rigour were accounted for.

Despite the employment of a comparatively objective method of literature review, some remained unconvinced about the promise of rehabilitation, and sceptical of the validity of the results of meta-analyses conducted by academics known to be proponents of the rehabilitative ideal. In answer to calls from sceptical academics that meta-analytic data available at the end of the 1980s required objective evaluation by those who did not share the enthusiasm of proponents of rehabilitation (Logan et al., 1991, cited in Lösel, 1995), Losel conducted a synthesis of the 13 published meta-analytic studies of corrections outcomes available at that time, including Garrett's. This synthesis drew on over 500 studies. However, this aggregate sample included overlapping samples, which resulted from the integration of earlier studies within later meta-analyses. Once again, the overall effect sizes identified fell within the 'small' range, between +.05 and +.36, and it is arguable whether the magnitude of some of the identified effect sizes are clinically significant. However, Losel himself argues that the average effect size found suggests a 10 per cent reduction in recidivism for those offenders who received treatment, and that this does carry with it some practical significance. Indeed, in contrast to the effect size reported in some medical clinical trials, the effect sizes reported here are an order of magnitude larger.

While this synthesis adds to the mounting evidence that some approaches to rehabilitation can be effective in reducing recidivism, as previously mentioned, the quality of meta-analyses and any syntheses thereof, are only as good as the original studies. It must be noted that within Losel's synthesis, one meta-analysis provided the majority of the overall sample. Lipsey (1995) conducted a meta-analysis of over 400 studies of correctional treatment, which represented a sample that exceeded 40,000 participants. The sample consisted of juvenile offenders, and included only studies conducted with a control group. All of the studies included had been published since 1950, in the English language. Within this analysis, over half (64%) of the studies were identified as illustrating positive treatment effects, with an aggregate effect size indicating a 10 per cent reduction in reoffending associated with treatment, which was maintained when methodological and design variations were accounted for. Despite the overall effect size falling within the 'small' range (Cohen, 1988), these findings provided added strength to the developing conclusion that something does in fact work with offenders. However, there are several caveats to this conclusion.

First, the over-representation of juvenile samples within the early meta-analytic literature is problematic in terms of the relevance of these findings, and associated clinical implications, for non-juvenile populations (which are also inherently gender biased towards males). Second, the conclusions based on the selected English language studies also introduce an additional source of bias, and prevent these findings from being generalized to other non-English speaking cultures. Third, as evident in Garrett's seminal meta-analysis, a substantial proportion of the original primary research studies employed designs that are fundamentally flawed, for example, through the use of non-equivalent control groups, pre-post designs with no control groups and so on. Such threats to the internal validity of the research render it impossible to actually determine whether the observed 'treatment effects' and associated effect sizes reflect the true impact of the treatment (Larzelere, Kuhn & Johnson, 2004; evaluation design considerations are examined in Chapter 6).

It has been argued by many that the only truly valid research design sensitive enough to identify true treatment effects is that of the randomized controlled trial (Berk, 2005). However, while this is an ideal to aspire to within corrections research, this has rarely been achieved and in some instances the randomness of allocation to treatment and non-treatment groups at the point of sentencing is compromised by the discretion of the judge (e.g. Feder & Forde, 2000). Moreover, there are compelling ethical arguments against the random allocation to treatment and non-treatment groups, particularly if one group could be perceived as benefiting from group allocation, while potentially beneficial treatment is withheld from another group (Dobash & Dobash, 2001). In addition, it has been argued that such designs lack ecological validity (Pawson & Tilley, 1997).

A fourth consideration is the extent to which publication bias influences the conclusions of meta-analytic studies. Several commentators argue that there is a selection bias inherent in meta-analytic studies in general, resulting in a focus on the secondary analysis of published data that report significant treatment effects, to the neglect of findings that have not been published, which typically identify smaller treatment effects (Lipsey & Wilson, 1993; McGuire, 2001). Within the corrections field, it appears that the evidence for the presence of this bias is mixed. Some researchers have included unpublished work in their meta-analyses, and specifically Redondo et al. (1996, cited in Vennard et al., 1997) found that when included, there were no significant differences in the estimated treatment effects between published and unpublished studies.

Despite these limitations and caveats, and the very small effect sizes resulting from the most methodologically rigorous evaluations, the results from both narrative reviews and meta-analytical studies during this period were interpreted as offering clear optimism regarding the promise of offender rehabilitation programmes.

British Developments in the Provision of Men's Programmes

During this time, although evidence of the potential positive impact of rehabilitation strategies was accumulating in the international corrections field, it was only in the mid-1980s that therapeutic interventions for male IPV perpetrators really developed in the UK. The Men's Centre in London, set up in 1985, was the first treatment centre in Europe dedicated to the treatment of men who are violent towards family members (Jukes, 1999), and employed a psychodynamic feminist model. From this perspective, violent and abusive behaviours are viewed as the tools of control within intimate relationships and, consistent with pro-feminist programmes, men are viewed as solely responsible for their behaviour. In addition, the nature of the attachments formed with others is also examined with a view to addressing intimacy issues.

In 1989 and 1990 two programmes were set up in Scotland, the CHANGE programme (Moran & Wilson, 1997), and the Lothian Domestic Violence Probation Project (LDVPP). Both of these programmes were developed with reference to existing North American programmes, particularly those of Duluth, and Man Alive (Dobash, Dobash, Cavanagh et al., 2000). Both programmes adopted a pro-feminist cognitive behavioural model influenced by the Duluth model, whereby men's violence is viewed as reflecting the patriarchal social context, and men are re-educated into the use of non-violent and controlling behaviours through the adoption of cognitive behavioural techniques. Both programmes worked in alliance with women's support services, although CHANGE was community based and LDVPP was probation based (the effectiveness of these programmes is discussed in Chapter 8). Both groups provided services to court-mandated IPV perpetrators and while some level of inter-agency working existed perpetrators were referred to attend the group, not to an overarching monitoring system as in the original DAIP. At the time, these were the only two justice-based programmes operating the UK (Dobash et al., 1992), although Duluth-informed programmes had influenced British practice since 1983 (Bilby & Hatcher, 2004).

Even in the mid-1990s, fewer than 25 programmes were identified in the UK (Scourfield & Dobash, 1999). Scourfield and Dobash found that of the 23 programmes identified in 1994, the majority (16) were provided by voluntary sector agencies, six were provided within criminal justice agencies and one was provided by a health authority. More than half (57%) provided services to men who volunteered to participate, and just over a quarter (26%) provided services to both court-referred and voluntary referrals. Programmes within the criminal justice service had been developed at a local level in relation to the perceived need at that time (Bowen, Brown & Gilchrist,

2002). It has been suggested that the difference between the USA and the UK is that the extent of programme provision for IPV perpetrators reflects fundamental cultural differences between the two countries. Of particular note is the importance placed on individualism in the USA, and the mental health movement, which resulted in the acceptance of therapeutic ideals and models of intervention and the development of a 'therapeutic society' (Dobash & Dobash, 1992, p. 215).

It was 1993 before the importance of directly addressing men's violence through rehabilitation programmes was formally acknowledged in the UK, when a the Home Affairs Select Committee recommended the development and implementation of perpetrator programmes within the prison service (Parliament, House of Commons, 1993, cited in Dobash et al., 2000). However, it took over a decade for such systematic programme development to occur, finally resulting in the implementation of the Healthy Relationship Programme in a small number of prisons. At the same time, two programmes were systematically rolled out across the regional probation areas after a period of development, evaluation and accreditation (details of these programmes are presented in Chapter 6). This shift reflected the broader influence of the international 'What works' movement in offender rehabilitation which had identified clear principles of effective practice.

'What Works?' and the Move Towards Accredited Programmes

In the mid-1990s, attitudes towards the potential of rehabilitation grew more optimistic as the results of the meta-analyses previously examined were more widely disseminated (Hollin, 1999). The results primarily indicated that when treatment groups and non-treatment groups are compared, there is a positive effect on recidivism, which is generally taken to indicate a 10 per cent reduction in offending (Lösel, 1995). A secondary finding was that, under some circumstances, the impact on reoffending may be greater, even as high as a 20 per cent reduction (Lipsey, 1992). As already alluded to, some of the meta-analytic findings pointed to specific forms and modes of intervention being particularly effective. Through consideration by academics a consensus of opinion arose to support the view that the combined results across available meta-analyses and associated syntheses were sufficient for principles of effective practice to be identified (McGuire, 2000). These principles have since been labelled the 'What works?' principles (Hollin, 1999). The characteristics of particularly effective programmes included the following:

1 a clear theoretical framework and rationale for the methods employed;
2 incorporated the risk assessment of offenders and offered appropriately targeted interventions;
3 targeted offending behaviours or risk factors that were possible to change;
4 adopted a clearly structured programme which employed treatment approaches that matched offenders learning styles;
5 employed multi-modal, skills focused and cognitive behavioural approaches;

6 were based in the community;
7 delivered the programme components as intended. (McGuire, 2000)

Alongside these characteristics, and indeed reflected in the intention of some of them, are four principles of effective assessment and treatment identified by the Carleton University Group (Andrews, Bonta & Hoge, 1990; Andrews, Bonta & Wormwith, 2006) as being of particular clinical relevance. Indeed Lipsey (1989, cited in Andrews & Bonta, 2006) suggested that the most effective programmes were those characterized as the most 'clinically relevant' or 'appropriate' (Andrews et al., 1990) by this group.

The first principle, the risk principle, asserts that offending behaviour can be predicted, in other words, an individual's risk for offending can be identified and, consequently, intervention strategies should match the risk posed by the individual (Andrews, 1989). Andrews and Bonta (2006) argue that while high-intensity intervention should be targeted at high-risk offenders and may result in a modest treatment effect (Andrews & Dowden, 2005), minimal intervention efforts should be expended on low-risk offenders, as even if high-intensity treatment were offered to low-risk offenders the resulting treatment effect would be negligible and would represent a waste of resources.

The second principle, the need principle, draws attention to the differentiation between the needs of offenders that are, and are not, related to their offending behaviour, and also makes a distinction between those needs that can, and cannot, be changed (Andrews, 1989). Criminogenic needs are considered to be a subset of an offenders risk level, in that they are amenable to change (i.e. dynamic), and that when changed, expected changes in criminal behaviour are also observed. These can be contrasted to clinical needs, which may also be dynamic, but which are less directly associated with criminal behaviour (Hollin, 1999). Following on from this, Andrews and Bonta argue that it is therefore most appropriate for treatment programmes to target criminogenic needs identified within a given offender population. In practice, criminogenic needs are intermediate treatment goals, therefore the theoretical and practical fit between the intervention and the criminogenic need is vitally important as mismatches are unlikely to lead to reductions in recidivism.

The third principle, the responsivity principle, relates to the development and delivery of programmes that take into consideration, and are tailored to, individual differences in learning styles within offender populations (Andrews, 1989). This principle therefore reinforces the use of cognitive behavioural approaches, owing to the evidence base regarding their effectiveness. Bonta (1995, cited in Cooke & Philip, 2001) identifies additional personal characteristics that need to be considered under this principle, these include (but are not limited to): interpersonal sensitivity, verbal intelligence and anxiety, in addition to personality traits associated with psychopathy (Cooke & Philip, 2001). It is likely that individuals for whom these characteristics are relevant are less likely to successfully adapt to the demands of an offending behaviour programme. Evidence for the clinical importance of these principles has been provided by Andrews et al. (1990), Andrews, Zinger et al. (1990) and Gendreau, Little and Goggin (1996) who found that programmes which adhered to all three principles achieved the largest effect sizes. In contrast, Antonowicz and Ross (1994) found support for two principles, but not for the risk principle. It has been suggested by Lösel (1998, cited in Cooke & Philip, 2001) that a curvilinear relationship exists between risk and programme effectiveness, such that very high risk offenders are also likely to be characterized by factors that may impede their responsivity (e.g. personality disorder), whereas in low risk offenders there is likely to exist some level of spontaneous remission. Indeed, Brown (2005) notes that in many instances, high-risk offenders are typically medium risk, as very high risk offenders are screened out of programmes on account of traits which are believed to make them resistant to change (e.g. denial, high PCL-R scores, depression). Consequently, any claims made regarding programme effectiveness with 'high risk' offenders may be spurious.

Finally, Andrews (1989) added the principle of professional discretion, which refers to the appraisal of risk, need and responsivity on an individual basis in order to inform a decision which reflects ethical, humanitarian, legal and effectiveness considerations (p. 11). This principle emphasizes the role of appropriate and sensitive assessment, conducted by appropriately trained personnel prior to the allocation of offenders to treatment, in the hope of maximizing individual treatment gains.

In addition to these principles, there is mounting evidence that the extent to which the programme is delivered as intended, referred to as 'programme integrity' (Hollin, 1995), is also centrally important in determining the effectiveness of programmes (Cooke & Philip, 2001; Shaffer & Pratt, 2009). Encapsulated within the term treatment integrity are the notions of good programme management, programme design and accomplished practitioners (Hollin, 1995), which include appropriately trained staff alongside the employment of appropriate methods for the effective monitoring of programme delivery (Leschied et al., 2001). Cooke and Philip also include the use of programme manuals, institutional commitment, resourcing, contingency planning and integrated evaluation as components of treatment integrity. Hollin (1995) identifies three methods through which treatment integrity may fail; these are through programme drift, programme reversal and programme non-compliance.

Programme drift occurs when the aims of a programme change over time, which may occur when emphasis on the therapeutic aims of the programme is reduced in light of increasing emphasis on programme administration and management (Hollin, 1995). Programme reversal occurs when some component or components of a programme work in opposition to the overarching treatment aims. Programme non-compliance refers to a process of change within a programme, often initiated by well-meaning practitioners on an ad hoc basis. Such change may result in different session content and/or aims, or even the omission of particular components of a programme, which when new staff are trained on the adapted programme, results in a process of change that Hollin likens to Chinese whispers. Consequently, across repeated iterations, over time, the programme becomes unrecognizable. Although a case for programme development can be made on the basis of ongoing evaluation and consideration of responsivity factors, programme non-compliance occurs when such change is not managed and is uncoordinated.

The relative importance of programme integrity cannot be overstated. In fact, it has been suggested that in circumstances where an inappropriate programme is delivered with high levels of programme integrity, reoffending may actually increase (Hill,

Andrews and Hoge (1991, cited in Andrews & Dowden, 2005). Cooke and Philip note, however, that it is much easier to define programme integrity than it is to monitor it and to ensure that it is achieved in practice. Andrews and Dowden observe that, despite the acknowledgement of its importance, little literature has specifically examined the impact of treatment integrity on treatment outcome.

In their meta-analysis, Andrews and Dowden (2005) examined the results of 230 primary treatment evaluation studies with a view to analysing the net effects of programme integrity variables on the outcomes of appropriate and inappropriate programmes. Appropriate programmes were those that adhered to two of the three principles (risk, need or responsivity). The studies selected were those in which treatment and non-treatment controls were examined; a follow-up period was included, as was a measure of recidivism (rearrest, parole failures, revocations or reconviction all counted); and sufficient study information was presented from which to compute an effect size. Ten indicators of treatment integrity were examined and included: the use of a specific programme theory, selection of workers, appropriately trained workers, clinical supervision of workers, use of training manuals, use of structured monitoring procedures, adequate dosage, recently developed programme, small sample (n = <100), and programme design/delivery or supervision provided by the evaluator. The results of the meta-analysis were surprising, given the perceived importance of such issues.

For example, only 5 per cent of the 273 tests of treatment examined provided evidence of a management focus on the selection of staff, and, perhaps even more surprisingly, evidence that staff had been trained to deliver the specified programme was available in only 52 per cent of cases. Indeed, the most widely cited indicator of integrity, adherence to a specific treatment model, was only present in 59 per cent of cases. When effect size was regressed on to all of the treatment integrity indicators, only selection of staff, evaluator involvement and small sample size achieved significant relationships with effect size. When the relationships between treatment integrity indicators and the provision of appropriate (and inappropriate) programmes were examined it was found that no significant relationship existed between any integrity indicator and inappropriate treatment (effect sizes ranged from .00 – .07). This suggested that enhancing the integrity of inappropriate treatments does in no way contribute to greater reductions in recidivism. Conversely, when appropriate treatment was considered, mean effect sizes were significantly greater in programmes that incorporated some elements of integrity; in this case a specific model (.24), staff selection (.34), trained staff (.24), clinical supervision (.26), small sample (.29) and evaluator involvement (.28; Andrews & Dowden, 2005, p. 181). These results reinforce the potent combination of high treatment integrity when implemented within appropriate treatment programmes.

The influence of this body of research cannot be underestimated, and the principles of effective practice identified have led to the development of accreditation criteria and an associated process for the provision of offending behaviour programmes within the English and Welsh criminal justice system and, similarly, registration and/or licensing in the USA. Such changes to practice were initiated in the mid-1990s (Hollin & Palmer, 2006). In 1999 the Joint Accreditation Panel (renamed the Correctional Services

Accreditation Panel (CSAP) in 2002) was developed to oversee the development and implementation of offending behaviour programmes within the British criminal justice system (both prison and probation based), in accordance with these principles. The remit of CSAP is to review the criteria for the design of such programmes, make recommendations for change; to accredit programmes, to authorize audit procedures for programme delivery, and to authorize the annual quality assessment of delivery; to conduct an annual review of the evidence base; to advise on programme design; to advise on training; and to examine reports of effectiveness returned from programme sites. The criteria by which programmes are assessed are detailed below.

Accreditation criteria

There currently exist 10 accreditation criteria outlined by the Correctional Services Accreditation Panel (CSAP) that must be met in order for programmes to achieve accredited status.

1. Programmes must a have an explicit, evidence-based model of change
It is necessary that all programmes should be designed around a clear model of change for which there exist sufficient empirical support to justify its basis. The evidence concerning predictors of recidivism for any particular population is considered as a starting point in programme development. It must be specified which offender population the programme is for, which criminogenic factors the programme targets, the methods employed to elicit change, the core achievements during each substantive component of the programme, and a theoretical justification for the combination of factors targeted and the choice of methods employed (Lipton et al., 2000).

2. Justification of the selection of offenders
How appropriate offenders for the proposed programme are selected has to be detailed, including criteria such as offence type, race and gender, along with more subtle criteria such as motivation to change/treatment readiness, learning style and risk. Exclusion criteria should also be detailed along with appropriate strategies for dealing with those who, after acceptance on to a programme, are found to be unsuitable.

3. A range of dynamic risk factors should be targeted
Each programme must address a range of dynamic or changeable risk factors (criminogenic needs) in the identified offender population for which it is designed. The factors that are targeted need to be justified, and measures put in place to assess the extent to which such factors are successfully targeted (Hollin & Palmer, 2006). The underlying assumptions of this criterion are that relevant criminogenic needs can be identified, will exist in the offender population that has been targeted, and that improvement will be found upon completion of the programme (Lipton et al., 2000).

4. Programmes should use methods that are proven to be effective
The weight of evidence supports the use of cognitive behavioural therapy techniques with a range of offender populations (Vennard et al., 1997). Consequently, it would be expected that all proposed programmes incorporate such methods. In all instances, the methods used need to be appropriately justified based on empirical literature. Cognitive behavioural programmes are those which Lipton et al. (2000) identified as including an 'appropriate' combination of:

> cognitive restructuring, training in self-monitoring, self-instructional training, training in problem-solving techniques, role-reversal and role-rotation, modelling, role playing, graduated practice with feedback, contingency management, behaviour therapy and behaviour modification. (p. 1718)

However, it is not sufficient for programmes to use these techniques in an ad hoc manner; their use and application need to be justified within the context of social learning theory (Lipton et al., 2000).

5. Skills orientation
In addition to targeting the cognitive and affective characteristics associated with offending, programmes should also include targets that are skills oriented. These components should aim to provide offenders with additional life and social skills that will help them to avoid offending and may enable them to achieve other rewards. Such skills may include numeracy, literacy, relationships skills and general problem-solving skills. Programmes have to specify which skills are to be taught and how they are to be taught, along with outcome measures such as the expected level of skill to be taught, and how changes will be assessed and evaluated. The link between the acquisition of the identified skill(s) and how this would facilitate an individual to remain crime free also needs to be made explicit (Lipton et al., 2000).

6. Sequencing, intensity and duration
Each programme should attempt to match the 'dosage' provided (in terms of the number and frequency of sessions), to the individual learning styles of offenders, and the overall length of the programme should match the level of risk posed by each individual. Such programme intensity needs to fully consider the range of static and dynamic risk factors for each individual offender. In addition, should offenders take part in more than one programme, consideration should be given to their overall treatment needs when sequencing programme attendance (Hollin & Palmer, 2006). It has been argued that programmes are not suitable for offenders deemed to be at low risk of reoffending (Lipton et al., 2000). Lipton et al. (2000) suggest as guidelines, that medium-risk offenders will probably required between 50 and 90 hours of 'treatment' across a duration of 4–6 months; whereas high-risk offenders, or highly repetitive offenders may require at least nine months' residential treatment delivered in prison,

preferably over a duration of 12–18 months, with follow-up work conducted in the community on release. The precise format and dosage, however, needs to be justified in relation to the methods and format of the programme, and the responsiveness of the offender population targeted.

7. Engagement and motivation
All programmes aim to increase offender motivation even if attendance or referral is not based on pre-treatment assessments per se (Hollin & Palmer, 2006). Programmes, therefore, need to ensure that appropriate methods are employed to facilitate the development of motivation, and that there are sufficient monitoring practices in place to examine reasons for non-attendance and drop-out.

8. Continuity of programmes and services
Programmes are embedded within the broader sentence handed down to an offender and are therefore subject to inter-agency information sharing in order to facilitate sentence planning, inform victim-centred work and monitor offender progress and risk.

9. Ongoing monitoring of programme integrity
Ensuring that appropriately trained and selected staff is delivering the programme as intended, and that the infrastructure is in place to support the provision of a programme, is central to the provision of effective programmes. Failures in any of these components can undermine the effectiveness of programme delivery and impact (Hollin, 2001).

10. Ongoing evaluation
Programmes should engage with ongoing evaluation strategies in order to determine whether programmes are successfully targeting and reducing risk in the identified areas and also, whether reoffending is reduced as a consequence. Such evaluations should combine a focus on programme process variables (change in dynamic risk factors) as well as outcome variables (reoffending).

The 'What Works' Movement and Domestic Violence Perpetrator Programmes

In contrast to other areas of offending behaviour programme development (e.g. sex offender treatment programmes, general offending programmes), the development of programmes for perpetrators of IPV appears to have been less directly influenced by the 'What works?' movement. As previously mentioned, cognitive behavioural programmes aimed at reducing IPV proliferated in the 1980s (Polaschek, 2006). These programmes conceptualized IPV as an anger-related problem, and did not incorporate an analysis of socio-cultural influences on behaviour, although it was also common for programmes that did focus on the socio-cultural context to incorporate cognitive behavioural techniques (Saunders, 1989). Despite reflecting the 'gold standard' approach to offender rehabilitation identified latterly, such programmes were accused of actually increasing the risk of violence against women owing to their reliance on a naive conceptualization of the causes of IPV (Gondolf & Russell, 1985). Such was, and continues to be, the strength of pro-feminist opposition to anger management approaches, despite no empirical evidence to support their claims, that the pure form of cognitive behavioural intervention has dwindled. More importantly, such approaches have actually been contraindicated in US state standards governing the development and provision of men's programmes (Austin & Dankwort, 1999).

Despite this, there continues to be considerable conceptual overlap between the pro-feminist programmes cast in the Duluth mould, and the few cognitive behavioural programmes that persist as typically both include components of each other, with the emphasis placed on the role of socio-cultural factors varying accordingly (Gondolf, 2004). Indeed, it is the Duluth model that forms the basis of the Integrated Domestic Abuse Programme (IDAP), accredited in 2003, and employed by the majority of probation areas in England and Wales (see Chapter 6 for a detailed overview of this programme). Although some have claimed that its incorporation of cognitive behavioural techniques means that it conforms to the 'What works?' principles (Gondolf, 2007), others believe the ideological basis of the Duluth men's programme to be incompatible with the ethos of cognitive behaviourism (Dutton & Corvo, 2007). While this may indeed be the case, Gondolf identifies clear similarities between the two forms of cognitive behaviourism in the allegedly opposing models. In the UK, the Duluth model is considered as the 'gold standard' approach to intervention with IPV offenders, and also forms the model of choice for those tasked with the registration of programmes for non-mandated men (Rivett, 2006; Respect, 2008).

It is interesting to note, however, that while the socio-cultural explanation of men's violence against women forms the bedrock of one accredited programme, it plays a lesser role in the Community Domestic Violence Programme, and also the prison-based Healthy Relationships Programme (see Chapter 6 for details). Both programmes incorporate a multi-factor explanation of IPV, wherein socio-cultural beliefs or expectations are viewed as only one component of an ecological risk framework. Based on the Correctional Service Canada's Family Violence Prevention Programme, the underlying model was developed in response to an acknowledgement that there was insufficient empirical evidence to support the notion that there is one superior treatment model that is most effective with IPV perpetrators (see Chapter 6 for a discussion of the empirical evidence relating to this point), despite the ideological favour proffered to the Duluth model (Stewart, Gabora & Hill, 2001). Moreover, by adhering to the 'What works?' principles and acknowledging the diversity of IPV perpetrator populations and the multiplicity of contexts within which violence may arise, a multi-factor model was deemed most appropriate.

Conclusion

In this chapter the history of treatment approaches designed to reduce IPV has been examined and integrated within the wider changes in criminological and penal thinking regarding the evidence for effective programmes. It is apparent that only recently has there been a systematic move towards the provision of rehabilitation programmes, and that this appears not to have been directly influenced by changing attitudes towards rehabilitation, but motivated by a perceived local need. The current gold standard approach involves a coordinated community response through which the offender is held accountable by a range of agencies, while being provided with a pro-feminist rehabilitation programme to facilitate personal change. The development of evidence-based practice guidelines provides a point of tension with this model. The extent to which this, and the alternative accredited programmes adhere to the principles of risk, need and responsivity, are discussed in Chapter 6 within the context of a broader description of current practice relating to the risk assessment and treatment of IPV offenders in the UK.

5

Current Practice: The Risk Assessment and Management Context

Chapter 3 showed how changes to penal philosophy and our understanding of the causes of IPV have led to the development of rehabilitation programmes aimed at changing violent men, and most recently, in line with broader governmental policy, the moves towards evidence-based practice in this area. The approach towards the rehabilitation of partner violent men typically includes a coordinated community response involving multi-agency working to effectively appraise and manage the risk posed by IPV perpetrators. This multi-agency risk management context and the specific approaches to risk assessment used are examined in this chapter. A descriptive analysis of the current rehabilitation programmes offered by UK probation and prison authorities is presented in Chapter 6, along with a critique of the underlying programme theory assumptions.

The Multi-Agency Risk Management Context: MAPPAs and MARACs

Multi-agency public protection arrangements (MAPPA)

In 2001, a formalized multi-agency approach to the risk management of the most serious sexual and violent offenders was developed in the form of multi-agency public protection arrangements (MAPPA; NOMS, 2009). The function of MAPPA is to draw

The Rehabilitation of Partner-Violent Men, by Erica Bowen

together offender management expertise from within probation, police and prison services. Together, these three organizations form the MAPPA responsible authority, and additional community agencies have a duty to cooperate with this authority in order to ensure the safety of known and future victims. Consequently, the main emphasis of MAPPA is the sharing of relevant information between agencies about known offenders in order to facilitate comprehensive risk assessment, and the development and implementation of risk management plans.

The offenders for whom MAPPA arrangements are most appropriate include those who are subject to the notification requirements of the Sexual Offences Act 2003, and certain other violent, and other, offenders who are deemed to pose a risk of serious harm to the public. Such offenders are likely to have been incarcerated for a minimum 12-month period either in an adult prison, young offenders' institution or hospital if sentenced under the Mental Health Act 1983. Sexual offenders thus defined form 'category 1 offenders', violent offenders form 'category 2 offenders' and other offenders form 'category 3 offenders'. Within MAPPA arrangements, offenders are managed at one of three levels.

Level 1: Ordinary agency management

Offenders managed at level 1 are those whose perceived risk can be managed by the sole agency responsible for the case management of the offender. In such circumstances it is considered unnecessary for multi-agency involvement, although this does not preclude the involvement of additional agencies if it is deemed appropriate. Offenders managed at this level will have been categorized as presenting at a low or medium risk of serious harm.

Level 2: Active multi-agency management

Offenders managed at this level are identified as posing a significant risk of serious harm, and the risk management plan will have identified a requirement for multi-agency involvement in order to effectively manage the risks identified. Alternatively, an offender may be managed at this level if he has previously been managed at level 3 but the seriousness of risk posed is deemed to have diminished.

Level 3: Active multi-agency management

Offenders managed at this level will have been identified as being of high or very high risk of serious harm, and the risks identified require a complex multi-agency arrangement in order for them to be effectively managed. This might arise owing to the complexity of the risk identified or because of the level of resourcing required. Alternatively, individuals who have attracted media attention, or for whom the likelihood of public interest in the management of the case is high, may also be managed at this level. It is also possible that offenders who have previously been managed at level 2, and whose risk of serious harm is assessed as having increased because of changes in personal circumstances, will be managed at this level.

Multi-agency risk assessment conferences (MARACs)

The MARAC system has been developed in order to protect the most high-risk IPV victims from re-victimization. Similar to MAPPA, the MARAC functions through meetings designed to facilitate multi-agency information sharing, with a view to implementing an agreed-upon risk management and victim safety plan. However, the remit of MARAC is restricted to cases of IPV with a focus on victim safety, whereas any offenders who meet the relevant criteria can be managed under MAPPA with a focus on public protection more broadly. In addition, MAPPA have statutory authority in accordance with their role in the criminal justice response to crime, whereas MARAC arrangements do not. This is due to the fact that the victim identified to MARAC may not have an abusive partner who is currently being managed by the police or probation services. The current vision for victim safety is that there will be a MARAC forum in each part of England and Wales, and that these will be provided in areas where a specialist domestic violence court (SDVC) is in operation, with a view to aiding victims through the criminal justice proceedings. At the time of writing, however, there are twice as many MARACs as there are SDVCs, as MARACs have formed independently.

Rather than being identified by a responsible authority, any agency can identify and refer the most serious IPV cases to MARAC. An independent domestic violence adviser (IDVA) team exists in all areas where a MARAC has been established, and will conduct an assessment of the perceptions and nature of risk that the IPV victim currently faces, in order to determine the overall level of risk involved. The highest risk cases will then be referred to MARAC at which the IDVA team will represent the victim's interests and a victim protection plan will be devised. Where appropriate, liaison with additional agencies, in order to safeguard additional potential victims (e.g. children), will be initiated in order to ensure that the plan meets the needs of the victim(s) and can be successfully implemented.

The intersection of MAPPA and MARAC

Not all MARAC cases result in a court appearance. The perpetrator may, however, have previous convictions and may be under the management of police/probation services as a result. If this is the case, it is possible that such management may include MAPPA management at level 2 or 3. If the perpetrator is not managed under MAPPA, then information presented to MARAC may be used to initiate MAPPA management at levels 2 or 3. Where an individual is already managed at level 2 or 3 MAPPA, the MAPPA meeting takes precedence over MARAC, owing to its statutory role. If both members of a dyad are subject to MARAC and level 2 or 3 MAPPA respectively, the IDVA team is invited to the MAPPA meeting in order to enhance the development and implementation of the MAPPA risk management plan. Consequently, although MAPPA and MARAC exist as separate entities, with reference to cases of IPV, these two systems merge to heighten the accuracy of perpetrator risk assessment and victim safety planning. These aims, however, are dependent on our ability to fully understand, identify and assess the nature of risk posed by any given IPV perpetrator.

Risk and Risk Assessment

Kropp (2004) notes that our understanding of IPV risk has lagged behind efforts to understand the risk associated with criminal behaviour and violence in general, and violence committed by specific offender subgroups, such as the mentally ill. Despite this, the nature of risk is now at the forefront of treatment targeting and intervention with domestic violence perpetrators. In Chapter 2, reference was made to the current sentencing guidelines for domestic violence cases. These guidelines highlight the appropriateness of non-custodial sentences, with conditions to attend an accredited domestic violence perpetrator programme (DVPP), for a proportion of IPV offenders who have not exhibited an entrenched pattern of abusive behaviours, and who may feasibly be considered as low risk. Such advice stands in opposition to the CSAP programme accreditation criteria (Chapter 4), which specify that the nature and extent of intervention should be appropriate to the level and nature of the risk posed by the individual, and that, more importantly, group-based programmes should be offered to offenders identified as at least medium risk (Hollin, 2006). It therefore seems that while the link between risk and intervention planning is acknowledged, there is some disparity between agencies regarding how this principle is applied in practice. Nevertheless, within a discussion of current DVPP approaches, it seems fitting to spend a little time examining the nature of risk and its assessment, and the role of risk in the rehabilitation of domestic violence offenders. Therefore, the next section examines the following issues: the nature of IPV risk, risk factors for IPV and current approaches to risk assessment.

The nature of IPV risk

Current practice in the UK embraces the idea of risk, with rehabilitation groups targeted at offenders who pose a medium or high risk of reoffending. However, it is acknowledged that the concept of risk is shrouded in ambiguity, with little consensus in the empirical and theoretical literature regarding what is meant when we refer to the risk of IPV (Kropp, 2004). Most commonly, studies that examine the risk of IPV recidivism define risk as the *likelihood* of an incident of violence occurring at some point in the future. Such a conceptualization of risk places great emphasis on the prediction of behaviour without considering the individual context involved. In practice, the consideration of risk is multi-faceted, and does not simply focus on whether it is likely that an individual will or will not be violent in the future, but also examines the nature of the risk posed (e.g. the type of violence, severity of violence, imminence), and the circumstances under which such risk may be elevated or reduced (Douglas & Kropp, 2002). It must be acknowledged, however, that in some professional contexts an assessment of the statistical likelihood of IPV may be all that is of interest (see actuarial risk assessment below).

In Chapter 1 the constellation of behaviours that might constitute IPV were considered, only some of which may be legally considered 'violence', and many of which would be considered abusive. It is necessary when appraising risk that practitioners work with a clearly defined concept of IPV, and that this is articulated in all formal communications and reports. In other words, if risk of physical violence towards an intimate partner has been considered, this should be made explicit. If a broader conceptualization of IPV has been used, then the relevant parameters should be stated. Good practice guidelines for the assessment of court-mandated IPV perpetrators are provided by Sonkin and Douglas (2002).

Risk factors for non-lethal IPV

A considerable body of empirical research has been conducted with a view to identifying characteristics of IPV perpetrators that are predictive of future IPV in treatment and non-treatment populations. However, owing to the dearth of available longitudinal studies, at best, such evidence highlights a range of risk markers rather than risk factors (Stith & McMonigle, 2009). Such factors include offender attitudes, use of control, gender role beliefs, history of abuse as a child and witnessing interparental violence, insecure attachment styles, alcohol and drug use and personality disorder. The empirical evidence and hypothesized theoretical mechanisms underlying the association between these factors and IPV were examined in Chapter 3, and will not, therefore, be examined here. However, some consideration of the factors associated with lethal IPV will be included, owing to the comparatively scant literature in this area, its clinical importance and utility.

Risk factors for lethal IPV

Stith and McGonigle (2009) classify the risk factors for lethal IPV into four categories:

- victim perceptions
- offender history of violence
- offender characteristics
- situational characteristics.

Despite the multi-agency approach to intervening in IPV that is currently in vogue in the UK, it is likely that individuals who are involved in the management of IPV perpetrators are more likely to have access to perpetrator rather than to victim information. However, research evidence indicates that the information provided by victims about their perceptions of the risk that they currently face can contribute valuable information to risk assessment, more broadly. In a recent study, Bennett Cattaneo, Bell, Goodman and Dutton (2007) found that, consistent with previous research (e.g. Bennett Cattaneo & Goodman, 2003; Heckert & Gondolf, 2004; Weisz, Tolman & Saunders, 2000), victims were more likely to be accurate than inaccurate in their appraisal of personal IPV risk over an 18-month period. Indeed, Heckert and Gondolf (2004) found that the appraisals of personal IPV risk by women whose partners were involved in a DVPP significantly predicted re-assault over a 15-month period at least as well as two out of three risk assessment instruments examined. Such information highlights the utility and importance of incorporating victim appraisals into the risk assessment of IPV perpetrators, which is emphasized by current structured assessment protocols (see spousal assault risk assessment, p. 104).

It has been argued that the utility of victim appraisals may reflect their status as proxy assessments of other risk factors, such as the offender's history of violence, which has been consistently identified as an important predictor of future and lethal IPV. More specifically, with regard to the history of violence, it has been found that femicide is more likely to occur after a period of escalating violence within the relationship (Campbell et al., 2003), and that escalation characterizes severe rather than moderate non-lethal IPV (Caetano, Field, Ramisetty-Mikler et al., 2005). Evidence also indicates that threats of harm by the perpetrator, and threats to kill others or themselves should be viewed as important risk markers, and have been found to be associated with severe and lethal IPV, with more than 80 per cent of cases of partner homicide being characterized by threats of death prior to the fatal incident (Moracco, Runyan & Butts, 1998). In addition, the association between homicide and suicide within domestic contexts has been identified. Stack (1997) found that the likelihood of a homicide offender committing suicide increased eight times if the victim was a current spouse and more than 12 times if the victim was an ex-spouse. Evidence also exists to support a link between severe and/or lethal IPV and the experience of forced or coerced sexual intercourse (e.g. Gondolf, 1988; Weisz et al., 2000), prior non-fatal strangulation (Campbell et al., 2003), and victim pregnancy (McFarlane, Parker & Soeken, 1995).

In addition to prior offender behaviours and associated behavioural characteristics, two offender characteristics have been identified as most important when assessing the risk of lethal IPV. An important correlate of violence repetition, escalation, severity and lethality is jealousy. For example, Campbell (1992) found that approximately two-thirds of intimate partner homicide cases were committed within the context of jealousy. In addition, jealousy-related stalking behaviours have also been associated with partner homicide, with stalking occurring prior to partner homicide in nearly one quarter of cases (Moracco et al., 1998). Finally, and consistent with the evidence examined in Chapter 1, IPV perpetrators who have a history of using violence against non-intimates are at an increased risk of more severe and frequent IPV than those without such a history. Gondolf (1988), for example, found that in contrast to a subgroup of IPV offenders labelled as 'moderate', those in the 'anti-social' group were considerably more likely to have prior arrests for non-IPV violence (6% vs 69% respectively). This was found to be the most substantive difference between offender subgroups. Campbell (1992) found that just fewer than 70 per cent of offenders arrested for partner homicide offences had a prior arrest for non-IPV violence.

The final category of offence characteristics to examine is that of situational characteristics. Again, two features have been identified as of particular concern when examining risk for future severe and/or lethal IPV. First, although no empirical evidence exists to link access to weapons to the risk of IPV in general, there is some evidence that access to weapons increases the likelihood of lethal IPV. For example, Campbell et al. (2003) found that the two features that discriminated femicide victims from non-lethal IPV victims was perpetrator access to a gun, and prior threats with a weapon. Second, severity of IPV and the likelihood of lethal IPV has been found to be associated with attempts on the part of the victim to leave or end the relationship. For example, Moracco et al. (1998) found that 50 per cent of women killed by their intimate partners had threatened, attempted or successfully left their partner. Wilson and Daly (1993) found that in contrast to homicide cases involving cohabiting couples, IPV was a feature in 80 per cent of homicide cases of separated couples (in contrast to 35%).

The findings of a British study of partner murderers suggests that the characteristics previously identified may cluster into meaningful spousal murderer subtypes akin to those hypothesized by Holtzworth-Munroe and Stuart (1994, see Chapter 1). Dixon, Hamilton-Giachritsis and Browne (2008) examined, through the use of multidimensional scaling, the characteristics of both offence and offender based on two underlying dimensions of psychopathology and criminality. The results identified three subtypes, two of which shared features with Holtzworth-Munroe and Stuart's (1994) generally violent/antisocial and borderline/dysphoric groups, and were labelled the high criminality/low-moderate psychopathology and moderate-high criminality/high psychopathology groups, respectively. The offender characteristics associated with the first group, which comprised of nearly half of the sample, had the most extensive criminal history, which was most likely to involve convictions before the age of 16, and convictions for extra-familial violence. Notably, the offence characteristics of the latter group, which represented just over a third of the sample, included stalking behaviours prior to the offence, suicide attempted after the murder, and offences motivated by estrangement and characterized by overkill (15 blows or more). This suggests that not only do offender characteristics cluster, but that these characteristics may also be associated with specific offence characteristics.

Current Approaches to IPV Risk Assessment

The identification of meaningful risk factors is central to the conduct of valid and defensible risk assessment practice. Approaches to the risk assessment of IPV reflect the general trends in risk assessment development. That is, assessments broadly fall within three categories: clinical, actuarial and structured professional judgement approaches (see Moore, 1996 and Quinsey, Harris, Rice & Cormier, 2006 for more comprehensive accounts of this field). Kropp (2004) argues that of these three approaches or 'generations' of risk assessment, unstructured clinical assessment continues to be the most widely used, which is, in part, due to the general lack of structured assessment instruments available to practitioners. This approach requires the clinician to make risk assessment decisions through the idiosyncratic appraisal of information deemed relevant to each individual case. Consequently, the nature and scope of information reviewed varies unsystematically across cases (Doyle & Dolan, 2008). Within the violence risk assessment more broadly, this approach has received harsh criticism, owing to the lack of validity, reliability and accountability associated with it (Grove & Meehl, 1996). Moreover, the empirical evidence regarding the validity of this approach suggests that clinical risk predictions are only slightly above chance, and that competence in this area varies significantly between clinicians.

In contrast, the 'second generation' actuarial approach to risk assessment relies on the use of statistical methods to predict future behaviour (Douglas, Cox & Webster, 1999). Such approaches may use statistical equations (statistical prediction), actuarial tables and/or algorithmic programmes (Grove, Zald, Lebow et al., 2000). The term actuarial is also used to refer to the selection of predictor variables, based on the weight of empirical evidence that supports their statistical association with violent outcomes in representative samples, and the combination of these factors based on increases in incremental validity (Hilton, Rice, Rice et al., 2004). Kropp (2004) notes that the aims of actuarial prediction are two-fold: to predict violence in a relative sense by comparing the individual to population norms, and to predict violence in an absolute sense by identifying a precise probabilistic estimate of the likelihood of future violence (Kropp, 2004, p. 681). Grove and Meehl (1996) conducted a meta-analysis of 136 studies comparing first and second generation risk assessment methods and found that in eight studies first generation approaches were superior, in 64 cases second generation approaches were superior and in 64 studies there were no significant differences between the two. This approach has also been criticized, owing to the inability of such approaches to include an appraisal of the risk context, thereby resulting in limited practical utility of such assessments (Hart, 1998).

The 'third generation' structured professional judgement or 'empirically validated structured decision-making' (Douglas et al., 1999) approach facilitates the systematic assessment of a number of specified risk factors through the provision of guidelines, but requires the individual professional (who may or may not be clinically trained, Kropp, 2004) to base their overall judgements of the nature of the risk posed by an individual offender on their clinical understanding of the case (Douglas and Kropp, 2002). The set of identified risk factors is deemed to be the minimum on which an appraisal of risk should be conducted. This approach has a flexibility that is not apparent in purely actuarial approaches, but more rigidity than unstructured clinical judgement and, consequently, changes the emphasis from one of prediction associated with earlier approaches to one of risk management (Doyle & Dolan, 2008).

Actuarial IPV risk assessments

Currently there exist only two purely actuarial risk assessments that are IPV specific, the Ontario domestic assault risk assessment (ODARA; Hilton et al., 2004), and the domestic violence risk appraisal guide (DVRAG; Hilton, Harris, Rice et al., 2008).

Ontario domestic assault risk assessment
The ODARA is designed to be used by frontline police officers and, consequently, the items included are those that can be scored based on information that is readily available to police officers. It consists of 13 weighted items that reflect IPV specific risk factors, and also more general risk factors for criminal behaviour (Hilton et al., 2004). Specifically, the items refer to:

- previous domestic assault;
- previous non-domestic assault;
- previous custodial sentence of at least 30 days;
- previous failure of conditional release;
- threats of harm or to kill during index offence;
- victim being held against their will during index offence;
- victim's fears future repeat violence;
- victim and/or offender having more than one child;
- offender as stepfather in index relationship;
- offender violent to non-family members;
- offender having substance abuse problem indicated by more than one piece of evidence;
- offender having used violence against the victim during her pregnancy;
- victim with at least one barrier to support.

In each instance, the item is rated as present (1) or absent (0), and an individual's scale score may range from 0 to 13. The authors derived seven score categories based on the distribution of scores and computed the associated recidivism rate during a follow-up period of nearly five years for a sample of 589 Canadian offenders. On this basis, 5 per cent of offenders with a score of 1 recidivated during this period, in contrast to 41 per cent of those with a score of 4, and 70 per cent with a score between 7 and 13. In total, 80 per cent of those who recidivated had scores between 1 and 4 on the scale. Some evidence of concurrent validity between the ODARA and other risk assessment instruments was found, including the Spousal Assault Risk Assessment ($r = .60$; see below for details of the SARA), and the Danger Assessment ($r = .43$), although in both cases the correlation coefficients were not large, and suggest only a moderate level of association.

Domestic violence risk assessment guide (DVRAG)
The DVRAG was developed from the ODARA through the addition of clinically relevant information that is not routinely available to the police (Hilton et al., 2008). Such information included scores on other IPV specific, and general violence risk assessments (SARA; DA; Domestic Violence Screening Instrument, Williams & Houghton, 2004; PCL-R, Hare, 1991; VRAG, Harris, Rice & Quinsey, 1993). It was found that PCL-R scores provided the greatest improvement in predictive validity from the basic ODARA scores (ODARA ROC area = .65; DVRAG ROC area = .70, $p < .05$).

Consequently, the 14 DVRAG items include all 13 ODARA items along with an item accounting for PCL-R scores. However, rather than the dichotomous scoring adopted for the ODARA, the DVRAG scoring system uses the Nuffield weighting system, consistent with the VRAG. Adopting the same approach to identifying seven score categories as detailed for the ODARA, but with a sample of 649 Canadian offenders, Hilton et al. found that the top 3 per cent were all recidivists in contrast to only 14 per cent of those in the lowest score category. As might be expected, given that this measure has only recently been published, there exists no data concerning its utility that has not been provided by the test constructors.

In the case of both of these actuarial IPV risk assessments, considerable work is needed to validate them on British IPV perpetrator samples prior to their being adopted with any confidence. However, even if such work were completed, it is questionable whether they would achieve any popularity among those charged with assessing the risk of IPV posed by forensic clients. The main criticism of actuarial approaches to risk assessment is that as they only consider historical information, an individual's level of risk is likely to remain the same, regardless of the potential impact of intervention strategies (Home Office, 2002). As a result, such assessments might have some utility in determining the magnitude of risk management approaches needed in a particular case, but will provide little useful information regarding the specific nature of such strategies. In addition, Douglas and Kropp (2002) note that such approaches also fail to fit with the underlying principles of treatment programmes, which target dynamic rather than static risk factors. Consequently, in line with the 'What works?' principles of risk, need, intensity and responsivity which dominate offender rehabilitation in the UK (see Chapter 4), the approaches to risk assessment that are currently favoured in the UK either combine actuarial and clinical approaches or emphasize structured clinical judgement. Specifically, there exist two risk assessment frameworks that are currently used to determine the nature of risk posed with domestic violence perpetrators, the spousal assault risk assessment (Kropp et al., 1999), and the offender assessment system (OASys).

Alternative approaches

The Spousal assault risk assessment (SARA)

The SARA provides those charged with the responsibility of assessing IPV risk with a checklist of 20 empirically validated IPV risk factors, along with guidelines for best practice in evidence gathering and evaluation (Kropp et al., 1999). The rationale behind the SARA is that non-clinicians should be able to make use of it in order to validate their decisions, and ensure that defensible risk management decisions are made. To this end, each item is associated directly with one or more risk management strategies, depending on its nature (Dutton & Kropp, 2000).

The first three items of the SARA reflect criminal history, specifically a prior history of assaulting family members and strangers and past violation of conditional release or community supervision requirements. Items 4–10 reflect psychosocial risk factors including relationship problems, employment problems, experience/witness of family violence during childhood/adolescence, recent substance abuse/dependence, recent suicidal/homicidal ideation/intent, recent psychotic and/or manic symptoms, personality disorder with anger, impulsivity or behavioural instability. Items 11–17 examine specific details of the history of IPV including past use of physical violence and sexual assault or jealousy, use of weapons, recent escalation, violation of restraining orders, and extreme minimisation or denial of IPV history and pro-IPV attitudes. The final three items consider details of the index offence such as the incorporation of severe/sexual assault, use of weapons/credible death threats and violation of restraining order. The SARA has been conceptualized as two parts, with Part 1 consisting of items 1–10, which are general violence recidivism risk factors, whereas those in Part 2, which consists of items 11–20, are deemed to be IPV specific risk factors (Grann & Wedin, 2002).

Each item has a specific evidentiary definition in order to justify the coding of it as either present, sub-threshold or absent. Items are scored on a scale of 2, 1 and 0 depending on the extent to which each item appears to be present from the available evidence (0 = absent, 2 = present). That some of the items reflect clinical constructs may potentially cause problems for non-clinician risk assessors, but the SARA allows for the consideration and incorporation of clinical opinion and the results of more structured clinical assessments. Kropp et al. (1999) also note that in some instances (e.g. denial/pro-IPV attitudes), additional evidence may be gathered through the use of validated scales, and cross-validating perpetrator report with victim report where available. It is also noted that relevant additional items can be included if they are deemed relevant to an individual case. The SARA should, therefore, be considered a starting point for best practice, and not a prescriptive assessment framework.

Although numerical item scores are derived, and total scale scores are possible, the SARA cannot and must not be used as an actuarial measure except for research purposes (Kropp et al., 1999). In contrast, clinicians should derive broad risk categories as either low, medium or high. Although Kropp et al. note that the SARA assumes a general linear association between the number of items present and risk categorization (i.e. the more risk factors present the higher the risk is deemed to be), the authors also highlight the potential importance of critical items. These are risk factors that, if present, may be sufficient by themselves to categorize the perpetrator as presenting a high risk of imminent harm in the absence of other factors. These decisions can only realistically be made through adopting a scenario planning approach, through which the assessment of the relevance of each risk factor to the individual's risk is examined, and plausible possible future scenarios are explored (Kropp, 2007). Such an approach renders it important for all risk assessment practitioners to be fully aware of the minutiae of each case, and ensure that the most valid and reliable evidence is reviewed.

Although not an actuarial measure, and likely in response to actuarial conventions, some research has been conducted to determine the predictive validity of the SARA and inter-rater reliability of the SARA items. Kropp and Hart (2000) detail the reliability and validity of SARA judgements in a sample of 2,681 male Canadian offenders obtained from probation (n = 1671) and prison (n = 1010). In general, across the items inter-rater reliability was high (> .80). However, the inter-rater reliability for Part 1 total scores and Part 1 items present, and agreement on summary ratings (low vs Moderate vs High or Low/moderate vs High) was less than ideal (0.50 – 0.68) with the identification of critical items particularly poor (0.18 , Part 1 and 0.38 Part 2). Evidence was found for criterion-groups validity, comparing the ratings assigned to inmates with and without a documented history of IPV, with those who had such a history being scored consistently higher than those without. When comparing the assessments of recidivist and non-recidivist offenders, a series of significant differences were identified on SARA scores. For example, although the total and Part 1 scores did not differ significantly between groups ($p < .07$ in both cases), significant differences were found between groups for the total number of factors and the number of factors on Part 2, and the total number of critical items and those within Part 2, providing more (albeit inconsistent) evidence for the criterion validity of the measure.

Concurrent validity was assessed by examining associations with the PCL-SV, a measure called the GSIR (Nuffield, 1982) which is an actuarial scale for the assessment of general criminality, and the VRAG (Quinsey, Harris, Rice et al., 1998). In general some, evidence for the concurrently validity when examined in relation to scores on the PCL-SV was identified, but there were no significant associations between SARA total scores and scores on the other two measures. As might be expected, however, Part 1 scores, which reflect a general predisposition towards violence, were significantly associated with scores on all measures, as were the number of factors present on Part 1.

In a Swedish study, Grann and Wedin (2002) examined the predictive validity of actuarial scale scores and item scores derived from the retrospective file-based SARA assessments of a sample of 88 court referred IPV perpetrators followed up for a period of seven years. It was found that the Part 1 and 2 scores performed only marginally better than chance in predicting recidivism during this period. In addition, three items were found to significantly predict recidivism: past violation of conditional release/ community supervisions, personality disorder with impulsivity/anger/behavioural instability and extreme denial or minimization of spousal assault history. Taken together, these studies indicate that the SARA has some validity and reliability, although this is perhaps not as clear as might be expected. Moreover, the reliability and validity of British practice is yet to be actually determined.

OASys: Integrated offender management

OASys is the risk assessment and management tool used by both prison and probation services, and it is also the risk assessment used to inform both MARAC and MAPPA proceedings. It combines a static likelihood of reconviction tool (Offender Group Reconviction Scale – OGRS 3, Howard, Francis, Soothill & Humphreys, 2009), and an assessment of dynamic risk factors linked to both the likelihood of recidivism and of causing serious harm. Whilst OASys is appropriate for assessing the risk of most offenders, it is recommended that in the case of IPV, it should be used in conjunction with the SARA (NOMS, 2009). Specifically, OASys is designed to:

- assess the likelihood of an offender being reconvicted;
- identify offending-related needs, basic personality traits and cognitive behavioural problems;

- assess the risk of serious harm, risk to the individual and other risks;
- contribute to the management of the risk of harm;
- link the risk assessment of serious harm to the sentence plan;
- flag requirements for additional specialist assessments;
- assess individual change during a sentence.

According to the user manual, the main aim of OASys is to 'help practitioners to make sound and defensible decisions' (Home Office, 2002, p. 3).

An OASys assessment comprises five elements which, include the assessment of risk of reconviction and offending-related factors; risk of serious harm to self and others, and other risks; a summary sheet; a supervision and sentence planning component, and an offender self-assessment to obtain self-report where relevant. Within the first section, the assessment of risk of reconviction and offending-related factors, there are 12 subsections of risk factors to be assessed, which have been empirically linked with reconviction. Within each section, the assessor is required to provide evidence of the functional relationship between the risk factor and risk of serious harm and offending behaviour. Items are scored as either present or absent (yes/no) or, where an opinion regarding the extent of a problem is required, as 0, 1 or 2. The item scores within each section are then summed and a weighting applied to reflect the strength of the relationship between each category of risk factors, and reconviction as is evidenced in the empirical literature. The sections are listed in table 5.1 and are presented in decreasing order of weights applied. Weighted scores for each section are then summed and a risk of reconviction score is calculated which may range from 0 to 168 with high scores deemed to reflect an increased risk of reconviction. Three risk categories are defined on the basis of scores obtained as either Low: 0–40, Medium: 41–99 and High: 110+.

Two components of this section of the OASys assessment reflect IPV. The first is whether the current offence involved a partner being physically attacked. The second,

Table 5.1 OASys risk of conviction and offending related factors subsections

Item category
Criminal history
Thinking style
Lifestyle and associates
Drug misuse
Current offence
Attitudes
Employability/education/training
Accommodation
Relationships
Financial management and income
Alcohol misuse
Emotional/psychological factors

Table 5.2 Risk of harm categories and definitions

Risk of harm category	Definition
Low	No significant, current indicators of harm
Medium	Identifiable indicators of risk of harm. The offender has the potential to cause harm but is unlikely to do so unless there is a change in circumstances
High	Identifiable indicators and the potential event could happen at any time, and the impact would be serious
Very high	Imminent risk of serious harm and the impact would be serious

within the relationships section, is designed to determine whether the perpetrator has a history of relationships characterized by IPV. This latter section is not scored, and does not therefore contribute to the risk of reconviction. However, should the information collected at this point indicate that IPV has been a problem, this information can be used to determine that further assessment is required. In contrast, if IPV is a feature of the current offence, this should immediately indicate the need for further assessment. Where further assessment is required, a SARA should be completed.

There are three risk of serious harm categories, details of which are presented in table 5.2. Risk of harm is defined as 'a risk which is life threatening and/or traumatic, and from which recovery, whether physical or psychological, can be expected to be difficult or impossible (Home Office, 2002, p. 128). The OASys risk of harm assessment requires a consideration of harm to self, harm to children, risk to the individual (suicide, self-harm, coping in custody/hostel), and other risks including the risk of absconding/escape, control issues and breach of trust.

There is a limited corpus of literature examining the reliability and validity of the OASys system in general, and none has examined explicitly its predictive validity versus that of the SARA in cases of IPV specifically. Morton (2009) conducted an examination of the inter-rater reliability of OASys. It was found that in general only moderate agreement on OASys items was obtained. Although the total scores were highly consistent across raters, the individual section scores that contributed to the total scores were less consistent. In particular, the least reliable sections were financial management, alcohol misuse, thinking and behaviour and risk of serious harm. Howard (2009) conducted a study to examine the two-year predictive validity of OASys for predicting violent and non-violent reoffending (based on police data). Specific risk indices for violent and non-violent offending were derived from the OASys dynamic risk factors and examined to determine whether they were more accurate in predicting reoffending than the OGRS-3 actuarial scale and the standard OASys scores. It was found that both of the derived risk indices outperformed the alternatives when predicting violent and non-violent reoffending, respectively. For non-violent reoffending the area under the curve (AUC) increased from 76 per cent (OASys standard score) and 78 per cent (OGRS-3) to 80 per cent (non-violent reoffending index score). For violent reoffending, the AUC increased from 68 per cent (OASys standard score) and 70 per cent (OGRS-3) to 74 per cent (violent reoffending index score). In a further study, it was found that the relationships section did not have adequate internal reliability (Chronbach's alpha > .70; Moore, 2009). In addition, when the items were factor analysed, a 15-factor solution was found to account for only 60 per cent of variance. Three of the OASys subsections were found to each load across two factors. It was also found that scores on the relationships, lifestyles and associates and emotional well-being were found not to be predictive of reoffending, thereby questioning the criminogenic nature of these problems.

Taken together, these data indicate that as is currently used, OASys has only moderate predictive validity of all reoffending, and this is reduced further when violent reoffending is considered. Such data highlight the importance of employing additional assessments for violence risk in general, and IPV in particular.

Through undertaking the risk of reconviction and serious harm assessments and, where appropriate, additional specified assessments (e.g. SARA) the information gleaned is used by both probation and prison staff in sentence planning activities. The remit of sentence planning within both of these sectors includes reducing and managing the risk posed by the individual through addressing offending-related needs, and increasing public protection and rehabilitation (according to National Probation Standards and PSO2200, respectively). Consequently, it is at this point that accredited offending behaviour programmes may be considered relevant and appropriate to the offenders needs.

Post-treatment risk appraisal

While not commonly used, the prison service has developed an additional risk and needs assessment for IPV perpetrators, the domestic abuse risk and needs assessment (DARNA, HM Prison Service/NOMS, undated). This assessment is conducted in order to ascertain the impact of treatment on identified risk factors, and any outstanding areas of risk or need for IPV perpetrators. Within this assessment, details of the historical and psychological context of the offence are noted in addition to the risk appraisal arising from a SARA assessment. The assessment also requires an appraisal of relevant dynamic risk factors, the offender's insight into their relevance for their behaviour, and any progress that has been made in modifying these risk factors. A fourth section examines current functioning and risk, and incorporates PCL-R assessment details and offence-paralleling behaviours that might have been observed within prison. This is followed by a consideration of how risk might change, either for the better or worse, and the conditions that might contribute to any such change. The final substantive section requires the assessor to determine what strategies are required to maintain successful risk management of the offender post-release. Such recommendations should be based on what is feasible, given the likely conditions to which the offender will be returned. Currently, there is no published data available regarding the reliability or validity of this assessment.

6

Current Practice: Programmes for Partner-Violent Men

Currently two different models of group-based intervention for male IPV perpetrators are offered by probation services, the Integrated Domestic Abuse Project (IDAP) and the Community Domestic Violence Programme (CDVP). CDVP is based on the same underlying model as the Healthy Relationships Programme (HRP), which is provided within custodial settings. These two models are described and discussed in turn. The descriptions are based on those contained within the programme theory manuals, as, according to the CSAP accreditation criteria examined in Chapter 4, the theory manual should contain an evidence-based theory of change, and that, 'The evidence concerning predictors of recidivism for any particular population is considered as a starting point in programme development. Specifically it must be stated which offender population the programme is for, which criminogenic factors the programme targets, the methods employed to elicit change.' The aim of this chapter, therefore, is to explicitly examine the extent to which these issues seem to have been addressed within current programmes. To this end, comparisons will be drawn across theoretical background, programme structure and focus, and the empirical evidence associated with the main treatment targets identified within each programme. Table 6.1 summarizes the structure, format and techniques used within each of the four programmes arising from these two models, and table 6.2 summarizes the main treatment targets identified within the respective theory manuals.

Table 6.1 reveals a great deal of conceptual overlap between the two main treatment models as both focus to a greater, or lesser, extent on the role of gender socialization and cognitive characteristics. Although the programme manuals of both IDAP and CDVP note that the programmes reflect the Nested Ecological Model (Dutton, 1985),

The Rehabilitation of Partner-Violent Men, by Erica Bowen

Table 6.1 Programmatic features of the main IPV perpetrator programmes offered in England and Wales

Component	Programme			
	IDAP	CDVP	MHRP	HHRP
Setting	Community	Community	Prison	Prison
Treatment model	Duluth psycho-educational	Nested ecological model	Nested ecological model	Nested ecological model
Therapeutic approach	Cognitive-behavioural	Cognitive-behavioural/ Rational emotive behaviour therapy	Cognitive-behavioural/ rational emotive behaviour therapy	Cognitive-behavioural/rational Emotive behaviour therapy
Referral criteria	Male perpetrator, 18+ years old, Heterosexual Moderate/high risk SARA	Male perpetrator Adult Heterosexual Moderate/high risk SARA	Male perpetrator Adult Heterosexual Moderate risk SARA One previous incident of violence against female partner	Male perpetrator Adult Heterosexual High risk SARA Established pattern of violence against women partners
Exclusion criteria	Severe learning difficulties English as second language Substance misuse Length of licence Failure to sign statement of understanding/ release of information	Severe learning difficulties English as a second language Emotional instability Severe substance use problems Severe mental health problems Poor motivation	Severe learning difficulties English as a second language Emotional instability Severe substance use problems Severe mental health problems Poor motivation	Denial of assault Emotional instability English as second language

Number and length of sessions	3 × pre-group sessions 27 group sessions 4+ post group sessions Midpoint assessment Endpoint assessment	1 × pre-group orientation session 26 × 2 hour core group sessions delivered once per week 3 pre-group, 2 during group, 4 post group individual sessions	29 × 2 hour sessions Individual sessions with tutors	68–70 hours of 2.5 hour sessions delivered 3 or 4 times per week Individual sessions with tutors
Rolling or fixed intake?	Rolling – intake at the start of each module	Fixed intake	Fixed intake	Fixed intake
Module topics	Non-violence (3 sessions) Non-threatening behaviour (3 sessions) Respect (3 sessions) Support and trust (3 sessions) Accountability and honesty (3 sessions) Sexual respect (3 sessions) Partnership (3 sessions) Responsible parenting (3 sessions) Negotiation and fairness (3 sessions)	Motivational enhancement (2 sessions) Awareness and education (7 sessions) Managing thoughts and emotions (7 sessions) Social skills (4 sessions) Relapse prevention and risk management (4 sessions) Healthy relationships (1 session)	Motivational enhancement (3 sessions) Awareness and education (8 sessions) Managing thoughts and emotions (7 sessions) Social skills (5 sessions) Relapse prevention and risk management (4 sessions) Healthy relationships (2 sessions)	Motivational enhancement (5 sessions) Awareness and education (4 sessions) Cultural issues (3 sessions) Autobiography (2 sessions) Thinking skills (5 sessions) Managing emotions (12 sessions) Social skills (6 sessions) Parenting (3 sessions) Relapse prevention (15 sessions) Healthy relationships (4 sessions)

(***Continued***)

Table 6.1 (*Continued*)

Component	Programme			
	IDAP	**CDVP**	**MHRP**	**HHRP**
Specific methods	Re-enacting violent events Videos Vignettes Self-assessment and monitoring Role play Rehearsal of new skills Small group discussion Control log Action plan Time out Self-talk Power and Control Wheel Equity Wheel	Lectures Socratic questioning Exercises/case studies Group inquiry/debate Mental imagery/visualisation Role playing Modelling Power and Control Wheel ABCD model Commentary of skills steps Feedback Self-evaluation Relapse prevention plans Risk management plans Cognitive restructuring Autobiographies Relapse prevention Homework	Lectures Socratic questioning Exercises/case studies Group inquiry/debate Mental imagery/visualisation Role playing Modelling Power and Control Wheel ABCD model Commentary of skills steps Feedback Self-evaluation Relapse prevention plans Risk management plans Cognitive restructuring Autobiographies Relapse prevention Homework	Lectures Socratic questioning Exercises/case studies Group inquiry/debate Mental imagery/visualisation Role playing Modelling Power and Control Wheel ABCD model Commentary of skills steps Feedback Self-evaluation Relapse prevention plans Risk management plans Cognitive restructuring Autobiographies Relapse prevention Homework
Skills taught	Time outs Self-talk Emotion identification Victim empathy Assertive behaviour Emotion management skills Communication skills Conflict resolution Parenting skills	Reflection Perspective taking Self-talk Emotion identification Emotion management skills Time out Thought stopping Communication skills Conflict resolution Parenting skills	Reflection Perspective taking Self-talk Emotion identification Emotion management skills Time out Thought stopping Communication skills Conflict resolution Parenting skills	Personal goal setting Reflection Self-talk Emotion identification Emotion management skills Time out Stress management skills Thought stopping Listening skills Perspective taking Negotiation Conflict resolution Parenting skills

Table 6.2 Treatment targets within all four accredited domestic violence perpetrator programmes

	IDAP	CDVP	MIDVT	HIDVT
Denial, minimization, blame	*	*	*	*
Attitudes supporting domestic violence	*	*	*	*
Thinking errors supporting domestic violence	*	*	*	*
Reduction in anger	*	*	*	*
Reduction in hostility		*	*	*
Management of anxiety		*	*	*
Management of depression		*	*	*
Conflict resolution	*	*	*	*
Assertive communication	*	*	*	*
Emotion management	*	*	*	*
Positive parenting	*	*	*	*
Victim perspective taking	*	*	*	*
Motivation to change	*	*	*	*

Note: IDAP = Integrated domestic abuse programme; CDVP = Community domestic violence programme; MIDVT = Moderate intensity domestic violence treatment; HIDVT = High intensity domestic violence treatment

it is evident that the IDAP programme adopts this with respect of the range of levels of support and intervention (cf. Edleson & Tolman, 1992), which is reflected in the broad multi-agency context previously described. In contrast, according to the theory manual, at least (which obviously might differ in practice), CDVP targets a range of individual risk factors that arise from different levels of the ecology (e.g. pro-violence attitudes which, it can be argued, arise from the macrosystem). It is interesting to note, however, that regardless of the apparent differences drawn between these two models, both at least superficially address identical treatment targets (see table 6.2).

The information contained in table 6.2 further reinforces the notion that the programmes, despite apparently reflecting different models, appear to focus on almost identical treatment targets. It is only when the details of the programme content are examined explicitly that the real differences between these programmes emerge.

Overview of IDAP

IDAP is based on the Duluth model of intervention (see Chapter 4) with respect of both the intervention project curriculum (cf. Pence & Paymar, 1993), and the ideology of placing such a programme within a wider multi-agency intervention system. It is interesting to note, however, that despite being allegedly based on the Duluth curriculum, the theory manual adopts the nested ecological model as its etiological framework for understanding risk for IPV. Moreover, the programme is described as multi-modal, incorporating intervention strategies from motivational enhancement, cognitive behavioural therapy, rational emotive behaviour therapy, stress inoculation, relaxation training, skills training and relapse prevention. Through adopting the therapeutic principles of cognitive behaviour therapy, IDAP is designed to 'challenge participants' patterns of thinking and rationalisations that underpin and maintains their violent and abusive behaviour' (p. 37). Moreover, this approach enables participants to be trained in a range of relevant skills deemed to be required for the development of non-controlling relationships. The ultimate goal of IDAP is to eliminate violent and abusive behaviour towards women and their children, and these behaviours are all viewed as a conscious means of control by male perpetrators. According to the manual this will be achieved by:

- developing perpetrators' insight into risk factors for abuse and violence;
- increasing their awareness of the range of abusive attitudes and behaviours used towards partners and children;
- increasing participants' understanding of the impact of these behaviours;
- developing a sense of responsibility for the behaviours;
- replacing abusive and controlling attitudes and behaviours with non-abusive and non-controlling alternatives.

Programme eligibility criteria

The programme is suitable for adult male perpetrators who are violent towards female intimate partners. No mention is made in the theory manual of any potential exclusion criteria relating to English language competence, screening for personality disorders or emotional fragility, or motivation to change. While it is stated that 'it is difficult to make a case for total deniers to be included, as, if they maintain that "nothing happened" then there is "nothing to say"' (Offending Behaviour Programmes Unit, undated, p. 79), however, within the theory manual it is not explicitly stated whether total deniers are excluded. Rather a more elaborate discussion of stages of change and treatment matching is provided, although this appears aimed at awareness raising concerning the different stages of motivation that might be encountered by practitioners, rather than as proposing a model of how such principles are adhered to within the programme.

Programme content

The programme consists of nine, three-session modules, each of which relates to a specific theme (identified in table 6.1). Each of the themes reflect a segment on the Equality Wheel (see Chapter 4), and these, in turn, represent the intended outcome of the programme – that is, that men will have replaced the behaviours depicted in the Power and Control Wheel (see Chapter 4) with those from the programme. Men are recruited on to the programme through a rolling intake policy at the start of each module. Each theme is examined in exactly the same way across three group sessions. Thus, the format is as follows:

- Check-in (same each week).
- Week 1: Definition of the theme, 3–5 minute video vignette of perpetrator exhibiting behaviours identified within the theme, which is then analysed by participants using the control log, perpetrators to identify one target for change and one specific step to take towards achieving that goal using the action plan.
- Week 2: perpetrators examine their own behaviour relevant to whichever theme is being explored using a control log, and each perpetrator is required to identify an abusive tactic that he has used, in order for this to be discussed in the group
- Week 3: group members role-play non-controlling behaviours that contrast to those identified within the theme, using an abusive incident that they have logged from the previous week.

Additional sessions

Within the orientation session, which takes place prior to the groupwork programme, perpetrators are taught the skills of 'time out' and 'self talk' and are also introduced to the 11 non-controlling behaviour strategies that feature in the main programme. These are: taking time out, recognizing anger cues, using positive self-talk, coping with jealousy, acknowledging women's fear, using assertive behaviour, accepting women's anger, being aware of non-verbal cues, communicating thoughts and feelings, letting go and conflict resolution. In pre-treatment sessions with their offender manager and programme facilitators, perpetrators are introduced to the control log in order to complete an offence analysis. The pre-group offence analysis serves to try and make perpetrators open to the honest reporting of their behaviours.

Overview of CDVP and the Moderate Intensity Healthy Relationships Programme

Central to the treatment ethos of CDVP is the assumption that IPV is not caused by one sole factor and, consequently, the pro-feminist ideal of patriarchy as the principle cause is directly challenged, and the extent to which such factors are acknowledged is reduced (OBPU, 2005). The programme combines techniques from cognitive behavioural therapy, rational emotive behaviour therapy, feminist-based and solution-focused therapies, cognitive therapy, and motivational interviewing, along with an appraisal of stages of change, within a relapse-prevention framework. The ultimate treatment goal of the programme is the elimination of men's violence against women and, in addition, a further three intermediary goals are identified. These are to:

- assist participants to develop insight into their risk factors as well as to assist them to develop relationship skills, thinking skills and emotion management skills;
- encourage participants to accept responsibility for their behaviours and encourage them to actively participate in changing their behaviour;

- help participants to increase their awareness of abusive attitudes and behaviours towards women and children and the negative effects of these behaviours.

The CDVP and HRP moderate intensity programmes are based on, and delivered from, the same programme manual. The main difference between the two programmes, aside from the location of delivery (community versus prison), is that the prison-based programmes are typically delivered with more sessions per week than those in the community. The two HRP programmes differ with regard of the amount of time spent examining different factors. For example, in the moderate intensity programme, the social skills module consists of five sessions, covering communication skills, conflict resolution skills and parenting skills, whereas in the high intensity programme parenting forms the basis of an individual module and the social skills module consists of six sessions. The two prison-based programmes require offenders to engage in one-to-one sessions with programme tutors in between group-based sessions so that matters arising from the group sessions can be explored further if needed. Within the programme, men are required to identify those components that are most relevant to their experience of using violence in intimate relationships (Garrett, 2010, personal communication).

Programme eligibility criteria

The CDVP is available to individuals who are male, adult and heterosexual, and who have a history of IPV against female partners and have been assessed as either moderate or high risk on the SARA (specific risk entry criteria apply for both HRP programmes, see table 6.1). In addition, males must be emotionally stable and have sufficient proficiency in the English language to be able to comprehend the programme. It is acknowledged that the programme is suitable for some individuals who may have some features of borderline personality disorder, but practitioners are urged to ensure that assessments are conducted to guarantee that the level of impairment present would not preclude the individual from attending. It is interesting to note, however, that in the theory manual at least, although offender typology literature is examined, there is no clear reference to which of these borderline traits might be appropriate for this programme. Additional inclusion criteria refer to motivation to change, in that those individuals who have low levels of motivation to change are not appropriate for the programme, despite it being acknowledged that motivation to change is also viewed as a treatment target.

Programme content

The programme consists of 25 group sessions, one pre-group orientation session, and an additional nine individual sessions are also incorporated. The group operates on a fixed intake basis on the understanding that the skills and knowledge from the previous modules help individuals to use the skills and knowledge in latter modules.

Module 1

The first module, which consists of two sessions, is designed to start the motivation enhancement process by getting participants to identify their individual therapeutic goals, which they aim to achieve by the end of the programme. The development of a therapeutic climate starts with the disclosure of personal information to facilitate the development of cohesion and trust.

Module 2

The second module, which lasts for seven sessions, uses the Power and Control Wheel from the Duluth model to facilitate awareness raising around issues of what does and does not constitute IPV. This leads into a discussion regarding risk factors for IPV that arise from thoughts, beliefs and attitudes, and individuals are subsequently required to identify the etiological factors in their use of IPV. It is within this module that the role of cultural and subcultural factors are examined in relation to the way they influence the development of relationship attitudes and values.

Module 3

This module last for seven sessions, and forms the initial thinking skills training component of the programme. Within this module, the ABC model is introduced and links between irrational beliefs, negative attitudes and emotions are examined with reference to violent behaviour. The emotion management component trains individuals in self-control techniques in order to deal effectively with emotions associated with abuse (e.g. anger, jealousy).

Module 4

According to the manual, 'the social skills module trains participants in communication skills, negotiation and reviews some parenting skills' (Offending Behaviour Programmes Unit, p. 62). This module lasts for four sessions.

Module 5

Across the four sessions of this module, participants are able to identify their personal risk factors and the situations in which they are at high risk of engaging in IPV behaviours. Personal relapse prevention and risk management plans are devised, within which the importance of ongoing intervention and support is emphasized.

Module 6

This is a single session module which requires participants to draw on their prior learning to define healthy relationships, and participants will reflect on the extent to which they have achieved the goals that they set at the start of the programme.

Additional sessions

There are also three individual pre-programme sessions with a case manager, one pre-programme orientation session, two individual session with a case manager throughout the running of the group programme and a minimum of four mandatory post-programme individual sessions with a case manager. The circumstances under which the number of these sessions might increase, or the role of these sessions is not explicitly detailed within the programme manual.

Overview of the High Intensity Healthy Relationship Programme

As shown in table 6.1, the main organizational difference between the moderate and high intensity versions of the healthy relationship programme relates to the increased number of sessions, which allows for specific content to be expanded into separate modules. For example, the following three modules do not exist in the moderate intensity programme, but broadly reflect similar content.

Module 3
This module consists of three sessions, which examine socio-cultural issues and how cultural messages relate to men's use of violence in intimate relationships. It is interesting to note that this was not a stand-alone module in the original Canadian programme.

Module 4
This module consists of two sessions, which require offenders to analyse their own personal risk factors and how they relate to the patterns of abusive behaviour that they have evidenced in relationships. The aim of the module is to increase awareness of personal risk factors and personal responsibility for perpetuating abusive behaviour.

Module 8
This module examines the IPV offender and child relationship. It enables IPV offenders to identify behaviours that constitute child abuse, and integrates victim empathy issues by examining the impact of both direct abuse and witnessing IPV on children. In addition, the module examines positive parenting practices including effective non-abusive parenting, and also incorporates risk management issues concerning risky situations that arise for some when discussing co-parenting arrangements. Within the high intensity HRP, three sessions are allocated to this topic.

Critique of the Programme Theories

Both manuals provide an examination of the theory and empirical research linking specific risk factors to IPV, and some appraisal of the offender typology literature is also included to reaffirm the point that not all IPV perpetrators have the same risk factors, and that some also have additional personality traits of clinical relevance for intervention planning. However, in neither case is there any mention of how the programmes directly deal with these issues, aside from ensuring that individuals who are referred are screened for 'emotional instability'. Quite what this means is never clarified, within the theory manuals at least. Reference is also made to the need principle, in that interventions should target dynamic risk factors that are associated with IPV behaviour. It is interesting to note that only in the IDAP manual is there is any acknowledgement that the literature in this area is insufficient from which to draw firm conclusions regarding the nature of criminogenic need in IPV offenders.

Within the CDVP manual, the dynamic treatment targets identified are referred to as: attitudes/thinking errors supporting IPV, reduction in anger and hostility, management of anxiety and depression, assertive communication, conflict resolution, positive parenting and motivation. Within the IDAP manual, the broad treatment targets are identified as: distorted thinking (minimization, denial, victim blame), emotional mismanagement (anger, hostility, jealousy, fear of abandonment), skills deficits (cognitive, coping, non-controlling behaviours, parenting, communication, assertiveness, conflict resolution), self-regulation (relapse prevention, reflection), and motivational enhancement.

There seems to be a lack of conceptual clarity within the programme manuals with regards to the potential role of some of the hypothesized dynamic risk factors. For example, it is unclear to what 'positive parenting' refers to in the CDVP manual, although within the IDAP manual reference is made to 'using positive, appropriate discipline and responding to the needs of children who have witnessed abuse' (p. 47). What is lacking, however, is any attempt to provide the theoretical rationale for the inclusion of such skills training – aside from incorporating them under the general rubric of 'social skills deficits'. It is possible that IPV can be conceptualized both as a risk marker for child maltreatment, and that child maltreatment can be conceptualized as a form of controlling behaviour. Indeed, within the Power and Control Wheel, the use of children and child contact arrangements is identified as a form of controlling behaviour. It is perhaps surprising, then, that within IDAP especially, there does not seem to be an explicit examination of these issues (as far as can be understood from the programme manual). Moreover, while evidence exists to suggest that depression and anxiety might differentiate violent from non-violent men, it is less clear whether these issues are predictive of recidivism or whether such features arise as a consequence of the behaviours of interest.

However, this is an argument that can be levelled at the evidence surrounding the vast majority of so-called risk factors for IPV (see Chapter 3). Also, despite the intermediary treatment target of 'Help participants to increase their awareness of abusive attitudes and behaviours towards women and children and the negative effects of these behaviours' no reference is made to the literature regarding the evidence to suggest that empathy plays a role in IPV despite the fact that direct reference is made to empathy training as a communication skill within the CDVP manual (p.42). Within the IDAP manual, victim empathy is explicitly identified as a 'relationship skill' that is taught. In this way it seems that empathy is conceptualized as a skill used to address an associated treatment target (relationship skills) rather than arguably a treatment target itself.

Both programmes incorporate components of motivational interviewing and the Stages of Change model (Prochaska & DiClimente, 1984) in order to facilitate motivational enhancement in relation to the stage of change an individual presents with at the start of the programme. Although it is a requirement of all accredited programmes to address motivation to change, and both programmes make reference to this characteristic to varying degrees, within the IDAP manual it is explicitly acknowledged that (at the time of writing), there was little evidence to support the links between denial, stage of change, in-treatment motivational enhancement and reducing reoffending (p. 49). This issues is addressed in more detail in Chapter 9.

Both manuals make the point that the single factor theories reviewed have yet to be fully supported and that an integrated model is, therefore, required. Within the IDAP manual, the case is then made for integrating individual and cultural contexts. It is stated that 'such interventions may aim to target systems as well as the individuals within those systems. IDAP is an example of such an intervention … the approach of IDAP thus seeks to impact preventatively and remedially' (p.25). It is proposed that this is achieved through integrating victim input, and addressing offence supportive factors at local and societal levels. While this might be a legitimate aim of the intervention system as a whole, it seems a little out of place to include this within a description of a perpetrator programme theory. Moreover, little is said about how this is actually achieved and the role of the perpetrator programme within this.

Both programme manuals examine the nested ecological model as an etiological model central to both programme theories. However, there is little attempt to examine any literature that might serve to validate this model, aside from the observation that the previous single-factor theories are incomplete. It is arguable that all the nested ecological model does is provide a useful heuristic within which to arrange and examine the potential links between identified risk factors and IPV, and on this basis it possibly has some clinical relevance. However, the full explanatory power of this model is yet to be ascertained with reference to IPV. Consequently, it seems that while both programmes provide thorough coverage of relevant literature regarding the available evidence in support of existing theories of IPV, and provide adequate accounts of the major therapeutic techniques and approaches used, there is less theoretical clarity with regard to the potential role of the dynamic targets challenged within both programmes. This is perhaps not surprising, given the lack of a coherent British research agenda focusing on understanding the antecedents of IPV, the impact of different treatment models, and the association between in-treatment change on dynamic risk factors and recidivism (see Chapters 8 and 9 for a discussion of these issues).

How Do the Programmes Differ?

From comparing the two written descriptions of the programmes in relation to the general topics covered and the techniques employed, it seems that there are few differences between the two programmes. However, the main differences seem to reflect the organization and delivery of the programmes. One of the main differences is the extent to which the Power and Control Wheel and, consequently, the feminist analysis of IPV, is central to the programme organization. Within IDAP, the Power and Control Wheel forms the organizing framework for the content of the programme, whereas within CDVP it is viewed as simply another tool that might be useful in enabling perpetrators to examine their own behaviour. Another point of contrast is the number of sessions per module with IDAP having a fixed three-session groupwork format and CDVP varying the number of sessions depending on the content being delivered. Moreover, within the prison-based alternatives, the two group formats differ in terms of duration and intensity depending on the level of risk posed by the individuals referred.

The Empirical Validity of Treatment Targets

It is evident from the previous critique of the programme manuals that the evidence in support of some of the major treatment components and treatment targets is not particularly coherent. The questionable empirical evidence for the validity of the role of patriarchal values and gender-role expectations in IPV has been examined in Chapter 3. In addition, the theoretical literature linking IPV to anger and emotion dyscontrol has also been examined. Consequently, this section examines in more depth the empirical data concerning the validity of the remaining treatment targets identified in table 6.2. These broadly reflect social cognitive characteristics such as denial, minimization, victim blame, cognitive distortions, perspective taking and empathy, as well as parenting. The aim of this section is to determine to what extent the evidence supports the notion that these factors are risk factors for IPV.

Cognition: Denial, minimization, victim blaming and cognitive distortions

It is normal for individuals to blame personality traits for the behaviour of others, but look to blame situations and circumstances for their own behaviour, the so-called 'correspondence bias' (Gilbert & Malone, 1995). The denial of socially unacceptable behaviour, or individual responsibility for engaging in such behaviour is also common across a range of psychological problems that have negative or harmful consequences for others (Scott & Straus, 2007). This has been a focus of considerable attention within research on sexual offenders. However, despite the fact that the clinical importance of denial, minimization and victim blaming in IPV has been acknowledged, rarely has it been the focus of empirical research (Scott & Straus, 2007).

Scott and Straus (2007) observe that denial, minimization and blame represent at least two dimensions (p. 852). The first dimension ranges from outright denial of behaviour to complete admission of all details and facets of such behaviours and their consequences. In contrast, blaming refers to attributing causality to factors external to the self. Barbaree (1991) observes that 'denial and minimisation are the results of a psychological process involving distortion, mistaken attribution, rationalisation, and selective attention and memory. The process serves to reduce the offender's experiences of blame and responsibility for their offences. Denial is extreme and categorical, minimisation is graded' (p. 2).

Although both treatment models adopted in the UK examine these factors, the IDAP model focuses on these behaviours as explicit forms of abuse along with more overt behaviours (e.g. physical, financial abuse), as well as strategies for reducing personal responsibility for other abusive behaviours, or as indicators of poor motivation to change. Moreover, individuals who are deemed to exhibit total denial are typically excluded from these programmes, although generally there is weak evidence that denial mitigates against successful treatment (Laws, 2002). From a feminist perspective, it is expected that IPV perpetrators will deny, minimize or deflect blame for their abuse within contexts that actively sanction such behaviour, and admit to these behaviours when in circumstances that endorse such behaviours. Some evidence to support this has been reported by Heckert and Gondolf (2000) who found that, prior to intervention, men were more likely than their partners to minimize the severity of their assaults, and overall they were more likely to minimize than to deny. During a post-treatment follow-up period the extent of minimization increased, which was attributed to the increased likelihood of ongoing or more severe sanctions owing to intense post-programme monitoring.

A corpus of studies has examined the cognitive characteristics of IPV perpetrators, focusing specifically on attributional style in order to determine whether particular attributional styles directly contribute to the occurrence of IPV (Murphy & Eckhardt, 2005). Studies have found consistently that IPV perpetrators believe that relationship conflicts are caused by their partner, regardless of the nature of these conflicts. For example, Dutton (1986, cited in Murphy & Eckhardt, 2005) found that within his sample of perpetrators, one third attributed the cause of their violence to their wives, a further 21 per cent blamed their violence on situational circumstances. Although a majority (79%) accepted responsibility for their behaviour, they justified their actions through blaming the victim. The findings of this particular study are difficult to interpret, however, given that Dutton did not use a comparison group. The extent to which such findings represent the correspondence bias that would be expected by chance, rather than clinically meaningful discrepancies in denial, minimization and blame are, therefore, not clear. It has also been found that higher levels of blaming are strongly correlated with IPV men's use of coercion, intimidation, emotional abuse and isolation (Dutton & Starzomski, 1997).

Murphy and Eckhardt (2005) argue that one of the most significant cognitive processes for IPV perpetrators is the tendency to interpret partner behaviour in a negative light (p. 201). Bradbury and Fincham (1990) suggest that there are two attributional processes at play within these scenarios: causal attributions and responsibility attributions. Murphy and Eckhardt go on to explain that in conjunction with the correspondence bias detailed earlier, partner blame arises from the increased likelihood of making attributional inferences in response to negative rather than positive relationship events. Indeed, there is some compelling evidence to suggest that IPV men are more likely than non-violent men to make hostile attributional inferences in relation to perceived partner behaviour. For example, Holtzworth-Munroe and Hutchinson (1993) provided maritally violent, maritally distressed-non-violent and maritally satisfied-*non-violent* husbands with nine vignettes that depicted problematic relationship scenarios. Each individual was asked to imagine themselves in each scenario. Questionnaire measures were used to determine the extent to which the men believed that the wife in each scenario acted with negative intent and deserved to be blamed for her actions, and the extent to which the wife acted in relation to five specific negative intentions. Significant differences between the violent and satisfied non-violent groups were identified in relation to attributing the cause of the conflict to negative intentions and blameworthiness of the wife. Similar findings have been reported elsewhere (e.g. Eckhardt, Barbour and Davison, 1998; Moore, Eisler & Franchina, 2000). More recently, it has been argued that these findings might actually reflect an 'overattribution bias'. Schweinle, Ickes and Bernstein (2002) found that self-reported aggression against partners was positively associated with the extent to which men overattributed critical and rejecting thoughts and feelings to women in general, indicating the relevance of a general perceptual bias.

Evidence also exists to suggest a sensitization effect, with individuals who have experience of using violence being more likely to minimize the seriousness of controlling and domineering behaviour than those with no such prior experience (Ehrensaft & Vivian, 1999), which mirrors similar findings regarding the perceived acceptability of violence within relationships (e.g. Arias & Johnson, 1989). Using the Articulated Thoughts in Simulated Situations paradigm with a sample of 17 violent and 16 non-violent college males, Eckhardt and Jamison (2002) identified several between group differences on measures of cognitive biases, hostile attributional biases, irrational beliefs and anger control statements. Specifically, it was found that in contrast to the non-violent men, violent individuals articulated a higher level of global irrational beliefs and cognitive biases. More interestingly, it was found that unit increases in the tendency to derive conclusions in the absence of evidence (arbitrary inference) were associated with a 23-fold increase in the likelihood of being in the IPV group (p. 303). In addition, similar increases in the tendency to make rigid demands upon people almost doubled the odds of group membership.

Although contention surrounds the empirical association between denial and treatment failure with offenders in general, there exists some evidence to indicate that individuals who exhibit high levels of denial and minimization encounter greater difficulties when engaged in a treatment programme (e.g. Murphy & Baxter, 1997; Scott & Wolfe, 2003). This evidence is reviewed within the 'motivation to change' section below. Taken together, these studies indicate that there is some validity to the assumption that cognitive characteristics may differentiate IPV from non-IPV men, with hostile attributional biases seeming most important, in this respect. In addition, there is tentative evidence that denial might be of clinical relevance to treatment progression. What is less clear is the extent to which such biases are causal in relation to IPV. For example, no attention seems to have been paid to the question of whether changes in these cognitive traits are directly associated with changes in IPV behaviour – a requirement for the validation of criminogenic needs (Hollin, 2001). It would be useful for research to determine whether the presence of such biases prior to the use of violence increases the likelihood of violence being used within intimate (or other) relationships, as well as whether interventions are effective in reducing these traits, and whether such changes then lead to behavioural change.

Perspective taking and empathy

Batson (2009) identifies eight separate phenomena within the literature that have been labelled as 'empathy' – such is the theoretical ambiguity surrounding this term. Across all of the various phenomena the notion of being able to share in the perceptions, thoughts and feelings of another is central, although the extent to which such abilities present at a social or neuronal level vary. Within IPV programmes, reference is typically implicitly made to increasing perpetrator empathy by making them aware of the impact of their behaviour upon their victims (Dobash et al., 2000). Within CDVP, for example, reference is made to enabling offenders 'to understand their partner's and children's response to abuse and violence' (OBPU, 2005, p. 49). The underlying assumption is that such individuals would not be violent if they understood beforehand the likely impact of their behaviour on their victims (Jolliffe & Farrington, 2004). Indeed, such has been the popularity of this assumption that

> Increasing empathy is often seen as the key to reducing the likelihood of offending against others. Some form of empathy training is, therefore, a common treatment component of those convicted of crimes such as assault, robbery, murder and sexual assault. (Mulloy, Smiley & Mawson, 1999, p. 16)

However, such a simple assumption may be interpreted within seven of the eight phenomena identified by Batson. For example, in order to make an individual aware of the impact of their behaviour and, consequently, for such an impact to serve as a punishment and inhibit future IPV behaviours, the individual would need to:

1. know another person's internal state including thoughts and feelings;
2. come to feel as the other person feels;
3. be able to project themselves into the other person's situation;
4. be able to imagine how another person is thinking and feeling;
5. imagine how they would feel in the other's place;
6. feel for the person that is suffering;
7. feel distress at witnessing the other person's suffering.

Each of these facets has independently been identified as 'empathy', but it is clear that each involves a range of independent, yet associated, skills.

As with the literature regarding the role of minimization, denial and blame in IPV, the literature on the role of empathy in offending is far greater within the general violence and sexual offender arenas than it is within the IPV field. The findings of this line of enquiry, however, are at best equivocal (see Walker & Brown, submitted. For a review of these findings, see Marshall, Hudson, Jones and Fernandez 1995). The lack of attention paid to the role of empathy in IPV is perhaps surprising, given the level of intimacy that characterizes the relationships within which the violence occurs and, in particular, owing to the evidence which suggests that relationship satisfaction is associated with levels of empathy (e.g. Fincham, Paleari & Regalia, 2002; Verhofstadt, Buysse, Ickes et al., 2008). Moreover, as might be expected, given the range of definitions of empathy alluded to previously, the literature as it stands is somewhat incoherent, owing to the focus on different facets of empathy and lack of standardized approach to its measurement.

Of the five empirical studies that have examined the relevance of different aspects of empathy to IPV perpetrators, three have focused on the ability of violent individuals to accurately judge and infer the thoughts and feelings of other people – so-called 'empathic accuracy' (Ickes, 2009). The first of these studies by Schweinle et al. (2002) was designed to determine whether aggressive men's attention to women's criticism and/or rejection reflected a perceptual bias or an enhanced ability to accurately decode and discriminate between women's thoughts and feelings. After watching video vignettes of three women discussing relationship problems with a male therapist (two concerning divorce, one concerning role conflict) and discriminating between expressed emotions, it was found that aggressive men exhibited biased rather than exceptionally accurate perceptions of women's critical/rejecting thoughts and feelings (p. 155). Moreover, this finding related to women in general, suggesting that aggressive men have a general empathy deficit. It was also found that the ability to distinguish women's critical/rejecting thoughts and feelings from non-critical thoughts and feelings was associated with men's self-reported relationship satisfaction, suggesting that this ability serves a functional role within the control and resolution of conflict. Caution surrounds the identification of aggressive men in this study, however, as an aggregate self-reported verbal and physical aggression score was derived which, in reality, included a majority of verbally but not physically aggressive men.

In a replication and extension of the study by Schweinle et al., Schweinle and Ickes (2007) incorporated an examination of attention and emotion into their analysis of empathic accuracy. The main finding of the earlier study (overattribution of criticism and rejection to women) was replicated with a sample of 85 men. In addition, it was found that men who reported feeling more concern or sympathy for the target women in the vignettes were more likely to accurately infer the content of the target's thoughts and feelings. In contrast, men who reported feeling uncaring were less accurate. In addition, the men's attention to the female target in the tape was also associated to the strength of their bias in inferring criticism and rejection from women, and also to the level of aggression towards their own wives. Attentional disengagement was associated with lower marital satisfaction, biased inferences of women's criticism and rejection, and to increased wife-directed aggression (p. 194).

A later study conducted by Clements, Holtzworth-Munroe, Schweinle and Ickes (2007) examined empathic accuracy within 71 heterosexual couples, 38 of which were identified as physically violent (both partners reported physical violence on the CTS).

This extended the original methodology detailed by Schweinle et al. (2002) by including an additional component in which each dyad discussed a relationship problem that was relevant to them. Each member of the dyad then independently had to determine the specific content of their partner's thoughts and feelings through examining the video-recorded discussions. It was found that when their partner was the target, violent men exhibited significantly lower levels of empathic accuracy than non-violent men in non-distressed relationships, and objective male observers. No differences were identified between violent, and non-violent distressed men, although the extent of violence rather than marital distress predicted the extent of the relative deficit in empathic accuracy. When the targets were female strangers there were no between-group differences. Non-distressed, non-violent men had significantly higher levels of empathic accuracy for their female partner than for strangers. This suggests that the deficit might actually be specific to female partners rather than a general deficit as was reported in the earlier study by Schweinle et al. (2002).

These three studies suggest that IPV men are more likely to exhibit biased and inaccurate interpretations of women's thoughts and feelings, with preliminary evidence that this might be wife-specific, and that it is the internal social cognitive processes, rather than wife behaviour, that are linked to IPV behaviours. Ickes (2009) suggests that these data indicate that men are motivated to avoid understanding their intimate partners' thoughts and feelings in order to maintain control within the relationship (p. 62).

A different approach to examining empathic deficits was taken by Covell, Huss & Langhinrichsen-Rohling (2007). In their study, a clinical sample of 107 IPV perpetrators (29% self referred), completed the Interpersonal Reactivity Index (IRI; Davis, 1980) and a modified version of the CTS-2 (Straus et al., 1996). The IRI is a self-report measure of four components of empathy – perspective taking, fantasy, empathic concern and personal distress. Perspective taking refers to the ability to adopt the perspective of another person. The fantasy scale relates to the ability to take on the feelings and actions of fictitious characters in books, films and plays. The empathic concern scale refers to the feeling of sympathy in relation to unfortunate others, and the personal distress scale measures the individual's feelings of unease and discomfort in relation to the emotions of other people.

It was found that perspective taking had the strongest (negative) association with self-reported psychological aggression and CTS total scores, but was not associated with either physical or sexual violence. In addition, personal distress was positively associated with physical assault and total CTS scores. In a series of multiple regression analyses it was found that increases in self-reported total violence were associated with two independent empathy profiles: a) high perspective taking, high personal distress, and low fantasy, and b) low fantasy, low personal distress and low perspective taking. Physical assault increased when personal distress and empathic concern were high, and perspective taking was low. Psychological assault increased when fantasy and perspective taking were low and personal distress was high. Finally, sexual coercion increased when perspective taking was high and personal distress was high. In addition, sexual coercion increased when both perspective taking and personal distress were low. While these results indicate a potentially complex association between self-reported IPV and self-reported empathy within clinical samples of IPV men, the findings have to be interpreted with caution, owing to the lack of comparison groups and lack of control for social desirability. As a result, the extent to which these findings are valid and are of clinical relevance is unclear.

In the final study, Babcock, Green and Webb (2008) examined the extent to which IPV perpetrators have deficits in decoding facial affect (i.e. recognizing facially expressed emotions) – what might be considered to be a fundamental socio-cognitive skill in the process of empathy. A sample of 101 (69 violent) men were asked to identify six emotions depicted in still portrait photographs. Based on classifying the violent group into the family-only, borderline/dysphoric and generally violent/anti-social groupings identified by Holtzworth-Munroe and Stuart (1994), a differential pattern of inaccuracy was identified, relative to non-violent men. Specifically, the borderline/dysphoric group were the most accurate violent group, and the generally violent were the least accurate. *Non-violent* men were less able to accurately recognize disgust and fear compared to the violent groups. In contrast to the borderline group, the generally violent group were less accurate at recognizing anger, happiness, neutral and surprise. The generally violent group were more likely to mistake neutral emotion for disgust. In addition,this group, in contrast to the *non-violent* and family-only groups, was more likely to misidentify anger as disgust. In contrast to all other groups, the generally violent subtype were more likely to misidentify anger as happiness. The same group were more likely than the *non-violent* and family-only groups to misidentify happiness as sad, and in contrast to all other groups, happiness as surprise. Finally, the generally violent group were more likely than the *non-violent* and family-only groups to misidentify surprise as fear.

The results of these five studies taken together provide preliminary evidence that deficits in empathy might be relevant to IPV perpetrators, although the question of whether such deficits are global or victim specific is unclear, because of the dearth of evidence. In addition, reaching coherent conclusions is difficult as varying facets of empathy have been investigated and different methodologies employed. What can be surmised is that IPV perpetrators appear to exhibit social information processing deficits particularly in relation to decoding social stimuli. The evidence also suggests that such deficits, which result in the misinterpretation of neutral stimuli as provocative, might be more prevalent within IPV perpetrators who are also violent outside of intimate relationships. The extent to which such deficits clearly and meaningfully differentiate violent from non-violent men is unclear. What is clear, however, is that substantially more research is required to determine the validity of the programme assumption that empathy training is required for all IPV perpetrators and that such characteristics are criminogenic needs. It seems that, currently, some of this evidence base remains unpublished. For example, Ferguson (2004) found in his MA research that the Canadian high intensity family violence prevention programme (on which the HRP programme is based) elicited statistically significant increases in victim and non-victim (but not child-oriented) empathy in individuals who completed the programme. In a study which focused on the differential treatment response of subtypes of IPV perpetrators, Huss and Ralston (2008) noted that there were no pre-post differences on the Interpersonal Reactivity Index scores across their sample, challenging the notion that programmes directly target empathy. However, owing to the identified associations between empathy and other known risk factors (e.g. IQ and socio-economic status, Jolliffe & Farrington, 2004), the independence of any such associations and observed changes needs to also be determined.

Parenting

Within all of the IPV perpetrator programmes provided in criminal justice settings, attention is paid to the parenting characteristics of IPV men. From examining the IDAP and high intensity HRP manuals it becomes apparent that, despite being targeted at men who have been violent in heterosexual intimate relationships, an examination of the impact of cruelty to children, on children, is also included, with emphasis placed on the use of appropriate discipline. Cummings and O'Reilly (1997, cited in Guille, 2004) note that there are three pathways through which children are affected by marital quality. These are: marital quality affecting the parent–child relationship; the direct exposure of marital relationship quality on the child, and the impact of marital quality on the psychological functioning of parents, which then impacts child development. The majority of research examining links between IPV and parenting has focused on the impact of IPV on the parenting capacity of female victims in their role as primary caregiver. There is a comparatively smaller evidence base, which indicates that IPV perpetrators are likely to be deficient, if not abusive parents, and that they are likely to undermine the main IPV victim's parenting role (Jaffe, Johnston, Crooks & Bala, 2008). This evidence has arisen predominantly from clinical observation rather than empirical enquiry (Guille, 2004). It must be acknowledged, however, that a proportion of IPV perpetrators are good parents despite the behaviours exhibited towards their female partners (Bancroft & Silverman, 2002). Although a range of parenting behaviours have been observed by IPV perpetrators from abusive to 'good enough', it is typically found that where negative parenting occurs, the abuse tactics displayed in relation to female partners are mirrored in their interactions with their children (Bancroft & Silverman, 2002; Jaffe et al., 2008). The association between IPV and child maltreatment and abuse is much more widely documented. In general it is estimated that IPV and child abuse/maltreatment co-occur at a rate of approximately 41 per cent (Appel & Holden, 1998).

It has been found that the parenting style of men who engage in violence against their female partners is characterized by a lack of warmth, increased coercion and increased rejection of their children (e.g. Anderson & Cramer-Benjamin, 1999, cited in Jaffe et al., 2008). In addition, when actively involved in the discipline of their children, it is an authoritarian parenting approach that is adopted. Holden and Richie (1991) found, based on maternal reports, that abusive men were more frequently angry at their children, 'spanked' their children more than twice as often that non-IPV men, and were also more likely to spank them 'hard'. It has also been observed that the parenting styles of IPV men often changes, swinging from authoritarian to permissive, or from involved to uninvolved (e.g. Adams, 1991, cited in Bancroft & Silverman, 2002; Roy, 1988). It has also been found that fathers typically do not understand the impact of their behaviour on their children. Salisbury, Henning and Holdford (2009) examined male IPV offender attitudes towards the impact of their behaviour on children in a large, primarily, African American sample (n = 3234, 83 per cent of whom were African American). It was found that two-thirds of these men acknowledged that children would have been exposed to interparental conflict. However, less than one-third acknowledged that this exposure would have affected the child. Believing that children had been affected was associated with older offenders, those with a higher level of education and those who had witnessed interparental violence during their own childhood.

Bancroft and Silverman (2002) provide a general clinical impression of IPV men as fathers who expect their children to obey their every whim and who are intolerant of challenge or resistance from their children. IPV men are often intolerant of the presence of children and view them as an annoyance, and generally fail to take interest in their children's lives. In contrast, should they decide to interact with their children, it has been observed that this form of interaction tends to be exaggerated in terms of energy, humour and the extent to which the children are treated as 'special'. This, in effect, may undermine the quality of the relationship between the child and the mother who is less likely to be in a position to be able to act in a similar way towards her children through her relationship dynamics with their father. In addition, they appear less able to follow the parenting lead from their partners who may be more inclined to model nurturing behaviours towards their children. Moreover, childcare is typically viewed as the duty of the female partner.

The limited empirical evidence reviewed here indicates that IPV men have characteristics that place them at risk of child abuse and that they are unlikely to be responsive parents. It is unclear, however, despite this evidence, how these characteristics fit within a programme as a potential 'criminogenic need' for IPV or 'domestic violence' – that is, as a treatment target. This is even more confusing when the Power and Control Wheel and Equality are re-examined. If the IDAP programme uses the segments as its focus, then the 'using children' segment within the Power and Control Wheel, which refers to behaviours such as threatening to take the children away, using contact arrangements to perpetuate abuse and accusing the partner of being a poor parent, becomes the 'responsible parenting' segment in the Equality Wheel, which refers to 'sharing parental responsibilities and being a non-violent role-model' (Pence & Paymar, 1993). Although the identified results of transformation as evidenced by the Equality Wheel reflect the documented knowledge base examined previously, how these arise from the position detailed in the Power and Control Wheel is not at all clear. Specifically, it is unclear how the opposite of 'using children' and its associated components is 'responsible parenting' as defined within the Equality Wheel. In addition, it is not specified how tackling this issue fits with the broader programme aims of reducing violence against women.

It is at this point that a question arises – if programmes seek to target family violence (i.e. violence at more than one level within the family), then why adopt a pro-feminist analysis of the problem, which focuses on explaining male violence towards women? This is not to suggest that accounting for the child's experience should not be addressed, but simply indicates a lack of clarity on the part of the programme theories, and perhaps suggests that, as in the case of substance abuse, such specific interventions should be provided on the basis of clearly assessed needs as part of the broader sentence planning process rather than relying on a small section of a comparatively brief programme to adequately address these needs.

In summary, it is evident from the empirical literature reviewed here and in Chapter 3, that the basic theoretical premises of the IPV programmes that are currently in vogue within British corrections have questionable empirical support. Overall, it seems that many of the underlying programme theory assumptions have not been clearly tested, and that the evidence which does exist has methodological and conceptual vagaries that lead to difficulties in interpretation. This calls for a more expansive programme of research internationally, but particularly within the UK in order to determine more clearly the validity of these assumptions.

International Practice

North America

Owing to the increased use of pro-arrest strategies in the USA and increasing numbers of IPV perpetrators requiring intervention, along with the diverse array of interventions that proliferated in the 1980s (see Chapter 4), domestic violence workers have endeavoured to develop practice guidelines aimed at standardizing the form of intervention offered (Gondolf, 1992). This has been met with ongoing criticism and opposition. Austin and Dankwort (1999) conducted a survey of 37 state standards that were in force in 1997. (It should be noted that at that time only three states were not in the process of developing standards if none were currently available.) It was found that in 81 per cent of cases victim safety was identified as the primary focus of intervention programmes, and 70 per cent cited patriarchy as causing or maintaining men's violence against women. The importance of a coordinated community response to IPV was cited in 92 per cent of standards and 84 per cent stated that intervention programmes should work closely with, or be accountable to, women's support services. The format of intervention was typically identified as groupwork based (86%), and as reflecting a psychoeducational/cognitive-behavioural/feminist approach (or combinations of all three, in 57% of cases). When components of the intervention philosophy were provided, they typically included an examination of power and control, the effects on women and children, pro-IPV attitudes, offender responsibility, and the socio-cultural basis of IPV. In contrast, couples counselling was identified as inappropriate and potentially dangerous in the majority (73%) of standards, and in 68 per cent of cases individual intervention was also deemed to be inappropriate. Similar findings are reported in a more recent survey (Maiuro & Eberle, 2008).

These findings indicate that while no specific programme (e.g. Duluth) is identified, programmes which share many of the basic principles of the Duluth model are favoured across the USA, and are provided as the only solution to the problem of IPV although the faith placed in their effectiveness belies the actual research evidence available (see Chapter 8). Indeed, the Duluth model has been hailed as 'one of the most successful community-based projects for violent men anywhere in the world' (Dobash et al., 2000, p. 48).

Canada

In Canada, two main programmes are offered to offenders within an institutional setting; the moderate and the high intensity family violence prevention programmes

(FVPP), which form the basis of the UK HRP programme. These programmes function within a broader context whereby, initially, offenders are assessed for their treatment readiness and motivation to change. For individuals that are deemed not to be currently suited for the FVPP, a treatment primer consisting of a resource pack aims at increasing awareness and motivation (Correctional Services Canada, CSC, 2009). The pack can be used in combination with one-to-one work *prior* to attending the FVPP. In addition, after IPV offenders have attended one or other of the FVPPs, they are required to engage in a programme of aftercare. Within the institutional setting, this requires individuals to attend the Family Violence Maintenance Program, and, within the community, the Community Maintenance Program. This takes the format of either an individual or a group-based programme with one facilitator per 10 offenders, and is designed to help offenders maintain their knowledge, understanding and newly acquired skills. The programme sessions are two hours in length and, within an institutional setting, individuals are required to attend one session per month for six months. In the community, offenders are required to attend at least three sessions. A high intensity programme has also been designed for Aboriginal Canadians, which is a culturally appropriate version of the standard high intensity programme. These programmes are offered throughout Canada, and are also used within the State of Iowa in the United States and offered through the Volunteers of America.

European practice

Between 2006 and 2008, a survey of European practice with perpetrators was compiled as part of a Daphne II Project (www.work-with-perpetrators.eu). Data were compiled regarding the number and nature of perpetrator programmes across 28 countries within the European Union (EU). The information obtained related to the extent of IPV legislation (whether it was viewed as a crime), the extent of victim support services available, number of IPV perpetrator programmes and current approaches. These data are summarized in table 6.3.

It can be seen from table 6.3 that the only pattern to emerge from the survey is one of inconsistency. There is a considerable range of practice, which seems to reflect the extent to which IPV is formally acknowledged as a serious social problem. For example, in Hungary, Latvia and Lithuania, IPV is not viewed as a crime and there are no identified perpetrator programmes offered. In contrast to the picture of intervention that emerges from the USA and Canada, where perpetrator programmes are offered. there is less standardization of approaches, although the cognitive behavioural approach seems to be well represented.

Global practice

A survey of international IPV interventions was conducted by the World Heath Organization in 2001. This survey identified 56 IPV perpetrator programmes from across 38 countries excluding the USA, Canada and the UK. Just over a third (36%) were located within Europe, and a further third (34%) in the Americas. Eleven per cent

Table 6.3 Summary of main findings from Daphne II survey of practice within the EU

Country	IPV is a crime?	Perpetrator programmes	
		Number	Main approach
Austria	Yes	8	No standardized approach
Belgium	Yes	3	Cognitive behavioural, group (3), individual (1), couple (2)
Croatia	Misdemeanour	2	Cognitive behavioural groupwork
Cyprus	Yes	1	Systemic and cognitive behavioural
Czech republic	Covered by other laws	0	–
Denmark	Yes	3	Psychodynamic (2) and NLP (1)
Finland	Yes	1	Psychodynamic
France	Aggravated offence	30	Psychodynamic, cognitive behavioural and systemic (sometimes mixed)
Germany	Covered by other laws	66	Cognitive behaviour therapy or systemic (sometimes mixed)
Greece	Aggravated offence	0	–
Hungary	No	0	–
Italy	Yes	0	–
Latvia	No	0	–
Lithuania	No	0	–
Luxembourg	Aggravated offence	1	Psychodynamic
Malta	Unknown	1	Unknown
Northern Ireland	Yes	4	Duluth
Norway	Yes	15	Psychodynamic, cognitive and counselling models
Poland	Yes	1	Duluth
Portugal	Not specifically	5	Cognitive behavioural (3) eclectic/integrative (1) groupwork (2) couples (2)
Republic of Ireland	Yes	12	Duluth
Scotland	Covered by existing law	13	Duluth
Slovakia	No	0	–
Slovenia	Yes	1	Cognitive behaviour therapy (no written curriculum) groupwork
Spain	Yes	70+	50% cognitive behavioural, 50% other (gender, systemic, eclectic or integrated) groupwork (70%) couples work (20%)
Sweden	Yes	20	Cognitive behaviour therapy and eclectic
Switzerland	Yes	26	Unknown, 6 offer treatment to females in addition to male perpetrators

of the programmes were located in Africa, with a further 5 per cent in South-east Asia, 2 per cent in the eastern Mediterranean and 13 per cent in the western Pacific. On average, the programmes were developed in the mid-1990s although it was not until 2002, on average, that the programmes in the eastern Mediterranean were developed. The longest running programme identified was the Men Against Male Violence programme, which originated in Germany in 1983. Evidence suggests that the 'feminist' model subscribed to elsewhere is less popular, with only 34 per cent of providers adopting this description for their interventions (Rothman, Butchart & Cerda, 2003). However, when programmes were categorized according to their focus on the extent to which gender roles play a part in IPV, this figure rose to 73 per cent. Less than one-third (27%) reported that their underlying theory identified psychopathology as the main cause of IPV. The survey further examined the intervention topics included within programmes in the developing (n = 19) and developed (n = 31) nations. The relative frequencies are detailed in figure 6.1 below.

Figure 6.1 shows that, despite the range of programme theories offered across these countries, relatively little variation in curriculum topics was identified. Developed countries were more likely than developing countries to include social change as a focus of their programmes, although, overall, 62 per cent of programmes stated that their

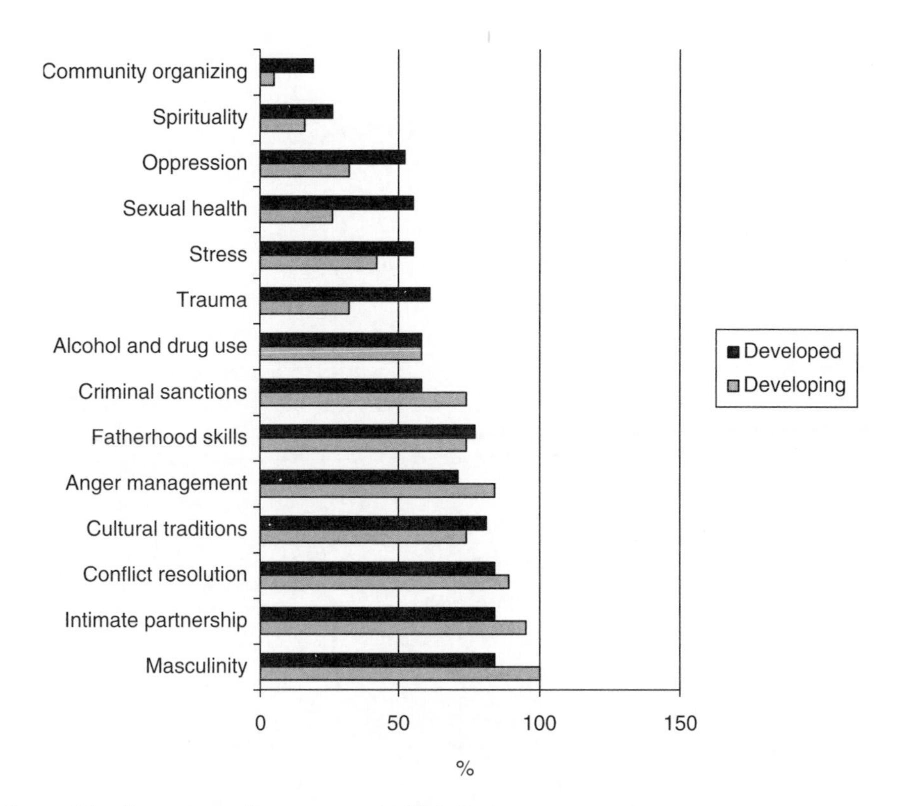

Figure 6.1 Programme theory content within European perpetrator programmes

overarching programme aims were to change attitudes and behaviours of systems which impact indirectly on the perpetrator (e.g. families, communities, society).

Summary and Conclusions

The evidence reviewed within this chapter indicates that intervention programmes for male IPV perpetrators around the world tend to focus on similar treatment targets. This is particularly clearly evidenced through the discussion of the two treatment programmes used in the UK. A dominant model is the pro-feminist psycho-educational model, which is also referred to as the 'Duluth' model, and this dominates practice in the UK and in the USA. That the same factors appear to be universally targeted within programmes would suggest that there is adequate evidence to support these principles. However, the evidence reviewed here and in Chapter 3 concerning the validity of the underling programme theory assumptions is mixed, with more convincing evidence for the role of cognitive factors than for the role of gender-role and patriarchal factors. In addition, the evidence with regard to the effectiveness of this approach is questionable, and suffers greatly from methodological weaknesses, which are discussed further in the next chapter.

7

The Effectiveness of Programmes: Issues in Programme Evaluation

So far, we have seen that the provision of group-based rehabilitation programmes for male IPV perpetrators has grown exponentially in the USA since the 1980s. While similar provision in the UK has been slower to get off the ground, the prison and probation services now offer accredited programmes for IPV men that have been developed from the 'What works?' principles of evidence-based practice. These programmes also reflect the dominant approach developed in the USA, which, as shown in the discussion of state standards in Chapter 6, has been endorsed to the exclusion, in some areas, of alternative models of intervention. However, the extent to which these programmes are effective, and alternatives are ineffective, is yet to be unequivocally determined, and debate persists regarding programme effectiveness (see Chapter 8 for a detailed examination of the empirical evidence). Within the CSAP accreditation criteria, the need for ongoing evaluation of intervention programmes is specified. While the need to adopt effective interventions has been formally acknowledged, however, it is also necessary to evaluate all programmes of intervention with IPV men, not only those already deemed to be effective. The aim of this chapter, therefore, is to provide a critical examination of the main issues to be considered when evaluating rehabilitation programmes for IPV men. This will help to lay the foundations for a critical review of the currently available published empirical evidence for the effectiveness of such programmes in Chapter 8.

Why Evaluate?

There are several reasons why the evaluation of programmes for IPV men is necessary generally, and specifically in the UK. First, the use of accredited programmes that

The Rehabilitation of Partner-Violent Men, by Erica Bowen

have been designed based on the theoretical principles of effective practice implies that such programmes are effective. However, it is not necessarily the case that each delivery of any given programme is going to be effective, as each programme delivery reflects an interaction between staff, offender, location and resource characteristics that will differ every time the programme is delivered. Moreover, the same programme delivered within one service is likely to change over time (Gondolf, 2004). Consequently, although the underlying theory manual adopted is the same across sites/services, the implementation of each group is likely to differ each time, so it cannot be concluded that because an evidence base exists to endorse the use of a particular intervention approach or theoretical framework, then this intervention will be effective *this* time, in *this* location, with *this* group of IPV men. Stakeholders should not therefore conclude that these programmes are, or will be, effective, but instead should acknowledge that under certain circumstances evidence indicates that they may be effective. Ongoing evaluation of new and established programmes is therefore required in order to determine under which circumstances programmes are particularly effective.

This understanding has serious implications for the victims of IPV who may be inclined to become reunited with a former abuser on the basis that he has attended an evidence-based programme and has been 'treated'. Indeed, the false advertising of programme effectiveness has been derided by women's advocates and researchers who emphasize the importance of providing realistic information to victims about the potential impact that any programme may have on their (ex) partner (Hague & Malos, 2005). Conversely, simply because a programme has not been accredited should not alone be taken as evidence that it is ineffective, unless there is sufficient empirical evidence to indicate this as being the case. Consequently, the evaluation of all programmes is needed to ensure that an evidence base exists from which stakeholders can make an informed decision about the most effective form of intervention, and from which realistic appraisals of programme effectiveness can be made and communicated to victims as part of victim safety planning and risk management. It is interesting to note, for example, that no published British outcome studies of the accredited programmes exist, and yet despite this apparent lack of evidence, they have been accredited nonetheless (see Chapter 7). This may simply reflect 'a tendency within the domestic violence field to jump on the bandwagon when a new approach emerges on the scene' (Shepard, 1999, p. 170).

A second justification for programme evaluation comes from the fact that IPV programmes in the UK are based on models that dominate practice in the USA. Therefore, the applicability and validity of the programme theory (the underlying assumptions about the nature of the programme and the characteristics of the target population – Rossi, Lipsey & Freeman, 2008) to a non-US population may be questioned. As noted in Chapter 5, although the Duluth model (or at least the men's programme) has been adapted for use in different countries, the comprehensive coordinated community response must be tailored to account for the different multi-agency contexts in different countries. Therefore, at a most fundamental level, the USA and UK intervention contexts differ with respect of the nature of services available, the basis of inter-agency agreements between agencies, and the potential influence of state law. Consequently, it might be expected that the impact of a men's programme within these contexts will also differ.

Finally, it is well documented that those IPV offenders who do not complete programmes are more likely to reoffend than those who do complete (e.g. Bowen, Gilchrist & Beech, 2005), and that failure to complete is associated with a range of pre-treatment factors (e.g. Bowen & Gilchrist, 2006; Cadsky, Hanson, Crawford & Lalonde, 1996; Daly & Pelowski, 1999). It is also possible that ineffective treatment may have an 'anti-therapeutic' effect (Yalom, 1985), which inadvertently increases the risk of reoffending. Consequently, all programmes must be evaluated to identify what is effective, in addition to identifying those programmes which are not only ineffective, but which also actively increase the risk posed by participants, for the sake of public protection.

At its most basic, evaluation research can be useful to all stakeholders involved in programme development and provision by providing information about how the programme functions, which may then guide decision making and resource allocation (Shepard, 1999). However, although the requirement for programme evaluation is clear, in practice, conducting evaluation research which adequately addresses the range of questions posed, and provides valid and clinically practical results is a difficult endeavour for a number of methodological, ethical and practical reasons. What follows is a critical examination of these issues, many of which are relevant to generic evaluation research within criminal justice and/or mental health settings, and some of which are peculiar to conducting evaluation research around the effectiveness of programmes for IPV perpetrators. Specifically, the following five questions will be addressed:

- Which evaluation questions should be asked?
- What should be evaluated?
- Which research design should be used?
- Which methods should be employed?
- What is good practice in IPV programme evaluation?

Which Evaluation Questions should be Asked?

With the academic and policy focus of IPV programme evaluation being whether or not programmes reduce or stop reoffending, it might seem controversial to raise the issue of which questions should be asked and addressed by programme evaluations. It is not surprising, given the public safety implications of rehabilitation programmes, that outcome evaluations have been prioritized. However, a number of observers have questioned the adequacy of adopting evaluation practice which is so limited in scope and aims, particularly given the methodological difficulties associated with this endeavour, and the challenges of obtaining valid data. Indeed, it has been argued that while the question of 'What works?' is important, additional questions such as 'How do programmes work?', 'For whom?' and 'Under what conditions?' are equally pertinent (e.g. Bowen & Gilchrist, 2004; Friendship, Falshaw & Beech, 2003; Pawson & Tilley,

1997), particularly for programme development and validation. Indeed, the findings from the 'What works?' literature regarding the characteristics of effective programmes, and their ability to target intermediary risk factors or criminogenic needs, lead to the assumption that the therapeutic approach and underlying change mechanisms within programmes modify these components, and that such change thereby reduces the risk of reoffending. Consequently, the 'What works?' ethos requires that evaluations do not simply determine whether a programme does reduce reoffending, but also whether it does this in the manner specified by the programme theory explicated in the theory manual. Evaluations need to adopt at least a process and outcome approach to determine if this is indeed the case. Failing to do so will lead to false conclusions about the mechanisms underlying programme effectiveness (these issues are expanded in Chapter 9).

What should be Evaluated?

As examined in Chapter 4, rehabilitation programmes for IPV perpetrators typically operate, to a greater or lesser extent, within a multi-agency, or coordinated community response. It could be argued that some components of this broader context might also be deemed to be components of the 'programme'. Gondolf (2002) argues that, if programmes operate within a wider infrastructure that might include 'assessments, orientation, a crisis hotline, compliance monitoring, case management, discharge procedures, individual psychotherapy and alcohol treatment, as well as weekly counselling sessions' (p. 34), defining exactly what constitutes the programme becomes more complex, as these additional features may also exert an influence on the offender, either individually or cumulatively. Therefore, the effect of the 'men's programme' may be dependent on the added influence of components of this wider infrastructure, rather than independent of it. Evaluators need to consider the potential role that such broader contextual features may play, and how, if necessary, such influences will be accounted for within evaluation design. Consequently, isolating from that wider multi-agency infrastructure, the unique contribution of a therapeutic/rehabilitation programme to individual behavioural change, becomes a critical issue in determining specific treatment effects. The IDAP programme (see Chapter 5) for example, is designed to function as one component of an ecological response to IPV which involves the police, probation, MAPPA/MARAC, courts, magistrates/judges and CPS policies. Gondolf (2002) asserts that when such systems are designed 'to interact and reinforce one another in a way that makes the whole more than the sum of its parts' (p. 34), then it is the system as a whole that should be the focus of evaluation, rather than the men's programme in isolation. As will be seen in Chapter 8, the extant evaluation literature typically neglects to consider the potential impact and influence of the broader intervention context on individual change. This might have particular importance when identifying appropriate control and/or comparison groups as such groups ideally should be influenced by the same infrastructure as those in the programme, to enable the identification of programme effects.

What Research Design should be Used?

Obviously, the nature of the design employed in evaluations should be determined by the question to be answered, and evaluation must be sufficiently broad and comprehensive in the combination of designs employed to be able to address multiple questions, if necessary. Within corrections evaluations, the greatest contention surrounds the methods employed to determine the impact or outcome of any given programme, that is, to assess the extent to which the intervention effects the target population (Rossi et al., 2008). The methodological paradigm of choice for conducting such assessments is experimental design and a range of quasi-experimental alternatives (Lipsey & Cordray, 2000). However, the use of such an approach is not without its critics, and within corrections evaluations the use of experimental designs is particularly controversial for a number of reasons.

Experimental design

Ideally, outcome evaluations should be designed to identify whether any observed reduction in post-intervention reoffending can be *directly* attributed to the intervention of interest. Experimental designs, also referred to as randomized controlled trials (RCTs) or randomized field studies (RFSs) are theoretically most adept at isolating specific treatment effects (Rossi et al., 2008). However, the decision as to whether or not to employ experimental designs in programme evaluations is highly contentious for a number of practical, conceptual and ethical reasons (Gondolf, 2004).

The basic premise of a truly experimental evaluation is that similar participants are randomly allocated to one of two or more treatment conditions. One group of participants should receive the treatment being evaluated, while a second group should receive an alternative placebo intervention, in which an intervention is provided that is as close as possible to the experimental intervention, so that participants cannot identify which condition they have been assigned to (Cook & Shadish, 1994). Additional conditions might also include participants being allocated to a no-treatment or 'treatment as usual' condition, and a non-random comparison group of treatment non-completers may also be incorporated into the evaluation. All participants should be provided with identical treatment (or as close as possible) throughout the period of investigation. In addition, ideally those individuals directing the evaluation, those responsible for delivering the intervention, *and* the participants, should be unaware of, or blind to, the conditions into which participants have been allocated. The aim of such practice is to reduce systematic bias in the allocation of participants to treatment that might arise from a range of participant and experimenter or therapist factors (Cordray, 2000). At some future point, when it can be realistically assumed that the intervention would have elicited the desired effects (for example by the end of the programme delivery or after a post-intervention follow-up period), an assessment of the participants should be conducted in a manner appropriate to identify the expected effects. If each of the tenets of the RCT has been successfully achieved, then any post-intervention differences identified from the outcome measures of each group can be attributed to the programme being evaluated with some confidence (Boruch, Victor & Cecil, 2000). If however, any of these components have not been achieved, then the confidence in the validity of the results may be reduced, depending on which tenet has been violated. It is probably clear from this description that the practicalities involved in assessing interventions for IPV men, particularly those provided as part of a criminal justice response to IPV, render the implementation of experimental evaluation designs problematic.

The prospect of randomly assigning adjudicated offenders to treatment or no-treatment conditions has raised many procedural and ethical concerns. Such concerns are magnified when individuals are court-mandated to attend a particular intervention (Rosenbaum, 1992). In order for research to be conducted ethically, all participants need to be informed of the following:

1. that research is being conducted;
2. the likely impact on them (including the condition that they have been assigned to);
3. their right to withdraw at any time without receiving negative consequences;
4. that their permission to obtain collateral information should be sought. (Dobash & Dobash, 2000; Gondolf, 2000)

However, participant deception lies at the heart of the experimental design with regard to these issues, as 'blind' assignment to conditions is a fundamental tenet of experimental designs. Proponents of the experimental evaluation methodology argue that the use of a no-treatment control group is a necessity, particularly when experimental and alternative treatment groups are used (Dunford, 2000a), as it is only when baseline recidivism within a no-treatment group is compared to the recorded recidivism of treatment groups (whether experimental or not), that the impact of the target intervention can be truly identified. However, within multi-agency contexts such as those surrounding the provision of IPV programmes, a no-treatment condition may not actually represent a no-intervention condition. For example, if an offender was ordered to attend a programme as part of a community rehabilitation order or, alternately, to not participate in such a programme, the 'no-treatment' condition participants would still be subject to some form of intervention which might include attendance on different programmes, or merely traditional probation supervision with one-to-one intervention. The difficulty in these circumstances is associated with controlling for any variability between participants in the no-treatment condition, as it cannot be safely assumed that all participants will be receiving the same kind of 'non-treatment'.

It has been argued that a fundamental weakness of RFSs in particular is the emphasis on the random allocation of participants to conditions, to the exclusion of other forms of variance control, which are present in traditional experimental studies (Cordray, 2000). Cordray (2000) notes that, in field studies, the ability to control the level and duration of intervention, the uniformity of treatment conditions and the influence of external forces, is difficult to accomplish (p. 408), and leads researchers to erroneously trust the statistical methods used to control for any potential impact such variables may have. Such a position is particularly tenuous, given the range of non-significant treatment effects identified (see Chapter 7), as such results call into question the extent to which the results are unbiased. It is also possible that random allocation may still result in systematic non-equivalence between groups. However, statistical methods can be used to account for such non-equivalence, which, when obtained through this method, is inevitable (Cordray, 2000). Any differences that do exist after randomized allocation to conditions are likely to be less systematic, and hence pose a less serious threat to the internal validity of the evaluation, than differences which arise from other allocation methods.

A further consideration is that allocation to conditions should in no way increase the risk to women and children (Shepard, 1999). It has also been argued that preventing appropriate individuals from accessing potentially beneficial treatment is unethical, and that allocation into alternative treatment groups is only justifiable ethically if the alternative treatments are hypothesized to be as effective as the target intervention in achieving the same outcome (Rosenbaum, 1992). Indeed, owing to issues such as these, one of the fiercest proponents of experimental designs admitted that randomized experimental designs are not feasible under many social conditions (Boruch, 1976, cited in Dobash & Dobash, 2000). It has been suggested that one compromise regarding randomization is to allocate participants to either treatment or waiting list control (Boruch et al., 2000). By doing this, all participants are guaranteed to receive the intervention at some point, thereby addressing the ethical concerns of withholding treatment.

In addition to the practical considerations associated with experimental designs, Gondolf (2004) draws attention to conceptual issues concerning the basis on which individuals are assigned to treatment and no-treatment conditions. This rests on the intention-to-treat principle in which the two groups are compared on a particular outcome on the basis that there was an intention to treat the treatment group, regardless of how much of the programme was completed (or dosage). Gondolf therefore argues that by not accounting for dosage, and relying on the intention to treat principle when calculating treatment effects, the expected association between dosage and outcome may confound the results. For example if the 'treatment group' actually comprises individuals who attended 25 per cent and 100 per cent of the programme, it is likely that those low-dose individuals would exhibit a smaller treatment effect than the high-dose individuals. Indeed, Gordon and Moriarty (2003) found that the number of sessions attended (dose) was an important predictor of treatment outcomes, and that those offenders who attended every session were significantly less likely to be rearrested post intervention than those who did not attend all sessions. By including both groups in treatment effect analyses it is likely that the overall treatment effect will be reduced. Therefore 'the comparison of an experimental group versus control group may tell us less about treatment effectiveness and more about the procedures of referring men to, and retaining them in, a certain programme (Gondolf, 2004, p. 610). The alternative – using treatment actually received, however, leads to a violation of the random allocation of participants to conditions and simultaneously compares the most and least motivated offenders, thereby rendering it no more rigorous than a quasi-experimental design (Babcock, Green & Robie, 2004).

Quasi-experimental designs

As will become evident in Chapter 8, the majority of IPV programme evaluations have not adopted an experimental design, but have instead been conducted using some form of quasi-experimental approach that does not involve the random allocation of participants to groups. In the main, this has resulted from the practicalities associated with the experimental method examined above. Broadly speaking, within quasi-experimental designs, those individuals who are to receive treatment are compared to a selected control group or to individuals that are not expected to receive the intervention (Rossi et al., 2008). Whether evaluations conducted using this design will yield unbiased estimates of the treatment effect depends on the extent to which the systematic differences between treatment and control groups can be minimized. Consequently, evaluations that use quasi-experimental methods need to pay attention to these possible differences and ensure that sufficient data are collected to minimize their potential impact on treatment effect estimates. It should be recognized that the use of non-equivalent control group designs does not meet the American Psychological Associations standards for establishing empirically supported interventions (Chambless & Hollon, 1998).

Within the IPV programme evaluation literature, those individuals who complete treatment programmes (or a specified proportion of a programme) are compared to programme drop-outs (identified on the basis of either pre-programme or within programme attrition). Consequently, individuals who may have received a variable high dosage of a programme (e.g. 75–100%) are compared to individuals who may have received no, low or moderate dosage (e.g. 0–74%). Such an approach has been criticized as it is widely documented that these two groups are incomparable, owing to underlying differences in characteristics. For example, treatment drop-outs are known to be characterized as higher risk, and have greater lifestyle instability than treatment completers (e.g. Bowen & Gilchrist, 2006; Cadsky et al., 1996). The main problem with this approach is that of 'stacking the deck' (Babcock et al., 2004) in favour of treatment as a consequence of these between-group differences. Moreover, by not including a 'no-treatment' control group, identifying valid treatment effect estimates is very difficult.

As previously alluded to, the notion of 'drop-out' is also poorly and inconsistently defined within the literature. That an individual fails to complete a programme might reflect many different circumstances, some of which may be more closely aligned to risk than others. For example, programmes might have policies that, after a certain number of unauthorized missed sessions, a perpetrator is automatically withdrawn from the programme and identified as a drop-out. Alternatively, if an individual discloses or is known to have re-assaulted their partner, this might lead to withdrawal and inclusion in the comparison group (Gondolf, 2004). Such policies vary considerably across programmes described in the international literature with the result that the comparison of evaluation studies, and the derivation of valid conclusions regarding programme effectiveness is difficult (see Chapter 8). There are several ways in which the basic quasi-experimental design can be improved to increase the validity of results, although these are rarely attempted by evaluators of IPV programmes. These include matching, using regression-discontinuity designs, using reflexive controls and adopting statistical methods.

In a matched design, the group receiving treatment is initially specified and then a no-treatment comparison group is constructed by the evaluator by matching the two groups on selected characteristics (Rossi et al., 2008). Specifically, they are matched on characteristics that would cause them to differ on the outcome under conditions when neither of the two groups received the intervention (p. 275). Such a methodology requires the identification of appropriate variables, and matching can be achieved either on individual or aggregate terms. Individual matching requires that, for each member of the treatment group, there is an equivalent member of the non-treatment group who shares the same key characteristics (e.g. age, socio-economic background, previous convictions). Aggregate matching requires that within the two groups the variables of interest are equally distributed. Rossi et al. note, however, that regardless of how precise the matching process adopted has been, it is still possible for systematic differences between groups to exist. They propose that where such differences are known, matching on key characteristics while statistically controlling for the known differences between groups is a useful approach to adopt.

Regression-discontinuity designs (or cutting point designs) are deemed to provide less biased estimates of programme effects than other quasi-experimental designs. In this approach, participants are systematically selected into treatment or no-treatment control groups based on need, merit or another qualifying condition. Those identified as the neediest are put into the treatment group, while those deemed to have a lower need are assigned to the control group (Rossi et al., 2008), which then facilitates the statistical control of selection bias. When the known selection process is modelled correctly, this approach approximates randomized experiments in terms of their ability to yield unbiased programme effect estimates. This approach, however, requires that programmes have specific and precise rules for eligibility. Despite its apparent potential utility in the field of IPV programme evaluation, this approach has never been adopted.

As previously identified, Boruch et al. (2000) have argued that a plausible alternative to the experimental design is that of a waiting list control design whereby all individuals receive treatment but for some this is delayed by way of creating a no-treatment control group. A similar quasi-experimental approach uses reflexive controls – that is, the estimated programme effects are derived from individuals studied on two or more occasions, with at least one observation occurring prior to attendance on a programme. Inferences of programme effects are based on the assumption that during a no-intervention period, no change would be seen on the outcome variable. There are several variations on reflexive control designs, from the simple pre-post design (sometimes adopted in IPV programme evaluations), to the stronger time-series design in which several observations are conducted across a period of time spanning the intervention, e.g. six months and three months before the intervention, the start and end of intervention, three months and six months post intervention. This latter variation is yet to be presented within the IPV programme evaluation literature.

Finally, it is possible to statistically control for the identified between group differences, and this is typically done through adopting a logistic regression analysis. Such an approach requires that sufficient data about the characteristics of the groups is available, and that a large enough sample is employed to yield valid results (Gondolf, 2004).

However, Gondolf highlights a false assumption of logistic regression when used in this way. The analysis treats programme attendance or drop-out as an independent variable, whereas in reality it is dependent on many of the same factors that influence re-assault. An alternative statistical method known as propensity score analysis has been used to overcome this issue.

Propensity scores

The case against random allocation into treatment and control groups has been made in the case of IPV perpetrators. The practical and ethical constraints already detailed highlight to difficulties in achieving a completely randomized experimental design within programme evaluations of this nature. Ultimately, therefore, participants of treatment programmes within the criminal justice system are selected into programmes on the basis of pre-existing characteristics which are deemed to be relevant by the criminal justice agencies (see Chapter 5 for inclusion and exclusion criteria for programmes). The consequence of this for programme evaluation is that the estimates of treatment effects from the resulting quasi-experimental design may be biased (Luellen et al., 2005). It is possible that the differences between treatment and control groups which are interpreted as indicative of treatment effects are actually artefacts of the non-randomized allocation process employed. Recently, within the fields of epidemiology, economics, education and sociology, a statistical procedure has been developed and implemented to control for selection bias and balancing non-equivalent groups using propensity scores (Rosenbaum & Rubin, 1983). One notable example of programme evaluation in the IPV field is also available and will be examined.

A propensity score is the estimated probability for a given individual that they will either receive treatment or no-treatment, and is derived from a range of observed covariates which are used to predict the individual's condition (Rosenbaum & Rubin, 1983). An individual's propensity score ranges from 0 to 1, and within quasi-experimental designs, if a dummy variable is used to indicate treatment (1) or control (0) then scores greater than 0.5 indicate an increased likelihood of the individual receiving treatment, and those lower than 0.5 indicate an increased likelihood of the individual receiving no-treatment (Luellen et al., 2005). This approach requires that the evaluator can identify a range of relevant variables that are likely associated with allocation to treatment or no-treatment conditions (e.g. risk, history of IPV, motivation to change, denial, and personality traits). The entire sample is then stratified into quintiles based on the propensity score, with the result that the data in the treatment and non-treatment conditions will have the same distribution on the covariates within the propensity score quintiles. The basic assumption is that individuals with the same propensity score but which are allocated into different conditions are comparable as the 'distributions of their covariates are balanced' (Luellen, Shadish & Clark 2005, p. 532). Consequently, the emergent data resembles that which would have been obtained had a properly executed randomized experimental design been employed (Jones, D'Agostino, Gondolf & Heckert, 2004). This then enables a treatment effect to be calculated.

Jones et al. (2004) applied this approach to examining the programme outcomes from a quasi-experimental multi-site IPV programme evaluation. The three programmes from three different locations in the USA included in the evaluation reflected varying therapeutic philosophies and lengths. All operated a post-sentence intake, although participants were deemed to be self-selecting, in the acknowledgement that enrolment was not actively enforced. The authors employed propensity score analysis to calculate the likelihood of completing a programme and, subsequently, the likelihood of re-assault in relation to completing the programmes during a 15-month follow-up period. The variables used to derive the propensity scores included (but were not limited to) socio-demographic (age, race, education, employment, marital status, number of children), criminal status (court ordered, non-IPV arrest prior to intake, severe IPV prior to intake), and psychopathology characteristics (drug use, severe psychopathology, alcohol dependence). It was found that there was a 33 per cent difference in the probability of recidivism between those who did and did not complete the programme. For individuals who had been court ordered and who completed the programme, this difference approached 50 per cent, indicating that retaining court-ordered individuals in treatment can have enhanced benefits for victim safety. These findings contrast markedly with those of the few experimental studies which typically identify small to non-existent programme effects (e.g. Dunford, 2000b; Feder & Forde, 2000).

Alternative designs

Aside from the experimental/non-experimental discussion, others argue that both approaches are not sufficiently realistic (e.g. Dobash & Dobash, 2000; Pawson & Tilley, 1997), as, in order to impose random assignment, interventions are often manipulated. Such approaches might be sufficient when evaluating programmes that do not function within a multi-agency context. However, these approaches neglect to consider the context of the programme that might substantially contribute to the programme outcomes and which are a feature of the broader intervention programme. Therefore, a more realistic outcome might consider individual conditional factors as well as community resources and supports (Mulvey & Lidz, 1985).

The emphasis on naturalistic context and process is advocated by social constructivists, who argue that the process of conducting research and interpreting evidence in order to identify treatment effects is an interactive social process from which a subjective definition of the situation is derived (Guba & Lincoln, 1989, cited in Gondolf, 2004). Consequently, the process of evaluation is not viewed as an objective or scientific process that yields unbiased results but instead is a process with a subjective outcome. Such an approach is known as a fourth-generation evaluation. For example, Scott and Wolfe (2003) used qualitative methods to identify variables that were most important in the change process for nine men who had attended a Duluth-informed intervention, and who were verified by their partners as having been non-violent and non-psychologically abusive for at least six months. Interview transcripts were initially coded using 28 a priori categories, which reflected nine theories that were relevant to understanding the change process. It was found that across all 28 items four were endorsed consistently by at least 75 per cent of participants. These were: taking responsibility for past behaviour, developing victim empathy, improved communication and reduced dependency on their partner/self as autonomous. These factors are all central to the descriptions of treatment targets within current programmes, and their identification in this study (despite a lack of abusive comparison group), provides some evidence of their potential clinical relevance, despite the fact that, in the case of empathy and responsibility, taking the empirical literature supporting the relevance of these constructs to IPV perpetrators in general, and the change process in particular is lacking (see Chapter 5). Despite an intuitive appeal to this approach, the subjectivity of the resulting evaluations leads to problems of generalizability and consequently their utility for policy development.

What Methods should be Used?

Within the evaluation of IPV perpetrator programmes there are several methodological issues that need to be considered by evaluators, but the most important problem is the identification and operationalization of appropriate outcome measures (Gondolf, 2002), specifically with regard to what, how and when to assess programme outcomes. The identification of appropriate outcomes should be aligned with the programme theory assumptions about which traits or characteristics are treatment targets (Daponte, 2008; van Voorhis, Cullen & Applegate, 1995). As already argued, within a 'What works?' tradition, emphasis is placed on the association between changes in intermediary treatment targets (criminogenic needs) and outcome (reduced offending). Consequently, from the perspective of IPV programmes, the assessment of outcomes might feasibly include assessments of attitudes, emotion control, empathy and perspective taking as well as a behavioural outcome. Despite the heterogeneity of possible outcomes, the vast majority of evaluation research has focused only on behaviour. However, defining IPV behavioural outcomes is more complex than it might, at first glance, appear.

Within the sexual offending literature, a useful distinction has been made between three potential indices of post-conviction behaviour (reconviction, reoffending and recidivism) that might be used as outcome measures (Falshaw, Friendship & Bates, 2003), and which can be translated for use by evaluators of IPV programmes (Bowen, 2004). Within this context **Domestic violence reconviction** would refer to a subsequent conviction for a standard list offence, the context of which indicates that it reflects domestic violence; **Domestic violence reoffending** would refer to the perpetration of another illegal act, the context of which indicates that it reflects domestic violence (regardless of whether the perpetrator was caught or not); and **Domestic violence recidivism** would refer to behaviour associated with domestic violence, whether illegal or legal (e.g. controlling behaviours). Each form of outcome measure identified is prone to issues regarding validity and bias, and it is down to the individual evaluator to determine which outcome measure to adopt after considering these issues.

Domestic violence reconviction

It has been widely acknowledged that the reliance on official records of crime (e.g. police and/or court records) create an incomplete and systematically biased estimate of all types of crime (Dobash, Dobash, Cavanagh et al., 1999; Dutton, Bodnarchuk, Kropp et al., 1997; Friendship, Beech & Browne, 2002; Friendship et al., 2003; Lloyd, Mair & Hough, 1994). Reconviction rates are only a proxy measure of reoffending and also reflect the wider processes and potential biases associated with police and prosecution policies (Lloyd et al., 1994). As examined in Chapter 2, this is of particular relevance within the UK evaluation context, owing to the lack of a specific 'domestic violence' criminal offence. The current reliance on available statutes through which to prosecute IPV perpetrators means that although there might be some utility in examining the impact of treatment on general reconviction, there is no way to systematically identify convictions specifically for domestic violence. In addition, the pre-trial attrition rates are so high that it is likely that only the most serious and/or persistent offences will ever be brought to court, thereby rendering reconvictions (even if they were possible to use) a poor assessment of the true extent of behaviour. Moreover, although a court appearance might occur within a particular timeframe, owing to the lag between behaviour and court appearance, it might well be the case that a conviction which would be taken to indicate that a programme had failed, actually reflected pre-programme behaviour rather than behaviour which had occurred either while the perpetrator was attending, or after they had completed an intervention. These are known as pseudo-convictions (Lloyd et al., 1994).

Domestic violence reoffending

Domestic violence reoffending can be gauged in three primary ways – through police call-out data, perpetrator, and victim self-report. Like reconviction data, police call-out data is also likely to be a proxy of actual behaviour. As previously shown, victims are typically reluctant to involve the police, who consequently become involved only in a small proportion of the more serious offences. Therefore, while reoffending data are likely to also be a proxy measure, certainly of the frequency of IPV behaviours, they might be more valid markers of illegal IPV behaviours. Moreover, the ability to access police records for all known individuals identified through the process of programme evaluation reduces participation bias associated with other methods of data collection (see below). However, the validity of these data cannot be accepted at face value. It may be that the individuals who notify the police are not actually the victims themselves but bystanders, eyewitnesses or earwitnesses, and that an incident is perceived to warrant official intervention by the police does not necessarily reflect the true context of the behaviours exhibited. For example, earwitnesses might notify the police of an argument which they suspect has become violent, but which may in fact, never have become violent. Consequently, if the police did attend, it is unlikely in these circumstances that this could be recorded as an incident of 'reoffending' as previously defined. Therefore,

if such data are taken as an outcome measure, it is necessary for the evaluator to have access to sufficient detail of the incidents to determine their validity as a marker of reoffending. Using partner reports to expand on and validate police call-out data would also improve on the quality of these data.

It is generally accepted that the reliance on offender self-report is problematic because of under-reporting associated with social desirability biases, particularly when standardized measures are used (Arias & Beach, 1987; Edleson & Brygger, 1986). This might be particularly the case for individuals who are subject to criminal justice sanctions that have placed them in the programme. It is possible that this context might motivate individuals to under-report in fear of negative repercussions associated with their sentence if full disclosure is provided (Rosenbaum, 1992). In contrast, partner reports of behaviour tend to be less influenced by such biases. If victim reports were to be used to identify reoffending, however, it is unlikely that standardized self-report measures would be sufficiently detailed to be of use. Consequently, verbal accounts of particular incidents would provide better quality data from which it could be ascertained whether illegal behaviours had taken place. Such an approach would also require that the evaluator had a clear understanding of the relevant legislative framework to determine whether particular incidents would have been classified as 'illegal' had they been officially responded to. Depending on the length of time that such reports were expected to cover, it is possible that such accounts might be contaminated by memory and/or recall effects.

Feder and Wilson (2005) note, however, that if victims are aware of their partner's allocation to treatment or no-treatment groups, such knowledge might also influence decisions to report revictimization to official agencies. As reviewed in Chapter 2, there is a range of factors relating to prior knowledge of, and beliefs about, the criminal justice response to IPV influence victims' decisions to report victimization. A victim might wish her partner to remain in treatment rather than go to jail and, consequently, withhold relevant information from agencies. Alternatively, a victim's preconceptions of the programme as either effective or ineffective might increase or decrease the likelihood of them reporting violent or abusive behaviours to the police.

Domestic violence recidivism

This outcome measure is typically gauged through victim self-report and is viewed as the 'gold-standard' outcome measure (Gondolf, 2004). Although victim reports are widely accepted as the most sensitive reports of partner abusive behaviours, they are not without their own sources of bias. Partner (victim) report is open to participation (self-selection) bias, problems with memory and/or recall, as well as socially desirable responding (Rosenbaum, Rabenhorst, Reddy et al., 2006).

Further issues concern the precise method of obtaining victim report. For example, an inventory such as the CTS might be appropriate, but the question arises of whether dimensional or dichotomous scoring is used. Aside from the issues regarding the item construction and context of the CTS items (Dobash, Dobash and Wilson & Daly, 1992), the danger with dichotomous scoring is that if a victim reports that, within a given time period, their partner 'hit, kicked or slapped' them, then their partner might be considered to have re-assaulted and, therefore, be a programme failure, even if this happened only once during a given follow up period (Dobash et al., 1992). A dimensional approach in which frequencies of re-assault are calculated might provide a more sensitive measure of programme impact. However, the question then arises regarding what will be taken as a clinically meaningful reduction in the frequency of assault. Consequently, the issues of measuring outcomes require evaluators to determine what criteria need to be met in order for re-assault to have been deemed to occur, and for clinically meaningful change to be identified (Henry, 2002). There remains no consensus as to what is an appropriate expectation of programme success (Dutton et al., 1997), although it has been argued that only complete abstinence from violence can be taken to indicate treatment success (Rosenbaum, 1988).

As recidivism relates to a range of behaviours associated with IPV, it seems that relying on re-assault as a marker of programme impact will lead to an underestimation of the incidents of recidivism. Ideally, obtaining reports of violent, non-violent, controlling and abusive behaviours, particularly if programmes adopt this broader definition of IPV, would be the most appropriate approach to take when measuring programme outcomes (Gondolf, 2004). Moreover, if the aim of a programme is to increase the quality of life of victims, then such measures should also be taken (Dobash et al., 2000). Hamberger and Hastings (1988) found that, whereas physical assaults were reduced in participants that completed an intervention, psychological abuse was maintained. In addition, Gondolf (1997) found substantially higher rates of non-physical assaults, verbal abuse and threats than physical assaults at a 15-month follow-up of a multi-site evaluation.

The one underlying assumption to the collection of domestic violence recidivism data from victims as an outcome measure of programmes is that the victim is in continuing contact with the partner during and after they have participated in a programme from which outcome data can be obtained. In many instances this is not the case. It is possible that a new 'potential' victim exists by way of a new relationship, but if this relationship starts after the perpetrator has completed the programme, it is questionable whether such individuals could be identified, and whether ethically, they could be asked to participate in this component of an evaluation if their partner's previous behaviour is not known to them. Although it is current policy to require perpetrators to notify agencies of new relationships, if they are attending the IDAP programme, this requirement is only partially successful and is met with some resistance by programme attendees. There is, in addition, some international evidence that when new partners are contacted within the duration of an evaluation, they are less likely to report re-assault than existing partners (Gondolf, 1997). Therefore, it is questionable whether the potential costs to the evaluation in terms of loss of participants and the use of precious resources in finding this information is worth it, given the limited data that will result.

The use of multi-agency arrangements might facilitate the collection of these data, particularly if women's support services have an active link with perpetrator programmes and know whether they are providing support to women whose current or ex-partner is attending or has attended the programme. Indeed, women who have sought this form of help will be in a relatively protected environment in comparison to those who have not (Gondolf, 2000). However, obtaining this information in this manner for a non-treatment control group might be more problematic if such links cannot be used, and there is a genuine risk that such contact might increase the likelihood of assault. Owing to the risk of post-separation IPV behaviours it would also make sense for current and most recent former partners to contribute to the collection of recidivism data. However, it is possible that any such data might come at a personal cost to those women who volunteer such information and, consequently, evaluators need to ensure that the risks associated with such disclosure are considered when designing evaluation studies (Gondolf, 2000).

An additional consideration concerns the length of follow-up period employed in evaluation studies. In England and Wales, when reconviction studies are conducted the typical convention is to employ a follow-up period of two years (Falshaw et al., 2003). This tradition has developed to account for the lag between behaviour and conviction, and in view of the observation that most offenders who are going to be reconvicted will be reconvicted within two years of release (Kershaw, Goodman and White, 1999). However, owing to the issues raised previously, the evaluation of IPV programmes might require a different approach. These issues include the point at which it starts – for example, does the follow-up period start at programme intake, or after the group-based sessions have been delivered, and if programmes of different lengths are to be compared, should the follow-up period be adjusted to enable equivalent observation periods across programmes (Gondolf, 2004). Based on evaluation approaches in the alcohol recovery field, Gondolf suggests that a useful metric might be to consider how many days/weeks/months an individual has remained violence free, prior to the follow-up period end-point. When this is applied to the findings from Gondolf's multi-site evaluation, a considerably more positive picture emerges with regard to the programme impact. For example, although the cumulative re-assault rates (assessed from the point of intake through the follow-up period) at the 30-month follow-up was 38 per cent, when examined retrospectively, at this point, less than 20 per cent of the perpetrators had re-assaulted their partners during the previous 12 months.

What is Good Practice in IPV Programme Evaluation?

Based on the literature reviewed, as well as best practice guidelines issued by the UK Evaluation Society (UKES, 2008), there are several recommendations that can be made regarding good practice in this area. Evaluation activities should be developed in collaboration with the organization providing the programme so that the evaluator can obtain a clear understanding of both the programme theory and aims and the expectations of stakeholders for the results of the evaluation. The design employed should be appropriate to address the research questions derived through the process of collaboration. Gondolf (2004) notes, in particular, that impact evaluations of programmes that operate within a multi-agency framework ideally need to consider the impact of programme dosage, use modelling techniques to simulate a non-treatment control group, consider both dynamic and conditional outcomes and recognize contextual factors and collaborative interpretations (p. 612). However, programme impact might not be the only question of interest to stakeholders, and it is acknowledged that, in reality, this 'ideal' might be impossible to achieve and might be best viewed as an aspirational benchmark against which to assess evaluation activities.

All participants must be treated ethically, and the safety of women and children should be a foremost consideration when any IPV programme evaluation activities are planned, particularly with respect to the type of outcome data that will be obtained. Specifically, informed consent to participate should be obtained from IPV perpetrators and their (ex) partners (where appropriate) and participants should be fully aware of the likely consequences of participation, as well as their right to withdraw from the research at any point without experiencing negative consequences. While offenders may have been court-mandated to attend a programme, this should not be interpreted as meaning that they have also been court-mandated to participate in any research programme designed to evaluate the effectiveness of the programme. Participants need to be fully informed about how their data will be treated and clear details regarding data protection need to be provided. A final consideration relates to the communication of findings. Not only should all participants be able to access the findings of the evaluation, but the findings themselves should be appropriately worded to minimize the extent to which treatment effects, if identified, are exaggerated, thereby ensuring that only realistic interpretations of the evidence are available to stakeholders. Rubin and Parrish (2007) note that, although 70 per cent of 138 published outcome studies used designs from which causal inferences about change could not be drawn, in more than 60 per cent of these cases the authors reported the findings in such a way as to inflate the evidence base status. It is arguable that such practice fundamentally undermines the process of evidence-based practice, and in the case of IPV interventions may provide information that places women and children at risk.

8

The Effectiveness of IPV Programmes: International and National Evidence

There have been a considerable number of attempts to evaluate IPV perpetrator programmes since the early 1980s, with an almost doubling of published outcome studies within the last decade of the twentieth century (Babcock, Green & Robie, 2004; Dobash et al., 1999). However, the debate regarding whether the evidence indicates these programmes to be successful or not continues and remains a controversial issue. As reviewed in Chapter 7, the evaluation of IPV programmes is replete with methodological challenges, some of which are difficult, if not impossible, to overcome. Consequently, when observations about programme effects are made, methodological issues are always raised as a caveat to drawing firm conclusions, regardless of whether significant effects are identified. Driven by fears of committing both Type I errors (accepting as significant a result that is not), and Type II errors (accepting as non-significant a result that actually is significant), and in view of the widely understood impact of IPV and its potentially devastating consequences for women and children, the literature reads as though researchers are reluctant to give up hope on the effectiveness of programmes 'just in case', even if the emerging opinion within the literature is that it does not produce change. Owing to methodological challenges, it is unlikely that this issue will ever be conclusively proven one way or the other. Evaluation efforts, therefore, need to continue to employ the most rigorous methods possible, so that over time the emerging evidence base can be examined through meta-analysis to determine possible trends and patterns in treatment effectiveness. The aim of this chapter is to examine the available published outcome literature, with particular emphasis on the results of British studies, which are typically neglected in existing syntheses. The results of currently available meta-analyses are also examined with a view to determining consistent themes about programme effectiveness.

The Rehabilitation of Partner-Violent Men, by Erica Bowen

International Evaluation Studies

A substantial number of evaluation studies have been published in the international literature. In addition, several reviews of this literature have also been published (e.g. Davis & Taylor, 1999; Eisikovitz & Edleson, 1989; Hamberger & Hastings, 1993; Rosenfeld, 1992; Tolman & Bennett, 1990). Rather than discussing each of the individual empirical studies in detail, this section will discuss the findings from two substantive reviews of this literature that have been conducted to prevent over-analysis of a partially duplicated evidence base.

Review overview

In 1992, a review by Rosenfeld was published. Although intended to use meta-analytical techniques, Rosenfeld acknowledged that the existing variation in methodologies across the available studies rendered this not possible. The review examined 25 studies, some of which included interventions that were not solely for male perpetrators of IPV (Deschner & McNeil, 1986; Harris, 1988; Lindquist, Telch & Taylor, 1983) or which were presented as conference papers (Douglas & Perrin, 1987; Halpern, 1984; Leong, Coates & Hoskins, 1987; Shepard, 1987) or which were unpublished theses (Gruszski, 1988). Consequently, these studies are not presented in Appendix 1. In addition, Rosenfeld included all of the studies examined in an earlier review by Eisikovitz and Edleson (1989) as well as three others (Beninati, 1989; Edleson & Syers, 1990; Purdy & Nickle, 1982).

The majority of the studies reviewed were North American (n = 23), one was Canadian (Dutton, 1986) and another Australian (Baum, Brand, Colley & Cooke, 1987). As this review covers the earliest outcome literature, few of the studies adopted particularly rigorous methods. For example, sample sizes were typically small, ranging from eight participants (Baum et al., 1987) to 149 (Tolman and Bennett, 1990). Only six of the studies employed a quasi-experimental design, which was the most sophisticated design reported (Dutton, 1986; Edleson & Grusznski, 1988; Edleson & Syers, 1990; Hamberger & Hastings, 1986, Shepard, 1987; Waldo, 1988). The remaining studies either used pre-post designs (Rosenbaum, 1986), relied on perpetrator self-report (Beninati, 1989; Rosenbaum, 1986; DeMaris & Jackson, 1987) or did not employ comparison and/or control groups (Saunders & Hanusa, 1986). Three studies reported on outcomes from court-mandated programmes (Chen, Bersani & Myers et al., 1989; Dutton, 1986; Waldo, 1988).

From the studies examined, Rosenbaum observed that, on average (accounting for sample size), 22 per cent of treatment completers reoffended, in contrast to 27 per cent across all samples. In studies where partners provided data, this estimate increased to 36 per cent regardless of treatment status, while those studies that relied on official records led to an average 7 per cent recidivism (accounting for sample size). Three published studies compared IPV perpetrators who received treatment to those that did not (Edleson & Grusznski, 1989, study one and study three, Hamberger & Hastings,

1988). Within these studies only one identified a statistically significant difference in the recidivism rates between the groups in the expected direction (Edleson & Gruszinski, 1988, Study one). Across studies that examined recidivism in treatment drop-outs (regardless of design), an average recidivism rate of 39 per cent was estimated (accounting for sample size). The estimated recidivism rates for untreated samples across three studies based on police report was 20 per cent. When five studies of court-mandated treatment were examined, it was found that only two studies (Dutton, 1986; Waldo, 1988) identified statistically significantly lower levels of recidivism in the treated versus untreated (Dutton, 1986) or unreferred (Waldo, 1988) groups. Based on the data reviewed, Rosenfeld (1992) concluded that there was little evidence to suggest that court-mandated programmes had substantive effects on recidivism, and that with or without specific psychotherapeutic interventions, it seems that legal system responses significantly reduce future violent behaviour.

Davis and Taylor (1999) reviewed the outcome literature with the aim of answering three questions:

1 Does treatment reduce violence relative to no-treatment?
2 Do some forms of treatment work better than others?
3 Does treatment work better for some batterers than for others? (p. 69)

The authors identified and examined 33 studies (and include details of two more that, at the time, had no outcome data) some of which also included data from evaluations of couples treatment. However, owing to a substantial number of missing references, it is difficult to verify the origin of all of the studies. Consequently, those that could be identified as published reports focusing on IPV perpetrator rather than couples interventions are included in Appendix 1. The studies were reviewed in relation to study design, through which it was identified that 15 studies had employed a post-test design only (including Beninati, 1989; DeMaris & Jackson, 1987; Edleson & Gruszinski, 1989, study two; Purdy & Nickle, 1982, Tolman et al., 1987 reviewed by Rosenbaum, 1992, and, in addition, Hamberger & Hastings, 1990). A further six had used a one group pre-post test design, six had used a quasi-experimental design comparing treatment completers to drop-outs, four had employed a quasi-experimental matched design, and four experimental studies had been conducted, although results were available at the time for only two (Davis & Taylor, 1999; Palmer, Brown & Barrera, 1992).

It was found that the answer to whether treatment reduces violence relative to no-treatment depended on the methodology employed. Deciding to focus on the most rigorous studies, Davis and Taylor calculated mean effect sizes for the three quasi-experimental studies that compared treated to untreated groups, and the two experimental studies. The mean effect size of the former group of studies was 0.416, whereas the mean effect size for the latter group of studies was 0.412. Despite the particularly small sample of studies analysed, Davis and Taylor concluded that 'these studies provide a case for rejecting the null hypothesis that treatment has no effect on violent behaviour toward spouses' (p. 86). The findings of these two studies therefore provide contradictory conclusions about programme effectiveness.

The most common issues to emerge across these reviews, however, is the variation evident in both clinical practice and evaluation practice. Programme formats vary in respect of referral criteria, links to criminal justice agencies, session lengths and numbers of sessions delivered, as well as the treatment philosophy adopted, although on this latter point the majority of men's groups are described as either psychoeducational or cognitive-behavioural. What is difficult to ascertain from any of the primary studies, however, is just how comparable programmes are, even when on the basic features they appear to be similar. Turning to a point made in Chapter 6, as it is inevitable that each iteration of the same programme is likely to be different, not least, owing to the different participants, it is highly likely that two programmes based on the same manual will be different if they are delivered in different contexts. Therefore, when these variations are considered in addition to methodological variations, it is perhaps more of a surprise that any general conclusions can be drawn at all, particularly from using a narrative review approach.

Meta-analytic studies of programme effectiveness

As reported in Chapter 3, meta-analysis is a method of synthesizing the results obtained across several primary studies to determine aggregate effects based on a large cumulative sample. Despite the influence of this technique upon changes to penal policy and the re-emergence of the rehabilitative ideal, only two published and one unpublished meta-analyses of IPV programme outcomes exist (Babcock, Green & Robie, 2004; Feder & Wilson, 2005; Levesque & Gelles, 1998). This reflects the fact that until recently, relatively few well-conducted studies of IPV programme outcomes existed. Since the mid-1990s, there has been a move towards a more consistent methodology which has enabled researchers to conduct more precise meta-analytic examinations of this literature. In their unpublished study, Levesque & Gelles (1998) identified 38 outcome studies that had been published, completed or presented between 1980 and August 1997. Of these, 23 adopted a single group design, and 15 a between groups design. All had a sample of at least five participants, and all provided post-treatment measures of recidivism. Eighteen were included in their meta-analysis. For the seven studies that used partner reports of recidivism, an effect size of $h = .063$ was found, based on average recidivism rates of 31.9 per cent for treatment groups and 34.2 per cent for comparison groups. This result was statistically non-significant. A re-analysis of the data with the study by Harrell (1991) removed as this was identified as an outlier, yielded more positive results with an effect size of $h = .269$, reflecting average recidivism rates of 29.7 per cent for treatment groups and 42.3 per cent for comparison groups, a difference which was statistically significant. When an analysis of 11 studies using official records was conducted, an effect size of $h = .191$ was found, reflecting recidivism rates of 14.3 per cent for treatment groups and 21.8 per cent for comparison groups, which again represented a significant difference. This effect size was reduced to $h = .175$ when three studies were removed, owing to their potential influence as outliers (Dutton et al., 1997; Harrell, 1991; Waldo, 1988). This remained significant and reflected an average recidivism rate of 13.5 per cent for treatment groups and 20.3 per cent for comparison groups. Once study characteristics that were associated with effect size were examined, a mean weighted recidivism rate of 21.6 per cent for programme completers was calculated from all 38 studies. In concluding, the authors commented that treatment probably works 'a little', but that there was questionable evidence for the increased effectiveness of favoured treatment models.

Taking up the challenge of comparing the effectiveness of treatment modalities, Babcock et al., (2004) conducted a meta-analysis in order to improve on the methods used in previous studies. For example, Levesque and Gelles (1998) reported the effect sizes of interventions in terms of Cohen's *h*, a statistic which is typically used in power analysis, and which does not enable sample size to be taken into account. Consequently, in their analysis, Cohen's *d* was adopted instead to enable sample size to be examined. For reference, effect sizes based on the *d* statistic are reported in standard deviation units. Consequently if $d = 0.50$ then this refers to an improvement of one half of a standard deviation compared to no-treatment. Effect sizes are deemed to be small if they are in the region of 0.20, medium at 0.50 and large at 0.80 and above (Cohen, 1988).

Broadly speaking, Babcock et al. (2004) compared recidivism rates across programmes that were identified as being based on a 'psychoeducational model' (cf. Duluth), a 'cognitive-behavioural model' and 'other' models. Their initial literature search identified 68 outcome studies. Those included in the meta-analysis had to include a comparison group, and had to have used either partner reports or police records as an indicator of recidivism. Consequently, 48 studies were not included, and analyses were based on 36 effect sizes (17 Duluth, 11 CBT, 7 'other' programmes). As well as treatment type, recidivism rates were calculated in relation to respondent type and also study design (quasi-experimental or experimental) and the interaction between these three factors was also considered. Overall, based on police reports, recidivism rates for non-treated offenders were estimated at 21 per cent, and 35 per cent based on partner reports. No evidence of potential publication bias was found.

It was found that across both police and partner reports, effect sizes were equivalent ($d = 0.18$). When study design and respondent were examined it was found that experimental studies that used police report resulted in a small effect size ($d = 0.12$). Quasi-experimental studies that used police reports resulted in a higher but still small effect size ($d = 0.23$), and the difference between these two effect sizes was non-significant. Taken together, these findings suggest that treatment had a significant but small impact on the recidivism rates as measured.

When partner reports were examined, it was found that the effect size obtained from experimental studies was very small indeed ($d = 0.09$), which was not significantly different from zero. In contrast, when quasi-experimental studies that used partner reports were examined, the effect size was substantially higher ($d = 0.34$), and represented a significant but still small treatment effect. The difference between these two effect sizes was significant. When treatment type was examined, the following results were obtained. For experimental studies of the Duluth model that used police reports, the resulting effect size was small ($d = 0.19$). Unfortunately, there were insufficient experimental studies of CBT and other models for effect sizes to be calculated. These data, therefore, indicate that the Duluth model exerts a significant but small effect on recidivism when assessed using police reports. For quasi-experimental studies of the Duluth model that used police reports, the resulting effect size was higher ($d = 0.32$). The effect size for CBT models examined using the same methodology was lower ($d = 0.12$), while the effect size for the Other treatment models fell in between the two ($d = 0.27$). The effect size for the CBT models did not differ from zero, while the other two did, but both represented small effects.

For studies that employed partner reports, the effect size of experimental studies of the Duluth model was small ($d = 0.12$), and the Other models resulted in a smaller effect size ($d = 0.03$). There were insufficient studies of the CBT model to calculate an effect size. For quasi-experimental studies of the Duluth model that employed partner reports, the effect size was substantially larger ($d = 0.35$), and studies of the CBT model revealed a slightly lower effect size ($d = 0.29$). There were insufficient studies of Other treatment models to enable a treatment effect to be calculated.

Overall, the results of this meta-analysis indicated that both study design and recidivism measure impact on aggregate estimates of the effectiveness of treatment programmes. Across all analyses, however, the resulting effect sizes were in the 'small' range, with the most rigorously designed studies that employed experimental designs and partner reports of behavioural outcomes yielding among the lowest effect sizes obtained. The authors observed that the results across experimental studies suggested that treatment is responsible for a one-tenth of a standard deviation reduction in recidivism, or a 5 per cent increase in success rate that is due to treatment. Such a finding would equate to roughly 42,000 fewer women in the United States being free from violence (Babcock et al., 2004, p. 1044). However, the authors also caution that such a small effect size might in fact reflect measurement error and underlying methodological issues associated with the nature of the research, and that, in reality, the actual effects stand to be larger. It is interesting to note that, in general, the effect sizes obtained for the Duluth and CBT models were similar, and non-significantly different. This finding challenges the naive assumption made by policy makers that the Duluth model is most effective. It is likely, however, that such equivalence in effect sizes reflects the equivalence in programme content and overlap between these two models. However, for more reliable comparative conclusions to be drawn, primary studies which compare more than two treatment modalities are required.

In an effort to examine only the most rigorous studies, Feder and Wilson (2005) conducted a meta-analysis of those outcome evaluations of court-mandated programmes which had adopted either an experimental design, or which had incorporated some effort to determine between groups equivalence through either matching or statistical controls. In addition, studies that compared two treatments but which did not have a no-treatment control were excluded, and studies also had to have a post-treatment follow-up of at least six months, use objective measures of recidivism (partner or official reports) and have been conducted in 1986 or later. This resulted in a sample of 15 studies that reflected 10 separate studies. The results were analysed by examining outcome type (official reports, victim reports), and design type (experimental, quasi-experimental with no-treatment comparison group, quasi-experimental with drop-outs as comparison group).

Where official reports were used, the mean effect size for experimental studies was small ($d = 0.26$). The quasi-experimental studies using a no-treatment control group yielded a negative and small effect size ($d = 0.14$), and those using drop-outs as a comparison group yielded a positive and significant effect ($d = 0.97$). Where partner reports were used, the resulting effect sizes were smaller (experimental studies: $d = 0.01$; quasi-experiments with no-treatment control: $d = -0.11$) and non-significant in all cases.

One study, conducted by Palmer, Brown and Barrera (1992) obtained the highest individual effect size greater than +0.75 and, consequently, provides the strongest empirical evidence of a positive treatment effect. However, closer examination of the study identifies a number of issues that need to be considered when accepting these data. The programme evaluated consisted of a 10-week group programme described as psychoeducational and, whilet it is acknowledged that the programme reflects other established programmes (cf. Duluth), it is deemed to be 'more flexible' (p. 279). This apparently means that the single counsellor who provided the intervention took a client-centred approach, which seems to suggest a lack of a manualized format, with intervention not delivered in blocks or modules. The specific course content was, therefore, explicitly covered when issues arose naturally from the course of the group sessions. This would suggest that what appears to be a successful programme was likely to have low levels of treatment integrity, which is due to the emergent nature of the course content.

The participants consisted of 59 men (including 29 controls) who had been court-referred and placed on probation. The control group were initially identified as individuals appropriate for the target treatment but for whom no programme was available for at least three weeks. However, ethical concerns led to a decision to enable probation officers to refer on to alternative treatments. Of the 17 controls who completed post-treatment questionnaires, two of these had actually received some alternative form of intervention and were subsequently removed from the evaluation. Furthermore, one of the controls died, leading to an actual sample of 56 men (30 treatment, 26 controls). Of the 30 men in the treatment group, 70 per cent 'completed' the programme (attended 7/10 sessions or more). A post-treatment follow-up period of between 12 and 24 months was used, during which police records were examined. On the basis of these data, 20 per cent of the sample used either serious threats or physical violence towards their partners, and this reflected a recidivism rate of 31 per cent for the control group and 10 per cent of the treatment group. No dose response relationship was identified. Both the small sample size and measure of recidivism indicate that these results need to be interpreted with caution and illustrate the extent to which a potentially promising intervention has been let down by poor evaluation methodology.

Overall then, the findings of this meta-analysis are less optimistic than those provided by Babcock et al. (2004), and suggest that IPV programmes, when rigorously evaluated, are shown to exert small and non-significant effects on recidivism as assessed by partners. In contrast, quasi-experiments, where treatment drop-outs are used, identify large and significant treatment effects when official records are used to assess recidivism. The disparity between the findings of these two meta-analyses may reflect underlying differences in the meta-analytic methods used, including inclusion criteria and the methods through which the aggregate effects were estimated. In particular, Feder and Wilson (2005) draw attention to the fact that in the earlier study, all quasi-experimental effects were assessed together rather than separately depending on the nature of the comparison group. Such practice might have biased the results towards providing higher estimated effects.

Conclusions from meta-analyses

The main conclusion to be drawn from the meta-analyses is that when more rigorous experimental and quasi-experimental designs are employed, which use victim reports as an outcome measure of recidivism, the identified effect sizes are small, typically not significantly different from zero, and generally do not differ significantly across treatment modalities. This could, therefore, lead to the conclusion that IPV perpetrator programmes are not effective in reducing recidivism, or indeed as Feder and Wilson (2005) note, that 'the existing evidence cannot ensure that these programmes are, in fact, helpful and not harmful'. However, although this is what the data indicate, authors remain reluctant to accept such conclusions. Babcock et al. (2004) refer to comments made by McCartney and Rosenthal (2000, cited in Babcock et al., 2004, p. 178) which argue that, '[g]iven that the stakes are so high, we should be wary of accepting the null hypothesis when it might very well be false – as it almost always is'. This statement reflects the fact that effect sizes are sensitive to methodological variations and, in particular, that measurement error within an outcome variable will lead to a reduction in the observed effect size. Therefore, it is likely that the small, non-significant effect sizes identified from the most rigorous studies are underestimates of actual effects, as they rely on victim report which is known to be biased (see Chapter 6 for a discussion of this issue). However, it is not possible to determine whether the 'actual' effect sizes would be significantly higher.

These issues suggest that a psychometrically sound outcome measure of victim experience is required to minimize measurement error as much as possible. Whilst self-report measures are available, and have been used in some outcome studies, it is likely that repeat measures within a follow-up period would be needed so that potential memory biases are reduced, rather than relying on victim report at the end of a follow-up period only. However, recent data questions the test-re-test reliability of the most common self-report measure (Vega & O'Leary, 2007). Of greater concern with such an approach, however, is the high level of study attrition particularly associated with victim participation. Feder and Wilson (2005) note that 'high attrition raises the possibility that the victims lost to follow-up in the treatment group may differ in meaningful ways to those lost to follow-up in the control group' (p. 255). Consequently, the facy that such small effect sizes have been obtained when victim reports are used, might reflect the possibility that the programme really is ineffective or, alternatively, that the actual effect is hidden by the effect of differential attrition.

A second issue to arise from the meta-analytic results is that when non-equivalent control groups are used, even when matching or statistical controls are employed, the resulting large effect sizes indicate that men who complete these programmes do recidivate at a significantly lower rate than the non-completers. Feder and Wilson (2005), however, question the utility of this finding, and in particular the extent to which statistical models adequately account for between-group differences. They provide as an example the fact that motivation to change is rarely assessed in such studies, let alone matched between groups. Therefore, such findings are open to interpretation as an artefact of a third unmeasured variable or, alternatively, as indicating that those who complete treatment represent a subset of offenders who would be more successful at changing their behaviour regardless of whether an intervention were provided or not.

British Studies

To date, despite the previously examined plethora of international evaluation studies of group-based interventions for partner violent men, the British literature regarding criminal justice based programmes for IPV perpetrators remains comparatively limited. In addition, British evaluations have never been included in the sophisticated literature reviews detailed previously. This is of some concern, given the recent growth in the provision of such interventions as documented in Chapter 4. This section therefore provides a critical examination of the available British literature, which is drawn from both published and unpublished sources.

CHANGE and LDVPP

The first criminal justice based group interventions for partner violent men were developed in Scotland. The CHANGE programme (Morran & Wilson, 1997), funded by Urban Aid (Dobash et al., 1999) embodied some of the main principles underlying the Duluth programme. Services were designed to run in coordination across probation and within the community in order to provide a programme for male perpetrators as well as training and information for a range of voluntary and statutory agencies. In contrast, the LDVPP was provided by Lothian Social Work Department, and operated as a stand alone court-mandated probation-based perpetrator programme. Although the LDVPP adhered to a similar treatment philosophy as the CHANGE programme, some variations in delivery between the programmes were observed (Dobash, Dobash, Cavanagh et al., 1996) although the evaluation team report that these variations were not substantive differences in philosophy, but small differences in delivery.

Both the CHANGE and the LDVPP programmes focused on holding male perpetrators accountable for their abusive behaviours. Voluntary referrals to the programmes were not accepted, as all men who attended the intervention were court mandated to attend after being found guilty for an offence involving violence against their female partner, and their attendance formed a condition of a probation order (Dobash et al., 1999). Both programmes comprised of weekly group sessions across 24 weeks (CHANGE) and 27 weeks (LDVPP) respectively.

The evaluation

Design

A context-specific quasi-experimental non-equivalent comparison group design was employed, whereby the offending behaviour of individuals referred to the programmes (Men's Programme Group; MPG) was compared to that of individuals who received alternative sanctions (Other CJ; OCJ).

Sample

The two groups were developed by drawing cases of all men sentenced for an offence involving IPV in the two courts located in the region of the programmes. All individuals were in either marital or marriage-like relationships. This led to the identification of 313 cases, of which 84 were MPG cases and 229 were OCJ cases. Three periods of data collection were completed. At the first, 226 (122 men, 134 partners) individuals participated. Within this cohort, 95 couples were identified. This sample included 51 men in the MPG condition, and 71 men in the OCJ condition. At time 2 (3-month follow-up), 80 per cent of the men (83% women) in the MPG group, and 72 per cent of the men (77 per cent women) in the OCJ group who participated at time 1 also participated at time 2. At time 3 (12-month follow-up), 57 per cent men (60% women) in the MPG and 49 per cent men (57% women) in the OCJ group participated.

Methods

In-depth interviews were conducted at time 1 with all participants. The focus of the interviews was to determine the nature and consequences and dynamics of behaviours experienced and/or perpetrated. At the second and third data collection periods, participants were sent postal questionnaires that included a measure of the behaviours identified through the initial interviews, as well as measuring quality of life. In addition to self and partner reports, court records were monitored for each of the men involved in the study.

Main findings

Impact on behaviour

It was found from court records that of the 42 men in the MPG, only three (7%) were reconvicted for a domestic violence related incident throughout the 12 months of the study. In contrast, eight of the 80 men (10%) in the OCJ group were reconvicted. A substantially different picture emerged from the partner reported data. At the three-month follow-up, 62 per cent of women in the OCJ group, in contrast to 30 per cent of the women in the MPG group, reported that their partner had re-assaulted them. At the 12-month follow-up assessment, 70 per cent of the women in the OCJ group and 37 per cent of the women in the MPG reported that they had been re-assaulted. Moreover, 37 per cent of the women in the OCJ group and only 7 per cent of the women in the MPG reported experiencing at least five incidents of violence during the follow-up period.

In addition to measuring assaults, a measure of controlling behaviour was also administered. It was found that at both follow-up points, the scores for men in the

MPG group had significantly reduced from those at time 1. In contrast, the scores for men in the OCJ group, although lower, were not significantly so. In addition, at time 3, men in the MPG had significantly lower frequency scores than at time 1, whereas again those for the OCJ group although lower were not significantly so.

The domestic abuse intervention project (DAIP)

In 1998, Burton, Regan and Kelly published a process evaluation of the violence prevention programme (VPP) provided by DAIP in Hammersmith, London, which reported data collected between October 1994 and September 1996. The overarching philosophy of the VPP is based on the understanding that men's violence against women is a control tactic through which they exert power. Therefore, the overriding intervention aimed to both empower women, and stop men's violence against them. Core to the programme is the conceptualization of men's violence as instrumental and the result of a conscious decision to engage in violent behaviour. In addition, it is assumed that violent men employ a range of justifications for their behaviour which serve to disguise its instrumental nature.

The objectives of the VPP include:

- providing educational workshops for men that define violence as an array of intended behaviours used to assert power;
- encouraging men to take full responsibility for their behaviour and reducing the extent to which they employ excuses to account for their behaviour (e.g. alcohol use, childhood experiences);
- changing the attitudes and beliefs that support this behaviour.

The VPP is one of several elements of intervention provided by DAIP, the other main element being a female victim support service. At the time of evaluation DAIP was unique in providing joined-up services for both male perpetrators and associated female victims of partner violence.

The VPP accepted both court and self-referred male perpetrators, with the majority of referrals being voluntary. All VPP groups have rolling entry to prevent prolonged waiting lists for attendance. The VPP consisted of one-to-one assessment and ongoing individual work with men, and a group programme split into three stages. The first stage consists of 12 sessions, the second 20 sessions and the optional third stage support group has no fixed time frame.

The VPP employs an eclectic range of techniques during the first phase of the group programme, which is aimed at ending the use of physical violence through targeting and changing the attitudes associated with the use of violence. Such techniques draw on cognitive, behavioural and social learning theory and include the teaching of relationship skills, the use of role play, brainstorming, re-enactment and discussion. The second stage of the programme focuses on aspects of control that do not include physical violence with a similar focus on examining and challenging intentions, and beliefs. The third stage of the programme occurs at least 34 weeks after the start of the intervention and consists of a support group that aims to provide ongoing support for men to maintain the changes that they have made.

In order to be responsive to the needs and risks of individual men, progress through the group is not necessarily linear. For example, the transition from the first to second stages of the group programme is contingent upon there being no evidence of violent behaviour towards female partners for at least eight weeks. In addition, in circumstances where such relapse was reported, the men would be returned to the first stage of the group regardless of the point of their current involvement (e.g. the second or, indeed, third stages).

The evaluation

Design

As noted previously, the evaluation of the VPP is best described as a process rather than an outcome evaluation, thus providing predominantly descriptive information about the success of participant assessment and retention, as well as some tentative information regarding the impact of the programme on men's violence and women's safety. The overall design is therefore a single sample longitudinal cohort design (Rossi et al., 2008), in which participant engagement, attendance and compliance are the main foci.

Sample

The complete sample of referrals consisted of 351 men during the two-year observation period (log sample). Of these, 174 participated in at least one element of the evaluation (the evaluation sample). Basic demographic data comparing the log sample to the evaluation sample is provided although, in places, missing data is problematic. In general, the data suggest that those individuals who participated in the evaluation did not differ substantially from the overall sample although no specific statistical analyses are reported.

The evaluation sample consisted of men typically aged between 31 and 40 years (43% of sample), who were employed (53%), and who were typically not referred by probation (35% probation referrals) but from other men's programmes (20%), the police (21%), or other agencies (25%). Just over one third of the log sample reported having previous convictions. Within the evaluation sample, 41 per cent (of 57 for whom data were available) reported a conviction of actual or grievous bodily harm related to a partner violence incident; 8 per cent reported convictions for common assault, criminal damage and breach of the peace each associated with a partner violence context, and 23 per cent reported convictions for other violence. In addition, 26 per cent reported previous convictions for theft or robbery.

Methods

A range of data collection methods were employed by the evaluation team which broadly consisted of questionnaire and interview data collected from male perpetrator and female victims, as well as the audio-taping of a small number of group sessions and interviews with project workers.

Male perpetrators completed questionnaires at the point of pre-intervention assessment (something that was not achieved for the whole sample, and which resulted in retrospective file reviews), during the middle and at the end of the first stage of the group programme as well as at an unspecified point during the second stage. In addition to questionnaire data, qualitative data were obtained through interviews conducted with 31 men and 14 women.

Main findings

Pre-attendance attrition

Burton et al. (1998) report that 12 per cent of the men who completed an assessment were subsequently refused places on the VPP. In the main, this was due to the men refusing or being unwilling to either take responsibility for their violence or to see it as a problem that required intervention. Of the 351 men in the log sample, records identified 122 who attended at least one first-stage group session, although incomplete data suggest that this is an inaccurate estimate. Despite data quality issues, this indicates substantial pre-attendance attrition within this programme.

Drop out

Just under one third (32%) of those who attended the first-stage group only attended between one and five sessions. However, if individuals continued toattend beyond this point they were less likely to drop out, with 55 per cent completing more than 10 of the 12 sessions. The court-mandated men were more likely to complete this stage and to attend more sessions on average, with 81 per cent of the 16 court-mandated men attending more than 10 sessions.

But of some concern is the small number of men who proceeded to the second stage of the group programme. Only 31 individuals achieved this within the observation period. However, the second stage was not subject to such high levels of drop-out with 29 per cent of men attending up to five sessions, 64 per cent attending more than 10 of the 20 sessions (with 28% attending more than 17 sessions).

Attrition

Overall, pre-attendance and within programme attrition had a marked impact on the ability of evaluators to gain a clear picture of the manner in which the VPP operates. Over two-thirds (69%) of the log sample and nearly three-quarters (73%) of the evaluation sample did not complete the programme. In general, this equates to over half (57%) of all men accepted on to the programme failing to complete it. However, little is known about the reasons for non-completion or of potentially clinically relevant characteristics of those who are unsuccessful.

Programme impact

A strength of the evaluation of VPP is that, through providing services to both male perpetrators and female victims, it is possible to obtain accounts of change from the victim perspective rather than relying on perpetrator self-report or police data, both of which are widely acknowledged as less reliable data sources (see Chapter 6). However, programme attrition and the voluntary participation associated with the women's support service component means that the actual sample used for this is very small.

Indeed, the impact analysis considers the views of '36 men where women participated and/or the men who substantially completed stage one and/or stage two of the programme' (Burton et al., 1998, p. 30) and then focuses on six men and women where both individuals participated in the evaluation. Questionnaire data obtained from women mid-way through the first stage revealed that of the 20 women who responded, 8 reported experiencing no abuse, 7 reported experiencing quite a bit less and 5 reported experiencing a little less. At the end of the first stage, of the 15 women who provided data, 4 reported experiencing no abuse, 8 quite a bit less and 3 a little less.

The Cheshire domestic violence prevention programme (CDVPP)

Skyner and Waters (1999) detail the provision of a community-based perpetrator programme delivered by Cheshire Probation Area, in partnership with the National Society for the Prevention of Cruelty to Children (NSPCC). Initially offered as a court-mandated programme, the remit had broadened to include 20 per cent voluntary referrals from domestic violence units.

The programme philosophy of the domestic violence prevention programme is based on the Duluth model and incorporates cognitive behavioural techniques within a pro-feminist analysis of domestic violence. The programme includes a range of learning styles and was completed across a period of 15 months, which consisted of two phases. In the first programme session, basic offence details and offending history are examined and detailed. In the second, the individual is required to storyboard the index offence, which provides the basis of initial group work during the early phases of the programme.

Prior to attendance, all offenders were assessed during two assessment interviews. Offenders who were assessed as exhibiting psychopathic traits, morbid jealousy, or who had mental health problems were screened out of the programme based on evidence gathered from a pilot programme which indicated that such individuals were unsuitable for the programme. A parallel support programme was offered to current and ex-partners and children, which was provided by NSPCC workers. The aims of the support programme were to demystify the nature of the programme for partners, and ensure that a realistic appraisal of the potential outcomes associate with programme attendance was obtained.

The first phase of the group programme comprised 10, two-hour weekly sessions in which intake was fixed. The focus of this phase was to introduce group processes, examining minimization, victim blame and the nature of physical abuse. The emphasis is on moving offenders towards acknowledging their abusive behaviours. The second stage of the programme comprised a rolling intake where offenders attended a two-hour session every fortnight. This element of the programme built on the material covered in the initial phase and focused on examining the use of power and control within relationships. Nine modules based on the content of the Power and Control Wheel (Pence & Paymar, 1993) were provided in order to change the offender's behaviour and attitudes with a view to them developing more egalitarian relationships. It is unclear from the programme description, however, how long the second phase of the programme was and no details are provided regarding the process surrounding individuals who fail to complete.

The evaluation

Design

The most basic reflexive control design, the pre-post test design was adopted to evaluate this programme. Participants were required to complete a battery of psychological and behavioural questionnaires at the start and end of each of the programme stages.

Participants

At the time of the publication, three stage one programmes and one stage two programme had been completed. Thirty-one offenders were referred to the stage one programme, of which 25 started, and 21 completed this component.

Measures

Although the authors refer to a range of psychological and behavioural measures, the precise identities are not provided. However, details of a two-year reconviction study were provided.

Main findings

Impact on psychological characteristics

A significant reduction in offence supportive attitudes was found at the end of the first phase of the programme. In addition, a statistically significant increase in their acceptance of responsibility was also identified at this point. It must be noted that this was only on the basis of one iteration of the stage one programme and, consequently, the numbers were very small indeed (n = 10). No measure of social desirability was used and the validity of these results is, therefore, questionable.

Impact on behaviour

The results of the two-year reconviction study indicated that, of the 10 individuals who had completed both stage one and stage two of the programme, two (40%) had been reconvicted and that in one case this was for an IPV-related offence. Of those who only completed the first component of the programme, three (60%) were reconvicted, but none of these offences were domestic violence related.

The West Midlands Probation domestic violence perpetrator programme (WMDVPP)

The most recently published British evaluation data is based on an evaluation of a non-accredited programme that was offered by West Midlands Probation Area, that I conducted for my doctoral research between 2000 and 2003 (Bowen, 2004). For the purpose of this chapter, however, this discussion focuses on the behavioural and psychological impact data obtained.

The DVPP was a 26 session psycho-educational programme that was based on the manuals of both the Duluth model (see chapter 4) and the CHANGE programme. The programme consisted of five modules delivered over twenty-four 2-2.5-hour sessions and five, monthly follow-up sessions of 2.5 hours. The five modules examined the nature of domestic violence, male socialization, victim empathy, sexual respect within relationships and accountability (see Bowen et al., 2005 for a full description of the content covered).

The evaluation

Design

A quasi-experimental design was chosen to assess the impact of completing the programme in contrast to not completing the programme on psychological treatment targets and alleged reoffending behaviour.

Sample

The original sample consisted of 142 men who attended an induction session between March 2001 and April 2002. Of these, five refused to participate and 17 had not been assigned to a programme within the observation period. Consequently, the evaluation sample consisted of 120 offenders, of whom the majority (68%) completed the programme and had attended on average 89 per cent of the scheduled programme. Of those who failed to complete, where information was provided, the most common reason was for re-assaulting a partner (18.4%) or being removed by programme staff (10%).

Methods

Participants in the evaluation were required to completed psychometric measures at three time points: pre-treatment, end-treatment and post-treatment. The end-treatment assessment coincided with the final core group session, and the post-treatment assessment coincided with the final follow-up session. The psychometric measures used were chosen on the basis of their apparent relevance to the programme, which was determined through inspecting the programme manual and discussing their selection with programme personnel. Consequently, the measures reflected anger (Novaco, 1994), interpersonal dependency (Hirschfield, Klerman and Gough et al., 1977), pro-domestic violence attitudes (Saunders et al., 1987), locus of control (Levenson, 1974), motivation to change (Levesque, Gelles & Velicer, 2000), and social desirability (Paulhus, 1984).

Attempts were made to contact the victims of men who were referred to the programme by liaising with regional women's support services with whom the probation area had a signed multi-agency information sharing agreement. However, it was soon determined that, owing to the confidentiality and anonymity policies held by some of these agencies at the time, it would not be possible to identify women whose partners were attending or referred to the group. This was due to the women's support services not necessarily knowing the true identity of women they were providing support to and whether their current or former partners were referred to the programme. Moreover, as the uptake of support services was left for women to decide, and no parallel women's programme was offered per se, it was likely that potential participants might access the service at any point, not necessarily at the start of the programme, may decide to withdraw from support at any point, and would number a minority relative to the men on the programme. Consequently police call-out data or 'alleged reoffending' data were used.

In order to obtain alleged reoffending data, police records of incidents involving the known offenders were examined. The records were either crime reports (official records of a crime being logged), command and control logs (records of incidents at which an officer had attended, which incidents may not have been logged subsequently as a crime), and family protection unit logs (e.g. reports of an incident by victims or children).

The length of the follow-up period used was determined by trying to balance obtaining the longest observation period with achieving the largest sample possible. The staggered scheduling of programmes and varied programme formats used (12 or 24 weeks) made this process difficult within a restricted data collection period. Although offenders attended follow-up sessions during the first five months after the core programme sessions, offenders are not sanctioned for non-attendance and in many cases do not attend. Therefore, a decision was taken to combine the five-month follow-up period of the programme with a six-month post-follow-up period, allowing a total observation window of eleven months.

Main findings

Impact on psychological characteristics

As with all evaluations, this study also suffered from high study attrition rates, which did not reflect programme attrition. Of the 120 offenders who completed questionnaires at time 1, 52 were completed at time 2, and 43 completed them at time 3. Only 28 completed questionnaires at all three time points. This was taken to reflect the fact that a participant could be deemed to be a completer by attending all but two sessions, and that some individuals would therefore decide not to attend the final group session in which the psychometrics were administered, knowing that there would be no sanctions for non-attendance. In addition, although the follow-up sessions were deemed to be a component of the programme, offenders were rarely sanctioned for non-attendance.

At the end of the core treatment sessions programme, completers reported significantly lower levels of external locus of control and physical abuse of their partner. No significant pre-post differences in pro-domestic violence attitudes, interpersonal dependency, anger and motivation to change were identified when social desirability was controlled. At the end of the follow-up sessions, offenders reported significantly higher levels of behavioural reactions when angry, and significantly lower levels of psychological and physical abuse of their partners than at the pre-treatment assessment. Analyses of the data obtained at all three time points indicated that, where significant gains were made in this small group of offenders (reduced external locus of control, reduced pro-domestic violence attitudes and physical abuse of partners), this change was not typically maintained throughout the follow-up period.

It has been argued by some that rather than relying upon statistically significant levels of change at a group level, assessments of the clinical utility of change at an individual level are more appropriate (Bowen et al., 2008). Consequently, the equation for assessing statistically reliable and clinically significant change proposed by Jacobson and Truax (1991) was also used to determine for each offender, the subscales on which reliable and clinically meaningful positive and negative change was achieved. It was found that across all subscales in nearly 50 per cent of cases the change achieved was unreliable, that is not statistically significant. In addition, across the subscales on average, only 15 per cent of offenders achieved clinically significant positive change at the end of the core treatment sessions. Moreover, this varied depending on the subscale examined (50% physical abuse; 20 psychological abuse; 16% external locus of control; 17% pro-IPV attitudes; 5% anger, Bowen et al., 2008). This indicates, if nothing else, that offenders appear to be more sensitive to some messages within the programme than others. For example, the disparity in reductions of self-reported physical and psychological abuse might simply reflect the fact that the programme was understood to be focusing on reducing these behaviour, with more emphasis placed on physical than psychological abuse.

Impact on alleged reoffending

Post-treatment alleged reoffending data were available for a subsample of 86 offenders. Of these, the majority (68) did not reoffend, according to police contact data during the 11-month follow-up period (Bowen et al., 2005). Of those offenders who dropped out of the programme, 33 per cent were deemed to have reoffended within this period, in contrast to 15 per cent of those who completed the programme. In addition, programme completers took longer to reoffend than did drop-outs (304 days vs 279 days, respectively), although this difference was not significant. These results led to a small and non-significant effect size estimate ($w = 0.20$, $p < .06$).

The integrated domestic abuse programme (IDAP)

In order to become an accredited programme, IDAP has been evaluated. While the preliminary findings from a process evaluation have been published (Bilby & Hatcher, 2004), the results of the impact evaluation to date have not. What follows here, therefore, is a description of the overall design and major findings taken from two unpublished sources (Hatcher, Palmer, Clark et al., 2005; Leicester-Liverpool Evaluation Group, 2005). The decision to refer to unpublished data in this way has been taken because of the importance of the IDAP programme, given its centrality in the official response to IPV.

Details of the main IDAP modules and treatment targets were provided in Chapter 6 and will not be reiterated here. However, it is interesting to note, that despite the range of potential treatment targets that were identified from the IDAP manual, the evaluators of this programme focused on assessing the effectiveness of the programme in relation to the four main treatment targets of the original Duluth programme. Consequently, the evaluation aimed to determine the following:

- a reduction in offender minimization and victim blaming;
- an increase in responsibility taken by offenders for their behaviour;
- change in the underlying beliefs associated with IPV;
- a reduction in violent, controlling and injurious behaviour.

The evaluation

Design

Two methodologies were adopted within this evaluation. The first consisted of a basic reflexive control pre-post design from which the programme impact on psychological characteristics and victim- (and self-) reported abusive behaviours was determined for programme completers only. In the second study, a quasi-experimental non-equivalent comparison group design was adopted in which the reconviction rates for completers, non-completers and non-starters were compared.

Sample

The IDAP programme was piloted within three areas, West Yorkshire, South-west London and South-east London. A maximum number of 404 offenders who were required to attend the programme as part of either a community rehabilitation order, or community punishment and rehabilitation order between September 2001 and September 2002 took part in the evaluation. Of the 339 offenders for whom data were available, roughly one third completed the programme, one third started but dropped out, and the final third never started the programme.

Methods

A combination of offender self-report measures of psychological constructs and behaviour, in addition to victim reports of behaviour were used. Although the evaluation team requested police call-out data to use as a behavioural outcome, existing data protection protocols prevented such data from being disclosed in a manner suitable for its use as an outcome measure. Consequently, the effectiveness (and subsequent accreditation) of this programme was based on the available victim reports which presented substantially less than half of the offender sample (Leicester-Leeds Evaluation Group, 2003).

More recently, the authors have conducted a quasi-experimental reconviction study in an attempt to determine the impact of IDAP on offending behaviour (Hatcher et al., 2005). The data used comprised records for known offenders obtained from the Offenders Index (Office for National Statistics, 2003) which is a Home Office database of standard list offence convictions, and from which it is not possible to identify domestic violence related convictions.

Main findings

Impact on psychological characteristics

In relation to the specific hypotheses, the following were observed among the treatment completers (maximum n = 114):

- A significant post-treatment reduction in scores on the Revised Attitudes Towards Offence Scale: This measure is taken to reflect the level of disclosure, minimization and victim blaming used by offenders. These results are taken to reflect higher levels of disclosure and a reduction in minimization and victim blame by offenders at the end of the programme.
- A significant post-treatment reduction in scores on a modified version of the Inventory of Beliefs About Wife Beating (Saunders, Lynch, Grayson & Linz, 1987): These results are taken to reflect a reduction in pro-IPV attitudes.
- A significant post-treatment increase in scores on a measure of locus of control (Craig, Franklin & Andrew, 1984): These results are interpreted as indicating that, at the end of treatment, offenders are more likely to believe that external rather than internal forces have control over life events.

Impact on behaviour

A significant post-treatment reduction in IPV behaviours was found, as measured by checklists of violent, controlling and injurious behaviours (Dobash et al., 1996). At both pre- and end-treatment, offenders were identified as reporting lower levels of these behaviours than their partners reported experiencing. However, even when partner reports are taken, a significant reduction is found in both the prevalence and frequency of these behaviours.

Reconviction data were available for a subsample of 262 offenders. It was found that overall, approximately half of this sample were reconvicted between starting the programme and the end of April 2003 when the data were collected. Those who were reconvicted were significantly younger, were significantly higher risk (OGRS2), had significantly more previous convictions and were at risk for a significantly longer period of time than were those who were not reconvicted. Programme completers were least likely to be reconvicted (29%), followed by the non-starters (55%) and non-completers (70%). Completers were 82.6 per cent less likely than non-completers to be reconvicted, and the non-starters were 60.6 per cent less likely to be reconvicted than were the non-completers.

Although these data suggest superficially at least that the programme achieved its four stated aims within the sample of programme completers, the behavioural impact data using victim reports was obtained on less than one tenth of the original sample (n = 41), and therefore the validity of the findings is questionable. The authors themselves note that the small numbers preclude generalizability of the findings and restrict the interpretation of programme impact. A key point, however, which is in no way addressed by the authors, is the clinical relevance of the psychological and behavioural change identified. What is more, despite using self-report measures, no attempt is made to account for, and examine, the impact of socially desirable responding, despite ample empirical evidence that such biases exist (e.g. Dutton & Hemphill, 1992). The lack of comparison group data, moreover, renders any identified change as being of questionable origin, as no comparison with the 'non-starters' that could have been a useful no-treatment comparison group, is made.

These data do also appear to show some evidence of a treatment effect on reconviction. However, owing to the issues identified in Chapter 7 with reconviction as an outcome measure generally, and in relation to domestic violence specifically, these data can only be interpreted with the utmost caution. Taken together, the results of the two impact evaluations have little to say about the potential effectiveness of the IDAP programme. In addition, it is perhaps of some concern that despite operating within a multi-agency framework, the inability to share information across boundaries rendered it impossible to obtain vital information about the potential effectiveness of the programme. Consequently, these studies have more to say about the inadequacy of the coordinated community response at the time of study, than they do about the impact of the IDAP programme. It is, therefore, of even greater concern that the programme achieved accredited status on the basis of the information obtained.

Emergent Themes from the British Evaluation Evidence

It is evident from the British studies reviewed that the progress of evaluation research in this area in this country has been slow, despite the seeming willingness of policy makers to adopt these forms of interventions. Taken together, the studies suggest, superficially at least, that programmes exert a positive effect on at least one outcome measure. However, as has been noted in previous international studies, these effects although positive are small, and methodological inconsistencies render the ability to draw firm conclusions difficult. The studies vary in their strengths and weaknesses. For example, although three studies were able to draw upon victim report (Dobash et al., 1999; Leicester-Liverpool Evaluation Group, 2005; Burton et al., 1998), this was achieved at a cost of numbers, thus rendering estimated effects potentially unreliable. In contrast, one study obtained police call-out data (Bowen et al., 2005) but, through adopting a quasi-experimental design, was not able to attribute any identified effects directly to the programme. Instead, as Feder and Wilson (2005) note, this approach answers the question: 'Among men who are court-mandated to batterer intervention, do those who choose to attend and complete this programme do better than those who do not?' (p 256), and not, 'Do court-mandated batterer intervention programmes reduce offender's likelihood of re-offending' (p. 256).

Overall, however, the studies indicate that even with backing from government agencies, evaluators have difficulty in accessing valid behavioural outcome data, although more success might be possible working through local multi-agency agreements where a specific partner can identify known offenders and obtain usable data. It seems, therefore, that these studies have more to say about the feasibility of conducting evaluation research within the UK, than they do about programme effectiveness per se. Moreover, these studies highlight that ongoing evaluation of programmes is required, particularly given the extent to which such programmes are endorsed within the criminal justice system.

Summary

In summary, despite the enthusiasm with which IPV perpetrator programmes have been developed and offered as a potential source of rehabilitation (and hope), there is questionable evidence that these programmes, regardless of their underlying therapeutic approach, are effective in initiating and maintaining change. Scott (2004) notes that across studies, on average, two-thirds of IPV perpetrators will cease being abusive for a considerable period of time. What is less clear is whether IPV programmes contribute to this cessation. What is more, within a British context, the decision to adopt these models has occurred recently despite the availability of the extant international literature which questions their efficacy, and meagre British data from which less robust conclusions can be drawn. It seems, therefore, that the decision to intervene in this way reflects a commitment to doing something, in the wake of broader policy shifts that have recognized the magnitude of the problem of IPV, regardless of the quality of the evidence base regarding what works. The data examined in this chapter indicate that the most consistent characteristic of the outcome literature is a lack of standardized procedures. The variation in methods, designs, outcomes and samples makes determining programme effectiveness difficult. Consequently, what is needed is a set of minimum standards to which programme evaluators should adhere, in order that a consistent body of research emerges over time from which meta-analytical studies can draw more reliable results. Such a move will then lead to a more viable evidence base from which policy decisions can be made with greater confidence about the potential implications for women and children.

9

Evaluation Issues: What Else should We be Considering?

We have seen that current data concerning the effectiveness of IPV perpetrator programmes has been marred by several methodological limitations specifically with regard to internal validity. Consistent with the wide array of corrections evaluations that have been conducted to date, evaluations of IPV perpetrator programmes have typically employed one outcome measure – official recidivism. However, as suggested in Chapter 6, recidivism data alone does not increase our understanding of the relationship between the mechanisms of change within the programmes and the resultant impact on behaviour. The central argument of this chapter is not new, as several commentators have suggested similar expansions to evaluation research in other corrections areas, and yet it is only more recently that these issues have been considered within the context of IPV programme evaluation, hence their inclusion.

Research indicates that treatment responsivity is influenced by the characteristics of the programme theory; the implementation and integrity of the programmes and the characteristics of the offender sample (Andrews & Bonta, 1994). Therefore, in order to understand how and for whom rehabilitation works, evaluations need to incorporate assessments of both programmes process variables (implementation and integrity) and multiple outcome measures (psychological and behavioural), in addition to the assessment of offender characteristics and needs. Broadening the conceptualization and assessment of offender rehabilitation programme effectiveness has been increasingly advocated during the last decades (e.g. Pawson & Tilley, 1997; Friendship, Falshaw & Beech, 2003) and it is this issue that provides the focus of this chapter. The overall shape of the chapter reflects that of an earlier published paper (Bowen & Gilchrist, 2004b), and includes an updated and expanded analysis of some of the issues presented in this earlier work that have not already been addressed elsewhere in this book.

The Rehabilitation of Partner-Violent Men, by Erica Bowen

Emphasis in this chapter is placed on the practicalities of the evaluation process and how by expanding the focus of this practice, evaluators are in a prime position to clarify issues concerning the validity of theory as well as identifying good and best practice. The comprehensive evaluation approach advocated by Rossi et al. (2008) is used as a conceptual framework within which current theory and practice are critiqued and areas for additional focus are discussed. It is argued specifically that the characteristics of offenders, their potential heterogeneity and the resulting response to treatment should be assessed routinely within evaluations. Moreover, the precise relationship between pre-treatment motivation to change, programme attendance and behavioural change requires refinement. In addition, programme implementation and integrity variables need to be quantified and examined in relation to the mediating variable of the therapeutic environment.

The Comprehensive Evaluation Approach

Rossi et al. (2008) define evaluation as 'the use of social research procedures to systematically investigate the effectiveness of social intervention programmes' (p. 4). Social intervention programmes are understood to be planned, and ongoing activities carried out for the purpose of improving some social condition. Programmes for IPV perpetrators that aim to reduce recidivism are an example of this category of social programme.

'Comprehensive evaluation' is a term given to evaluations that encompass the five 'programme domains' postulated by Rossi et al. (1999, 2008; see table 9.1).

It has been suggested that only through the careful integration of these five domains will it be possible to understand what works, for whom and under what conditions (Lipsey and Cordray, 2000). Within this chapter each of these domains will be examined with reference to what is known, what can be learned about the problem of IPV, and the characteristics of best practice.

Needs Assessment: What is Domestic Violence and Who are the Perpetrators?

As presented in table 9.1, a needs assessment refers to several interlinked components that form the basis for identifying and understanding the nature of the social problem for which an intervention programme is required. Conducting a needs assessment might not always be needed, depending on the underlying purpose of the evaluation, and conducting a comprehensive needs assessment for IPV is not an easy (and perhaps an impossible) task. However, it is possible that part of the reason that we have such poor evidence of programme outcome in IPV corrections is due to a poor understanding of the nature of the problem. Consequently, where practicable, a needs assessment

Table 9.1 The five programme domains within the Comprehensive Approach and their aims

Domain	Aim
Programme need	To identify the extent of the problem, the targets for intervention, and the needs of the intervention targets
Programme theory	To analyse the implicit and explicit assumptions within the programme about the nature of the problem being addressed, and the most appropriate methods through which the problem will be tackled
Programme process	To document key aspects of the performance of the programme that indicate whether the programme is functioning as intended or according to an appropriate or documented standard
Programme outcome	To measure whether the social programme is achieving its desired outcomes with each and every client who is subject to the programme
Programme efficiency	To determine whether the financial costs entailed through the provision of the social programme are reasonable, given any identified benefits associated with running the programme.

should be undertaken for each programme. The questions that can be addressed through a needs assessment might include:

- What are the nature and magnitude of the problem to be addressed?
- What are the characteristics of the population in need?
- What are the needs of the population?
- What services are needed?
- How much service is needed and over what time period?
- What service delivery arrangements are needed to provide those services to the population? (Rossi et al., 2008, p. 77)

The predominance of offending behaviour programmes for male IPV perpetrators suggests that there is only one type of perpetrator and one, clearly defined form of IPV. However, as was extensively examined in Chapter 1, this is an oversimplification of a complex social phenomenon. 'Domestic violence', 'intimate partner violence', 'wife abuse' and 'family violence' (to name but a few) are all terms that have been used to refer to the occurrence of violence within heterosexual adult relationships. The multiplicity of these terms has in part arisen owing to the use of differing methodological assessments of the magnitude of the problem samples and theoretical interpretations of the resulting data (Johnson, 1995). A contemporary development has been the conceptualization of two distinct forms of domestic violence: 'common couple violence' and 'patriarchal terrorism' (Johnson, 1995). Common couple violence is viewed as being less a product of patriarchy and more the product of less gendered causal factors leading to minor forms of violence by male, female or both partners. Patriarchal terrorism on the other hand is theorized to be that violence which is a product of the patriarchal tradition of men's rights to control 'their' women. As discussed in Chapter 1, it seems that these perspectives arise from adopting different methodologies to access 'victims', with clinical samples identifying their experiences as intimate terrorism and population-based samples identifying their experiences as common couple violence.

Rossi et al. (2008) note that, fundamentally, needs assessments are political tools which reflect the common or dominant understanding of social issues at any one time. Consequently, it is perhaps not surprising that the current focus of intervention is based on the dominant ideological view of patriarchy as the primary cause of IPV. However, assuming that all perpetrators who come into contact with formal intervention services (whether community or criminal justice based) are going to be proponents of the patriarchal terrorism form of IPV, if a holistic assessment of the problem is not conducted, this might inadvertently lead to a level of misclassification and, consequently, client–treatment mis-match. Therefore, it is my view that evaluators should work from a scientific perspective whereby the underlying assumptions of stakeholders about the nature of programme need are directly and empirically tested rather than assumed to be accurate, as errors in conceptualization will have fundamental consequences for programme success. However, this is a fundamentally difficult task which is complicated by issues concerning the validity of data sources and the requirement of: a) access to the most recent partner and/or victim of the index offence, and b) accurate, unbiased responding from all involved. It is also likely that stakeholders that employ external evaluators will be reluctant to have the validity of their understanding and conceptualization of the problem scrutinized.

Assessing Programme Theory

Several authors have pointed out that the conceptualization and design of a programme must reflect valid assumptions about the nature of the target problem and represent a well-founded and feasible approach to resolving it (Dobash et al., 1999; Rossi et al., 1999; Lipsey & Cordray, 2000). This places the validity of a programme's theory central to the success of a programme, as some argue that if the theory is faulty the intervention will fail, regardless of how well it is conceived and implemented (Chen, 1990). Some of the questions addressed through the process of assessing programme theory might include:

- What clientele should be served?
- What services should be provided?
- What are the best delivery systems for the services?
- How can the programme identify, recruit and sustain the intended clientele?
- How should the programme be organized?
- What resources are necessary and appropriate for the programme? (Rossi et al., 2008 p. 77)

It is clear that these questions lead on from the evidence that informs the needs assessment, and it is likely that the identified clientele will reflect the assumptions made about the nature of the problem. Therefore, while, internationally, at least there has been some recognition of females as perpetrators and victims within heterosexual and lesbian relationships (Eaton et al., 2008), and males as perpetrators and victims within gay relationships (Hellmuth, Follansbee, Moore & Stuart, 2008), practice remains dominated by the conceptualization of heterosexual males as perpetrators and heterosexual females as victims.

Questions concerning the nature of services and modes of service delivery have been less widely debated in the international literature. This in part, reflects the adoption of regional and national standards and accreditation criteria (see Chapter 8). The consensus among all standards is that a group-based format should be adopted. Murphy and Meis (2008) note, however, that this is a departure from the usual individual (one to one) interventions developed to address a broad range of psychosocial problems, which, after evaluation, has proven their effectiveness, are then typically adapted into groupwork formats for relatively homogeneous groups of individuals. As shown in Chapters 3 and 6, the empirical support for many of the treatment targets within group-based programmes is weak, and Murphy and Meis (2008) expand to suggest that many of the therapeutic techniques within such programmes are often very poorly implemented with little understanding of whether, and how, they will apply to groups of IPV perpetrators.

While the adoption of group approaches can be easily justified economically, and a therapeutic justification made with reference to groupwork theory, less is known about the comparative benefits of a groupwork versus individual versus couple intervention model. Dunford (2000b) conducted the only experimental evaluation which incorporated the allocation of violent Navy personnel to either a 26-week cognitive-behavioural groupwork programme (with six follow-up sessions at monthly intervals), a 26-week multi-couple cognitive-behavioural treatment programme (followed by six monthly follow-up sessions), a 'rigorously monitored' condition (social worker engagement once a month for 12 months) or no-treatment. No significant differences were found in victim reported injuries, feeling endangered, or in the frequency of being hit or pushed at either the six-month or 12-month follow-up period.

Although these results might lead to the interpretation that all forms of intervention are equally beneficial, there are several important limitations to the study. First, the focus on military personnel reduces the ecological validity of the findings as even those individuals in the 'no-treatment' group were likely to experience negative consequences from their superior officers if their violent behaviour continued. In addition, although a multi-couple group programme was implemented, the relative number of female partners who participated was small (two women to every five men). Therefore, such groups rarely consisted of complete couples. This might reflect the fact that although the men who were in active duty were mandated to attend, their female partners who were typically civilian were not, and therefore may simply have chosen not to participate. Consequently, this intervention appeared to focus on male perpetrators in the presence of females rather than provide a holistic conjoint analysis of IPV.

Given the very poor outcomes from group-based approaches, it is clear that a greater emphasis needs to be placed on the comparative evaluation of multiple approaches to IPV 'treatment' in order to determine which approaches are most effective with this client group, or subgroups thereof.

Validating programme theory: Do programmes target criminogenic need?

As reviewed in Chapters 4 and 6, the dominant approach to group-based rehabilitation of male domestic violence perpetrators is that forged from the feminist Duluth model (Pence & Paymar, 1993). Feminist explanations of domestic violence attribute its cause to the existence of patriarchy as a dominant construct within society (Dobash & Dobash, 1979). According to this view, men are socialized into aggression, and taught directly or indirectly that it is an appropriate means of problem solving and a method demonstrating authority in certain circumstances. The Duluth programmeme employs a 'knowledge–attitude–behaviour' meta-theory of change (Weiss, 1997) in which changes in behaviour are presumed to be a function of changes in attitudes, which, in turn, depend on the acquisition of knowledge (Lipsey & Cordray, 2000). The primary treatment target within this approach is the male offender's patriarchal attitudes that condone domestic violence and the subordination women (Mederos, 1999). Secondary treatment targets include responsibility taking and victim empathy.

Evaluations of domestic violence offender programmes commonly assess the association between offender characteristics (demographics and psychopathology) and treatment outcome (for example, Babcock & Steiner, 1999; Chen, Bersani, Myers et al., 1989; Dunford, 2000a; Edleson & Grusznski, 1988; Gondolf, 2002; Gondolf & White, 2001; Hanson & Wallace-Capretta, 2000a). To date, few evaluations have examined the impact of treatment on the psychological characteristics that are hypothesized to be criminogenic needs (for example pro-offending attitudes, anger, attitudes towards women, locus of control), and targeted by the programmeme (see Feder & Dugan, 2002; Hamberger & Hastings, 1988; Harrell, 1991; Palmer, Brown, Maru & Barrera, 1992; Russell & Jory, 1997; Tutty, Bidgood, Rothery & Bidgood, 2001; Wolfus & Bierman, 1996 for notable exceptions). In other cases, victims' feelings of safety have been used as an outcome measure (e.g. Gondolf, 1999).

In instances where these assessments are made, methodological limitations such as biased control groups (Hamberger & Hastings, 1988; Wolfus & Bierman, 1996), and lack of behavioural data (Russell & Jory, 1997; Tutty et al., 2001; Wolfus & Bierman, 1996), preclude the ability to relate these changes to recidivism. As Hanson and Wallace-Capretta (2000b) note, in order to determine the criminogenic nature of a psychological factor, treatment-induced psychological change must be found to be associated with changes in offending behaviour. However, it has been argued that if clients present pre-treatment with clinical level symptoms (e.g. anger), and at post treatment the symptoms are still reported as being within a clinical range, albeit significantly reduced from pre-treatment, behavioural changes associated with psychological change should not be expected (Hanson & Wallace-Capretta, 2000b). Therefore, outcome studies need to determine the proportion of offenders who achieve 'clinically significant change'

(Jacobson & Truax, 1991) and relate this change to the proportion of offenders who also achieve behavioural change in order to validate the 'criminogenic' status of the targeted need.

The calculation of clinically significant change when used within corrections has typically followed the methodology popularized by Jacobson, Roberts, Berns and McGlinchey (1999). This requires the calculation of clinical cut-offs – a score below or above which will be taken as indicating that the individual has achieved a score which places them within a distribution of a non-clinical population on that measure. The clinical cut-offs (C) are derived from the following equation:

$$C = \frac{(SD^1)(MEAN^2) + (SD^2)(MEAN^1)}{SD^1 + SD^2}$$

Where SD^1 refers to the standard deviation of the non-offender population, and $MEAN^1$ refers to the mean non-offender score. SD^2 refers to the standard deviation of the offender population and $MEAN^2$ refers to the offender group mean score.

In addition, a reliable change (RC) index is calculated, which is used to verify that the extent of the change recorded is statistically reliable. The RC was derived from the following equation:

$$RC = \frac{(\text{post-treatment}) - (\text{pre-treatment})}{S_E}$$

Where S_E refers to the standard error of the measure used. The standard error is calculated from the following equation:

$$S_E = SD\sqrt{(1 - r_{xx})}$$

Where r_{xx} is the test-re-test reliability (or internal consistency; Jacobson, Follette & Ravenstorf, 1984) of the measure used. In order for any pre-/ post change to be classified as significant, the RC has to exceed 1.64 for a one-tailed test (Beech, Fisher & Beckett, 1999). To date, only one study has taken such an approach within the evaluation of an IPV perpetrator programme.

Bowen, Gilchrist and Beech (2008) examined explicitly the relationship between psychological change and post-treatment behaviour. The psychological constructs assessed reflected the broad aims of a psycho-educational programme, but were identified not from a coherent programme theory manual (as this did not exist), but from discussion with stakeholders and the empirical literature. Consequently, the evaluation examined in treatment change in anger, pro-domestic violence attitudes, locus of control, interpersonal dependency and self-reported abusive behaviours. The behavioural outcome measure consisted of alleged reoffending as determined from police contact data (call-out logs, command and control logs) and was obtained for a follow-up period of 11 months after the last core group session. Like many evaluation studies that require information from offenders at more than one time point, the study suffered from in-treatment attrition, which resulted in a sample of 52 offenders with self-report data at pre- and end-group timepoints, and alleged reoffending data were only available for 37 of these individuals.

Drawing on work by Jacobson et al. (1999), offenders were categorized according to the nature of the change attained. The definitions of these categories were as follows:

1 Normal: individual starts in 'functional' group and remains within this group regardless of whether the change is statistically reliable;
2 Recovered: clinically significant change;
3 Improved: statistically reliable change in the direction of functional population but remaining within the range of scores of the dysfunctional population;
4 Deteriorated: begins in the dysfunctional population and scores indicate statistically reliable deterioration;
5 Regressed: starts within the functional population and moves to the dysfunctional population with statistically reliable change;
6 Unreliable: statistically reliable change, regardless of the direction or relationship to cut-off.

A substantial proportion of offenders (27.2%) did not achieve reliable change across measures. A further 26.5 per cent were categorized as Normal, that is both pre- and post-treatment scores were within the range of the normal population. Of those offenders who did achieve reliable change, the most frequent categorization on average was clinically significant change (Recovered), with 17.3 per cent achieving this status. The least frequent categorization was Regressed (5%). In general, the data indicate a pattern of positive change where reliable change was achieved.

The profile of change achieved within the sample varied according to the construct assessed. For example, offenders were most likely to achieve unreliable change in levels of behavioural reactions to anger provocation, and were least likely to achieve unreliable change in pro-domestic-violence attitudes. Moreover, offenders were most likely to achieve clinically significant change and to be categorized as Improved on the Inventory of Beliefs about Wife Beating (IBWB) and least likely to achieve clinically significant change in their reported cognitive mediation of anger responses, a scale for which offenders were most likely to be categorized as Normal.

Of the 37 offenders for whom alleged reoffending data were available, it was found that four (10.8%) reoffended within the observation period. Contrary to expectations, reoffending is neither associated with achieving clinically significant change on the Cognitive, Arousal and Behavioral domains of the Novaco Anger Scale (NAS), nor reductions in pro-domestic-violence attitudes and external locus of control. In addition, there was no association between the number of scales on which clinically significant change was achieved and reoffending. The findings from this study, therefore, question the underlying assumptions of the programme theory as it was operationalized. In addition, the study illustrates the contribution that such an approach can make to validating theoretical assumptions about the nature of a phenomenon. Such an approach does require, however, that the underlying assumptions are accurately operationalized and that the resulting theoretical constructs are measured accurately – something which is difficult when relying on self-report measures.

Implicit assumptions of programme theory: Do all members of the target population have the same needs?

Some elements of programme theory are not explicitly stated in programme manuals (Rossi et al., 1999). It is therefore, necessary, to determine the validity of these assumptions where possible. The question of whether all offenders respond in the same way to offending behaviour programmes has come under scrutiny in contemporary research (Lindsay & Brady, 2002). High attrition rates, consistent discriminating characteristics of treatment drop-outs and increasing numbers of studies identifying systematic heterogeneity within offender samples suggest that this is simply not the case. Indeed, Murphy and Meis (2008) argue that the extent of heterogeneity evidenced within IPV perpetrator populations is one of the greatest threats to group intervention success.

Treatment drop-outs are consistently identified as being higher risk than treatment completers. They are younger, have more extensive criminal histories, and higher levels of lifestyle instability factors (e.g. many jobs, moving between locations, substance use) than those who complete treatment (Bowen and Gilchrist, 2006; Cadsky et al., 1996; Daly & Pelowski, 1999; DeHart, Kennerly, Burke et al., 1999; DeMaris, 1989; Healey et al., 1998; Rondeau, Brodeur, Brochu et al., 2001; Rooney & Hanson, 2002). As such, these individuals share a number of characteristics with the 'generally violent/anti-social' subtype of IPV perpetrator identified by Holtzworth-Munroe & Stuart (1994), who are characterized by anti-social personality traits, extensive criminal histories, and substance and alcohol problems (Holtzworth-Munroe & Stuart, 1994; Waltz, Babcock, Jacobson et al., 2000). It is also acknowledged that individuals with anti-social personality traits are less likely to conform to the demands of treatment (Davison & Neale, 1997).

This offender type stands in contrast to emotionally volatile or borderline/dysphoric offenders who are characterized by borderline personality characteristics (high dependency, high anger, high levels of depression), similarly have substance/alcohol abuse problems, but less extensive legal involvement and less generalized violence (Hamberger et al., 1996; Holtzworth-Munroe & Stuart, 1994; Holtzworth-Munroe et al., 2000; Saunders, 1992; Tweed & Dutton, 1998). This category of offender will rarely present themselves for therapy and, some argue, will never truly benefit from traditional offender programmes, owing to the intractable nature of the disorder (Beck & Freeman, 1990; Davison & Neale, 1997). Indeed, American Psychiatric Association (2001) guidelines recommend a combination of extended psychotherapy and pharmacotherapy for such clients with no advantage of group over individual therapy.

Both of these categories of offender are most common within court-referred samples and stand in stark contrast to 'family only' offenders who evidence little or no psychopathology, low levels of anger, pro-domestic violence attitudes and low levels of legal/criminal involvement with violence restrained to family members (Holtzworth-Munroe et al., 2000; Waltz et al., 2000).

The consistent identification of offender subtypes has direct implications for offender responsivity. The risk, need and responsivity principles of Andrews and Bonta (1994), which underpin the CSAP accreditation criteria, endorse the matching of treatment provision to the offender's levels of risk, criminogenic needs and learning styles. As these offender types exhibit different crimnogenic needs, which in turn impact upon an offender's risk level, it can be hypothesized that their response to rehabilitation may differ. A number of studies explicitly examine the association between offender heterogeneity and treatment outcome.

In a comparatively early (for this line of enquiry) and, as yet, unpublished study, Bowen (2004) identified three offender types within her British sample based on their psychometric profile. The three types broadly fitted the Holtzworth-Munroe and Stuart (1994) typology previously detailed. It was found that the type which paralleled the 'family only type' (low deviance) were least likely to reoffend (9%) followed by the 'emotionally volatile' (similar to borderline/dysphoric; 22%) and the anti-social (similar to the generally violent/anti-social; 33%) although, owing to small numbers, this overall association was not significant. However, when time to first alleged reoffence was calculated, it was found that the anti-social group reoffended significantly more quickly, post-group, than did the low deviance group. However, on average the anti-social group took 276 days to reoffend which is the equivalent of just over nine months, in contrast to an average of 319 days or just over 10 months for the low deviance group.

In a more recent published study Huss and Ralston (2008), examined similar issues to Bowen (2004), but in a larger sample of 175 IPV perpetrators. Again, a trimodal typology reflecting the types identified by Holtzworth-Munroe and Stuart (1994) were derived from measures of depression, empathy, self-reported abusive behaviour, personality pathology and self-reported anger. It was found that the family-only group completed significantly more sessions than did the other two groups, although the generally violent and borderline/dysphoric groups did not differ significantly from each other in attendance. The generally violent/anti-social group recorded the greatest pre-post intervention change in levels of self-reported anger, empathy and abusive behaviours, without controlling for social desirability. According to official records, 10.6 per cent of the family only, 23.9 per cent of the borderline/dysphoric and 39.1 per cent of the generally violent/anti-social group reoffended – differences that were statistically significant. In addition, it was found that the generally violent/anti-social group were quicker to reoffend than were the other two groups, but the time to reoffend did not differ significantly between the family-only and borderline/dysphoric groups. The generally violent group were also more likely than the other two groups to reoffend repeatedly.

There is additional evidence that offender subtype may be more clinically meaningful in relation to predicting treatment outcome than motivation to change. In their sample of 199 predominantly (46%) African American IPV perpetrators, Eckhardt, Holtzworth-Munroe, Norlander et al., (2008) replicated the four-cluster typology initially reported by Holtzworth-Munroe et al. (2000), which included a low-level antisocial group in addition to the better established subtypes. It was found that motivation to change (assessed by the URICA-DV, Levesque, Gelles & Velicer, 2000) was not associated with treatment completion, whereas subtype was, with the generally violent and borderline/dysphoric groups more likely to drop out than the family-only group. Stages of change clusters were also not associated with post-treatment adjudication during a 13-month time period. In contrast, stages of change subscale scores did predict re-arrest, specifically higher precontemplation scores. Perpetrator subtype was also associated with re-arrest, with the borderline/dysphoric and generally violent/anti-social groups significantly more likely to have been arrested than the other two groups but the family-only group the least likely of all subtypes to be re-arrested.

There is additional evidence that different offender types may benefit from different approaches to rehabilitation. In an experiment in which offenders were randomly assigned to either process-psychodynamic or pro-feminist psycho-educational group interventions, Saunders (1996) identified an interaction between offender characteristics and treatment. Those offenders who had dependent personality profiles benefited from the psychodynamic approach, and anti-social offenders benefited from the pro-feminist psycho-educational approach. While this is only one study with a resulting small treatment effect, it does provide preliminary evidence that treatment outcomes can be affected by participant characteristics.

It is apparent that research is increasingly suggesting that there is more than one subgroup of domestic violence offenders and that treatment compliance and outcomes may be mediated by this heterogeneity. As a result, it may be beneficial when assessing the programme theory to determine the presence of subcategories of offender from the analysis of pre-treatment crimnogenic need. The outcomes associated with subgroup membership, if apparent, would provide information about which offenders may be most appropriate for the treatment approach being evaluated.

Motivation to change: selection criteria or treatment target?

A second implicit assumption of domestic violence offender programmes, and an influential referral criterion is that offenders are 'adequately' motivated to change, and have some insight into their offending (Home Office, 1999). Some authors argue, however, that increasing an offender's motivation to change is a primary goal of rehabilitation, and therefore high levels of pre-treatment motivation to change may not necessarily produce the most reliable outcomes (McMurran, 2002). Indeed, it is within the CSAP accreditation criteria that all programmes should enhance, and therefore target, motivation to change (see Chapter 4). However, Levesque et al. (2000a) found that the manuals of five domestic violence offender programmes failed to relate to models of motivation to change and incorporate motivation enhancement into their content. The previous description of the IDAP and CDVP/HRP programmes offered currently in the UK (Chapter 6) showed that both refer to motivation to change as a treatment target and incorporate the consideration of a theoretical model of change, the Transtheoretical model, within their programme descriptions.

The Transtheoretical model of change, and its controversial stage of change (SoC) model are now conceptualized within many accredited offending behaviour programmes (McConnaughty, Prochaska and Velicer, 1983; Prochaska & DiClimente,

1982). The SoC model hypothesizes that individuals who are trying to change behaviour move through different categories of motivation to change (McConnaughty et al., 1983). These include, most commonly, precontemplation (an individual having no insight into or awareness of problem behaviour and need to change), contemplation (an individual has some insight into problem behaviour but is ambivalent about change), action (an individual is actively changing behaviour) and maintenance (an individual has modified behaviour successfully and is trying to maintain the change achieved; Miller & Rollnick, 1991). As Murphy and Baxter (1997) note, clinical experience, high attrition rates and research findings suggest that the majority of offenders who attend treatment do so in response to extrinsic factors (such as a threat to the relationship). As a result, rather than being classified as in the 'action' stage (an implicit assumption of many behaviourally-oriented batterers' programmes that emphasise skills training), offenders are more likely to be in the precontemplation, or contemplation stages of change. Moreover, it is likely that within any given group of IPV perpetrators a range of stages of change will be evidenced (Murphy & Meis, 2008).

Although this model is quite explicit, in terms of identifying stage-based strategies for increasing motivation to change, the current IPV programmes in the UK seem to pay little attention to adopting these strategies within the programme content. Rather, if an individual is deemed to be particularly resistant to change (in denial) then they are required to undergo one-to-one motivational interviewing. However, as far as is detailed in the theory manuals, the use of motivational enhancement strategies do not appear to be sensitively matched to the individual's stage of change, as no formal assessment of motivation to change is detailed. Moreover, there is no explicit statement of which stage of change participants need to be in, in order to be eligible for the group programmes, aside from not 'in denial'. The presence, therefore, of individuals in a group who might be at different stages of change presents a direct challenge to the group facilitators, and may also impact negatively on the therapeutic climate if manualized materials emphasize working in a manner more appropriate for one particular stage of change than others (Murphy & Meis, 2008). It seems, therefore, on the face of it at least, that there is scope for more detailed individual assessment and intervention prior to an offender attending programmes which, if successful, might improve the overall treatment effect. Indeed, there is mounting debate and equivocal evidence regarding the ability of adopting stage-based intervention approaches to improve treatment outcomes.

Levesque, Gelles and Velicer (2000) identified eight subtypes of domestic violence offender based on cluster analysis of their scores on the four domains described previously. It was found that those offenders assigned to clusters representing low levels of motivation to change were significantly less likely to have stopped being violent and reported employing fewer behaviour change strategies in the last six months than those identified in high motivation clusters. Men in the higher stage clusters also valued the advantages of violence cessation significantly more than those in less motivated clusters. Hanson and Wallace-Capretta (2000b) found that, while mandated offenders were more likely to recidivate than volunteers, neither pre- nor post-treatment motivation to change was related to recidivism. Studies of attrition from treatment, however, have found that implicit rather than explicit measures of motivation predict completion (for example, Cadsky et al., 1996; Daly & Pelowski, 1999; Rooney & Hanson, 2002).

More recently, studies have examined the potential benefits of additional motivational enhancement strategies to the outcomes of standard intervention programmes. For example, Musser, Semiatin, Taft and Murphy (2008) examined the impact of attending a two-session motivational interviewing (MI) intake module prior to attending a 16-week cognitive-behavioural groupwork programme on engagement and treatment outcomes. A total of 108 offenders were assigned in blocks of 12 to either the MI or an alternative structured intake module. It was found that those individuals in the MI condition were more likely to complete homework tasks, and more constructive behaviour during the early group sessions as rated by therapists. In addition, those in the MI condition were more likely to engage in additional help-seeking from a greater number of sources than those in the alternative condition. Although victim reports of physical assault were half the number by men in the MI group than the structured intake group, small sample sizes and low base rates rendered these differences non-significant.

In a second study, Kistenmacher and Weiss (2008) conducted a small sample (n = 33) randomized controlled trial of a different two-session motivational interviewing (MI) pre-group module and assessed the impact of attendance on readiness to change and external attributions of blame for offending. It was found that, in contrast to the control group, who received no additional intervention, those individuals in the MI condition reported increased action towards, and contemplation of, change, whereas those in the control group reported no such gains. In addition, those in the MI condition reported significant reductions in external attributions of blame for offending. Taken together, the results of these two studies suggest that an additional MI component might indeed impact upon treatment readiness, engagement and possibly outcome. These data illustrate that a more systematic exploration of motivation to change and the impact of treatment upon motivation to change is required. Understanding the influence of programme attendance on motivation to change will enable the development of clinical strategies to address motivation-related deficits, both within existing programmes and as pre-programme additions.

Assessing Programme Process: Is the Intended Treatment Delivered?

Assessments of programme process or the conduct of a 'formative evaluation' (Kropp & Hart, 1994) determine whether the programme received by the target population was that as intended. Specific questions that might form the basis of an assessment of programme process might include:

- Are administrative and service objectives being met?
- Are the intended services being delivered to the intended persons?
- Are there needy but unserved persons that the programme is not reaching?

- Once in service, do sufficient numbers of clients complete service?
- Are the clients satisfied with the services?
- Are administrative, organisational, and personal functions handled well? (Rossi et al., 2008 pp. 77–8)

As Kropp and Hart (1994) note, the majority of these questions focus on issues that are of primary concern to service providers. Such evaluations can be conducted several times throughout the course of a running programme, in order to ensure that processes are being effectively monitored, and, where evidence indicates this is necessary, modified. An example of a process evaluation is that published by the Home Office in relation to the implementation of the IDAP programme in the UK (Bilby & Hatcher, 2004).

The scope of the process evaluation that was conducted through interviewing 30 staff members who were directly involved in the implementation of the programme, was to:

> obtain information on the staffing levels, staff experience, staff training, accommodation, communication internally and externally, programme material, delivery style and techniques, dosage and intensity, duration of the programme and the compliance with monitoring and integrity procedures … the structure of organisations and the processes through which the programme is being developed. (Bilby & Hatcher, 2004, p. 5)

It is evident that these goals reflect a situation of agency self-monitoring and feedback whereby information is obtained about the extent to which procedures around the implementation of the programme are followed. The findings of this survey illustrated (among other issues) that the IDAP programme is resource intensive, requires properly trained staff with detailed knowledge of domestic violence, demands a sensitive multi-agency information-sharing context, and requires that group facilitators are aware of, and responsive to, the individual needs of offenders who attend the programme.

Questions regarding whether the appropriate targets received the service, whether there exists a group of targets who are never provided with the service, and whether acceptable numbers of targets completed the service provided, are less well examined in the literature. It is documented, however, that owing to the apparent popularity of referring offenders on to a court-mandated programme, waiting lists often far exceed the length of an offender's community rehabilitation order, of which attendance on the programme is a condition (Home Affairs Select Committee, 2008). Consequently, it therefore seems that there is a substantial proportion of needy individuals who are never provided with the service required.

Within the process evaluation domain described in table 9.1, the importance of two elements of programme functioning are implied, both of which focus on the treatment group, rather than the individual, as the unit of analysis. These are programme integrity and the therapeutic environment.

Programme integrity

Programme integrity refers to the delivery of programmes in relation to the explicit guidelines contained within manuals relating to content, timing, staffing, scheduling and delivery of services (Hollin, 1995). High programme integrity has been identified as a characteristic of effective offender programmes (Dane & Schneider, 1998; Leschied, Bernfield & Farrington, 2001). As Hollin (1995) notes, for the results of outcome studies to truly reflect the impact of intervention, it must be shown that all participants followed the same programme.

Although programme integrity is acknowledged as central to programme success, it has been acknowledged that in many instances it remains the 'forgotten' variable (Gendreau, Goggin & Smith, 1999). This has been the case with domestic violence evaluations. Typically, evaluators acknowledge the role of treatment integrity, and report the monitoring processes used such as observations of selected sessions and interviews with programme facilitators used to verify that the content delivered was as planned (e.g. Hanson & Wallace-Capretta, 2000a). However, this information is rarely quantified in a method that enables it to be entered into analyses of treatment outcomes.

It makes intuitive sense that variations in programme delivery and treatment facilitators could impact on treatment outcome. There are many reasons why the integrity of a programme could be compromised. Harrell (1991) employed multiple outcome measures in her experimental evaluation of three programmes that differed in their emphasis on the role of patriarchal values and control in violence. It was found that a significantly smaller proportion of offenders in treatment abstained from physical aggression than did those not in treatment. No significant difference was identified in post-treatment measures of pro-domestic violence attitudes between the offender groups after controlling for pre-treatment differences. Overall a negative treatment effect was recorded. Harrell (1991) hypothesizes two reasons for this failure. It is possible that the treatment programmes were of insufficient intensity or that they lacked an accurate conceptualization of the causes of domestic violence (inappropriate programme theory), and, as a result, were targeting factors not associated with domestic violence. Alternatively, they could have been targeting appropriate factors, but as programme implementation varied substantially between programmes, they were ineffectively targeted. This study illustrates the potential detrimental impact of poor treatment integrity upon treatment outcomes. It further illustrates that the measurement and incorporation of these variables into outcome analyses is required in order to determine that the outcome of treatment actually relates to the nature of the treatment delivered.

Therapeutic environment

The second element of process evaluation alluded to within programme process is that of the therapeutic environment. Programme integrity as discussed, relates to the mechanistic delivery of the programme. A secondary implicit goal of programme process is the attainment of an environment conducive to behavioural and psychological change (Corey & Corey, 1997). Evaluators of psychotherapy, in general, have argued that the examination of the therapeutic environment is essential if we are to understand the dynamics of therapy that enforce change (Dies, 1985). Despite this request, this is one area of research that has been largely ignored by evaluators of domestic violence offender programmes.

An explicit assumption of groupwork-based programmes is that the group format reduces a participant's sense of isolation and provides an atmosphere that facilitates the sharing of inner secrets with persons who can relate to and understand them. As the primary goal is to change the abuser's attitudes, peer acceptance support and validation of changing attitudes are crucial to the treatment process (Sakai, 1991). Thus, an implicit assumption is that the development of a therapeutic group provides a motivational atmosphere, which can increase an individual's intrinsic motivation to change (Murphy & Baxter, 1997), while offering a supportive environment within which problematic behaviour can be challenged.

Authors have noted that group processes are the driving force behind group treatment (Bloch & Crouch, 1985; Yalom, 1985). Group processes consist of a finite number of therapeutic factors. A therapeutic factor is 'an element of group therapy that contributes to improvement in a patient's condition and is a function of the actions of the group, therapist, other group members and the patient himself' (Yalom, 1985, p. 4). It is suggested that these factors can work both for and against an individual's attempt to change and produce either therapeutic or anti-therapeutic effects (Bloch & Crouch, 1985). Therefore, it is reasonable to expect different treatment groups to respond differently to similar treatment as a consequence of the unique developmental ecology of each group (Bednar & Kaul, 1978; Mackensie & Livesley, 1986). Several factors that appear central to effective therapy have been identified. These can be divided into group variables and leader variables.

Group variables

In their review of over 300 articles, Corsini and Rosenberg (1955) identified ten dynamics of effective groups (see Bloch & Crouch, 1985 for an in-depth examination of these factors and their role in group therapy). Acceptance or cohesiveness was identified within the majority of articles reviewed as being of central importance, and this has been maintained by more contemporary research (Bednar & Kaul, 1978; Evans & Dion, 1991; Yalom, 1985). Cohesiveness refers to feelings of acceptance and belonging within the group experienced by group members (Corsini & Rosenberg, 1955; Moos, 1994), and has been likened to the therapeutic alliance in individual therapy (Yalom, 1985). Theorists argue it is the attainment of a cohesive environment that leads to self-disclosure by participants, the challenging of attitudes and behaviour, and an increase in participant's commitment and motivation to change (Yalom, 1985). Hanson and Wallace-Capretta (2000a) observed selected sessions of the domestic violence treatment programmes that were evaluated in order to determine levels of cohesiveness, and found that different theoretical approaches to treatment had different levels of perceived cohesion. An interaction between group cohesion, integrity and outcome was identified such that the least cohesive group also had the lowest levels of integrity (poor structure and staffing) and reported the highest rates of post-treatment reoffending. Schwartz and Waldo (1999) explored the availability of eleven therapeutic factors identified by Yalom (1985) within a Duluth men's programme and their relationship to time spent in the programme. The programme was characterized by the 'imparting information', 'socializing techniques', and 'cohesion' factors confirming its psycho-educational format. A significant relationship was identified between the length of participation in treatment and the factors of cohesion and universality (identifying that they are not the only ones with a problem). Universality occurred relatively early on in attendance whereas cohesion did not emerge until they had prolonged experience in the group.

Leader variables

It has been argued that the most important element of group functioning is the style employed by group facilitators, rather than the existence of cohesion per se. Theorists argue that it is the role of the group leaders to manipulate group dynamics and foster a cohesive environment (Dies, 1985). Corey and Corey (1997) suggest that effective leaders are supportive, innovative within the group sessions, trustworthy and open, and instil a sense of hope in participants, foster group norms and encourage disclosure (Burlingame & Fuhriman, 1990). Indeed, research has illustrated that groups in which leaders reinforced clients' statements reflecting cohesion, showed greater symptomatic improvement in comparison to control groups, and that a supportive caring style of leadership was an essential component of cohesive groups (Hurst, 1978).

The therapeutic environment literature suggests that group members' socio-demographic and other personal attributes are only minimally related to their perceptions of group social climate (Moos, 1994). Therefore obtaining information about individual's perceptions of group climate and leadership style would enable a greater understanding of the interaction between group characteristics and treatment outcomes. One such study measured the perceived therapeutic environment of twelve sex offender treatment groups. Supportive leadership style was associated with a feeling of belongingness in the group and was a feature of well-organized groups, which were task oriented and focused on problem solving. It was also found that the groups that were highly cohesive, well organized, promoted independent action and which had supportive leaders produced higher levels of short-term treatment change than those groups that did not share these characteristics (Beech & Fordham, 1997).

Taken together, these findings illustrate that in order to begin understanding 'how' rehabilitation works, the impact of variation in treatment integrity and therapeutic environment upon outcomes needs to be explored. It is arguable that these two factors may moderate treatment outcomes independently of individual factors, possibly by enhancing motivation to change. As a result, evaluations that report small overall effect sizes for a large sample may be confounded by differences in treatment integrity and therapeutic environment at a treatment group level.

To date, only one evaluation study has been published which explicitly examines the characteristics of the therapeutic environment and how they might be associated to treatment outcomes. Bowen (2010) used the Group Environment (Moos, 1994) as a measure of therapeutic factors within her evaluation of a British IPV programme. The study aimed to identify characteristics of well functioning groups, and the impact of variations in programme delivery factors (session length (2 or 2.5 hours), programme length (12 or 24 weeks), numbers of staff involved), and attendance on perceptions of the therapeutic environment. In addition, the relationship between therapeutic factors and outcomes (psychological change and alleged reoffending) was examined.

It was found that group members' perceptions of group cohesion and leader support were significantly and positively associated with other therapeutic factors indicative of a positive therapeutic environment. Cohesion was associated with task orientation, self-discovery, order and organization, leader support and expressiveness. Leader support was associated with the same subscales as cohesion, but in all instances was more strongly associated with them than perceived cohesion was. Both group formats were perceived as adequately cohesive and with above average levels of leader support. In contrast, those groups conducted with sessions of 2.5 hours were not perceived as expressive but those conducted with sessions of two hours were perceived as emphasizing the open expression of feelings and problems. On the personal growth dimension, the emphasis on independent action was perceived as average. The focus on task completion was greater in groups with longer sessions. The groups with longer sessions were perceived as better organized and with more leader control but less openness to change than groups with shorter sessions. In both group formats, organization and leader control were high.

Programmes with sessions of 2.5 hours were generally perceived as fostering, within the group, significantly less disclosure, significantly less expression of anger and aggression, and significantly lower levels of innovation than the groups delivered with sessions of two hours. Furthermore, the groups with longer sessions were reported to be significantly more organized and have leaders that are more controlling of the group than those programmes with shorter sessions.

It was found that the number of staff involved in running the programme was not associated with perceptions of the therapeutic environment, whereas the number of hours perpetrators attended was positively associated with perceptions of the groups as well organized, although there was no association between the percentage of offenders who completed each group and overall perceptions of the therapeutic environment.

Finally, it was found that the number of psychometric subscales upon which individuals achieved clinically significant in-treatment change was positively associated with perceptions of group leaders as supportive. There was no association between therapeutic environment and alleged reoffending during the 11-month follow-up period.

Programme Outcome

As examined in some depth in Chapter 8, there is considerable variation in the evidence concerning the effectiveness or outcome of IPV perpetrator programmes. This evidence is not reviewed here. However, Rossi et al. (2008) note that there are additional questions relating to programme outcome which are also useful to consider within evaluation strategies. These include:

- Are the outcome goals and objectives being achieved?
- Do the services have beneficial effects on the recipients?
- Do the services have adverse side effects on the recipients?
- Are some recipients affected more by the services than others?
- Is the problem or situation the services are intended to address made better? (Rossi et al., 2008, p. 78)

As discussed in Chapter 7, the question of whether or not the goals of a programme are achieved, and whether the social problem is improved, requires programme developers and evaluators to specify a metric from which such questions can be answered. Such a metric needs to clearly operationalize the behaviour(s) of interest, as well as specify the rate of change that will be taken to be meaningful. As Gondolf (2002) notes, this is yet to appear in the literature, as providers and evaluators remain uncertain as to what constitutes clinically meaningful change. Moreover, it is unlikely that any such metric will appear soon unless evaluators can be assured access to data that provides a valid estimate of treatment impact from all programme providers. The lack of these data means that evaluators will be less inclined to make declarative statements about treatment effectiveness just in case measurement error may be masking real effects that contradict the identified impact. Murphy and Eckhardt (2005), in their specification of an individual cognitive behavioural intervention for IPV perpetrators, make a useful distinction between recidivism and relapse, and one which is rarely considered when operationalizing the outcome variables of interventions. Recidivism is defined as any repeat incident of a problem behaviour during a defined interval (p. 246), whereas relapse is defined as any such behaviour after an identified period of successful and meaningful behaviour change. It is likely that by taking a nomothetic approach to outcome evaluations, the distinction between recidivism and relapse has been lost. Consequently, a more idiographic approach to identifying recidivistic behaviours, within and out with the context of prior successful and meaningful behavioural change, is required in order to obtain a more realistic and sensitive assessment of programme success.

The previous discussion of the heterogeneity of offender samples also indicates that such heterogeneity in need is linked to differential treatment impact and outcome. It has also been noted that not all individuals who participate in such programmes improve their behaviour. For example, in the summary of a multi-site evaluation Gondolf (2002) noted that between 10 per cent and 15 per cent of the partners of men who attended a programme reported that their lives had worsened as a result. A fifth of the partners reported ongoing physical assault, injuries and experiencing heightened fears. Analyses of risk markers to identify the group of most severely and persistently violent programme attenders found that the situational variable of drunkenness increased the likelihood of violence 3.5 times. In addition, if a man was intoxicated nearly every day, the likelihood of re-assault increased by 16 times. This variable was most important in predicting recidivism among this group of offenders and highlights the potential importance of addressing alcohol use issues within this sample alongside or before addressing issues of IPV, in order to increase women's safety while attending IPV programmes.

In addition to identifying the most serious offenders, Gondolf (2002) also reports on the use of non-physical aggression throughout the evaluation period, including a 30-month follow-up period. It was observed that by the end of the 30-month follow-up period 76 per cent of men had used verbal abuse, 49 per cent had threatened a partner, and 38 per cent had re-assaulted a partner, indicating that, although physical violence might be most clearly targeted by programmes, the use of non-physical violence was less so. Indeed, 22 per cent of men had neither physically nor verbally assaulted their partner, 21 per cent had re-assaulted their partner on more than one occasion, and a further 12 per cent had only re-assaulted their partner once. More than one quarter (26%) were only verbally abusive or controlling and the remaining 20 per cent had made threats but were not physically abusive (p. 125). The longitudinal findings from this study indicate that although the majority of IPV perpetrators stop using physical violence eventually, the period of time during which re-assaults are most common is actually during the time that they are attending the programme. Consequently, in order to fully determine the impact of a programme, multiple longitudinal assessments of behaviour are required.

Evaluations of IPV programmes have been criticized for neglecting the subjective experiences of women whose partners are subject to the conditions of the programme (e.g. Dobash et al., 2000). It has been argued that simply because physical or psychological violence reduces in frequency or severity does not mean that the subjective experience or quality of life of women improves. Findings from the multi-site evaluation, however, suggest broadly that if physical assault stops, then women's quality of life improves (Gondolf, 2002). Specifically, it was found that approximately two-thirds of partners indicated that they were 'better off' than when their partners were referred to the programme, and that such reports coincided with a cessation of physical abuse in 93 per cent of cases.

These results indicate that while standard outcome assessments may provide one marker by which the impact of a programme can be assessed, taking a holistic approach and broadening the conceptualization of service users to include women themselves enables a triangulation of data from which evaluators can obtain greater confidence in their conclusions regarding the effects and impact of a programme.

Programme Efficiency

Assessments of programme efficiency are typically conceptualized as either cost–benefit or cost–effectiveness analyses. Such assessments of programme efficiency are usually undertaken at one of two time points relative to the programme running. In the first example, analyses of programme efficiency might be undertaken during the design and development phase of a programme, before the programme is established. This is known as *ex ante* efficiency analysis (Rossi et al., 2008 p. 338). Conversely, such an analysis might be undertaken once the programme is established and has been demonstrated to be effective through the results of an impact evaluation. This might be undertaken if the possibility of expanding a programme or making it a permanent service is being considered. This is known as *ex post* efficiency analysis (Rossi et al., 2008 p. 338). The questions that might be addressed through an assessment of programme efficiency may include:

- Are resources used efficiently?
- Is the cost reasonable in relation to the magnitude of the benefits?
- Would alternative approaches yield equivalent benefits at less cost? (Rossi et al., 2008, p. 337)

Owing to the financial restraints affecting all sectors that are involved in providing IPV programmes for male perpetrators, offering a service which is cost-effective is vital to ensure that scarce resources are not being misdirected (Friendship et al., 2003). The difficulty in addressing the second and third questions above comes from the fact that: a) there has been no systematic evaluation of either IDAP or CDVP/HRP, which provides sufficiently detailed and sensitive data to determine their effectiveness, and b) the lack of real alternative intervention models within the criminal justice system. Welsh and Farrington (2001) note that any economic evaluation of offender programmes is only as rigorous as the outcome study upon which it is based. Consequently, more rigorous empirical evaluations of UK IPV programmes is needed before any such economic analyses can be undertaken.

As reported in Chapter 7, even when allegedly different approaches have been evaluated in North America very similar results have been found, owing to the underlying conceptual similarity (Babcock et al., 2004). It is known that it costs £7,262 (approximately US$11,300 at the time of writing) for every offender to attend and complete the CDVP programme, and £7,250 for IDAP (Home Affairs Select Committee, 2008). It is possible that a partial answer to the third question stated above might come from a multi-site evaluation of IPV perpetrator programmes, which is currently being conducted in the voluntary sector, although the relative cost estimates would also need to account for the criminal justice context in order to make them applicable.

Conclusion

In conclusion, the 'comprehensive evaluation' framework outlined in this chapter provides a method of ensuring that evaluators operate scientifically and neutrally to determine in as objective a manner as possible whether programmes are based on valid assumptions. By taking this approach, a more nuanced evaluation method is proposed, which requires the consideration of a range of intervening factors that might influence the measured outcome of programmes and attenuate the conclusions about programme effectiveness that can be drawn. Only by adopting such an approach will we move closer to understanding more about how programmes work, and why they may only work for a proportion of individuals who are referred to them.

10

Conclusions and Future Directions

The literature reviewed shows that considerable change has occurred in the way in which IPV is perceived and responded to during the course of the last forty years. Specifically, IPV is now formally acknowledged and responded to, thanks to the groundbreaking work of feminist scholars and activists in the 1970s. However, despite the fact that IPV is now acknowledged and formal criminal justice responses have been defined and implemented to a greater or lesser degree around the world, the evidence indicates that such a response is of limited utility in reducing the likelihood of future IPV. The role that IPV programmes play in this response is even less certain given the paucity of sound empirical evidence testifying to their effectiveness. This situation raises questions about what is needed to improve the response to, and impact of, interventions for IPV, particularly those tertiary interventions aimed at reducing recidivism. In light of this and the evidence reviewed, the aim of this chapter is to provide some thoughts about the future direction of intervention practice and evaluation science. It is argued that the future lies in taking an objective, idiographic approach to defining, understanding and intervening in the problem, coupled with a more holistic approach to evaluation, but acknowledging that as tertiary interventions can only address the needs of the few, alternative primary interventions are required to help reduce the future burden placed on the criminal justice system by adults in need of tertiary intervention.

The Future Understanding of IPV: A Move towards an Evidence-Based Definition

It is apparent that current intervention policy is framed around a conceptualization of IPV as the use of violence by men against women, which was formed early in the

The Rehabilitation of Partner-Violent Men, by Erica Bowen

evolution of responses to this social problem. While this may well be the case for a proportion of clients who are mandated to treatment programmes, it is unlikely to reflect the reality for all clients, particularly with the escalating endorsement of pro-arrest policies, which have led to increasing numbers of lower risk, lower pathology perpetrators being identified (Apsler, Cummins & Carl, 2002). Moreover, the evidence reviewed in Chapter 6 illustrates that no one factor (and particularly patriarchal constructs) is sufficient to explain IPV behaviours, and that the phenomenon is multi-determined through the interaction of a range of factors within different ecological systems. Despite the acknowledgement of such heterogeneity within clinical offender samples (Holtzworth-Munroe & Stuart, 1994; Holtzworth-Munroe et al., 2000; Waltz et al., 2000), the assessment and treatment options available remain focused on the conceptualization of men as sole perpetrators and females as sole victims of male-perpetrated IPV. Moreover, current pro-feminist models of intervention fail to fully acknowledge the potential functional role of individual risk factors such as alcohol, drug use, emotional and psychological disorders. As Young, Cook, Smith et al. (2005) remark, although such approaches which focus on 'power and control' might be suitable for a proportion of offenders, in the majority of cases this conceptualization does not fit with the experiences of the majority of men and women for whom IPV is a more complex and varied phenomenon. Moreover, such discrepancies have been associated with treatment dropout and recidivism (Lee, Uken & Sebold, 2009). Young et al. (2005) note that the labelling of individuals as victims and perpetrators oversimplifies the dynamics that are active within abusive relationships, as such labels will differ, depending on the time at which an assessment is conducted, and will also shift over time as the relationship evolves.

It is particularly telling that Ellen Pence, who contributed to the creation of the Duluth model, has even acknowledged the discrepancy between programme philosophy and the subjective reality of the men for whom it was designed:

> By determining that the need or desire for power was the motivating force behind battering, we created a conceptual framework that … did not fit the lived experience of many of the men and women. (Pence, 1999, p. 29)

It is interesting that despite this disclosure over a decade ago – and the mounting evidence which refutes the validity of the central tenets of programmes based on this ideology – policy, certainly in the UK at least, is yet to be formally reconciled with the existing evidence base. Indeed, outside of court-mandated intervention in the UK, Respect, a national organization for practitioners who work with perpetrators of IPV, has devised accreditation criteria for community based programmes. Yet within the criteria which were only published in 2008, the following features of programmes that are eligible for accreditation are stipulated. Such programmes must include 'a written model of their work … which staff are required to follow and which is based upon … the following principles' (Respect, 2008, p. 40):

1 The safety of the perpetrator's victim(s) is the main focus of the programme.
2 The use of abusive or violent behaviour towards a current or former partner and her children is unacceptable.

3 The perpetrator is 100 per cent responsible for his use of abusive behaviour and the use of such behaviour is a choice.
4 The use of abusive behaviour is instrumental and functional.
5 A willingness to choose to use violent and abusive behaviour towards a partner is influenced by learnt expectations and a gender-based sense of entitlement. (pp. 40–1)

Consequently, we are again presented with a vision of IPV that is perpetrated by men against women and children, for which a gendered socialization process is responsible, and which fails to draw on the existing evidence base. Moreover, in line with North American state standards, the use of alternative methods are questioned, specifically those based on couples intervention, for which it is stated that if couples therapy has been recommended as appropriate this is because 'the violence is being understood as a relational/systemic problem. This type of intervention is problematic and potentially dangerous ...' (p. 57). In addition, practitioners are cautioned against offering services based on their understanding of one form of IPV (i.e. that specified by the criteria) to other client groups (e.g. perpetrators of violence within same sex relationships). What is not specified, however, is what services are appropriate (or available) for such client groups. That such restrictions on the provision of programmes exist, however, means that the evidence base, such that it is, will remain biased and restricted, owing to the under-development of our clinical and academic knowledge in this area.

As noted in Chapter 9, conducting a needs assessment is vital prior to developing interventions for any social problem and should, in my opinion, form the preliminary stages of programme evaluations even when programmes are established. The effective assessment of IPV cases is fundamental to the development and provision of appropriate treatment. Given the debate and evidence concerning the heterogeneity of IPV, it is necessary for a comprehensive holistic assessment of the individual within the context of their relationship and family to be conducted, which includes as a minimum the following issues:

- The true dynamics and victim relationships within each IPV situation, including the extent to which children are victims (Hamel, 2005; Young et al. 2005), and the extent to which both adults in the relationship are responsible for initiating violence: where possible this must include information from both parties;
- The nature of the risk posed, based on a consideration of a full range of static and dynamic risk factors as they are deemed to be relevant to each individual which is also informed by both parties;
- A full assessment of the antecedent history for both parties to determine the extent to which such antecedents have a functional relationship with the behaviour;
- Clinical assessments of substance use and personality disorder traits where such features are considered relevant.

This level of information will enable the identification of criminogenic needs for each individual case as well as issues concerning responsivity, which can then inform decisions regarding the availability of appropriate programmes or the requirement for specialist services or programme development. As a result, if the victimization of children is an issue, for example, then appropriately focused systemic treatments may be offered (if deemed to be suitable to the individual case). This would be a stark improvement on the current practice of including a tacit examination of the potential risk to children posed by men who are violent to female partners for all IPV perpetrators, regardless of whether they have children or not (see Chapter 6). The resulting information could then also be systematically collated by agencies and, in liaison with academic partners, this information could be examined in order to inform and develop an evidence base of the characteristics and needs of individuals and/or families who present with IPV-related problems. This would ultimately lead to a greater evidence-based understanding of the nature of IPV within court-mandated samples. Such knowledge could then be used to identify or develop alternative, appropriate treatment models, and modify existing theoretical frameworks. In order for this to happen, however, we need to move away from the ideologically based definition of IPV, so that practitioners can be allowed to ask about women's use of violence, abuse and control in a relationship, rather than assuming that this is not a relevant issue for court-mandated male clients. This would further require that ideologically based programme standards and accreditation criteria are removed so that practitioners can develop and implement alternative models. As Gelles (2001) notes,

> Standardizing treatment programs before we know what works, for which men, under what circumstances, limits and eliminates the development of novel or innovative approaches to treating violent and abusive men. (p. 18)

The Future of Programme Development: What are the Alternatives?

Despite the dominance of the pro-feminist treatment model for IPV rehabilitation programmes, and the focus given to this within this volume, a number of alternative approaches have more recently been publicized within the academic literature, by academics and practitioners who are frustrated by the emphasis on standardized practice. Of particular relevance are two publications, a special issue of the *Journal of Aggression, Maltreatment and Trauma* (2003, Vol. 7, No. 1/2), and a more recent book edited by Peter Lehmann and Catherine Simmons (2009a). In the former, Dutton and Sonkin (2003) identify three main treatment factors for male IPV perpetrators that have been neglected, which focus on traits associated with borderline personality disorder, primarily shame and attachment insecurity. These will now be briefly described.

Wallace and Nosko (2003) detail an intervention which focuses on the links between anger and shame through an affect theory approach. The IPV perpetrators for whom such an approach may be deemed suitable are those for whom anger and shame are linked. Such individuals are likely to have features consistent with borderline personality disorder. It is argued that such individuals have 'an unstable sense of self, masked dependency, intense and unstable relationships, and intense anger, demandingness and impulsivity' (p. 53). They are also deemed to have a 'shame-based personality' (p. 53) in which the experience of their self as defective is masked in a defensive script. The logic continues that shame and anger are co-assembled and linked to cognitive scripts, which regulate assumptions about the insecure and unpredictable nature of intimate relationships. Consequently, anger and violence become ways of ensuring that the partner does not leave, much in the same way that anger within attachment theory serves to discourage the attachment figure from leaving (Bowlby, 1988). Shame is, therefore, conceptualized as being central to the fear of abandonment. The therapeutic aim of the group approach outlined is to increase the individual's ability to cope with feelings of shame in a manner that reduces the angry affective response to these feelings, and without activating the defensive scripts. To this end, the programme combines shame inducement with cognitive behavioural interventions, such as cognitive restructuring and anger management skills training.

Sonkin and Dutton (2003) provide a rationale for the use of attachment psychotherapy with IPV perpetrators. The main tenets of attachment theory are explained in Chapter 3. Attachment therapy requires that the therapist takes on the role of surrogate mother figure with a view to encouraging the client to explore the world using the therapist as a 'secure base'. Framed within attachment theory, treatment is typically based on an individual rather than group approach. According to Bowlby (1988), there are five tasks that are central to therapeutic work from an attachment perspective. These include: creating a 'secure base' from which the client can explore thoughts, feelings and experiences regarding self and attachment figures; exploration of relationships with current attachment figures; exploring the relationship with the therapist as an attachment figure; exploring the relationship between early attachment experiences, and finding ways to regulate attachment anxiety when threat of abandonment is perceived.

The observed attachment heterogeneity within IPV perpetrator samples leads to hypotheses regarding the interactional style that these individuals may exhibit within a therapeutic setting. For example, Dutton and Sonkin (2003) propose that IPV men with an avoidant style fluctuate between being emotionally distant to being critical and controlling. In contrast, those with a preoccupied attachment style aim to please others in order to receive positive feedback, and aside from exhibiting extreme anger and clinginess when experiencing loss anxiety, will present as extremely self-controlled. Finally, IPV men with a fearful or disorganized attachment style may present with features of individuals with both avoidant and preoccupied styles, which do not represent a coherent pattern of responding to perceived abandonment. Consequently, the therapist has to be attuned to the individual strategies employed and interpret them in light of these styles. The ability to do so proficiently is theorized as leading the IPV perpetrator to modify their internal working models of relationships.

Finally, Waltz (2003), in the same volume, examines the principles underlying the use of dialectical behaviour therapy (DBT) with male IPV perpetrators who have borderline personality disorder (BPD). Originally developed as an intervention for chronically suicidal and self-harming individuals, DBT was then used to treat women with BPD. Given the heterogeneity of psychopathology within populations of IPV men, and the literature documenting the prevalence of BPD traits in approximately one quarter of court-mandated perpetrators, it is not surprising that the potential of DBT for intervening with this subgroup of IPV perpetrators has been examined. However, at the time of writing, Waltz noted that no outcome studies were available to validate this approach with IPV men. Several clinical features of IPV perpetrator samples are well suited to DBT. These include: excessive anger responses, multi-problem presentation (including alcohol/substance use and other Axis 1 disorders such as depression); life-threatening behaviour; poor compliance, and drop-out.

DBT is based on a biosocial theory of BPD (Linehan, 1993, cited in Waltz, 2003) which specifies that BPD results from the interaction between biologically based emotion dysregulation and an 'invalidating environment'. Within this framework, four components are proposed. The first is that BPD patients are more sensitive to emotive experiences. Second, the BPD patient has very intense emotional responses. Third, the BPD patient finds regulating an emotion, once triggered, very difficult; and finally, the individual experiences the triggered emotion for a considerably longer period of time that an individual without BPD. The invalidating context is deemed to arise during childhood and although it can take many forms, the central features are that the child is not treated as worthy, but the family communicate that the child is unimportant, crazy or unworthy and that feelings and emotions should not be responded to as they are not important.

Standard DBT typically incorporates both group and individual intervention. Group interventions are used to address behavioural skills deficits, and this represents the first function of DBT. The second assumption is that barriers to successfully using the new skills exist, and these barriers (e.g. motivation, emotions and relationships) are, therefore, explored during individual therapy sessions. In between individual and/or group sessions, additional support is offered through phone contact with clients or homework assignments in order to help them generalize the new skills to real world situations, difficulties with which form the third assumption. The treatment targets are examined in a specific hierarchical order and include:

1 suicidal and other life-threatening behaviours;
2 therapy-interfering behaviours;
3 quality of life interfering behaviours;
4 increasing skills.

The therapeutic aims of this approach focus on change and acceptance. Change-based interventions focus on eliciting, teaching and developing new behaviours; whereas acceptance interventions focus on accepting reality as it is, the acknowledgement of reality, and the validation of the client (p. 91). The edited volume also details interventions for couples, lesbian women, Aboriginal men, and violent women, indicating the range of treatment approaches being developed.

In their edited book, *Strengths-based Batterer intervention*, Lehmann and Simmons (2009a) bring together a number of authors who write from the position that, given the current knowledge and evidence base which typically adopts a deficit model of intervention whereby individual IPV perpetrators are thought of as being deficient in skills and aptitudes relevant to their use of violence, it might prove beneficial to focus on the strengths (talents, knowledge, capacities and resources) that individuals have instead. Consequently, interventions cast from this perspective place a greater emphasis on identifying the positive attributes of individuals (Lehmann & Simmons, 2009b, p. 26) and are forged from ideologies and processes that aid client led and directed change; and are fair and respectful of individual differences (Simmons & Lehmann, 2009). This volume is important as it marks a potential paradigm shift in terms of our thinking regarding the basic philosophy of intervention to take with IPV perpetrators, although the efficacy of the approaches described within the volume is yet to be established. Of particular interest are chapters detailing the potential benefits of solution focused approaches (Lee, et al., 2009), narrative therapy (Augusta-Scott, 2009), and the 'Good lives' model (Langlands, Ward & Gilchrist, 2009), which was originally developed for the treatment of sexual offenders.

According to Lee et al. (2009), taking a solution focused approach to IPV emphasizes a focus on the times during which clients are successful in refraining from using violence and making these experiences more readily accessible to them in order to learn what factors contribute to success. Solutions are identified as goals, and each individual is made accountable for their solutions rather than responsible for problems. The identification and definition of a goal is client-led – that is, the individual defines the nature of the changed state they wish to achieve, rather than relying on an externally imposed goal, thereby increasing intrinsic motivation to work towards goal achievement. The emphasis is, consequently, on the present and future and on helping the individual to identify a future that does not contain the problem behaviour. This requires the therapeutic relationship to be collaborative in nature, and draws solutions out of the individual rather than requiring the individual to learn new skills in order to change.

In contrast, the narrative approach described by Augusta-Scott (2009) involves examining the influence of dominant masculinity on the choices and behaviours of men, by engaging in a guided dialogue about the issues through the use of a statement of position map. This approach requires the IPV men to establish their position relative to a particular problem (i.e. masculinity) through defining the problem, identifying the effects of the problem on themselves and others, evaluating these effects as either positive or negative and justifying their evaluation of the problem. Through this guided discourse, the individual develops some insight into the socio-political forces, implicit assumptions and schema that have shaped their behaviour. It therefore seems that this approach might be better suited as the first of a range of interventions for individual clients, which raises their awareness of these issues and may also impact on an individual's empathic responding and perspective taking, before engaging with additional interventions that target alternative needs.

Finally, Langlands et al. (2009) explain that the good lives model (GLM) is fundamentally a strengths-based approach which aims to 'equip individuals with the necessary psychological and social conditions and resources to achieve well-being in socially acceptable and personally satisfying ways' (p. 219). It is argued that this approach is a comprehensive theory of offender rehabilitation, which combines the appraisal and management of risk with promoting individual strengths and goals. At the centre of this approach is the 'Good Lives Plan' which incorporates important and valued goals and activities that the individual seeks to achieve in order to lead the life that they have identified as their ultimate goal. These goals are typically referred to as 'goods' and can either be ultimate goals, or minor goals that contribute to the achievement of other 'goods'. As a therapeutic framework, the GLM aims to instil in offenders a range of skills and capacities (attitudes and resources) that are required for them to lead a different life. The underlying assumption regarding offending is that all individuals are goal (goods) seeking, but that offenders either seek goods through offending, or their offending results from the indirect effects of pursuing a basic 'good'. Risk factors or criminogenic needs are, therefore, either omissions or distortions in the internal and external conditions that are required to implement the good lives plan (p. 228). It is explained that, while this approach has not been used with IPV offenders, it has the capacity to increase the motivation of IPV perpetrators even within standard Duluth-informed programmes by including the client-led identification of goods and goals, much like solution-focused approaches, thereby emphasising the individual.

This section has briefly detailed existing and potential alternative models for intervening in IPV, and attests to the diversity of approaches that may be available to practitioners. However, in many cases, the evidence base with regard to their effectiveness is yet to be accumulated, and unless our attitude towards clinical freedom changes, we will continue to endorse an ideologically rather than evidence-based approach to tertiary intervention.

The Future of Evaluation Research

As we have seen, the evaluation literature is replete with arguments regarding whether or not randomized controlled trials lead to the best evaluation outcome appraisals. Objectively, I believe that the answer to this is yes, but in light of the framework presented in Chapter 9, I more firmly believe that we need to move beyond this unitary outcome focus and adopt a more holistic and comprehensive approach to evaluation and yet remain mindful of the practical realities of conducting research within a British corrections context. For example, regardless of how feasible such an approach might be, it is unlikely that the randomized allocation of individuals at the point of sentence to treatment or non-treatment conditions will ever be sanctioned, given the current level of publicity that surrounds IPV cases in the UK. This, therefore, limits the type of design that can be employed to, at best, a quasi-experimental approach. However, as examined in Chapter 7, there are several quasi-experimental designs available. Of particular relevance are those which employ a reflexive control design (Rossi et al., 2008). Such designs require that each individual acts as their own control and, consequently, do not require separate control groups of individuals who are assessed as appropriate but not given the opportunity at the outset to engage in a programme. The strongest reflexive control design is the time series which requires multiple assessments over time, and could include assessment at referral, repeated assessments at set fixed time points prior to attending a programme, directly before and after attending a programme, and then at set multiple time points after completing the programme. Particularly where programmes are aiming to address psychological criminogenic needs, a reflexive design would enable evaluators to determine whether periods of 'probation as normal' have any impact on these needs or, conversely, the stability of these traits, and whether 'probation with programme' has the expected greater impact.

When it comes to assessing impact, the outcome measures employed need to be diversified so that the focus does not simply remain on 'reoffending' but examines within-treatment change plus associations between the two. More sensitive measures are needed where impact is concerned, as it is not currently feasible to use reconviction data for IPV offending in the UK. While these are also biased to a greater or lesser degree, it seems that the emphasis has been placed on obtaining self- or partner-reports using itemized lists of behaviours, and that evaluation science has neglected to embrace more naturalistic and possibly ecologically valid measures that can be found in the international literature. For example, given that interventions as they are tend to focus on the social cognitive precursors of IPV, it would make more sense to examine such precursors within the context of ecologically valid scenarios. Such methods might, for example, include implicit association tests (Greenwald, McGhee & Schwartz, 1998), think aloud paradigms (Davison, Robins & Johnson, 1983), and perhaps controversially dyadic interaction assessments (cf. Holtzworth-Munroe & Hutchinson, 1993). Each of these forms of test have precedents in the literature, and whilst it is acknowledged that the implementation of these approaches requires expertise, if criminal justice and academic organizations worked more closely together such tests could be designed, validated and developed to be used as part of a coherent approach to evaluation.

Remaining focused on impact, evaluations would benefit from a time-based examination of violent/abusive incidents in order to more clearly determine whether the alleged outcome reflects the assumed recidivism, or alternatively relapse following successful behavioural change. Given the consistent findings that the majority of alleged/actual reoffending occurs during the period of intervention (Gondolf, 2002), it seems plausible that a substantial proportion of 'recidivists' might actually have relapsed instead. The consequences for conclusions regarding programme effectiveness are quite stark if these data are reinterpreted. As Murphy and Eckhardt (2005) note, relapse is suggestive of intervention which was at least partially effective, but which was insufficient to maintain positive change. In contrast, recidivism indicates treatment failure, that is, the inability of a programme to instil any form of positive change in the first place. In the former instance it might be that an increase in programme intensity or duration might elicit more positive results. In the latter, it is unlikely that any modification to current programme content will elicit any form of positive change. Therefore, in order to ensure that we minimize the risk of making a type II error when reaching conclusions about programme effectiveness, a much more subtle and nuanced idiographic approach to evaluation is required.

Aside from impact, evaluations need to objectively assess the validity of programme theory by determining the extent to which changes in theorized treatment targets are associated with behavioural change. Again, through adopting an idiographic approach in which the clinical significance of change is determined and correlated with behavioural outcome measures this might be possible (Hanson & Wallace-Capretta,

2000). What this approach requires if a self-report methodology is relied upon, are psychometric tests with adequate non-offender and offender norms. It is interesting to note that although IPV offenders who are engaged with accredited programmes are routinely required to complete psychometrics, no British non-offender normative data are currently available for any of the measures. This is something currently being addressed by myself and my colleague Dr Sarah Brown in conjunction with the Ministry of Justice.

Finally, as mentioned in Chapter 7, the vast majority of IPV programmes within the criminal justice system are tied to additional services. Consequently, evaluations would benefit from trying to determine the extent to which the programme is the active ingredient in successful change, or whether it is the system of which it is part that is most important (Gondolf, 2002; Hamberger, 2008)

Does the Future Lie in Tertiary Interventions?

A report written by a Home Affairs Select Committee in 2008 identified a number of concerns with the current provision of court-mandated programmes for IPV perpetrators. These included the lack of systematic evaluation evidence regarding their effectiveness. More pressing concerns identified by witnesses to the report, however, included the lack of programmes being offered within the probation service, and excessive waiting lists. In some areas waiting lists had been shut, resulting in magistrates being unable to even make referrals to programmes, whereas in other areas waiting lists were so excessive that they exceeded the length of some community rehabilitation orders, which meant that suitable offenders did not have the opportunity to attend before the end of their sentence. Probation areas specifically identified IPV programmes as a specific area in which they were unable to deliver. In addition, the lack of sustainable future funding available to probation programmes poses a direct threat to IPV intervention capacity. Indeed, this is something that was consistently identified as the major threat to the continuation of services by eight probation areas that I have recently surveyed (Bowen, submitted). Although these programmes form a core component of the official response to IPV, it must be remembered that as evidenced in Chapter 2, the likelihood of an individual who uses violence being arrested, prosecuted and referred to a programme is remote, even after the overhaul of policy across the criminal justice sector (Hester, 2006). Consequently, perpetrator programmes provided within the probation service will possibly only ever meet the needs of a very small proportion of individuals who have been convicted for IPV and for whom the behaviour is well entrenched, even if highly effective models are identified. The needs of undetected IPV perpetrators will remain unaddressed.

So, what other approaches need to be considered in order to ultimately reduce the prevalence of IPV and reduce further the number of adults who require tertiary-level interventions? According to the same HASC report, an emphasis needs to be placed on primary intervention – that is, population-level intervention which aims to prevent IPV before it has emerged. Indeed, there is growing consensus in the international literature that this is a much needed move (Whittaker, Morrison, Lindquist et al., 2006). Such a shift of focus to prevention forms one third of the British Government's *Together we can end Violence against Women and Girls* cross-government strategy that was launched in May 2009 (HM Government, 2009). The strategy emphasizes the importance of raising public awareness through media campaigns, school policies to reinforce the message that violence against women and girls is not acceptable, and secondary interventions aimed at identifying those at high risk, through parenting and family projects. It is of concern that this campaign remains focused on an ideological understanding of IPV. We will have to see what impact this policy has in the long term. At the time of writing, Britain is in the midst of the worst recession for three decades, and has a coalition government that has made dramatic changes to policy in a number of areas withints first four months in power. It is impossible, therefore, to know whether the future will be characterized by ongoing positive policy change in this area.

In conclusion, while there has been some change in terms of the shape of the official response to IPV in the UK and internationally during the last four decades. At a policy level at least, the development and provision of tertiary intervention programmes for IPV perpetrators within the criminal justice system has stagnated, owing to an over-reliance on an ideological rather than evidence-based approach. Consequently, there is much needed in terms of alternative programme development, and the evaluation of existing approaches which do not prescribe to the intervention model that is currently in vogue. However, owing to the current methodological limitations of published evaluations and an emphasis on outcomes at the expense of process, and understanding the links between the two, progress is also required in this field in order to ensure that we move closer to understanding what works, for whom and under what circumstances. Alongside this however, attention must be focused on reshaping the public view and understanding of violence within intimate relationships from childhood to ensure that, over time, fewer individuals require tertiary interventions at all, regardless of their gender or sexuality.

References

ACPO (2008). *Tackling Perpetrators of Violence against Women and Girls*. London: ACPO.
ACPO (2009). *Policy for prosecuting cases of domestic violence*. London: ACPO.
Adams, D. (1988). Feminist approaches. In P.L. Caesar. & L.K. Hamberger (eds). *Treating men who batter: Theory, practice and programs*. New York: Springer.
Ainsworth, M.D.S. (1991). Attachments and other affectional bonds across the lifecycle. In C.M. Parkes, J. Stevenson-Hinde & P. Marris (eds). *Attachment Across the Lifecycle*. London: Routledge, pp. 3–51.
Ainsworth, M.D.S., Blehar, M.C., Waters, E. & Wall, D. (1978). *Patterns of Attachment: A psychological study of the strange situation*. Hillsdale, HJ: Erlbaum.
American Psychiatric Association (APA) (1994). *DSM-IV Diagnostic and Statistical Manual of Mental Disorders*. Washington, DC: APA.
American Psychiatric Association (2001). *Treating Borderline Personality Disorder: A quick reference guide*. Arlington, VA: APA.
Anderson, C.A. & Bushman, B.J. (2002). Human aggression. *Annual Review of Psychology*, 53, 27–51.
Anderson, K.L. (1997). Gender, status, and domestic violence: An integration of feminist and family violence approaches. *Journal of Marriage and the Family*, 49, 655–69.
Andrews, D.A. (1989). Recidivism is predictable and can be influenced: Using risk assessments to reduce recidivism. *Forum of Correction Research* [online], 1, 11–18 (retrieved from www.csc-scc.gc.ca/tet/pblct/forum/e012/12j_e.pdf).
Andrews, D.A. & Bonta, J. (1994). *The Psychology of Criminal Conduct*. Cincinnatti, OH: Anderson Publishing Company.
Andrews, D.A. & Bonta, J. (2006). *The Psychology of Criminal Conduct* (4th edn).

Andrews, D. A., Bonta, J. & Hoge, R.D. (1990). Classification for effective rehabilitation: Rediscovering psychology. *Criminal Justice and Behaviour*, 17, 19–52.

Andrews, D.A., Bonta, J. & Wormwith, S.J. (2006). The recent past and near future of risk and/or needs assessment. *Crime & Delinquency*, 52, 7–27.

Andrews, D.A. & Dowden, C. (2005). Managing correctional treatment for reduced recidivism: A meta-analytic review of programme integrity. *Legal and Criminological Psychology*, 10, 173–87.

Andrews, D.A., Zinger, I., Hoge, R.D., Bonta, J., Gendreau, P. & Cullen, F.T. (1990). Does correctional treatment work? A psychologically informed meta-analysis. *Criminology*, 28, 369–404.

Antonowicz, D.H. & Ross, R.R. (1994). Essential components of successful rehabilitation programs for offenders. *International Journal of Offender Therapy and Comparative Criminology*, 38, 97–104.

Appel, A.E. & Holden, G.W. (1998). The co-occurrence of spouse and physical child abuse: A review and appraisal. *Journal of Family Psychology*, 12, 578–99.

Applegate, R.J. (2006). Changing local policy and practice towards the policing of domestic violence in England and Wales. *Policing: An International Journal of Police Strategies and Management*, 29, 368–83.

Apsler, R., Cummins, M. & Carl, S. (2002). Fear and expectations: Differences among female victims of domestic violence who come to the attention of the police. *Violence and Victims*, 17, 445–53.

Archer, J. (1999). An assessment of the conflict tactics scales: A meta-analytic review. *Journal of Interpersonal Violence*, 14, 1263–89.

Archer, J. (2000). Se differences in aggression between heteroseual partners: A meta-analytic review. *Psychological Bulletin*, 126, 651–80.

Archer, J. (2006). Cross-cultural differences in aggression between partners: A social-role analysis. *Personality and Social Psychology Bulletin*, 10, 133–53.

Archer, J. & Graham-Kevan, N. (2003). Do beliefs about aggression predict physical aggression to partners? *Aggressive Behavior*, 29, 41–54.

Archer, J. & Haigh, A.M. (1997). Do beliefs about aggressive feelings and actions predict reported levels of aggression? *British Journal of Social Psychology*, 36, 83–105.

Arias, I. & Beach, S.R.H. (1987). Validity of self reports of marital violence. *Journal of Family Violence*, 2, 139–49.

Arias, I. & Johnson, P. (1989). Evaluations of physical aggression among intimate dyads. *Journal of Interpersonal Violence*, 4, 298–307.

Augusta-Scott, T. (2009). Narrative therapy: addressing masculinity in conversations with men who perpetrate violence. In P. Lehman & C.A. Simmons (eds) Strengths based batterer intervention, New York: Springer Publishing, pp. 113–36.

Austin, J.B. & Dankwort, J. (1999). State standards for batterer programs: A review and analysis. *Journal of Interpersonal Violence*, 14, 152–68.

Averill, J. (1982). *Anger and Aggression: An essay on emotion*. Berlin: Springer.

Babcock, J.C., Green, C.E. & Robie, C. (2004). Does batterers' treatment work? A meta-analytic review of domestic violence treatment. *Clinical Psychology Review*, 23, 1023–53.

Babcock, J.C., Green, C.E. & Webb, S.A. (2008). Decoding Deficits of Different Types of Batterers During Presentation of Facial Affect Slides. *Journal of Family Violence*, 23, 295–302.

Babcock, J.C., Jacobson, N.S., Gottman, J.M. & Yerington, T.P. (2000). Attachment, emotion regulation and the function of marital violence: Differences between secure, preoccupied and dismissing violent and non-violent husbands. *Journal of Family Violence*, 15, 391–409.

Babcock, J.C. & Steiner, R. (1999). The relationship between treatment, incarceration and recidivism of battering: A programmes evaluation of Seattle's co-ordinated community response to domestic violence. *Journal of Family Psychology*, 13, 46–59.

Babcock, J.C., Waltz, J., Jacobson, N.S. & Gottman, J.M. (1993). Power and violence: the relation between communication patters, power discrepancies, and domestic violence. *Journal of Consulting and Clinical Psychology*, 61, 40–50.

Baldry, A.C. (2003). 'Sticks and stones hurt my bones but his glance and words hurt more': The impact of psychological abuse and physical violence by current and former partners on battered women in Italy. *International Journal of Forensic Mental Health*, 2, 47–57.

Bancroft, L. & Silverman, J.G. (2002). *The batterer as parent: Addressing the impact of domestic violence on family dynamics*. Thousand Oaks, CA: Sage.

Bandura, A. (1977). *Social learning theory*. Oford: Prentice-Hall.

Barbaree, H.E. (1991). Denial and minimization among se offenders: assessment and treatment outcome. *Forum on Corrections Research*, 3, 30–3.

Baron, L. & Straus, M.A. (1989). *Four theories of Rape in American Society: A state-level analysis*. New Haven, CT: Yale University Press.

Bartholomew, K. & Horowitz, L.M. (1991). Attachment styles among young adults: A test of a four category model. *Journal of Personality and Social Psychology*, 61, 226–44.

Batson, D. (2009). These things called empathy: Eight related but distinct phenomena. In J. Decety. & W. Ickes (eds) *The Social Neuroscience of Empathy*. Cambridge, MA: The MIT Press.

Baum, F., Brand, R., Colley, D. & Cooke, R. (1987) Preventing family violence: The evaluation of a group of men who are violent towards their partners. *Australian Journal of Sex, Marriage & Family*, 8, 173–83.

Beck, A.T. & Freeman, A.F. (1990). *Cognitive Therapy of Personality Disorders*. New York: Guildford.

Bednar, R.L. & Kaul, T.J. (1978). Experiential group research. In S. L. Garfield & A. E. Bergin (Eds). *Handbook of Psychotherapy and Behaviour Change* (2nd edn). Chichester: John Wiley & Sons.

Beech, A.R., Fisher, D. & Beckett, R.C. (1999). *An evaluation of the prison sex offender treatment programme* (UK Home Office Occasional Report). London: Home Office.

Beech, A. & Fordham, A.S. (1997). Therapeutic climate of seual offender treatment programs. *Seual Abuse: A Journal of Research and Treatment*, 9, 219–37.

Bell, K.M. & Naugle, A.E. (2008). Intimate partner violence theoretical considerations: Moving towards a contextual framework. *Clinical Psychology Review*, 28, 1096–107.

Beninati, J. (1989). Pilot project for male batterers. *Social Work with Groups*, 12, 63–74.

Bennett, L., Goodman, L. & Dutton, M.A. (1999). Systemic obstacles to the criminal prosecution of a battering parter. *Journal of Interpersonal Violence*, 14, 761–72.

Bennett Cattaneo, L., Bell, M.E., Goodman, L. & Dutton, M.A. (2007). Intimate partner violence victims' accuracy in assessing their risk of re-abuse. *Journal of Family Violence*, 22, 249–440.

Bennett Cattaneo, L. & Goodman, L. (2003). Victim reported risk factors for continued abusive behaviour: Assessing the dangerousness of arrested batterers. *Journal of Community Psychology*, 31, 349–69.

Berk, A. (2005). Randomized experiments as the bronze standard. *Journal of Experimental Criminology*, 1, 416–33.

Berk, S.F. & Loseke, D.R. (1981). 'Handling' family violence: Situational determinants of police arrest in domestic disturbances. *Law and Society Review*, 15, 317–46.

Berkowitz, L. (1993). *Aggression*. Boston: McGraw-Hill.

Bern, E.H. & Bern, L.L. (1984). A group program for men who commit violence towards their wives. *Social Work with Groups*, 7, 63–77.

Bilby, C. & Hatcher, R. (2004). Early stages in the development of the Integrated Domestic Abuse Programme: Implementing the Duluth domestic violence pathfinder. *Home Office online Report 29/04*. London: Home Office.

Bloch, S. & Crouch, E. (1985). *Therapeutic Factors in Group Psychotherapy*. Oford: Oford University Press.

Bograd, M. (1988). Feminist perspectives on wife abuse: An introduction. In K. Yllo & M. Bograd (eds) *Feminist Perspectives on Wife Abuse*. Thousand Oaks, CA: Sage (pp. 11–27).

Book, A.S., Starzyk, K.B. & Quinsey, V.L. (2001). The relationship between testosterone and aggression: a meta-analysis. *Aggression and Violent Behavior*, 6, 579–99.

Boruch, R.F., Victor, T. & Cecil, J.S. (2000). Resolving ethical and legal problems in randomized eperiments. *Crime & Delinquency*, 46, 330–53.

Bouffard, L.A., Wright, K.A., Muftic, L.R. & Bouffard, J.A. (2008). Gender differences in specialization in intimate partner violence: Comparing the gender symmetry and violent resistance perspectives. *Justice Quarterly*, 25, 570–94.

Bowen, E. (2004). 'Evaluation of a community-based rehabilitation programme for male domestic violence perpetrators'. University of Birmingham: Unpublished PhD thesis.

Bowen, E. (2010). Therapeutic environment and outcomes in a UK domestic violence perpetrator programme. Small group research, in press.

Bowen, E., Brown, L. & Gilchrist, E.A. (2002). Evaluating probation based offender programmes for domestic violence perpetrators: A pro-feminist approach. *The Howard Journal of Criminal Justice*, 41, 221–36.

Bowen, E. & Gilchrist, E. (2004a). Do court- and self-referred domestic violence offenders have the same characteristics? Comparisons of anger, locus of control and motivation to change. *Legal and Criminological Psychology*, 9, 279–94.

Bowen, E. & Gilchrist, E.A. (2004b). Comprehensive evaluation: a holistic approach to evaluating domestic violence perpetrator programs. *International Journal of Offender Therapy and Comparative Criminology*, 48, 215–34.

Bowen, E. & Gilchrist, E.A. (2006). Predicting drop out of court mandated treatment in a British sample of domestic violence offenders. *Psychology, Crime and Law*, 12, 453–573.

Bowen, E., Gilchrist, E.A. & Beech, A.R. (2005). An examination of the impact of community-based rehabilitation on the offending behaviour of male domestic violence offenders and the characteristics associated with recidivism. *Legal and Criminological Psychology*, 10, 189–209.

Bowen, E., Gilchrist, E.A. & Beech, A.R. (2008). Change in treatment has no relationship to subsequent reoffending in UK domestic violence sample: A preliminary study. *International Journal of Offender Therapy and Comparative Criminology*, 52, 598–614.

Bowlby, J. (1958). The nature of the child's tie to his mother. *International Journal of Psycho-Analysis*, I, 1–23.

Bowlby, J. (1980). *Attachment and loss, Vol. 3: Loss*. London: Pimlico.

Bowlby, J. (1984). Violence in the family as a disorder of the attachment and caregiving systems. *American Journal of Psychoanalysis*, 44, 9–27.

Bowlby, J. (1988). *A Secure Base: Parent–child attachment and healthy human development*. New York: Basic Books.

Bradbury, T.N. & Findham, F.D. (1990) Attributions in marriage. *Psychological Bulletin*, 107, 3–33.

Brady, S.S. (2008). Lifetime family violence eposure is associated with current symptoms of eating disorders among both young men and women. *Journal of Traumatic Stress*, 21, 347–51.

Brody, S.R. (1976). The effectiveness of sentencing: A review of the literature. *Home Office Research Study 35*. London: Home Office.

Bronfenbrenner, U. (1979). *The Ecology of Human Development: Eperiments by nature and design*. Cambridge, MA: Harvard University Press.

Brown, S. (2005). *An Introduction to Sex Offender Treatment Programmes*. Cullompton, UK: Willan Publishing.

Budd, T., Mattinson, J. & Myhill, A. (2000). *The Etent and Nature of Stalking: Findings from the 1998 British Crime Survey*. London.

Burlingame, G.M. & Fuhriman, A. (1990).Time limited group therapy. *The Counselling Psychologist*, 18, 93–118.

Burton, M. (2008). *Legal Responses to Domestic Violence*. London: Routledge-Cavendish.

Burton, S., Regan, L. & Kelly, L. (1989). *Supporting Women and Changing Men: Lessons from the Domestic violence Intervention Project*. York: Joseph Rowntree.

Buzawa, E.S. & Austin, T. (1993). Determining police response to domestic violence victims: the role of victim preference. *American Behavioral Scientist*, 36, 610–23.

Buzawa, E.S. & Buzawa, C.G. (2003). *Domestic Violence: The criminal justice response*. (3rd edn).Thousand Oaks, CA: Sage.

Buzawa, E.S. & Buzawa, C.G. (1993). Opening the doors: The changing police response to domesti violence. In R.G. Dunham & G.P. Alpert (eds), *Critical Issues in Policing*. Prospect Heights, IL: Waveland, pp. 551–67.

Buzawa, E. & Hotaling, G. (2000). *An Eamination of Assaults within the Jurisdiction of Orange District Court: Final Report*. Washington, DC.

Cadsky, O., Hanson, R.K., Crawford, M. & Lalonde, C. (1996). Attrition from a male batterer treatment program: Client treatment congruence and lifestyle instability. *Violence and Victims*, 11, 51–61.

Caetano, R., Field, C.A., Ramisetty-Mikler, S. & McGrath, C. (2005). The 5-year course of intimate partner violence among White, Black and Hispanic couples in the United States. *Journal of Interpersonal Violence*, 20, 1039–57.

Cahn, D.D. & Lloyd, S.A. (1996). *Family violence from a communication perspective*. Thousand Oaks, CA: Sage.

Campbell, J.C. (2002). Health consequences of intimate partner violence. *The Lancet*, 359 (9314), 1331–6.

Campbell, J.C. (1992). 'If I can't have you no one can': Power and control in homicide of female partners. In J. Radford & D.E.H. Russell (eds) *Femicide: The politics of women killing*. New York: Twayne, pp. 99–113.

Campbell, J.C., Webster, D., Koziol-McLain, J., Block, C., Campbell, D., Curry, M.A. et al. (2003). Risk factors for femicide in abusive relationships: Results from a multi-site case control study. *American Journal of Public Health*, 93, 1089–97.

Capaldi, D.M. & Clark, S. (1998). Prospective family predictors of aggression toward female partners for at-risk young men. *Developmental Psychology*, 37, 61–73.

Capaldi, D.M. & Owen, L.D. (2001). Physical aggression in a community sample of at-risk young couples: Gender comparisons for high frequency, injury and fear. *Journal of Family Psychology*, 15, 425–40.

Chambers, A.L. & Wilson, M.N. (2007). Assessing male batterers with the Personality Assessment Inventory. *Journal of Personality Assessment*, 88, 57–65.

Chase, K.A., O'Leary, K.D. & Heyman, R.E. (2001). Categorizing partner-violent ment within the reactive-proactive typology model. *Journal of Consulting and Clinical Psychology*, 69, 567–72.

Chambless, D.L. & Hollon, S.P. (1998). Defining empirically supported therapies. *Journal of Consulting and Clinical Psychology*, 66, 7–18.

Chen, H.T. (1990). *Theory Driven Evaluations*. Newbury Park: Sage.

Chen, H., Bersani, C., Myers, S.C. & Denton, R. (1989). Evaluating the effectiveness of a court sponsored abuser treatment programme. *Journal of Family Violence*, 4, 309–22.

Chermack, S.T. & Taylor, S.P. (1995). Alcohol and human physical aggression: Pharmacological versus epectancy effects. *Journal of Studies on Alcohol*, 56, 449–456.

Clements, K., Holtzworth-Munroe, A., Schweinle, W. & Ickes, W. (2007). Empathic accuracy of intimate partners in violent versus nonviolent relationships. *Personal Relationships*, 14, 369–88.

Choice, P., Lamke, L.K. & Pitman, J.F. (1995). Conflict resolution strategies and marital distress as mediating factors in the link between witnessing interparental violence and wife battering. *Violence and Victims*, 10, 107–19.

Cohen, J. (1988). *Statistical power analysis for the behavioral sciences* (2nd edn). Hillsdale, NJ: Erlbaum.

Coker, A.L., Smith, P.H., Bethea, L., King, M.R. & McKeown, R.E. (2000). Physical health consequences of physical and psychological intimate partner violence. *Archives of Family Medicine*, 9, 451–7.

Coleman, D. & Straus, M.A. (1986). Marital power, marital conflict and violence in a nationally representative sample of Americans. *Violence and Victims*, 1, 141–57.

Cook, D., Burton, M., Robinson, A. & Vallely, C. (2004). *Evaluation of Specialist Domestic Violence Courts/Fast Track Systems*. London: CPS/DCA.

Cook, T.D. & Shadish, W.R. (1994). Social eperiments: Some developments over the past fifteen years. *Annual Review of Psychology*, 45, 545–80.

Cooke, D.J. & Philip, L. (2001). To treat or not to treat? An empirical perspective. In C.R. Hollin (ed.) *Handbook of Offender Assessment and Treatment*. Chichester, UK: Wiley.

Cordray, D.S. (2000). Enhancing the scope of eperimental enquiry in intervention studies. *Crime & Delinquency*, 46, 401–24.

Cordova, J.Y., Jacobson, N.S., Gottman, J.M., Rushe, R. & Co, G. (1993). Negative reciprocity and communication in couples with a violent husband. *Journal of Abnormal Psychology*, 102, 559–64.

Corey, M.S. & Corey, G. (1997). *Groups: Process and Practice* (5th edn). Pacific Grove, CA: Brooks/Cole.

Correctional Services Canada (2009). Family Violence prevention programs. Available from: www.csc-scc.gc.ca/tet/prgrm/cor-pro-2009-eng.shtm (accessed 12 March 2010).

Corsini, P.J. & Rosenberg, B. (1955). Mechanisms of group psychotherapy: processes and dynamics. *Journal of Abnormal and Social Psychology*, 51, 401–11.

Corvo, K. (2006). Violence, separation and loss in the families of domestically violent men. *Journal of Family Violence*, 21, 117–25.

Covell, C.N., Huss, M.T. & Langhinrichsen-Rohling, J. (2007). Empathic deficits among male batterers: A multidimensional approach. *Journal of Family Violence*, 22, 165–74.

CPSI (1998) *Inspectorates report on cases involving domestic violence*. London: CPSI.

CPSI (2005a). *CPS Domestic Violence Good Practice Guidance*. London: CPS.

CPSI (2005b). *Domestic Violence Policy for Prosecuting cases of Domestic Violence*. London: CPS.

Craig, A.R., Franklin, J.A. & Andrew, G. (1984). A scale to measure locus of control of behaviour. *British Journal of Medical Psychology*, 57, 173–80.

Cretney, A. & Davis, G. (1997). Prosecuting domestic assaults: Victims failing courts or courts failing victims? *The Howard Journal*, 36, 146–57.

Critchlow, B. (1983). Blaming the booze: The attribution of responsibility for drunken behavior. *Personality and Social Psychology Bulletin*, 9, 451–73.

Crow, I. (2001). *The Treatment and Rehabilitation of Offenders*. London: Sage.

Cunningham, A., Jaffe, P.C., Baker, L., Dick, T., Malla, S., Mazaheri, N. et al. (1998). *Theory-derived Eplanations of Male Violence against Female Partners: Literature update and related implications for treatment and evaluation*. London: London Family Court Clinic.

Daly, J.E. & Pelowski, S. (1999). Predictors of dropout among men who batter: A review of studies with implications for research and practice. *Violence and Victims*, 15, 137–60.

Dane, A.V. & Schneider, B.H. (1998). Programmes integrity in primary and early secondary prevention: Are implementation effects out of control? *Clinical Psychology Review*, 18, 23–45.

Dankoski, M.E., Kelley, M.K., Thomas, V., Choice, P., Lloyd, S.A. & Seery, B.L. (2006). Affect regulation and the cycle of violence against women: New directions for understanding the process. *Journal of Family Violence*, 21, 327–39.

Daponte, B.O. (2008). *Evaluation Essentials: Methods for conducting sound research*. San Francisco, CA: Jossey-Bass.

Dasgupta, S.D. (1999). Just like men? A critical view of violence by women. In M.F. Shepard & E.L. Pence (eds) *Coordinating community responses to domestic violence: Lessons from Duluth and beyond*. Thousand Oaks, CA: Sage, pp. 95–222.

Davis, M.H. (1980). A multidimensional approach to individual differences in empathy. *Catalog of Selected Documents in Psychology*, 10, 85.

Davis, R., Smith, B. & Taylor, B. (2000). Increasing the proportion of domestic violence arrests that are prosecuted: A natural eperiment in Milwaukee. *Criminology and Public Policy*, 2, 263–82.

Davis, R.C. & Taylor, B.G. (1999). Does batterer treatment reduce violence? A synthesis of the literature. *Women and Criminal Justice*, 10, 69–93.

Davison, G.C. & Neale, J.M. (1997). *Abnormal Psychology* (7th edn). Chichester: John Wiley & Sons.

Davison, G.C., Robins, C. & Johnson, M.K. (1983). Articulated thoughts during simulated situations: A paradigm for studying cognition in emotion and behavior. *Cognitive Therapy & Research*, 7, 17–39.

Dawson, M. & Dinovitzer, R. (2000). Victim cooperation and the prosecution of domestic violence in a specialized court. *Justice Quarterly*, 18, 593–622.

DeHart, D.D., Kennerly, R.J., Burke, L.K. & Follingstadt, D.R. (1999). Predictors of attrition in a treatment programmes for battering men. *Journal of Family Violence*, 14, 19–34.

DeKeseredy, W.S. (2000). Current controversies on defining nonlethal violence against women in intimate heteroseual relationships: Empirical implications. *Violence Against Women*, 6, 728–46.

Delsol, C. & Margolin, G. (2004). The role of family-of-origin violence in men's marital violence perpetration. *Clinical Psychology Review*, 24, 99–122.

DeMaris, A. (1989). Attrition in batterer's counselling: The role of social and demographic factors. *Social Service Review*, 63, 142–53.

DeMaris, A. & Jackson, J.K. (1987). Batterers reports of recidivism after counselling. *Social Casework*, 68, 458–65.

DePaola, L.M., Lambert, L., Martino, T., Anderson, G. & Sutton, S. (1991). Effects of interparental violence on the psychological adjustment and competencies of young children. *Journal of Consulting and Clinical Psychology*, 59, 258–65.

Deschner, J.P. (1984). *The Hitting Habit: Anger control for violent couples.* New York: Free Press/Collier-Macmillan.

Deschner, J.P. & McNeil, J.S. (1986). Lowering the dropout rate in groups for battering couples. Paper presented at the Symposium for the Advancement of Social Work with Groups, Detroit (November).

Dies, R.R. (1985). A multidimensional model for group process research elaboration and critique. *Small Group Behavior*, 16, 427–46.

Dixon, L., Hamilton-Giachritsis, C. & Browne, K. (2008). Classifying partner femicide. *Journal of Interpersonal Violence*, 23, 74–93.

Dobash, R., Cavanagh, K., Dobash, R. & Lewis, R. (2000). Domestic violence programmes: A framework for change. *The Probation Journal*, 47, 18–30.

Dobash, R.E. & Dobash, R.P. (1979). *Violence against Wives: A case against the patriarchy.* New York: Free Press.

Dobash, R.E. & Dobash, R.P. (1990). How theoretical definitions and perspectives affect research and policy. In D.J. Besharov (ed.) *Family Violence: Research and Public Policy Issues.* Washington, DC: AEI Press, pp. 108–29.

Dobash, R.E. & Dobash, R.P. (1992). *Women, Violence and Social Change.* London: Routledge.

Dobash, R.E. & Dobash, R.P. (2000). Evaluating criminal justice interventions for domestic violence. *Crime & Delinquency*, 46, 252–70.

Dobash, R.P. & Dobash, R.E. (2001). Violence against women: A review of recent anglo-american research. *Journal of Conflict and Violence Research*, 3, 5–22.

Dobash, R., Dobash, R.E., Cavanagh, K. & Lewis, R. (1996). *Re-education programmes for violent men: An evaluation.* Home Office Research Findings, 46. London: Home Office Research and Statistics Directorate.

Dobash, R., Dobash, R.E., Cavanagh, K. & Lewis, R. (1999). *Changing Violent Men.* London: Sage.

Dobash, R.P., Dobash, R.E., Cavanagh, K. and Lewis, R. (2000). *Changing Violent Men Thousand Oaks*, CA: Sage

Dobash, R.E., Dobash, R.P., Wilson, M. & Daly, M. (1992). The myth of seual symmetry in marital violence. *Social Problems*, 39, 71–91.

Dodge, K.A., Bates, J.E. & Pettit, G.S. (1990). Mechanism in the cycle of violence. *Science*, 250 (21 December), 1678–83.

Douglas, K.S., Co, D.N. & Webster, C.D. (1999). Violence risk assessment: Science and practice. *Legal and Criminological Psychology*, 4, 149–84.

Douglas, M.A. & Perrin, S. (1987) Recidivism and accuracy of self reported violence and arrest. Paper presented at the Third National conference for Family Violence Research, University of New Hampshire, Durham.

Douglas, K.S. & Kropp, P.R. (2002). A prevention-based paradigm for violence risk assessment: Clinical and research applications. *Criminal Justice and Behavior*, 29, 617–58.

Doyle, M. & Dolan, M. (2008). Understanding and managing risk. In K. Soothill, P. Rogers & M. Dolan (eds). *Handbook of Forensic Mental Health.* Uffculme, Devon, UK: Willan Publishing.

Dunford, F.W. (2000a). Determining program success: The importance of employing eperimental research design. *Crime & Delinquency*, 46, 425–34.

Dunford, F.W. (2000b). The San Diego navy eperiment: An assessment of interventions for men who assault their wives. *Journal of Consulting and Clinical Psychology*, 68, 468–76.

Dutton, D.G. (1985). An ecologically nested theory of male violence towards intimates. *International Journal of Women's Studies*, 8, 404–13.

Dutton, D.G. (1986). The outcome of court-mandated treatment for wife assault: A quasi-eperimental evaluation. *Violence and Victims*, 1, 163–75.

Dutton, D.G. (1995a). Male abusiveness in intimate relationships. *Clinical Psychology Review*, 1, 567–81.

Dutton, D.G. (1995b). *The Domestic Assault of Women*. Vancouver, BC: UBC Press.

Dutton, D.G. (1994). Patriarchy and wife assault: The ecological fallacy. *Violence and Victims*, 9, 167–82.

Dutton, D.G. (1998). *The Abusive Personality*. New York: The Guilford Press.

Dutton, D.G. (1999). Limitations of social learning models in eplaining intimate aggression. In .B. Arriaga & S. Oskamp (eds), *Violence in Intimate Relationships*. Thousand Oaks, CA: Sage, pp. 3–87.

Dutton, D.G., Bodnarchuk, M., Kropp, R., Hart, S.D. & Ogloff, J.P. (1997). Wife assault treatment and criminal recidivism: An 11-year follow up. *International Journal of Offender Therapy and Comparative Criminology*, 41, 9–23.

Dutton, D.G. & Corvo, K. (2006). Transforming a flawed policy: A call to revive psychology and science in domestic violence research and practice. *Aggression and Violent Behavior*, 11, 457–83.

Dutton, D.G. & Corvo, K. (2007). The Duluth model: A data-impervious paradigm and a failed strategy. *Aggression and Violent Behavior*, 12, 658–67.

Dutton, D.G. & Hemphill, K.J. (1992). Patterns of socially desirable responding among perpetrators and victims of wife assault. *Violence and Victims*, 7, 29–40.

Dutton, M.A., Kaltman, S., Goodman, L.A., Weinfurt, K. & Vankos, N. (2005). Patterns of intimate partner violence: Correlates and outcomes. *Violence and Victims*, 20, 483–97.

Dutton, D.G. & Nicholls, T.L. (2005). The gender paradigm in domestic violence research and theory: Part 1 – the conflict of theory and data. *Aggression and Violent Behavior*, 10, 680–714.

Dutton, D.G. & Kropp, P.R. (2000). A review of domestic violence risk instruments. *Trauma, Violence & Abuse*, 1, 171–81.

Dutton, D.G., Saunders, K., Starzomski, A. & Bartholomew, K. (1994). Intimacy-anger and insecure attachment as precursors of abuse in intimate relationships. *Journal of Applied Social Psychology*, 24, 1367–87.

Dutton, D.G. & Sonkin, D. J. (2003). Introduction: Perspectives on the treatment of intimate violence. In D. Dutton & D.J. Sonkin (eds) *Intimate Violence: Contemporary treatment innovations*. New York: The Howarth Maltreatment and Trauma Press, pp. 1–6.

Dutton, D.G. & Starzomski, A.J. (1997). Peronality predictors of the Minnesota Power and Control Wheel. *Journal of Interpersonal Violence*, 12, 70–82.

Dwyer, D.C. (1995). Response to the victims of domestic violence: Analysis and implication of the British eperience. *Crime & Delinquency*, 41, 527–40.

Eaton, L., Kaufman, M., Fuhrel, A., Cain, D., Cherry, C., Pope, H. & Kalichman, S.E (2008). Examining factors co-existing with interpersonal violence in lesbian relationships. *Journal of Family Violence*, 8, 697–705.

Eckhardt, C., Barbour, K.A. & Davison, G.C. (1998). Articulated thoughts of maritally violent and nonviolent men during anger arousal. *Journal of Consulting and Clinical Psychology*, 66, 259–69.

Eckhardt, C., Holtzworth-Munroe, A., Norlander, B., Sibley, A. & Cahill, M. (2008). Readiness to change, partner violence subtypes and treatment outcomes among men in treatment for partner assault. *Violence and Victims*, 23, 446–75.

Eckhardt, C. & Jamison, T.R. (2002). Articulated thoughts of male dating violence perpetrators during anger arousal. *Cognitive Therapy and Research*, 26, 289–308.

Edleson, J.L. & Brygger, M.P. (1986). Gender differences in reporting in reporting of battering incidences. *Family Relations*, 35, 377–82.

Edleson, J.L. & Grusznski, R.J. (1988). Treating men who batter: four years of outcome data from the domestic abuse project. *Journal of Social Service Research*, 12 (1/2), 3–22.

Edleson, J.L. & Syers, M. (1990). Relative effectiveness of group treatments for men who batter. *Social Work Research and Abstracts*, 26, 10–17.

Edleson, J.L. & Tolman, R.M. (1992). *Intervention for Men who Batter: An ecological approach.* Thousand Oaks, CA: Sage.

Edwards, S. (1987). Provoking her own demise: From common assault to homicide. In J. Hanmer & M. Maynard (eds), *Women, Violence and Social Control.* London: Macmillan.

Edwards, S. (2000). *Reducing Violence: What Works? Use of the criminal law.* London: Policing and Reducing Crime Unit Home Office.

Edwards, S.S.M. (1985). Compelling a reluctant spouse: Protection and the prosecution process. *New Law Journal*, 11, 1076–8.

Edwards, S.S.M. (1986). Police attitudes and dispositions in domestic disputes: The London Study. *Police Journal*, 7, 230–41.

Edwards, S.S.M. (1989). *Policing 'Domestic' Violence: Women, the law and the state.* London: Sage.

Ehrensaft, M.K., Cohen, P., Brown, J., Smailes, E., Chen, H. & Johnson, J.G. (2003). Intergenerational transmission of partner violence: A 20-year prospective study. *Journal of Consulting and Clinical Psychology*, 71, 741–53.

Ehrensaft, M.K. & Vivian, D. (1999). Is partner aggression related to appraisals of coercive control by a partner? *Journal of Family Violence*, 14, 251–66.

Eisikovitz, Z.C. & Edelson, J.L. (1989). Intervening with men who batter: A critical review of the literature. *Social Service Review*, 37, 384–414.

Eley, S. (2005). Changing practices: The specialised domestic violence court process. *The Howard Journal of Criminal Justice*, 44, 113–24.

Evans, S.E., Davies, C. & DiLillo, D. (2008). Eposure to domestic violence: A meta-analysis of child and adolescent outcomes. *Aggression and Violent Behavior*, 13, 131–40.

Evans, C.R., Dion, K.L. (1991). Group cohesion and performance: A meta–analysis. *Small Group Research*, 22, 175–86.

Falshaw, L., Friendship, C. & Bates, A. (2003). Seual offenders – measuring reconviction, reoffending and recidivism. *Research Findings* 183. London: Home Office.

Fals-Stewart, W. (2003). The occurrence of partner physical aggression on days of alcohol consumption: A longitudinal diary study. *Journal of Consulting and Clinical Psychology*, 71, 41–52.

Fals-Stewart, W., Golden, J. & Schumacher, J.A. (2003). Intimate partner violence and substance use: A longitudinal day-to-day eamination. *Addictive Behaviors*, 28, 1555–74.

Feazell, C.S., Mayers, R.S. & Deschner, J. (1984). Services for men who batter: Implications for programs and policies. *Family Relations*, 33, 217–23.

Feder, L. (1998). Police handling of domestic and non-domestic assault calls: Is there a case for discrimination? *Crime & Delinquency*, 44, 335–249.

Feder, L. & Dugan, L. (2002). A test of the efficacy of court mandated counselling for domestic violence offenders: The Broward eperiment. *Justice Quarterly*, 18, 171–201.

Feder, L. & Forde, D.R. (2000). *Test of the Efficacy of Court Mandated Counseling for Domestic Violence Offenders: The Broward Eperiment, Eecutive Summary.* Washington: National Institute of Justice.

Feder, L. & Wilson, D.B. (2005). A meta-analytic review of court-mandated batterer intervention programs: Can courts affect abusers' behaviour? *Journal of Eperimental Criminology*, 1, 239–62.

Feeny, J.A. (1999). Adult romantic attachment and couple relationships. In J. Cassidy & P.R. Shaver (eds) *Handbook of attachment: Theory, research and clinical applications*. New York: Guilford, pp. 55–377.

Feldman, C.M. & Ridley, C.A. (2000). The role of conflict-based communication responses and outcomes in male domestic violence toward female partners. *Journal of Social and Personal Relationships*, 17, 552–573.

Ferguson, L.M. (2004). Assessing the correctional services of Canada high intensity family violence prevention programme. Unpublished MA thesis: University of Saskatchewan.

Fergusson, D.M., Boden, J.M. & Horwood, J. (2006). Eamining the intergenerational transmission of violence in a New Zealand cohort. *Child Abuse & Neglect*, 31, 89–108.

Ferraro, K.J. (1989). Policing woman battering. *Social Problems*, 46, 61–74.

Fincham, F.D., Paleari, F.G. & Regalia, C. (2002). Forgiveness in marriage: the role of relationship quality, attributions and empathy. *Personal Relationships*, 9, 27–37.

Finkelhor, D. & Yllo, K. (1985). *License to Rape: Seual abuse of wives*. New York: Free Press.

Flavin, J. (2001) Feminism for the mainstream criminologist: An invitation. *Journal of Criminal Justice*, 29, 271–85.

Follingstad, D.R., Rutledge, L.L., Berg, B.J., Hause, E.S. & Polek, D.S. (1990). The role of emotional abuse in physically abusive relationships. *Journal of Family Violence*, 5, 107–120.

Ford, D.A. (1991). Prosecution as a victim power response: a note on empowering women in violent conjugal relationships. *Law and Society Review*, 25, 313–34.

Ford, D.A. (1993). *The Indianapolis Domestic Violence Project Eperiment* (Final report submitted to the National Institute of Justice). Indianapolis: Indiana University-Purdue University Indianapolis, Department of Sociology.

Ford, D.A. (2003). Coercing victim participation in domestic violence prosecutions. *Journal of Interpersonal Violence*, 18, 669–84.

Fox, B.J. (1993). On violent men and female victims: A comment on DeKeseredy and Kelly. *Canadian Journal of Sociology*, 18, 320–24.

Franchina, J.J., Eisler, R.M. & Moore, T.M. (2001). Masculine gender role stress and intimate abuse: Effects of masculine gender relevance of dating situations and female threat on men's attributions and affective response. *Psychology of Men & Masculinity*, 2, 34–41.

Friendship, C., Beech, A.R. & Browne, K.D. (2002). Reconviction as an outcome measure in research: A brief methodological note. *British Journal of Criminology*, 42, 442–4.

Friendship, C., Falshaw, L. & Beech, A.R. (2003). Measuring the real impact of accredited offending behaviour programmes. *Legal and Criminological Psychology*, 8, 115–28.

Fusco, R.A. & Fantuzzo, J.W. (2009). Domestic violence crimes and children: A population-based investigation of direct sensory eposure and nature of involvement. *Children and Youth Services Review*, 31, 249–56.

Ganley, A. (1981). *Court Mandated Therapy for Men who Batter*. Washington, DC: Center for Women's Policy Studies.

Garcia-Moreno, C., Jansen, H.A.F.M., Ellsberg, M., Heise, L. & Watts, C.H. (2006). Prevalence of intimate partner violence: Findings from the WHO multi-country study on women's health and domestic violence. *The Lancet*, 369, 1260–9.

Garner, J.H. & Mawell, C.D. (2009). Prosecution and conviction rates for intimate partner violence. *Criminal Justice Review*, 34, 44–79.

Garrett, C.J. (1985). Effects of residential treatment on adjudicated delinquents: A meta-analysis. *Journal of Research on Crime and Delinquency*, 22, 287–308.

Geffner, R., Mantooth, C., Franks, D. & Rao, L. (1989). A psychoeducational, conjoint therapy approach to reducing family violence. In: P.L. Caesar and L.K. Hamberger (eds) *Treating Men who Batter: Theory, practice and programs.* New York: Springer, pp. 103–33.

Gelles, R.J. (2000). Estimating the incidence and prevalence of violence against women. *Violence against women*, 6, 784–804.

Gelles, R. (2001). Standards for programs for men who batter? Not yet. In R. Geffner & A. Rosenbaum (eds) *Domestic Violence Offenders: Current interventions, research and implications for policies and standards.* New York: Howarth Press.

Gendreau, P. & Andrews, D.A. (1990). Tertiary prevention: what the meta-analyses of the offender treatment literature tells us about 'what works'. *Canadian Journal of Criminology*, 32, 173–84.

Gendreau, P., Goggin, C. & Smith, P. (1999). The forgotten issue in effective correctional treatment: Programmes implementation. *International Journal of Offender Therapy and Comparative Criminology*, 43, 180–7.

Gendreau, P., Little, T. & Goggin, C. (1996). A meta-analysis of the predictors of adult offender recidivism: What works! *Criminology*, 34, 575–607.

Gendreau, P. & Ross, R.R. (1979). Effective correctional treatment: Biblotherapy for cynics. *Crime and Delinquency*, 25, 463–89.

Gilbert, D.T. & Malone, P. (1995). The correspondence bias. *Psychological Bulletin*, 117, 21–38.

Golding, J.M. (1999). Intimate partner violence as a risk factor for mental disorders: A meta-analysis. *Journal of Family Violence*, 14, 99–132.

Gondolf, E.W. (1988). 'Who are those guys?' Towards a behavioural typology of batterers. *Violence and Victims*, 3, 187–203.

Gondolf, E.W. (1992). Standards for court-mandated batterer counseling: A reply to Goldman. *Journal of Family Violence and Seual Assault Bulletin*, 8, 18–21.

Gondolf, E.W. (1997). Patterns of reassault in batterer programs. *Violence and Victims*, 12, 373–87.

Gondolf, E.W. (1999). A comparison of four batterer intervention systems. *Journal of Interpersonal Violence*, 14, 4 –61.

Gondolf, E.W. (2000). Human subjects issues in batterer program evaluation. In S.K Ward. & D. Finkelhor (eds) *Program Evaluation and Family Violence Research.* Binghampton, NY: The Haworth Maltreatment & Trauma Press.

Gondolf, E.W. (2002). *Batterer Intervention Systems: issues, outcomes and recommendations.* Thousand Oaks: Sage.

Gondolf, E.W. (2004) Evaluating batterer counselling programs: A difficult task showing some effects and implications. *Aggression and Violent Behaviour*, 9, 605–31.

Gondolf, E.W. (2007) Theoretical research support for the Duluth model: A reply to Dutton and Corvo. *Aggression and Violent Behavior*,12, 697–708.

Gondolf, E.W. & Russell, D. (1985). The case against anger control treatment programs for batterers. *Response*, 9, 2–5.

Gondolf, E.W. & White, R.J. (2001). Batterer programmes participants who repeatedly reassault: Psychopathic tendencies and other disorders. *Journal of Interpersonal Violence*, 16, 361–80.

Goode, W.J. (1971). Force and violence in the family. *Journal of Marriage and the Family*, 33, 624–36.

Goodman, L.A., Bennett, L. & Dutton, M.A. (1999). Obstacles to victim's cooperation with the criminal prosecution of their abusers: the role of social support. *Vioence and Victims*, 14, 427–44.

Goodwin, I. (2003). The relevance of attachment theory to the philosophy, organization and practice of adult mental health care. *Clinical Psychology Review*, 23, 35–56.

Gordon, J.A. & Moriarty, L.J. (2003). The effects of domestic violence batterer treatment on domestic violence recidivism: The Chesterfield County eperience. *Criminal Justice and Behavior*, 30, 118–34.

Gordon, M. (2000). Definitional issues in violence against women: surveillance and research from a violence research perspective. *Violence against Women*, 6, 747–83.

Gormley, B. (2005). An adult attachment theoretical perspective on gender symmetry in intimate partner violence. *Sex Roles*, 52, 785–95.

Grace, S. (1995). Policing domestic violence in the 1990s. *Home Office Research Study 139*. London: Home Office.

Graham, K., Plant, M. & Plant, M. (2004). Alcohol, gender and partner aggression: A general population study of British adults. *Addiction Research and Theory*, 12, 385–401.

Graham-Kevan, N. & Archer, J. (2003). Physical aggression and control in heteroseual relationships: The effect of sampling. *Violence and Victims*, 18, 181–96.

Graham-Kevan, N. & Archer, J. (2008). Does controlling behaviour predict physical aggression and violence to partners? *Journal of Family Violence*, 23, 539–48.

Grann, M. & Wedin, I. (2002) Risk factors for recidivism among spousal assault and spousal homicide offenders. *Psychology, Crime & Law*, 8, 5–23.

Greenwald, A.G., McGhee, D.E. & Schwartz, J.L.K. (1998). Measuring individual differences in implicit cognition: the implicit association test. *Journal of Personality and Social Psychology*, 74, 1464–80.

Grove, W.M. & Meehl, P. (1996). Comparative efficiency of informal (subjective, impressionistic) and formal (mechanical, algorithmic) prediction procedures: the clinical-statistical controversy. *Psychology, Public Policy and Law*, 2, 293–323.

Grove, W.M., Zald, D.H., Lebow, B.S., Snitz, B.E. & Nelson, C. (2000) Clinical versus mechanical prediction: A meta-analysis. *Psychological Assessment*, 12, 19–30.

Grusznski, R.J. (1986). Court ordered treatment of men who batter (Doctoral dissertation, University of Minnesota, 1985). *Dissertation Abstracts International*, 46, p. 3594B.

Grych, J.H., Jouriles, E.N., Swank, P.R., McDonald, R. & Norwood, W.D. (2000). Patterns of adjustment among children of battered women. *Journal of Consulting and Clinical Psychology*, 68, 84–94.

Guerra, N.G., Tolan, P.H. & Hammond, R. (1994). Prevention and treatment of adolescent violence. In L.D. Eron, J.H. Gentry & P. Schlegel (eds) *Reason to Hope: A psychosocial perspective on violence and youth*.Washington, DC: American Psychological Association, pp. 383–403.

Guille, L. (2004). Men who batter and their children: An intergrated review. *Aggression and Violent Behavior*, 9, 129–63.

Hagemann-White, C. (2001). European research on the prevalence of violence against women. *Violence Against Women*, 7, 732–59.

Hague, G. & Malos, E. (2005). *Domestic Violence: Action for change* (3rd edn). Cheltenham: New Clarion Press.

Hague, G. & Wilson, C. (2000). The silenced pain: Domestic violence 1945–1970. *Journal of Gender Studies*, 9, 157–69.

Halpern, M. (1984). Battered Women's Alternatives: The Men's Program Component. Paper presented at the meeting of The American Psychological Association, Toronto (August).

Hamberger, L.K. (2008). Twenty-five years of change in working with partner abusers – part II: Observations from the trenches in understanding of abusers and abuser treatment. *Journal of Aggression, Maltreatment &Trauma*, 17, 1–22.

Hamberger, L.K. & Hastings, J.E. (1986). Personality correlates of men who abuse their partners: A cross-validation study. *Journal of Family Violence*, 1, 323–41.

Hamberger, L.K. & Hastings, J.E. (1988). Skills training for treatment of spouse abusers: An outcome study. *Journal of Family Violence*, 3, 121–30.

Hamberger, L. K., & Hastings, J.E. (1990). Recidivism following spouse abuse abatement counseling: Treatment program implications. *Violence and Victims*, 5, 175–170.

Hamberger, L.K. & Hastings, J.E. (1993). Court-mandated treatment of men who assault their partner. In Z. Hilton (ed.). *Legal Responses to Wife aSsault: Current trends and evaluation.* Newbury, CA: Sage, pp. 188–229.

Hamberger, L.K., Lohr, J.M., Bonge, D. & Tollin, D.F. (1996). A large-sample empirical typology of male spouse abusers and its relationship to dimensions of abuse. *Violence and Victims*, 11, 277–92.

Hamberger, L.K., Lohr, J.M. & Gottlieb, M. (2000). Predictors of treatment dropout from a spouse abuse abatement program. *Behavior Modification*, 24, 528–52.

Hamel, J. (2005). *Gender Inclusive Treatment of Intimate Partner Abuse.* New York: Springer.

Hanson, B. (2002). Interventions for batterers: Program approaches, program tensions. In A.R. Roberts (ed.) Handbook of domestic violence intervention strategies. Oford: Oford University Press, pp. 419–50.

Hanson, R.K. & Wallace-Capretta, S. (2000a). *A multi-site study of treatment for abusive men.* Solicitor General Canada. Available from: www.sgs.cg.ca

Hanson, R.K. & Wallace-Capretta, S. (2000b). *Predicting recidivism among male batterers.* Solicitor General Canada. Available from: www.sgs.cg.ca

Hare, R. (1991). *The Hare Psychopathy Checklist Revised.* New York: Multi-health Systems.

Harrell, A. (1991). *Evaluation of Court-ordered Treatment for Domestic Violence Offenders. Final report.* Washington: The Urban Institute.

Hart, B. (1993). Battered women and the criminal justice system. *American Behavioral Scientist*, 36(5), 624–38.

Harris, J. (1986). Counseling violent couples using Walker's model. *Psychotherapy*, 23, 613–21.

Hart, S.D. (1998). The role of psychopathy in assessing risk of violence: Conceptual and methodological issues. *Legal and Criminological Psychology*, 3, 121–37.

Hartley, C.C. (2001). 'He said, she said': The defense attack of credibility in domestic violence felony trials. *Violence against Women*, 7, 510–44.

Hartley, C.C. (2003). A therapeutic jurisprudence approach to the trial process in domestic violence felony trials. *Violence against Women*, 9, 410–35.

Harris, G.T., Rice, M.E. & Quinsey, V.L. (1993). Violent recidivism of mentally disordered offenders: the development of a statistical prediction instrument. *Criminal Justice and Behavior*, 20, 315–35.

Harwin, N. (2006). Putting a stop to domestic violence in the United Kingdom. *Violence against Women*, 12, 556–67.

Hatcher, R., Palmer, E., Clark, C., Hollin, C., McGuire, J. & Bilby, C. (2005). Preliminary Outcome Findings of the Crime Reduction Pathfinder Project (Offending Behaviour): Duluth domestic violence programme. Unpublished report prepared for the correctional Services Accreditation Panel.

Hayes, J.A. & Mahalik, J.R. (2000). Gender role conflict and psychological distress in male counselling centre clients. *Psychology of Men and Masculinity*, 1, 116–23.

Hazan, C. & Shaver, P. (1987). Romantic love conceptualised as an attachment process. *Journal of Personality and Social Psychology*, 52, 511–24.

Healey, K., Smith, C. & O'Sullivan, C. (1998). *Batterer Intervention: Program Approaches and Criminal Justice Strategies.* Washington, DC: National Institute of Justice.

Heckert, D.A. & Gondolf, E.W. (2000). Assessing assault self reports by batterer program participants and their partners. *Journal of Family Violence*, 15, 181–97.

Heckert, D.A. & Gondolf, E.W. (2004). Battered women's perceptions of risk versus risk factors and instruments in predicting repeat re-assault. *Journal of Interpersonal Violence*, 19, 778–800.

Hellmuth, J.C., Follansbee, K.W., Moore, T.M. & Stuart, G.L. (2008). Reduction of Intimate Partner Violence in a Gay Couple Following Alcohol Treatment. *Journal of Homosexuality*, 54, 439–48.

Henning, K. & Feder, L. (2005). Criminal prosecution of domestic violence offences: An investigation of factors predictive of court outcomes. *Criminal Justice and Behavior*, 32, 612–42.

Hester, M. (2006). Making it through the criminal justice system: attrition and domestic violence. *Social Policy & Society*, 5, 79–90.

Hester, M., Pearce, J. & Westmarland, N. (2008). *Early Evaluation of the Integrated Domestic Violence Court, Croydon*. London: Ministry of Justice.

Hester, M., Pearson, C. & Harwin, N. (2007). *Making and Impact: Children and domestic violence: A reader* (2nd edn). Philadelphia: Jessica Kingsley Publishers.

Hester, M. & Westmarland, N. (2005). *Tackling Domestic Violence: Effective interventions and approaches*. Research study 290. London: Home Office.

Hester, M., Westmarland, N., Pearce, J. & Williamson, E. (2008). *Early Evaluation of the Domestic Violence Crime and Victims Act 2004*. London: Ministry of Justice.

Henry, G.T. (2002). Choosing criteria to judge program success: A values inquiry. *Evaluation*, 8, 182–204.

Hergenhahn, B.R. (1982). *An Introduction to Theories of Learning*. Englewood Cliffs, NJ: Prentice-Hall.

Hilton, Z.H., Harris, G.T., Rice, M.E., Houghton, R.E., Eke, A.W. (2008). An indepth actuarial assessment for wife assault recidivism: The Domestic Violence Risk Appraisal Guide. *Law and Human Behavior*, 32, 150–63.

Hilton, Z.H., Rice, G.T., Rice, M.E., Lang, C., Cormier, C.A. & Lines, K.J. (2004). A brief actuarial assessment for the prediction of wife assault recidivism: The Ontario Domestic Assault Risk Assessment. *Psychological Assessment*, 16, 267–75.

Hines, D.A. (2008). Borderline personality traits and intimate partner aggression: An international multisite, cross gender analysis. *Psychology of Women Quarterly*, 32, 290–302.

Hirschel, D. & Hutchinson, I.W. (2001). The relative effects of offense, offender, and victim variables on the decision to prosecute domestic violence cases. *Violence Against Women*, 1, 46–59.

Hirschfield, R.M.A., Klerman, G.L., Gough, H.G., Barrett, J., Kordin, S.J. & Chodoff, P. (1977). A measure of interpersonal dependency. *Journal of Personality Assessment*, 41, 610–18.

HMCPSI & HMIC (2004). *Violence at Home: A joint thematic inspection of the investigation and prosecution of cases involving domestic violence*. London.

HMCS (2007). *Domestic Violence: A Guide to Civil Remedies and Criminal Sanctions*. London: HMCS.

HMCS (2008). *Justice with Safety: Specialist Domestic Violence Courts Review*. London: HMCS, Home Office, Crown Prosecution Service.

HM Government (2009). *Together We Can End Violence against Women and Girls: A Strategy*. London: Author.

Holden, G. & Ritchie, K. (1991). Linking extreme marital discord, child rearing and child behaviour problems: Evidence from battered women. *Child Development*, 62, 311–27.

Hollin, C. (1995). The meaning and implications of programme integrity. In J. McGuire (ed.), *What works: Reducing reoffending: Guidelines from research and practice*. Chichester, England: Wiley, pp. 93–206.

Hollin, C.R. (1999). Treatment programs for offenders: meta–analysis, 'what works', and beyond. *International Journal of Law and Psychiatry*, 22 (3–4), 361–72.

Hollin, C.R. (2001). Rehabilitation. In E. McLaughlin & J. Muncie (eds), *The Sage Dictionary of Criminology*. London: Sage.

Hollin, C.R. (2006). Offending behaviour programmes and contention: Evidence-based practice, manuals, and programme evaluation. In C.R. Hollin & E.J. Palmer (eds) *Offending Behaviour Programmes: Development, application and controversies*. Chichester: John Wiley & Sons, pp. 33–68.

Hollin, C.R. & Palmer, E.J. (2006). Offending behaviour programmes: History and development. In C.R. Hollin & E.J. Palmer (eds), *Offending Behaviour Programmes: Development, application and controversies*. Chichester: John Wiley & Sons Ltd., pp. 1–32.

Hollin, C. & Palmer E. (2006). *Offending Behaviour Programmes: Development, application, and controversies*. Chichester, UK: JohnWiley & Sons, pp. 113–54.

Holmes, W.M. (1993). Police arrests for domestic violence. *American Journal of Police*, 12, 101–25.

Holtzworth-Munroe, A. & Hutchinson, G. (1993). Attributing negative intent to wife behavior: the attributions of maritally violent versus nonviolent men. *Journal of Abnormal Psychology*, 102, 206–11.

Holtzworth-Munroe, A., Meehan, J.C., Herron, K., Rehman, U. & Stuart, G.L. (2000). Testing the Holtzworth-Munroe and Stuart (1994) batterer typology. *Journal of Consulting and Clinical Psychology*, 68, 1000–19.

Holtzworth-Munroe, A., Meehan, J.C., Herron, K., Rehman, U. & Stuart, G.L. (2003). Do subtypes of martially violent men continue to differ over time? *Journal of Consulting and Clinical Psychology*, 71, 728–40.

Holtzworth-Munroe, A., Smutzler, N. & Bates, L. (1997). A brief review of the research on husband violence: Part III: Sociodemographic factors, relationship factors and differing consequences of husband and wife violence. *Aggression and Violent Behavior*, 2, 285–307.

Holtzworth-Munroe, A. & Stuart, G.L. (1994). Typologies of male batterers: Three subtypes and the differences among them. *Psychological Bulletin* (116), 476–97.

Holtzworth-Munroe, A., Stuart, G. & Hutchinson, G (1997). Violent versus nonviolent husbands: differences in attachment patterns, dependency and jealousy. *Journal of Family Psychology*, 11, 314–31.

Home Affairs Select Committee (2008). Sith report. Available from: www.publications.parliament.uk/pa/cm200708/cmselect/cmhaff/263/26312.htm (accessed 6 April 2009).

Home Office (1999). *What Works: Reducing Reoffending. Evidence based practice.* HO Communications Directorate.

Home Office (2000). *Domestic Violence: Break the Chain – Multi-Agency Guidance for Addressing Domestic Violence*. London: Home Office.

Home Office (2002). *Offender Assessment System OASys User Manual*. London: Home Office.

Home Office (2003). *Safety and Justice: The government's proposals on domestic violence*. London: Home Office.

Home Office (2005). *Domestic Violence: A national report*. London: Home Office.

Hotaling, G.T. & Buzawa, E. (2001). *An analysis of assaults in rural communities: Final report.* Federal grant #MA0095-400, US Department of Justice, Office of Community Oriented Policing Services.

Howard, P. (2009). Improving the prediction of re-offending using the Offender Assessment System. *Research Summary 2/09*. London: Ministry of Justice.

Howard, P., Francis, B., Soothill, K. & Humphreys, L. (2009). OGRS 3: the revised offender group reconviction scale. *Research Summary 7/09*. London: Ministry of Justice.

Hoyle, C. (1998). *Negotiating Domestic Violence: Police, Criminal Justice and Victims*. Oxford: Oxford University Press.

Hoyle, C. (2000). 'Being "a nosy bloody cow": ethical and methodological issues in researching domestic violence'. In R.D. King and E. Wincup (eds) *Doing Research on Crime and Justice*. Oxford University Press.

HM Crown Prosecution Service Inspectorate. (1998). *Cases involving domestic violence*. London: CPS.

HM Prison Service/NOMS (undated). *Domestic Assault Risk/Needs Assessment: Guidance Notes*. London: HM Prison Service.

Hunnicutt, G. (2009). Varieties of patriarchy and violence against women: Ressurecting 'patriarchy' as a theoretical tool. *Violence Against Women*, 15, 553–73.

Hurst, A.G. (1978). Leadership style determinants of cohesiveness in adolescent groups. *International Journal of Group Therapy*, 28, 263–79.

Huss, M.T. & Ralston, A. (2008). Do batterer subtypes actually matter: Treatment completion, treatment response and recidivism across a batterer typology. *Criminal Justice & Behavior*, 35, 710–24.

Ickes, W. (2009). Empathic accuracy: links to clinical, cognitive, developmental, social and physiological psychology. In J. Decety. & W. Ickes (eds). *The Social Neuroscience of Empathy*. Cambridge, MA: MIT Press, pp. 7–70.

Jacobson, N.S., Follette, W.C. & Ravenstorf, D. (1984). Psychotherapy outcome research: methods for reporting variability and evaluating clinical significance. *Behavior Therapy*, 15, 336–352.

Jacobson, N.S., Roberts, L.J., Berns, S.B. & McGlinchey, J. (1999). Methods for defining and determining the clinical significance of treatment effects: Description, application and alternatives. *Journal of Consulting and Clinical Psychology*, 67, 300–7.

Jacobson, N.S. & Truax, P. (1991). Clinical significance: A statistical approach to defining meaningful change in psychotherapy. *Journal of Consulting and Clinical Psychology*, 59, 12–19.

Jaffe, P.G., Johnston, J.R., Crooks, C.V. & Bala, N. (2008). Custody disputes involving allegations of domestic violence: Toward a differentiated approach to parenting plans. *Family Court Review*, 46, 500–22.

Jasinski, J.L. (2004). Pregnancy and domestic violence. *Trauma, Violence & Abuse*, 5, 47–64.

Jenkins, S.S. & Aube, J. (2002) Gender differences and gender-related constructs in dating aggression. *Personality and Social Psychology Bulletin*, 28, 1106–18.

Jennings, J.L. (1987). History and issues in the treatment of battering men: A case for unstructured group therapy. *Journal of Family Violence*, 2, 193–213.

Johnson, M.P. (1995). Patriarchal terrorism and common couple violence: Two forms of violence against women. *Journal of Marriage and the Family*, 57, 283–94.

Johnson, M.P. (2006). Conflict and control : Gender symmetry and asymmetry in domestic violence. *Violence against Women*, 12, 1–16.

Johnson, M.P. (2008). *A Typology of Domestic Violence: Intimate terrorism, violent resistance and situational couple violence*. Boston, MA: New University Press.

Jolliffe, D. & Farrington, D.P. (2004). Empathy and offending: A systematic review and meta-analysis. *Aggression and Violent Behavior*, 9, 441–76.

Jones, A.S., D'Agostino, Jr, R.B., Gondolf, E.W. & Heckert, A. (2004). Assessing the effect of batterer program completion on reassault using propensity scores. *Journal of Interpersonal Violence*, 19, 1002–20.

Jones, L., Hughes, M. & Unterstuller, U. (2001). Post-traumatic stress disorder (PTSD) in victims of domestic violence: A review of the research. *Trauma, Violence & Abuse*, 2, 99–119.

Jukes, A.E. (1999). *Men who Batter Women*. London: Routledge.

Kane, R. (1999). Patterns of arrest in domestic violence encounters: Identifying a police decision-making model. *Journal of Criminal Justice*, 27, 65–80.

Kennedy, LW. & Dutton, D.G. (1989). The incidence of wife assault in Alberta. *Canadian Journal of Behavioral Science*, 21, 40–53.

Kershaw, C., Goodman, J. & White, S. (1999). *Reconvictions of Offenders Sentenced or Discharged from Prison In 1995, England And Wales.* Statistical Bulletin No 19/99. London: Home Office.

Kershaw, C., Nicholas, S. & Walker, A. (2008). Crime in England and Wales 2007/08: Findings from the British Crime Survey and police recorded crime. *Home Office Statistical Bulletin 07/08.* London: Home Office.

Kessler, R.C., Molnar, B.E., Feurer, I.D. & Appelbaum, M. (2001). Patterns and mental health predictors of domestic violence in the United States: Results from the National Comorbidity Study. *International Journal of Law and Psychiatry*, 24, 487–508.

Kingsnorth, R.F. & Macintosh, R.C. (2004). Domestic violence: Predictors of victim support for official action. *Justice Quarterly*, 21, 301–28.

Kingsnorth, R.F., Macintosh, R.C., Berdahl, T., Blades, C. & Rossi, S. (2001). Domestic violence: The role of inter-racial/ethnic dyads in criminal court processing. *Journal of Contemporary Criminal Justice*, 17, 123–41.

Kingsnorth, R.F., Macintosh, R.C. & Sutherland, S. (2002). Criminal charge or probation violation? Prosecutorial discretion and implications for research in criminal court processing. *Criminology*, 40, 553–78.

Kistenmacher, B.R. & Weiss, R.L. (2008). Motivational interviewing as a mechanism for change in men who batter: A randomized controlled trial. *Violence and Victims*, 23, 558 –70.

Klein, A. & Tobin, T. (2008). Longidutinal study of arrested batterers, 1995–2005: Career criminals. *Violence against Women*, 14, 136–57.

Klostermann, K.C. & Fals-Stewart, W. (2006). Intimate partner violence and alcohol use: Eploring the role of drinking in partner violence and its implications for intervention. *Aggression and Violent Behavior*, 11, 587–97.

Kropp, P.R. (2007). Spousal assaulters. In C.D. Webster & S.J. Hucker (eds), *Violence risk assessment and management.* Chichester: Wiley, pp. 123–31.

Kropp, P.R. (2004) Some questions regarding spousal assault risk assessment. *Violence Against Women*, 10, 676–97.

Kropp, P.R. & Hart, S.D. (1994). *Evaluating Men's Treatment Programmes: An introduction for service providers.* Vancouver, BC: British Colombia Institute Against Family Violence.

Kropp, P.R. & Hart, S.D. (2000). The Spousal Assault Risk Assessment (SARA) guide: Reliability and validity in adult male offenders. *Law and Human Behavior*, 24, 101–18.

Kropp, P.R., Hart, S.D., Webster, C.D. & Eaves, D .(1999). *Manual for the Spousal Assault Risk Assessment Guide* (2nd Edition). Vancouver, BC: British Columbia Institute on Family Violence.

Kury, H., Obergfell-Fuchs, J. & Woessner, G. (2004). The etent of family violence in Europe: A comparison of national surveys. *Violence Against Women*, 10,749–69.

Kwesiga, E., Bell, M.P., Pattie, M. & Moe, A.M. (2007). Eploring the literature on relationships between gender roles, intimate partner violence, occupational status, and organizational benefits. *Journal of Interpersonal Violence*, 22, 312–26.

Kwong, M.J., Bartholomew, K. & Dutton, D.G. (1999). Gender differences in patterns of relationship violence in Alberta. *Canadian Journal of Behavioral Science*, 31, 150–60.

Lane, G. & Russell, T. (1989). Second order systemic work with violent couples. In P.L. Caesar. & L.K. Hamberger (eds). *Treating men who batter: Theory, practice and programs.* New York: Springer.

Langhinrichsen-Rohling, J., Huss, M.T.. & Ramsay, S. (2000). The clinical utility of batterer typologies. *Journal of Family Violence*, 15, 37–53.

Langlands, R.L., Ward, T. & Gilchrist, E.A. (2009). Applying the good lives model to male perpetrators of domestic violence. In P. Lehman. & C.A. Simmons (eds) *Strengths based batterer intervention*. New York: Springer Publishing, pp. 216–31.

Larzelere, R.E., Kuhn, B.R. & Johnson, B. (2004). The intervention selection bias: An underrecognized confound in intervention research. *Psychological Bulletin*, 130, 289–303.

Lawrence, E., Yoon, J., Langer & Ro, E. (2009). The independent effects of psychological aggression on depression and aniety symptoms. *Violence and Victims*, 24, 20–35.

Laws, D.R. (2002). Owning your own data: the management of denial. In M. McMurran (ed.) *Motivating offenders to change: A guide to enhancing engagement in therapy*. Chichester: John Wiley & Sons.

Lawson, D.M., Barnes, A.D., Madkins, J.P. & Francois-Lamonte, B.M. (2006). Changes in male partner abuser attachment styles in treatment. *Psychotherapy: Theory, Research Practice, Training*, 43, 232–37.

Lee, M.Y., Uken, A. & Sebold, J. (2009). Accountability for change: solution focused treatment of domestic violence offenders. In P. Lehman & C.A. Simmons (eds). *Strengths based batterer intervention)*. New York: Springer Publishing, pp. 55–86.

Lehmann, P. & Simmons, C.A. (2009a). *Strengths-based Batterer Intervention: A new paradigm in ending family violence*. New York: Springer.

Lehmann, P. & Simmons, C.A. (2009b). The state of batterer intervention programs: An analytical discussion. In P. Lehmann & C.A. Simmons (2009a). *Strengths-based Batterer Intervention: A new paradigm in ending family violence*. New York: Springer, pp. 3–38.

Leicester-Leeds Evaluation Group (2003). Duluth domestic violence reconviction study. Unpublished report: University of Leicester.

Leicester-Liverpool Evaluation Group (2005). 'Duluth domestic violence reconviction study'. Unpublished manuscript: University of Leicester.

Leschied, A., Bernfield, G. A. & Farrington, D.P. (2001). Implementation issues. In G.A Bernfield., D.P. Farrington. & A.W. Leschied (eds), *Offender Rehabilitation in Practice*, 3–24. Chichester: John Wiley & Sons, pp. 3–24.

Leonard, K.E. & Senchak, M. (1996). The prospective prediction of husband marital aggression by newlywed couples. *Journal of Abnormal Psychology*, 105, 369–80.

Leong, D., Coates, C.J. & Hoskins, J. (1987). Follow up of batterers treated in a court ordered treatment program. Paper presented at the Third National Conference for family Violence Research, university of New Hampshire, Durham.

Levenson, H. (1974). Activism and powerful others: distinctions within the concept of internal–eternal control. *Journal of Personality Assessment*, 38, 377–83.

Levesque, D.A & Gelles, R.J. (1998). Does treatment reduce recidivism in men who batter? Meta-analytic evaluation of treatment outcome research. Paper presented at the Programmes evaluation and family violence research conference. Durham, NH (July).

Levesque, D.A., Gelles, R. & Velicer, W.F. (2000). Development and validation of a stages of change measure for men in batterer treatment. *Cognitive Therapy and Research*, 24, 175–99.

Levesque, D.A., Driskell, M.M. & Prochaska, J.A. (2000a). Transtheoretical model of change processes used in batterer intervention programs. Unpublished manuscript.

Lie, G., Schilit, R., Bush, J., Montague, M. & Reyes, L. (1991). Lebians in currently aggressive relationships: How frequently do they report aggressive past relationships? *Violence and Victims*, 6, 121–135

Lieberman, A.F., Van Horn, P. & Ozer, E.J. (2005). Preschooler witnesses of marital violence: predictors and mediators of child behavior problems. *Development and Psychopathology*, 17, 385–396.

Lindquist, C.U., Telch, C.F. & Taylor, (1984) Evaluation of a conjugal violence treatment program: A pilot study. *Behavioral Counselling and Community Interventions*, 3, 76–90.

Lindsay, J. & Brady, D. (2002). Nurturing fragile relationships: Early reflections on working with victims of domestic violence on the National Probation Service's Duluth pathfinder. *Issues in Forensic Psychology*, 3, 59–71.

Lipsey, M.W. (1992). Juvenile delinquency treatment: A meta-analytic inquiry into the variability of effects: In T. Cook, D. Cooper, H. Corday, H. Hartman, L. Hedges, R. Light, T. Louis & F. Mosteller (eds) *Meta-analysis for explanation: A casebook*. New York: Russell Sage.

Lipsey, M.W. (1995). What do we learn from 400 research studies on the effectiveness of treatment with juvenile delinquents? In J. McGuire (ed.), *What Works: Reducing reoffending*. Chichester: John Wiley & Sons, pp. 63–78.

Lipsey, M.W. & Cordray, D.S. (2000). Evaluation methods for social intervention. *Annual Review of Psychology*, 51, 345–75.

Lipsey, M.W. & Wilson, D.B. (2001). *Practical meta-analysis* (Vol. 49). Thousand Oaks, California: Sage.

Lipton, D.S., Martinson, R. & Wilks, J. (1975). *The Effectiveness of Correctional Treatment: A survey of treatment evaluation studies*. New York: Praeger.

Lipton, D.S., Thornton, D., McGuire, J., Porporino, F J. & Hollin, C R. (2000). Program accreditation and correctional treatment. *Substance Use and Misuse*, 35, 1705–34.

Lloyd, C., Mair, G. & Hough, J.M. (1994). Eplaining Reconviction Rates: A Critical Analysis. *Home Office Research Study 136*. London: HMSO.

Logan, T., Shannon, L., Cole, J. & Swanberg, J. (2007). Partner Stalking and Implications for Women's Employment. *Journal of Interpersonal Violence*, 22, 268–91.

Lösel, F. (1995). The efficacy of correctional treatment: A review and synthesis of meta-evaluations. In J. McGuire (ed.), *What works: Reducing reoffending–Guidelines from research and practice*. Chichester: John Wiley & Sons, pp. 79–105.

Luellen, J.K., Shadish, W.R. & Clark, M.H. (2005). Propensity scores: An introduction and eperimental test. *Evaluation Review*, 29, 530–58.

Lussier, P., Farrington, D.P. & Moffitt, T.E. (2009). Is the antisocial child father of the abusive man? A 40-year prospective longitudinal study of the developmental antecedents of intimate partner violence. *Criminology*, 47, 741–80.

McConnaughty, E.A., Prochaska, J.O. & Velicer, W.F. (1983). Stages of change in psychotherapy: Measurement and sample profiles. *Psychotherapy: Theory Research and Practice*, 20, 368–75.

McGuire, J. (2000). *Cognitive-behavioural Approaches: An introduction to theory and research*. London: HM Inspectorate of Probation.

McGuire, J. (2001). What works in correctional intervention? Evidence and practical implications. In G.A. Bernfeld, D.P. Farrington & A.W. Leschied (eds) *Offender rehabilitation in practice: Implementing and evaluating effective programs*. Chichester: John Wiley & Sons.

McFarlane, J., Parker, B. & Soeken, K. (1995). Abuse during pregnancy: Frequency, severity, perpetrator and risk factors of homicide. *Public Health Nursing*, 12, 284–9.

McGuire, J. & Priestly, P. (1995). Reviewing what works: Past, present and future. In J. McGuire (ed.) *What Works: Reducing re-offending – Guidelines from research and practice*. Chichester, England: Wiley, pp. 3–34.

McKenry, P.C., Julian, T.W. & Gavazzi, S.M. (1995). Toward a biopsychosocial model of domestic violence. *Journal of Marriage and the Family*, 57, 307–20.

MacKensie, K.R. & Livesley, W.J. (1986). Outcome and process measures in brief group psychotherapy. *Psychiatric Annals*, 16:12, 715–21.

McKinney, C.M., Caetano, Ra., Ramisetty-Mikler, S. & Nelson, S (2009) Childhood family violence and perpetration and victimization of intimate partner violence: Findings from a national population-based study of couples. *Annals of Epidemiology*, 19, 25–32.

McMurran, M. (2002). Motivation to change: Selection criterion or treatment need? In M. McMurran (ed.) *Motivating Offenders to Change.* Chichester. John Wiley & Sons.

Macpherson, S. (2000). *Domestic Violence: Findings from the Scottish Crime Survey*. Edinburgh: Scottish Executive.

Magdol, L., Moffitt, T.E., Caspi, A., Fagan, J., Newman, D.L. & Silva, P.A. (1997) Gender differences in partner violence in a birth cohort of 21 year olds: Bridging the gap between clinical and epidemiological approaches. *Journal of Consulting and Clinical Psychology*, 65, 68–78.

Mahalik, J.R., Cournoyer, R.J., DeFranc, W., Cherry, M. & Napolitano, J. (1998). Men's gender role conflict in relation to their use of psychological defenses. *Journal of Counseling Psychology*, 45, 247–55.

Mair, G. (1997). Community penalties and the probation service. In M. Maguire, R. Morgan & R. Reiner (eds), *The Oford Handbook of Criminology*. Oford: Oford University Press, pp. 1195–32.

Maiuro, R.D. & Eberle, J.A. (2008). State standards for domestic violence perpetrator treatment: current status, trends and recommendations. *Violence and Victims*, 23, 133–55.

Margolin, G. & Berman, B. (1993). Wife abuse versus marital violence: Different terminologies, eplanations and solutions. *Clinical Psychology Review*, 13, 59–73.

Markowitz, F.E (2001). Attitudes and family violence: Linking intergenerational and cultural theories. *Journal of Family Violence*, 16, 205–18.

Marshall, W.L., Hudson, S.M., Jones, R. & Fernandez, Y.M (1995). Empathy in sex offenders. *Clinical Psychology Review*, 15, 99 –113.

Martin, D. (1976). *Battered Wives*. San Francisco: Guide Publications.

Martin, M.E. (1994). Mandatory arrest for domestic violence: the court's response. *Criminal Justice Review*, 19, 212–27.

Martinson, R. (1974). What works? Questions and answers about prison reform. *The Public Interest*, 22–50.

Mauricio, A.M. & Gormley, B. (2001). Male perpetration of physical violence against female partners. *Journal of Interpersonal Violence*, 16, 1066–81.

Mauricio, A.M., Tein, J.Y. & Lopez, F.G. (2007). Borderline and antisocial personality scores as mediators between attachment and intimate partner violence. *Violence and Victims*, 22, 139–57.

Mederer, H.J. & Gelles, R.J. (1989). Compassion or control: intervention in cases of wife abuse. *Journal of Interpersonal Violence*, 4, 25–44.

Mederos, F. (1999). Batterer intervention programs: the past and future prospects. In M.F. Shepard & E.L. Pence (eds), *Coordinating Community Responses to Domestic Violence*. London: Sage.

Miller, W.R. & Rollnick, S. (1991). *Motivational Interviewing: Preparing People to Change Addictive Behaviour*. New York: Guildford Press.

Miller, T.Q., Smith, T.W., Turner, C.W., Guijarro, M.L. & Hallet, A.J. (1996). A meta-analytic review of research on hostility and physical health. *Psychological Bulletin*, 119, 322–48.

Mirlees-Black, C. & Byron, C. (1999). *Domestic Violence: Findings from the BCS self-completion questionnaire*. London.

Moore, B. (1996). *Risk Assessment: A practitioner's guide to predicting harmful behaviour*. London: Whiting & Birch Ltd.

Moore, R. (2009). *The internal reliability and construct validity of the Offender Assessment System (OASys). Research Summary 6/09*. London: Ministry of Justice.

Moore, T.M., Eisler, R.M. & Franchina, J.J. (2000). Causal attributions and affective responses to provocative female partner behavior by abusive and nonabusive males. *Journal of Family Violence*, 15, 69–80.

Moore, T.M. & Stuart, G.L. (2004). Illicit substance use and intimate partner violence among men in batterer's intervention. *Journal of Addictive Behaviors*, 18, 385–89.

Moos, R.H. (1994). *Group Environment Scale Manual: Development, Applications and Research*. (3rd edn). California: Consulting Psychologists Press.

Moracco, K.E., Runyan, C.W. &Butts, J. (1998) Femicide in North Carolina. *Homicide Studies*, 2, 422–46.

Morran, D. & Wilson, M. (1997). *Men who are Violent to Women: A groupwork practice manual*. Lyme Regis: Russell House.

Morley, R. & Mullender, A. (1994). Preventing domestic violence to women. *Police Research Group Crime Prevention Series Paper No. 48*.London: Home Office.

Morris, A. & Gelsthorpe, L. (2000). Re-visioning men's violence against female partners. *The Howard Journal of Criminal Justice*, 412–28.

Morton, S. (2009). *Can OASys deliver consistent assessments of offender? Results from the inter-rater reliability study. Research Summary 1/09*. London: Ministry of Justice.

Mullender, A. (1996). Groupwork with male domestic abusers: Models and dilemmas. *Groupwork*, 9, 27–47.

Mulloy, R., Smiley, W.C. and Mawson, D.L. (1999). The impact of empathy training on offender treatment. *Focus on Corrections Research*, 11, 15–18.

Mulvey, E.P. & Lidz, C.W. (1985). Back to basics: A critical analysis of dangerousness research in a new legal environment. *Law and Human Behavior*, 9, 209–19.

Murphy, C.M. & Baxter, V.A. (1997). Motivating Batterers to Change in the Treatment Contet. *Journal of Interpersonal Violence*, 12, 607–619

Murphy, C.M. & Eckhardt, C.I. (2005). *Treating the abusive partner: An individualized cognitive-behavioral approach*. New York: Guildford.

Murphy, C.M. & Meis, L.A. (2008). Individual treatment of intimate partner violence perpetrators. *Violence and Victims*, 23, 173-186.

Murphy, C.M., Meyer, S.L. & O'Leary, K.D. (1994). Dependency characteristics of partner assaultive men. *Journal of Abnormal Psychology*, 103, 729–735.

Murphy, C.M. & O'Farrell, T.J. (1994). Factors associated wtih marital aggression in male alcoholics. *Journal of FamilyPsychology*, 8, 321–35.

Murphy, C.M., Winters, J., O'Farrell, T.J., Fals-Stewart, W. & Murphy, M. (2005). Alcohol consumption and intimate partner violence by alcoholic men: Comparing violent and non-violent conflicts. *Psychology of Addictive Behaviors*, 19, 35–42.

Musser, P.H., Semiatin, J.N., Taft, C.T. & Murphy, C.M. (2008). Motivational interviewing as a pre-group intervention for partner-violent men. *Violence and Victims*, 23, 539–557.

National Probation Directorate (2003). *Domestic violence policy*. London: National Probation Directorate.

Neidig, P.H. (1984). Women's shelters, men's collectives and other issues in the field of spouse abuse. *Victimology*, 9, 464–76.

NOMS (2009) *MAPPA guidance 2009 version 3.0*. London: National Offender Management Service Public Protection Team.

Norlander, B. & Eckhardt, C. (2005) Anger, hostility, and male perpetrators of intimate partner violence: A Meta-analytic review. *Clinical Psychology Review*, 25, 119–52.

Northern Ireland Office. (2008). *Eperience of domestic violence: Findings from the 2007/2008 Northern Ireland Crime Survey* (Vol. 16/2008). Belfast: Northern Ireland Office.

Nuffield, J. (1982). *Parole decision-making in Canada: Research towards decision guidelines. Ottawa.* ON: Solicitor General Canada.

Novaco, R.W. (1994). Anger as a risk factor for violence among the mentally disordered. In J. Monahan & H. Steadman (eds), *Violence and mental disorder: Developments in risk assessment*. Chicago: University of Chicago Press.

Offending Behaviour Programmes Unit (2005). *Community domestic violence programme: Theory manual.* London: Crown Copyright.

Offending Behaviour Programmes Unit (undated). *Integrated Domestic Abuse Programme: Theory manual.* London: Author.

Office for National Statistics (2003) Offenders Inde Database. Retrieved from: www.statistics.gov.uk/StatBase/Source.asp?vlnk=732&More=Y (16 February 2010).

O'Leary, K.D. (1988). Physical aggression between spouses. In V.B. Van Hasselt., R.L. Morrison., A.S. Bellack. & M. Henson (eds) *Handbook of Family Violence*. New York: Plenum, pp. 1–55.

O'Leary, K.D. (2000). Are women really more aggressive than men in intimate relationships? Comment on Archer (2000). *Psychological Bulletin*, 126, 685–9.

O'Neil, J.M. (1981) Male se role conflicts, seism and masculinity: Psychological implications for men, women, and the counselling psychologist. *The Counseling Psychologist*, 9, 61–80.

Pahl, J. (1985). *Private Violence and Public Policy*. London: Kegan Paul.

Palmer, S., Brown, R.A. & Barrera, M.E. (1992). Group treatment program for abusive husbands: Long-term evaluation. *American Journal of Orthopsychiatry*, 62, 276–83.

Palmer, S.E., Brown, R.A., Maru, E.W. & Barrera, M.E. (1992). Group treatment programmes for abusive husbands: Long term Evaluation. *American Journal of Orthopsychiatry*, 62/21, 276–83.

Palmer, T. (1975). Martinson revisited. *Journal of Research on Crime and Delinquency*, 12, 133–52.

Quay, H.C. (1977). The three faces of evaluation: What can be expected to work. *Criminal Justice & Behavior*, 4, 341–50.

Quinsey, L.V., Harris, T.G., Rice, E. M. & Cormier, A.C. (1998). *Violent Offenders: Appraising and Managing Risk*. Washington: American Psychological Association.

Pan, H.D., Neidig, P.H. & O'Leary, K.D. (1994). Predicting mild and severe husband-to-wife physical aggression. *Journal of Consulting and Clinical Psychology*, 62, 975–81.

Parliament of Australia (2006). *Domestic Violence in Australia – An Overview of the Issues.* Ebrief. Available from: www.aph.gov.au/library/intguide/SP/Dom_violence.htm (accessed 15 March 2010).

Paterson, E.J. (1979). How the legal system responds to battered women. In D.M. Moore (ed.) *Battered Women*. Beverly Hills, CA: Sage, pp. 79–100.

Paulhus, D.L. (1984). Two-component models of socially desirable responding. *Journal of Personality and Social Psychology*, 46, 598–609.

Pawson, R. & Tilley, N. (1997). *Realistic Evaluation*. London: Sage.

Pence, E. (1999). Some thoughts on philosophy. In M. Shepard & E. Pence (eds), *Coordinating community responses to domestic violence: Lessons from Duluth and beyond*. Thousand Oaks, CA: Sage, pp. 25–40.

Pence, E.L. & Paymar, M. (eds) (1993). *Education Groups for Men who Batter: The Duluth model.* New York: Springer.

Pirog-Good, M. & Stets-Kealey, J. (1985). Male batterers and battering prevention programs: A national survey. *Response*, 8, 8–12.

Pizzey, E. (1974). *Scream Quietly or the Neighbours will Hear*. Harmondsworth, Middlese: Penguin.

Plotnikoff, J. & Woolfson, R. (1998). Policing domestic violence: Effective organisational structures. *Police Research Series Paper 100*. London: Home Office.

Polaschek, D. (2006) Violent offender programmes: concept, theory and practice. In C.R. Hollin. & E.J. Palmer (eds). *Offending Behaviour Programmes: Development, controversies and applications* Chichester: John Wiley & Sons, pp. 113–54.

Reitzel-Jaffe, D. & Wolfe, D.A. (2001). Predictors of relationship abuse among young men. *Journal of Interpersonal Violence*, 16, 99–115.

Respect (2008). *The Respect Accreditation Standard: Full Version: Includes Guidance*. London: Author.

Povey, D., Coleman, K., Kaiza, P. & Roe, S. (2009). *Homicides, firearms incidents and intimate violence: Supplementary Volume 2 to Crime in England and Wales 2007/08* (Vol. 02/09). London: Home Office.

Prochaska, J.O. & DiClimente, C.C. (1984). Transtheoretical therapy: Toward a more integrative model of change. *Psychotherapy: Theory Research and Practice*, 19, 276–88.

Purdy, F. & Nickle, N. (1982) Practice principles for working with groups of men who batter. *Social Work with Groups* 4, 3–4.

Quinsey, V.L., Harris, G.T., Rice, M.E. & Cormier, C.A. (2006). *Violent Offenders: Appraising and Managing risk* (2nd edn). Washington, DC: American Psychological Association.

Radford, J. (2003). Professionalising responses to domestic violence in the UK: Definitional difficulties. *Community Safety Journal*, 2, 1, 32–9.

Rebovich, D.J. (1996). Prosecution responses to domestic violence: Results of a survey of large jurisdictions. In E.S. Buzawa & C.G. Buzawa (eds), *Do Arrests and Restraining Orders Work?* Thousand Oaks, CA: Sage.

Reece, H. (2006). The end of domestic violence. *Modern Law Review*, 69, 770–791.

Respect (2008). *The Respect Accreditation Standard*. London: Respect.

Ritmeester, T. (1993). Batterers' programs, battered women's movement, and issues of accountability. In E.L. Pence & M. Paymar (eds), *Education Groups for Men who Batter: The Duluth model*. New York: Springer, pp. 169–78.

Rivett, M. (2006) Treatment for perpetrators of domestic abuse: controversy in policy and practice. *Criminal Behavior and Mental Health*, 16, 205–10.

Roberts, N. & Noller, P. (1998). The association between adult attachment and couple violence: the role of communication patterns and relationship satisfaction. In J.Z. Simpson & W.S. Rholes (eds), *Attachment Theory and Close Relationships*. New York: Guilford Press, pp. 317–52.

Robinson, A.L. & Chandek, M.S. (2000). The domestic violence arrest decision: eamining demographic, attitudinal and situational variables. *Crime and Delinquency*, 46, 18–37.

Robinson, A. & Cook, D. (2006). Understanding victim retraction in cases of domestic violence: Specialist courts, government policy and victim-centred justice. *Contemporary Justice Review*, 9, 189–213.

Robinson, G. & Crow, I. (2009). *Offender rehabilitation: Theory, research and practice*. London: Sage.

Romig, D.A. (1978). *Justice for Our Children*. Lexington, MA: DC Heath.

Rondeau, G., Brodeur, N., Brochu, S. & Lemire, G. (2001). Dropout and completion of treatment among spouse abusers. *Violence and Victims*, 16, 127–43.

Ronfeldt, H.M., Kimerling, R. & Arias, I. (1998) Satisfaction with relationship power and the perpetration of dating violence. *Journal of marriage and the family*, 60, 70–8.

Rooney, J. & Hanson, R.K. (2002). Predicting attrition from treatment programs for abusive men. *Journal of Family Violence*, 16, 131–49.

Rosenbaum, A. (1986). Group treatment for abusive men: Process and outcome. *Psychotherapy*, 23, 607–12.

Rosenbaum, A. (1988). Methodological issues in marital violence research. *Journal of Family Violence*, 3, 91–104.

Rosenbaum, A. (1992). Court-ordered treatment of spouse abuse. *Clinical Psychology Review*, 12, 205–26.

Rosenbaum, P.R. & Rubin, D.B. (1983).The central role of the propensity score in observational studies for causal effects. *Biometrika* 70: 41–55.

Rosenbaum, A., Rabenhorst, M.M., Reddy, M.K., Fleming, M.T., Howells, N.L. (2006). A comparison of methods for collecting self-report data on sensitive topics. *Violence and Victims*, Vol. 21 (August), pp. 461–71.

Rosenfeld, B. (1992). Court-ordered treatment of spouse abuse. *Clinical Psychology Review*, 12, 205–226.

Ross, J.M. & Babcock, J.C. (2009). Proactive and reactive violence among intimate partner violent men diagnosed with antisocial and borderline personality disorder. *Journal of Family Violence*, 24, 607–17.

Rossi, P.H., Freeman, H.E. & Lipsey, M.W. (1999). *Evaluation: A Systematic Approach* (6th edn). London: Sage.

Rossi, P.H., Lipsey, M.W. & Freeman, H.E. (2008). *Evaluation: A Systematic approach* (7th edn). Thousand Oaks, CA: Sage.

Rothman, E.F., Butchart, A. & Cerda, M. (2003). *Intervening with Perpetrators of Intimate Partner Violence: A global perspective*. Geneva: World Health Organization.

Roy, M. (1988). *Children in the Cross-fire: Violence in the home – how does it affect our children?* Deerfield Beach, FL: Health Communications.

Rubin, A. & Parrish, D. (2007). Problematic phrases in the conclusions of published outcome studies: Implications for evidence based practice. *Research on Social Work Practice*, 17, 334–47.

Russell, R. & Jory, M.K. (1997). An evaluation of group intervention programs for violent and abusive men. *Australian and New Zealand Journal of Family Therapy*, 18 (3), 123–36.

Sackett, L. & Saunders, D.G. (1999). The impact of different forms of psychological abuse on battered women. *Violence and Victims*, 14, 105–17.

Sagrestando, L.M., Heavey, C.L. & Christensen, A. (1999). Perceived power and physical violence in marital conflict. *Journal of Family Issues*, 55, 65–79.

Sakai, C.E. (1991). Group intervention strategies with domestic abusers. *Families in Society: The Journal of Contemporary Human Services* (November) 536–42.

Salisbury, E.J., Henning, K. & Holdford, R. (2009). Fathering by partner-abusive men. *Child Maltreatment*, 14, 232–42.

Sansone, R.A., Reddington, A., Sky, K. & Wiederman, M.W. (2007). Borderline personality symptomatology and history of domestic violence among women in an internal medicine setting. *Violence and Victims*, 22, 120–6.

Saunders, D.G. (1988). Wife abuse, husband abuse or mutual combat? A feminist perspective on the empirical findings. In K. Yllo & M. Bograd (eds), *Feminist Perspectives on Wife Abuse*. Thousand Oaks, CA: Sage pp. 90–113.

Saunders, D.G. (1989). Who hits first and who hurts most? Evidence for the greater victimization of women in intimate relationships. Paper presented at the annual meeting of the American Society of Criminology, Reno, Nevada (November).

Saunders, D.G. (1992). A typology of men who batter: Three types derived from cluster analysis. *American Journal of Orthopsychiatry*, 62, 264–75.

Saunders, D.G. (1996). Feminist cognitive behavioural and process psychodynamic treatment for men who batter: Interaction of abuser traits and treatment models. *Violence and Victims*, 11, 393–414.

Saunders, D.G. & Hanusa, D. (1986). Cognitive-behavioral treatment of men who batter: The short-term effects of group therapy. *Journal of Family Violence*, 1, 357–72.

Saunders, D.G., Lynch, A.E., Grayson, M. & Linz, D. (1987). The inventory of beliefs about wife beaing: the development and initial validation of a measure of beliefs and attitudes. *Violence and Victims*, 2, 39–57.

Saunders, Daniel G. & Size, Patricia B. (1986). Attitudes about women abuse among police officers, victims and victim advocates. *Journal of Interpersonal Violence*, Vol. 1, 25–42.

Schechter, S. (1982). *Women and Male Violence: The visions and struggles of the battered women's movement*. Cambridge, MA: South End Press.

Schumacher, J.A., Feldbau-Kohn, S., Slep, A.M.S. & Heyman, R.E. (2001). Risk factors for male-to-female partner physical abuse. *Aggression and Violent Behavior*, 6, 281–352.

Schwartz, J.P. & Waldo, M.(1999). Therapeutic factors in spouse – abuse group treatment. *Journal for Specialists in Groupwork*, 24, 197–207.

Schweinle, W.E. & Ickes, W. (2007). The role of men's critical/rejecting overattribution bias, affect, and attentional disengagement in marital aggression. *Journal of Social and Clinical Psychology*, 26, 173–98.

Schweinle, W.E., Ickes, W. & Bernstein, I.H. (2002). Empathic inaccuracy in husband to wife aggression: the overattribution bias. *Personal Relationships*, 9, 141–58.

Scott, K.M. (2004). Predictors of change among male batterers. Application of theories adn review of empirical findings. *Trauma, Violene & Abuse*, 5, 260–84.

Scott, K.L. and Wolfe, D.A. (2003). Readiness to change as a predictor of outcome in batterer treatment. *Journal of Consulting and Clinical Psychology*, 71, 879–89.

Scourfield, J.B. & Dobash, R.P. (1999). Programmes for violent men: Recent developments in the UK. *The Howard Journal of Criminal Justice*, 38, 128–43.

Shaffer, D.K. & Pratt, T.C (2009) Meta-analysis, moderators, and treatment effectiveness: The importance of digging deeper for evidence of program integrity. *Journal of Offender Rehabilitation*, 48, 101–19.

Shepard, M. (1987). Intervention with men who batter: An evaluation of a domestic abuse program. Paper presented at the Third National Conference for Family Violence Researchers, University of New Hampshire, Durham.

Shepard, M.F. (1999). Evaluating a coordinated community response. In M.F Shepard & E.L Pence (eds). *Coordinating community responses to domestic violence: Lessons from Duluth and beyond*. Thousand Oaks, CA: Sage, pp. 69–194.

Shepard, M.F. & Campbell, J. (1992). The abusive behaviour inventory: A measure of psychological and physical abuse. *Journal of Interpersonal Violence*, 4, 291–305.

Schmidt, J. & Steury, E.H. (1989). Prosecutorial discretion in filing charges in domestic violence cases. *Criminology*, 27, 487–510.

Schmucker, M. & Losel, F. (2008) Does seual offender treatment work? A systematic review of outcome evaluations. *Psicothema*, 21 (1), 10–19.

Scott, K. & Straus, M. (2007). Denial, minimisation, partner blaming and intimate aggression in dating partners. *Journal of Interpersonal Violence*, 22, 851–71.

SGC (2002). *Rape: The panel's advice to the court of appeal*. London: Sentencing Guidelines Council.

Sheptyki, J.W.E. (1991). Using the state to change society: The eample of domestic violence. *Journal of Human Justice*, 3, 47–66.

Sherman, L. (1993). *Policing Domestic Violence: Eperiments and Dilemmas.* New York: Free Press.

Sherman, L. & Berk, R. (1984). The specific deterrent effects of arrest for domestic assault. *American Sociological Review*, 49, 261–72.

Simons, R.L., Lin, K-H. & Gordon, L.C. (1998) Socialisation in the family of origin and male dating violence: A prospective study. *Journal of Marriage and the Family*, 60, 467–78.

Simmons, C.A. & Lehmann, P. (2009). Strengths-based batterer intervention: A new direction with a different paradigm. In P. Lehmann & C.A. Simmons (2009a). *Strengths-based Batterer Intervention: A new paradigm in ending family violence.* New York: Springer, pp. 9–52.

Skyner, D.R. & Waters, J. (1999). Working with perpetrators of domestic violence to protect women and children: A partnership between Cheshire probation service and the NSPCC. *Child Abuse Review*, 8, 46–54.

Smith, D.A. (1987). Police response to interpersonal violence: defining the parameters of legal control. *Social Forces*, 65, 767–82.

Sonkin, D. & Douglas, L. (2002). The assessment of court-mandated perpetrators of domestic violence. *Journal of Trauma, Aggression and Maltreatment*, 6, 3–36.

Sonkin, D.J. & Dutton, D. (2003). Treating assaultive men from an attachment perspective. In D. Dutton & D.J. Sonkin (eds) *Intimate violence: Contemporary treatment innovations.* New York: The Howarth Maltreatment and Trauma Press, pp. 105–33.

Sorenson, S.B. & Telles, C.A. (1991). Self-reports of spousal violence in a Meican-American and non-Hispanic white population. *Violence and Victims*, 6, 3–16.

Spielberger, C.D. (1988). *State-Trait Anger Epression Inventory: Research edition professional manual.* Odessa, FL: Psychological Assessment Resources Inc.

Stack, S. (1997). Homicide followed by suicide: An analysis of Chicago data. *Criminology*, 35, 435–53.

Stark, E. (2006). Commentary on Johnson's 'conflict and control: gender symmetry and asymmetry in domestic violence'. *Violence against Women*, 12, 1019–25.

Stets, Jan E. (1992). Interactive processes in dating aggression: A national study. *Journal of Marriage & the Family*, Vol. 54, pp. 165–77.

Stewart, J. (2005). *Specialist Domestic/Family Courts within the Australian contet.* Sydney: Australian Domestic & Family Violence Clearing House.

Stewart, L., Gabora, N. & Hill, J. (2001). *The Moderate Intensity Domestic Violence Treatment Programme.* London: OBPU.

Stewart, D.E. & Robinson, G.E. (1998). A review of domestic violence and women's mental health. *Archives of Women's Mental Health*, 1, 83–9.

Stith, S.M. & Farley, S.C. (1993). A predictive model of male spousal violence. *Journal of Family Violence*, 8, 183–201.

Stith, S.M. & McMonigle, C.L. (2009). Risk factors associated with intimate partner violence. In D.J. Whittaker. & J.R. Lutzker (eds) *Preventing Partner violence: Resesarch and evidence-based intervention strategies.* Washington, DC: American Psychological Association, pp. 7–92.

Stith, S.M., Rosen, K.H. & Middleton, K.A., Busch, A.L., Lundberg, K. & Carlton, R.P. (2000). The intergenerational transmission of spouse abuse: A meta-analysis. *Journal of Marriage and the Family*, 62, 640–54.

Stith, S.M., Smith, D.B., Penn, C.E., Ward, D.B. & Tritt, D. (2004). Intimate partner physical abuse perpetration and vicimisation risk factors: A meta-analytic review. *Aggression and Violent Behavior*, 10, 65–98.

Straus, M.A. (1979). Measuring intra-family conflict and violence: The conflict tactics scale. *Journal of Marriage and the Family*, 75–88.

Straus, M.A. & Gelles, R.J. (eds) (1990). *Physical Violence in American Families: Risk factors and adaptations to violence in 8,145 families*. New Brunswick, NJ: Transaction Publishers.

Straus, M.A., Gelles, R.J. & Steinmetz, S. (1980). *Behind Closed Doors: Violence in the American family*. Garden City, NY: Anchor.

Straus, M.A., Hamby, S.L., Boney-McCoy, S. & Sugarman, D.B. (1996). The revised Conflict Tactics Scale (CTS-2): Development and preliminary psychometric data. *Journal of Family Issues*, 17, 283–326.

Sugarman, D.B. & Frankel, S.L. (1996). Patriarchal ideology and wife-assault: A meta-analytic review. *Journal of Family Violence*, 11, 13–40.

Tadros, V. (2005). *The distinctiveness of domestic abuse: A freedom based account*. In A. Duff & S. Green (eds) *Defining Crimes*. Oford: Oford University Press.

Taft, C.E., Resick, P.A., Panuzio, J., Vogt, D.S. & Mechanic, M.B. (2007). Coping among victims of relationship abuse: a longitudinal eamination. *Violence and Victims*, 22 (4), 408–18.

Thompson, Martie P., Kingree, J.B. (2006). The roles of victim and perpetrator alcohol use in intimate partner violence outcomes. *Journal of Interpersonal Violence*, 21, 163–77.

Thorne-Finch, R. (1992). *Ending the Silence: The origins and treatment of male violence against women*. Toronto: University of Toronto Press.

Ting, Laura, Jordan-Green, Lisa, Murphy, Christopher M., Pitts, Steven C. (2009). Substance use problems, treatment engagement, and outcomes in partner violent men. *Research on Social Work Practice*, Vol. 19, 395–406.

Tolman, R.M. (1989). The development of a measure of psychological maltreatment of women by their male partners. *Violence and Victims*, 4, 159–77.

Tuck, M (1992). *Domestic violence: Report of an inter-agency working party*. London: Victim Support.

Tolman, R.M. & Bennett, L.W. (1990). A review of quantitative research on men who batter. *Journal of Interpersonal Violence*, 5, 87–118.

Tutty, L.M., Bidgood, B.A., Rothery, M.A. & Bidgood, P. (2001). An evaluation of men's batterer treatment groups. *Research on Social Work Practice*, 11, 645–70.

Tweed, R. & Dutton, D.G. (1998). A comparison of impulsive and instrumental subgroups of batterers. *Violence and Victims*, 13, 217–30.

UKES (2008). *Guidelines for Good Practice in Evaluation*. London: UKES.

Umberson, D., Anderson, K., Glick, J. & Shapiro, A. (2009). Domestic violence, personal control, and gender. *Journal of Marriage and the Family*, 60, 442–52.

Van Voorhis, P., Cullen, F.T. & Applegate, B. (1995). Evaluating interventions with violent offender: A guide for practitioners and policymakers. *Federal Probation*, 59, 17–28.

Vega, E.M. & O'Leary, K.D. (2007). Test re-test reliability of the revised conflict tactics scales (CTS2). *Journal of Family Violence*, 22, 703–8.

Vennard, J., Sugg, D. & Hedderman, C. (1997). *Changing offenders' attitudes and behaviour: What works? Part 1: The use of cognitive-behavioural approaches with offenders: messages from the research*. London: Home Office.

Ventura, L.A. & Davis, G. (2005). Domestic violence: Court case conviction and recidivism. *Violence Against Women*, 11, 255–77.

Verhofstadt, L.L., Buysse, A., Ickes, W., Davis, M. & Devoldre, I. (2008). Support provision in marriage: The role of emotional matching and empathic accuracy. *Emotion*, 8, 792–802.

Vivian, C. & Malone, J. (1997). Relationship factors and depressive symptomatology associated with mile and severe husband-to-wife physical aggression. *Violence and Victims*, 12, 3–18.

Walby, S. & Allen, J. (2004). *Domestic Violence, Seual Assault and Stalking: Findings from the British Crime Survey*. London: Home Office.

Walby, S. & Myhill, A. (2001). New survey methodologies in researching violence against women. *British Journal of Criminology*, 41, 502–22.

Waldo, M. (1988) Relationship enhancement counseling groups for wife abusers. *Journal of Mental Health Counseling*, 10, 37–45.

Walker, L. (1979). *The Battered Woman*. New York: Harper & Row.

Wallace, R. & Nosko, A (2003). Shame in male spouse abusers and its treatment in group therapy. In D. Dutton & D.J. Sonkin (eds) *Intimate Violence: Contemporary treatment innovations*. New York: The Howarth Maltreatment and Trauma Press, pp. 47–74.

Wallis, M. (1996). Outlawing stalkers. *Policing Today*, 2, 25–29.

Walsh, C. (2001). The trend towards specialisation: West Yorkshire innovations in drug and domestic violence courts. *Howard Journal of Criminal Justice*, 40, 26–38.

Waltz, J. (2003). Dialectical behaviour therapy in the treatment of abusive behaviour. In D. Dutton & D.J. Sonkin (eds) *Intimate violence: Contemporary treatment innovations*. New York: The Howarth Maltreatment and Trauma Press, pp. 75–104.

Waltz, J., Babcock, J.C., Jacobson, N.S. & Gottman, J.M. (2000). Testing a typology of batterers. *Journal of Consulting and Clinical Psychology*, 68 (4), 658–69.

Ward, T., Polaschek, D.L.L. & Beech, A.R. (2005). *Theories of Seual Offending*. Chichester: John Wiley & Sons.

Weiss, C.H. (1997). How can theory based evaluation make greater headway? *Evaluation Review*, 21, 501–24.

Weisz, A.N., Tolman, R.M. & Saunders, D.G. (2000). Assessing the risk of severe domestic violence: The importance of survivors' predictions. *Journal of Interpersonal Violence*, 15, 75–90.

Welsh, B.C. & Farrington, D.P. (2001). Evaluating the economic efficiency of correctional intervention programs. In G.A Bernfield., D.P. Farrington. & A.W Leschied (eds) *Offender Rehabilitation in Practice*. Chichester: John Wiley & Sons, pp 45–66.

White, H.R. & Widom, C.S. (2003). Intimate partner violence among abused and neglected children in young adulthood: The mediating effects of early aggression, antisocial personality, hostility and alcohol problems. *Aggressive Behavior*, 29, 332–45.

White, J.W., Smith, P.H., Koss, M.P. & Figuerdo, A.J. (2000). Intimate partner aggression – what have we learned? Comment on Archer's meta-analysis. *Psychological Bulletin*, 126, 690–6.

Whittaker, D.J., Morrison, S., Lindquist, C., Hawkins, S.R., O'Neil, J.A., Nesius, A.M., Mathew, A. & Reese, L. (2006). A critical review of interventions for the primary prevention of perpetration of partner violence. *Aggression and Violent Behavior*, 11, 151–66.

Williams, K. & Houghton, A.B. (2004). Assessing the risk of domestic violence reoffending: A validation study. *Law and Human Behavior*, 24, 437–55.

Wilson, M. & Daly, M. (1993). Spousal homicide risk and estrangement. *Violence and Victims*, 8, 3–15.

Winstok, Z. (2007). Toward an interactional perspective on intimat partner violence. *Aggression and Violent Behavior*, 12, 348–63.

WNC (2004). *Violence Against Women Working Group response to the consultation paper on domestic violence and sentencing*. London: WNC.

Woodin, E.M. & O'Leary, K.D. (2009) Theoretical approaches to the etiology of partner violence. In D.J Whittaker. & J.R Lutzker (eds) *Preventing partner violence: research and evidence-*

based intervention strategies. Washington, DC: American Psychological Association, pp. 41–66.

Worden, Robert E., Pollitz, Alissa A. (1984). Police arrests in domestic disturbances: A further look. *Law & Society Review*, Vol. 18, 105–19.

Wolfus, B. & Bierman, R. (1996). An evaluation of a group treatment programmes for incarcerated male batterers. *International Journal of Offender Therapy and Comparative Criminology*, 40 (4), 318–33.

Worrall, J L., Ross, J.W. & McCord, E.S. (2006). Modeling prosecutors' charging decisions in domestic violence cases. *Crime and Delinquency*, 52, 472–503.

Yalom, I.D. (1985). *The Theory and Practice of Group Psychotherapy* (3rd edn). New York: Basic Books.

Yates, T.M., Dodds, M.F., Sroufe, A. & Egeland, B. (2003). Eposure to partner violence and child behavior problems: A prospective study controlling for child physical abuse and neglect, child cognitive ability, socioeconomic status and life stress. *Development and Psychopathology*, 15, 199–218.

Yodanis, C.L. (2004) Gender inequality, violence against women, and fear: A cross-national test of the feminist theory of violence against women. *Journal of Interpersonal Violence*, 19, 655–75.

Yllo, K. (1988). Political and methodological debates in wife abuse research. In K. Yllo & M. Bograd (eds), *Feminist perspectives on wife abuse.* Thousand Oaks, CA: Sage, pp. 28–50.

Yllo, K. & Straus, M. (1981). Interpersonal violence among married and co-habiting couples. *Family Relations*, 31, 339–47.

Yllo, K.A & Straus, M.A. (1990). Patriarchy and violence against wives: The impact of structural and normative beliefs. In M.A. Straus & R.J. Gelles (eds) *Physical Violence in American Families: Risk factors and adapatations to violence in 8,145 families.* New Brunswick, NJ: Transaction.

Young, C., Cook, P., Smith, S., Turtletaub, J. & Hazlewood, L. (2005). Domestic violence: New visions, new solutions. In J. Hamel & T.L. Nicholls (eds). *Family Interventions in Domestic Violence.* New York: Springer, pp. 601–19.

Index

Indexed by TERRY HALLIDAY
(HallidayTerence@aol.com)